# TRAPPED!

# TRAPPED!

## The Story of
## FLOYD COLLINS

Robert K. Murray and
Roger W. Brucker

THE UNIVERSITY PRESS OF KENTUCKY

Published 1982 by The University Press of Kentucky

Scholarly publisher for the Commonwealth,
serving Bellarmine University, Berea College, Centre College of Kentucky,
Eastern Kentucky University, The Filson Historical Society, Georgetown
College, Kentucky Historical Society, Kentucky State University, Morehead
State University, Murray State University, Northern Kentucky University,
Transylvania University, University of Kentucky, University of Louisville,
and Western Kentucky University.

*Editorial and Sales Offices*: The University Press of Kentucky
663 South Limestone Street, Lexington, Kentucky 40508-4008
www.kentuckypress.com

12 11 10 09 08   8 7 6 5 4

ISBN-10: 0-8131-0153-0
ISBN-13: 978-0-8131-0153-8

Originally published by G.P. Putnam's Sons.

Manufactured in the United States of America.

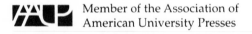 Member of the Association of
American University Presses

TO

MATTIE and BILL
whose support and love saved five
other persons from being trapped

JOAN
who provided love and plenty of
opportunities to fail cheaply

# Contents

*Illustrations follow page 160*

# Maps and Diagrams

# Acknowledgments

If we were to acknowledge fully the debt we owe to others in the researching and writing of this book, few pages would be left for the narrative. Such persons are legion, ranging all the way from young people half our ages to oldsters living on borrowed time, from semieducated hill folk to linguists and engineers with Ph.D.'s. Space requires that most of them remain nameless, but they know who they are and that they have our heartfelt thanks.

Some persons must be mentioned because of their particular or unusual help in bringing this book to completion. We are grateful to Stuart Forth, dean of libraries of the Pennsylvania State University, for encouragement in beginning this project; to Professor Stanley Weintraub and the Institute for the Arts and Humanistic Studies at the Pennsylvania State University for making travel and clerical monies available when needed; to Mrs. Shirley Rader, also of the institute, for her amazing typing ability; to Jane

Schott, Ruth Senior, Roxanne Shute, and Noelene Martin of the Pattee Library, Pennsylvania State University, for their patience in handling endless interlibrary loan requests; to Joan Lee, Pennsylvania State University, for her cheerful aid in tracking down sources; to Dr. Albert L. Ingram, director of the Mental Health Center, Pennsylvania State University, for useful psychiatric insights; to William J. Marshall, Jr., Department of Special Collections, Margaret I. King Library, University of Kentucky, for too many favors to list; to Nancy Baird and Jeanette Farley of the Margie Helm Library, Western Kentucky University, for dredging up old poems, sheet music, and ballad recordings; to Gus Wendel and John Beglin, Air Kentucky pilots, for flying their Beechcraft 99 at a very low altitude over the Mammoth Cave region one spring morning on a regularly scheduled flight from Cincinnati to Bowling Green; to June Dyer for letting us see Mary Frank Jones's scrapbook; to the National Park Service and to Superintendent Albert A. Hawkins of Mammoth Cave National Park for cooperation and assistance; to cavers Richard Zopf, Tom Brucker, Tom Gracanin, Greer Price, Scooter Hildebolt, Pete Lindsley, Jennifer Anderson, Don Coons, Curtis Weedman, and Sheri Engler, who helped take the measure of Sand Cave; to Philip M. Smith, founding president of the Cave Research Foundation, whose vision resulted in the oral history recording program carried on by James M. Dyer, Louise Storts, E. Robert Pohl, and others; to the directors of the Cave Research Foundation who provided field support and also placed at our disposal maps, photographs, tape recordings, and other records relating to Floyd Collins; to John P. Wilcox, Don F. Black, Stanley D. Sides, Richard A. Watson, and Harold Meloy, who gave editorial assistance and important information on the subjects of cave engineering, cave rescue, and cave history; and to our wives: Evelyn K. Murray, whose skill in literary composition is apparent on almost every page, and Joan W. Brucker, who compiled the index with the thoroughness of the librarian that she is.

Finally, our thanks go to Wiley Jennings of Lansing, Michigan, who suddenly appeared out of the surrounding foliage one sunny day in May 1977, while one of us was standing guard and the other was making our first clandestine hacksaw cuts in the heavy steel grating blocking the entrance to Sand Cave. Shoving a Nikkormat into his hand, we sought to distract him by requesting that he snap our picture. Never before nor ever again seen by either of us, he clicked the shutter and continued on his way, unsuspecting.

R.K.M. and R.W.B.

State College, Pennsylvania
Yellow Springs, Ohio
December 15, 1978

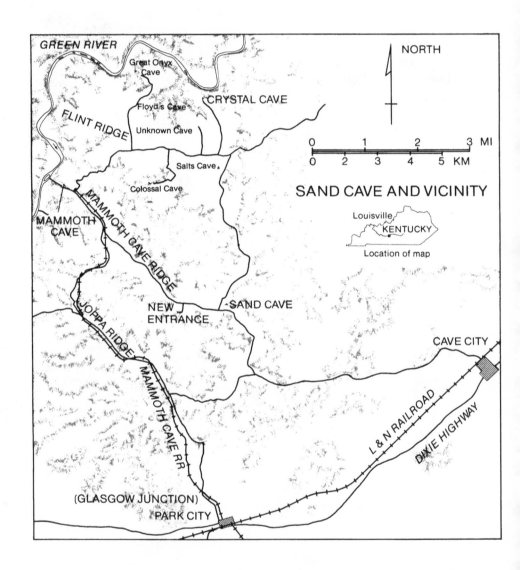

GREEN RIVER

Great Onyx
Cave

CRYSTAL CAVE

FLINT RIDGE

Floyd's Cave

Unknown Cave

Salts Cave

Colossal Cave

MAMMOTH
CAVE

MAMMOTH CAVE RIDGE

NEW
ENTRANCE

SAND CAVE

JOPPA RIDGE

MAMMOTH CAVE RR

CAVE CITY

L & N RAILROAD

DIXIE HIGHWAY

(GLASGOW JUNCTION)
PARK CITY

NORTH

| 0 | | 1 | | 2 | | 3 MI |
| 0 | 2 | | 3 | 4 | | 5 KM |

SAND CAVE AND VICINITY

Louisville
KENTUCKY

Location of map

# *Prologue*

"Hello . . . Roger Brucker? This is Robert Murray." With those words, the present book began.

How I, a blue-water sailor, and Roger Brucker, an expert caver, should have found each other is, in itself, the work of fate. A historian when not sailing, I had often run across the name of Floyd Collins and had accumulated considerable information about him in the course of nearly a quarter of a century of research on the social and political life of the American people during the 1920s. Brucker, an advertising executive when not caving, had also long possessed an interest in Collins and had collected much material about him and his caving exploits while conducting his own underground explorations in the Mammoth Cave region of Kentucky.

Unknown to each other, Brucker and I had started on paths that eventually converged. Following the publication in 1976 of his *The Longest Cave* (written in collaboration with Richard A. Watson), describing the various connections between the central Kentucky caves, Brucker intensified his gathering of data relating to Floyd, the Collins family, and Floyd's caving adventures. In that same year (1976), I also stepped up my own research on the Collins story following the appearance of my *The 103rd Ballot,* a study of the Democratic convention in Madison Square Garden in 1924. Since I was not a caver, I naturally felt the need to consult the latest speleological literature in order to gain an insight into that activity. Inevitably I came upon Brucker's 1976 volume. Captivated by his underground deeds and impressed by his knowledge of the "Collins cave country," I decided to phone him.

"I am writing a book about Floyd Collins," I began, "and am trying to uncover information about members of his family and details concerning his entrapment. I thought maybe you could help me."

Roger hedged. "How far have you gone in your research?"

"Why?" I countered, suddenly wary.

"Well," said Brucker, "I am beginning to write a book on Collins myself."

This was one of those awkward moments when two men realize that they are competitors. Normally, several brief platitudes are exchanged and a quick conclusion is brought to the conversation. I, however, detected that Brucker still wanted to talk. Aware that I did not have the caving experience required for a thorough investigation of the Collins matter, I sketchily reviewed for him my own progress. He urged me on, suspecting that I, as a professional historian, possessed some research skills he had not had time to develop.

As the minutes passed, the discussion switched back and forth. Gradually, we warmed to each other, our concern over competition giving way to the enthusiasm of finding another human being as interested in Floyd Collins as we individually were. Guarded speech and intermittent silences became less frequent. Finally we were asking each other, "Do you know this?" and "Do you know that?" ultimately confiding to the other even those nuggets of information no one else but ourselves had uncovered.

Suddenly Roger interjected, "Say, why don't we collaborate?"

I was surprised, even though such an idea was beginning to form in my own mind. "Why not," I replied, and sealed the bargain by saying: "Okay, Roger, you take the caving part and I'll take the history."

Not until two months later did we actually meet. It was at the end of January 1977. The eastern part of the United States was shivering through its worst winter in years and I skidded down from my State College, Pennsylvania, home to Roger's gasless, freezing house in Yellow Springs, Ohio. The roadsides were piled high with snow, public schools were closed, and industry had curtailed its hours because of the emergency. There in the Brucker living room, bundled in sweaters and drinking wine to ward off the chill, we hammered out the broad outlines of this book and assigned the remaining research tasks. It was also there that we decided to reopen Sand Cave in order to reconstruct the actual rescue circumstances as accurately as possible.

In the end, our research was conducted both above and below ground, in the local Kentucky countryside and in the nation's largest libraries. Our literary association became unique. It involved crawling on our backs and bellies, uncovering buried artifacts, viewing a fifty-two-year-old corpse, and tracking down rare books, personal manuscripts, poems, ballads, old radio programs, TV broadcasts, and movies. In addition, we held a number of oral interviews, shuttling from large, well-appointed New England country homes to backwoods Kentucky shacks. We handled some of these interviews jointly, taped some separately, and secured some from the archives of the Cave Research Foundation.

In the process I had to learn the rudiments of caving. Suffering nausea and claustrophobia, I apprehensively placed my welfare in the hands of my collaborator while deep in the caverns of Kentucky. More than once I moaned to Brucker, "My God, Roger, do I *have* to do this?" Finding myself in the dark beside a coffin a hundred and sixty feet underground was not my idea of fun. Roger, in turn, during the final stages of completing this manuscript, was introduced to the art of revising sentences and reading galleys while wedged in the transom berth of an oceangoing sailboat. Striving to maintain his equilibrium, he often allowed that a stable desk top would have been better. Clearly, each of us sacrificed something for this venture.

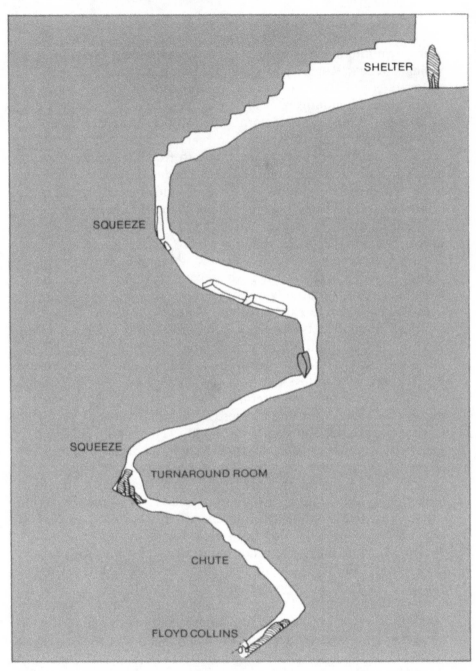

Cross-section diagram of Sand Cave with Floyd Collins trapped.

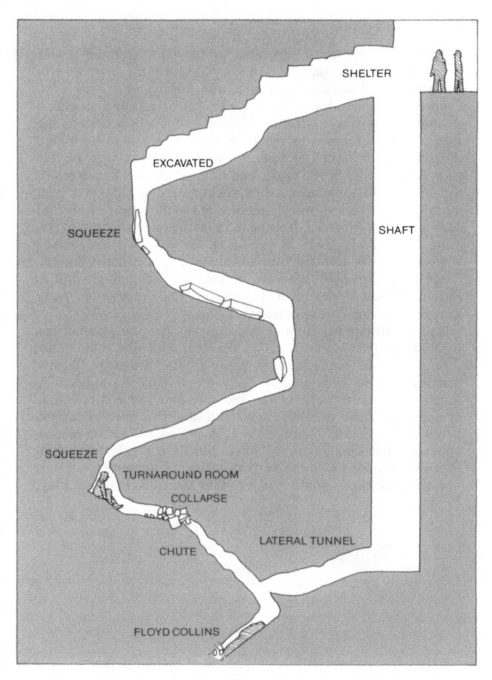

Cross-section diagram of Sand Cave showing the relationship of the rescue shaft and lateral tunnel.

Throughout, we were motivated by the hope that the reader would enjoy and be stimulated by this story as much as we were in researching and writing it. It is a true tale about a man who, trapped underground, precipitated what has been called America's greatest rescue story. Offering millions of his fellow citizens the most horrible example on record of what it is like to be buried alive, this man seemed to some to have been born trapped. He grew up in a large family at the end of a dirt road in a backwoods area. He was basically uneducated, spent most of his life on or near the farm where he was raised, and died at age thirty-seven only four miles from his birthplace. Yet, he led a fascinating life of discovery, living for the adventure of exploring the unknown and finding underground wonders that dazzled generations of caving followers. Despite his parochial existence, he knew the liberating world of excitement and challenge, and often met and surmounted grave dangers involving crucial personal decisions.

As with all fantastic true stories, this one has many paradoxes, surprises, and hidden threads. The reader is reminded at the outset that as wild or implausible as some of the situations, events, personalities, or conversations may seem, none have been invented. They are introduced and described here just as they existed or occurred. Some of these events and situations are still remembered by old-timers. Many are not. A few of the rescue personalities and participants are still alive. Most are not. But one thing they shared, along with the authors—all were connected and were brought together in some way or other by a caver named Floyd Collins. . . .

# 1

## *To Find a New Cavern*

The cave was only a short distance from Bee Doyle's house, and Floyd covered the ground quickly. It was not a morning to loiter. A chill westerly had pushed back the rain clouds, which, for the past two days, had brought extreme dampness to the area, and only a weak sun shone through. Winter runoff dripped everywhere and the earth underfoot was in a semisolid state that was neither ice nor mud.

Except for the battered kerosene lantern and a seventy-two foot rope slung over his shoulder, Floyd could have been any Barren County farmer setting out to cut ties for the Louisville & Nashville Railroad or to examine his land for winter damage. Floyd, however, was on a different mission this day. Earlier he had eaten a breakfast of salt pork, potatoes, corn bread, and a quart of coffee. Between bites he had told a worried Doyle that everything was going to turn out all right. Floyd smiled to himself as he recalled

Doyle's face. There was really nothing to be alarmed about—he had been through more difficult situations before. Floyd's smile suddenly faded as he continued his brisk pace. He should not have told Miss Jane about the angels and the falling rock. She had gotten everyone excited, and he remembered the ensuing family squabble with distaste. Old Man Lee had raged at his foolishness, and even Homer had failed to come to his defense.

Floyd descended a slippery path that skirted a cliff, and made a left turn. He admitted to himself that he would be glad to have this part over with. For three weeks he had been digging in this hole, trying to pick his way through the dangerous, crumbling passageway to solid limestone below. Four days earlier, he had set off a charge of dynamite to remove some of the last obstacles that blocked his path. Now it was mainly a matter of wriggling past the shattered rocks. During the last two days he had built fires at the cave's mouth hoping that the heat would dry it out. Alternate snow, freezing rains, and a mid-January thaw had turned the ground into a saturated sponge. At best, it was going to be a wet crawl.

The cave loomed ahead. The overhang of sandstone above it was splotched with patches of moss and lichen and was etched and split into sections like layered brick. Extending out about fifty feet, this ledge sheltered a circular area forty feet in diameter. At the back wall on the left was a passage entrance. To reach it, Floyd had dug out a crawlway—a trench roughly six feet deep and four feet wide. Shaded from the light, it led into the gloom. Arriving there, he took off his heavy outside woolen coat and hung it on a projecting rock. He figured he would still be warm enough and he needed to reduce his hundred-and-sixty-pound bulk for the work to come. Clothed in rough overalls, a blue jumper, a woolen shirt, and ankle-high hobnailed boots, Floyd now looked like what he was— one of central Kentucky's cavers. Somehow, though, he seemed older than his thirty-seven years, his face appearing gaunt behind a long, sharp nose, deep-set eyes, and a prominent gold front tooth. Hurriedly, Floyd lit his lantern, readjusted his rope, and ducked inside.

To many, a man who would crawl around under the earth rather than cultivate its surface might seem like a shiftless sort. Floyd

Collins was not. Caves provided his livelihood. Moreover, the same spirit that led others to scale mountain heights caused him to go into the depths. Even now, despite the danger, he thrilled at the thought of exploring the underground unknown. Ever since he had started to work in this cave in early January, he had been convinced that its treacherous passageway would lead to marvelous discoveries below, and he was determined to find them. Besides, they might also make him rich.

The cave's entrance passage sloped slightly downward for about fifteen feet and ended in a four-foot drop at a small square hole through which Floyd gently lowered himself. Bearing to the right, he was shortly forced onto his hands and knees as the passageway doubled back under itself once. The path then twisted and turned and divided into a number of false leads between tumbled limestone blocks before it narrowed to a squeeze that caused Floyd to squirm in order to get his body through. The way enlarged temporarily as it continued down at an angle of almost ten degrees. Suddenly it pinched to barely ten inches high, and bent sharply to the right. Not long afterward, the passage heightened into a small chamber that allowed Floyd to sit up. Here, earlier in the week, he had placed a crowbar, a shovel, and some burlap bags he had used for removing loose gravel and rock. He picked up the crowbar, lowered himself into the continuing passage, and resumed crawling on his belly. Shortly, he arrived at another squeeze, which opened into a ten-foot pitlike chute. At the bottom of the chute was a cubbyhole the size of the inside of a kneehole desk. Leading out of it was a crack about the circumference of a large wastebasket.

Floyd was now a hundred and fifteen feet from the mouth of the cave and fifty-five feet underground. He had reached this point several times before, but had always been stopped by a pile of rocks, a terminal breakdown. However, Monday's dynamite blast and his subsequent removal of the rock fragments had opened the way for him to continue. Here, in the bottom of the chute, there was so little room that he had been forced to work upside down to scrape out the last of the loose material. Today, he turned feetfirst into the chute and, hunching the rest of his body up in a ball, eased himself cautiously through the cubbyhole and into the crevice. He moved his rope coil ahead of him, shoving it as far as his arms could extend. Then he pulled himself out and repeated the procedure, this time pushing a lantern and checking some of the jagged ceiling rocks for stability as he went. Because this hole was a burrow through limestone rubble, it did not have solid bedrock sides and ceiling. Extreme care was therefore necessary. As Floyd moved again into the crack, he noticed the roof was one huge limestone block for a distance of about four feet. But the remainder of the ceiling was loose with smaller rocks protruding. One, which Floyd guessed to weigh about a hundred pounds, hung ominously down at the narrowest part of the crevice. Skillfully, he moved past it.

Floyd emerged onto a narrow ledge, caught his breath, and peered into a hole some sixty feet deep. Since its sides were sloping, he tied his rope to a boulder and descended easily with its aid. The walls of this pit appeared dark gray in his lantern light and revealed nothing interesting. If there was a "big cave," it still lay beyond. Yet Floyd was excited because this deep cavity gave promise of new passages out and down, and he looked around for possible leads. Suddenly his lantern flickered, telling him he had better leave. No matter, he thought. There would be ample time to explore further after he told Doyle and the others what he had found. Laboriously, he rope-walked his way up the steep pitch to the ledge above. He decided to leave the rope tied where it was because he could use it again later. Then, perspiring freely, he pushed his lantern ahead of him in the crevice as far as he could reach, turned over on his back, and entered, inching his body along by hunching his shoulders, twisting his hips, and pressing his feet against the walls and the floor.

At the narrowest part of the fissure he again moved his lantern ahead, this time shoving it into the cubbyhole, where it toppled over and went out. Floyd had been plunged into darkness many times before and it did not bother him. But in this particular situation it was a nuisance not to have light. He tucked his arms along his sides, compressed himself as flat as possible, and again began to combine shoulder and hip motions to wiggle through. Bringing his feet into play, he dug them hard into the sides and floor of the crack for better leverage. He guessed that he was just now emerging from under the large limestone block and kicked out with his right foot for a final surge. Inadvertently, he struck the hanging rock that he had so carefully avoided on the way in. It broke loose and fell. At that precise moment, Floyd's left foot was in a small V-shaped indentation in the floor of the crevice and the falling rock, dropping across his left leg at the ankle, pinned his left foot there. Hoping to free it, he kicked again with his right foot. This dislodged more rocks from above, further trapping his left foot and then his right one as well.

Floyd's head was lying toward the cave's entrance, just at the cubbyhole in the bottom of the ten-foot chute. He was reclining as if in a barber's chair, lying on his left side at an angle of about forty-five degrees. His left arm was partially pinned under him, his left cheek rested against the floor rock, and his right arm and hand were held close to his body by the crevice wall and the limestone boulder above. Coming to within a few inches of his chest, this block's flat undersurface prevented him from turning over. Entirely surrounded by rock and earth, Floyd was in a coffinlike straitjacket. His feet were pinned, his left hand and forearm could move only slightly, his right hand and arm were useless, and he could not roll over.

Panic seized him. Since he was in the dark, he could not fully assess the damage, but he knew he was in trouble. He first worked his abdominal and thigh muscles, struggling to free his feet. Next, he clawed at the gravel sifting around his legs. This loosened more debris which slid slowly onto his body, and soon his fingertips oozed blood from the futile effort. He twisted and humped his torso for relief from the sharp stones grinding into his back, but his lunges only shook down more dirt from above. Fragments of rock and sand drifted in around him, wedging his body more tightly and eventually immobilizing even his hands. When his panic finally subsided, he lay still, realizing belatedly that his every movement made his predicament worse. Over the wild beating of his heart, he could hear the soft rivers of dirt still sliding downward.

Although he knew it was useless, Floyd began to yell. He had no idea how long he screamed, but he soon lost his voice. Then he began to shiver. He was cold and wished he was wearing his heavy woolen coat. He felt miserable in his wet and sweaty clothing, and his left leg throbbed with pain. To add to his discomfort, a stream of water was running across the underside of the limestone boulder and a small tributary was dripping onto his face. Worse, his bladder felt like it was going to burst. Oh, God, he thought, I've got to piss! Was anyone ever trapped this way? To lie here even a few moments was agony; for hours it would be unbearable.

At last Floyd began to pray. Harboring vestiges of a hard-shell Baptist upbringing, he fervently begged God to help him. Finally, he lost track of time. He dozed fitfully, waking on several occasions but always mercifully slipping back into sleep. For now, exhaustion was his kindest friend, supplying the necessary drug that made his plight at all endurable. Jumbled thoughts alternated with his fretting and sleeping, but throughout he retained the belief that someone would ultimately find him. He had entered the cave at ten o'clock that morning. Along about noon, he had been trapped. Bee Doyle knew where he was and would surely begin searching for him when he failed to return. Doyle would raise the alarm, reasoned Floyd, and then aid would come.

That was Friday night, January 30, 1925.

The Green River in central Kentucky is formed from trickles that drain through limestone beds which, according to the natives, give the water a flavor that makes a lip-smacking whiskey. By percolating down the joints and fractures of this same limestone, the water also carves out fantastic subterranean caverns.

This process has been going on for 20 million years. Since the Tertiary period, water has seeped through the underlying Kentucky rock, gradually dissolving away the limestone and forming openings that over time have enlarged and become joined. Disintegration of the limestone has also continued on the top, bottom, and sides of these openings, and the draining water has cut passageways that interconnect at several levels. Simultaneously, water penetrating down and through the rock has not only created vertical shafts, horizontal tubes, and canyon passages, but has left behind spectacular crystalline formations on its way to reach the Green River.

Geologically known as the Central Kentucky Karst, this area is part of a huge limestone belt extending from southern Indiana, through Kentucky, and into Tennessee. More than elsewhere, however, the surface of the Central Kentucky Karst is riddled with sinkholes and its underground is shot through with caves. Literally thousands of them honeycomb the landscape. Appearing as depressions on the land's surface, the sinkholes are prominent funnels through which water seeps to seek its hydrological base at the Green River. The caves range from the simple (containing one passage of no more than a few yards) to the complex (possessing miles of interconnecting shafts and passageways). Historically and geologically, the most famous of these is Mammoth Cave, which has given its name to the entire surrounding region. Mammoth achieved notoriety almost fifty years before the California Gold Rush and before Yellowstone or Yosemite were even heard of. Over the years other caves have become known and commercially developed in Kentucky's cave region: Hidden River Cave, Diamond Caverns, Great Onyx Cave, Mammoth Onyx Cave, Crystal Cave, and Colossal Cavern, to name only a few.

Interest in Kentucky's caves has not been just a modern phenomenon. Three to four thousand years ago prehistoric peoples knew about the caverns and used them for various purposes. These ancient visitors left remnants of torches, sticks, and canes, as well as bone fragments, human feces, and at least five desiccated bodies as mute testimony to their presence. About thirty-five hundred years ago, prehistoric groups actually made their camps in Mammoth Cave and Salts Cave. With underground temperatures hovering at a year-round 54° F., these two caves provided shelter and comfort against the cold winter winds and the hot summer temperatures above. Walls and ceilings of parts of both Salts Cave and Mammoth Cave remain blackened to this day by the torches and fires of these prehistoric men.

There is also evidence that these prehistoric cavers mined the caves. They were interested in chert (a dull-colored flintlike silica), gypsum (a white powder that produces paint or plaster when heated and mixed with water), and mirabilite (a laxative and a salt substitute). Remains of human feces near quantities of mirabilite suggest that ancient peoples came there to cure their constipation. In 1935, a prehistoric body was discovered trapped under a seven-ton boulder in Mammoth Cave. The victim had been mining gypsum when he was crushed by the rockfall. Ancient men also engaged in some exploration of the caves. Several of their explorers ventured at least two miles back into the caverns. Torch fragments composed of reeds from the banks of the Green River indicate their routes. At least two sets of bare footprints preserved in mud reveal that a man and a woman followed interconnecting passages from Salts Cave to Unknown Cave, a remarkable feat. There is a question, however, about how much the successor to ancient man, the American Indians, knew of or used the caves. We know that they visited them but we have no evidence of their deep penetration.

According to popular myth, the first white man to show an interest in the Kentucky caves was a frontiersman named Houchins who chased a bear into the mouth of Mammoth in 1797. The next year, 1798, Valentine Simons registered a two-hundred-acre survey known as the "Mammoth Cave Tract," and began leaching saltpeter out of it. Mammoth's earth contains calcium nitrate, derived from nitrogen-fixing bacteria in the cave soil. But before it was suitable for making gunpowder it had to be converted into potassium nitrate, or "true" saltpeter. Simons operated such a conversion works just inside the mouth of the cave prior to the War of 1812. However, the low price of the product barely enabled him to survive, and in that year he sold Mammoth to Charles Wilkens, a saltpeter dealer, and Hyman Gratz, a wealthy Philadelphian. Happily for the new owners, the war suddenly dried up all overseas sources of saltpeter and the price soared. For a time Wilkens and Gratz even found it profitable to import gangs of slaves to work the cave's deposits.

After the war the demand for saltpeter again declined, and Mammoth began to be exploited as a tourist attraction. The discovery of ancient bones and a mummy helped fuel popular interest, and several eastern newspapers began publishing articles about the cavern. In 1828, Gratz took advantage of a drop in land values to buy out Wilkens and, expecting to capitalize on the tourist trade, added to his holdings until he owned about sixteen hundred acres. He also built a rustic inn with sleeping quarters at the cave in order to entice overnight visitors. But the venture failed as the frontier moved rapidly westward, leaving Mammoth in the backwater.

For a decade the fortunes of Mammoth remained at low ebb. Then, in 1838, Franklin Gorin of Glasgow, Kentucky, purchased the tract from the Gratz family for $5000, enlarged the rustic lodge to accommodate forty persons, and rechristened it the Mammoth Cave Inn. Gorin appointed as cave guide a slave named Stephen Bishop, who became one of the most famous cave explorers in the region's history. Although only seventeen years old at the time, Bishop skillfully added variations to the scenic tourist route and developed an attractive spiel. A self-educated man, he displayed a remarkable range of wit and humor and acquired considerable familiarity with geology. In his spare time he explored the depths of Mammoth on his own and discovered what are now called Gorin's Dome, the River Styx, Pensacola Avenue, Bunyan's Way, and Great Relief Hall. He also caught and displayed the first cave blindfish.

Gradually more tourists began to arrive at Mammoth, and by the spring of 1839 Gorin was doing a modest business. But his capital and foresight were limited and late in that same year he sold the cave, the inn, and Stephen Bishop for $10,000 to Dr. John Croghan, a Louisville physician. Croghan immediately converted the inn into the Mammoth Cave Hotel and, with the aid of the Kentucky legislature, got one road constructed from Cave City to Mammoth, another from Rowletts to Mammoth, and a third from Dripping Springs. These routes across semiwilderness permitted the Louisville and Nashville stage to reach the cave and stop overnight. As a result, Mammoth became a regular station on the way from Louisville to Nashville, offering travelers cave tours, rooms, and meals.

Bishop, in the meantime, added new delights to the cave trips by his continued discoveries—Mammoth Dome, the Snowball Room, and Cleaveland Avenue. Ultimately a visitor could select a guided tour of from two to nine miles. Bishop also drafted a map showing the various underground chambers and gave printed copies to the cave's guests. But Bishop did not share all of the cave's secrets and continued to make private explorations far beyond the end of the tourist trails. Because of what he found, he began to suspect that all of the caves in the Mammoth region were somehow interconnected.

In 1849, Croghan, a bachelor, died of tuberculosis, leaving Mammoth in trust to a succession of nieces and nephews. In his will he granted Stephen Bishop his freedom at the end of seven years. Ironically, only one year after Bishop was freed he also died, a young man of thirty-six. By that time the expansion of steamboat traffic, the connecting stage lines, and the completion of the Louisville & Nashville Railroad brought an ever-increasing number of tourists to the cavern.

The Civil War hurt Mammoth. Radical Reconstruction and continuing North-South animosities also worked against the tourist trade. Yet there were always those who were willing to brave almost any hardship to enjoy the sights of Mammoth, including such famous persons as Jenny Lind, the Swedish Nightingale, who is said to have sung arias under the arches in Gothic Avenue, and the actor Edwin Booth, who set the walls to ringing with Hamlet's soliloquy. Still, a revival in tourism did not occur until the mid 1880s when a narrow-gauge spur of the L&N Railroad was built directly to the mouth of the cave. Known as the Mammoth Cave Railroad, it ran from Glasgow Junction (now Park City) to the cave's entrance, a distance of nine miles. This service was first inaugurated in 1886, and the engine, "Hercules," thereafter carried in its two coaches a maximum of forty passengers each way on two trips a day. Other innovations and improvements in facilities rapidly followed, especially during the tenure of cave manager Henry C. Ganter. He supervised the cavern for many years and made Mammoth a commercial cave without peer. By World War I, forty thousand patrons were visiting it annually. At that time, souvenirs of all kinds were being sold at the cave and lunches were being prepared not only for those staying in the Mammoth Cave Hotel but for day visitors as well. As of 1920, it cost one dollar to get inside the cavern and four dollars to stay all day. All admission profits went to two elderly ladies in San Francisco who, as nieces of Dr. John Croghan, had inherited it.

An old-timer once said, "God gave Texas oil and He gave Kentucky Mammoth Cave. But He should have stopped when he finished and not made all those others."

From the outset, the residents of central Kentucky used the caves for a wide variety of purposes. They considered them as havens from windstorm and lightning. They cooled their milk, stored their canned goods, and kept their turnips and potatoes in them. Local children employed them in their games of hide-and-seek. And long before Prohibition, moonshiners made and stockpiled their whiskey there. But as Mammoth became a commercial success, some of the region's inhabitants grew less interested in the caves for these purposes and more interested in their potential for attracting tourists. Upland farmers, in particular, began to pursue a sideline of cave hunting and developing. For some of them, farming gradually became a sideline as they mastered the rudiments of geology and taught themselves the differences between the various types of crystalline formations. Unlike bottomland farmers, who specialized in corn, tobacco, and stockraising, many upland farmers owned soil that was none too good anyway—rocky, broken by hills and gullies—a hard land to tame. If Mammoth was any example, there was more money to be made by crawling around under the ground than tilling the top of it.

Since the Croghan estate controlled most of the land on the ridge housing Mammoth Cave (Mammoth Cave Ridge), early competitive commercial exploration shifted to neighboring Flint Ridge just across the way. Separated from Mammoth Cave Ridge for most of its distance by the narrow Houchins Valley, Flint Ridge merges with Mammoth Cave Ridge at its southeastern corner. Prior to the mid 1890s, major interest in the caves on Flint Ridge centered on Salts Cave, mainly because of the ancient artifacts it contained. Although actually under a remote piece of the Mammoth Cave property, Salts Cave was always an object of free-lance exploration and exploitation. Open to anyone, it was plundered by the natives of bushel baskets of old torches and moccasins and of at least one male mummy, discovered in 1875 by William Cutliff, who mistakenly named it Little Alice and sold "her" to Mammoth for display. Legend has it that at least three other mummies were hidden away by Cutliff before his death, but they never have been found. In 1897, the first modern cave accident of the region occurred in Salts when Pike Chapman, who was helping to dig a new entrance into the cavern, was trapped by a cave-in. Hauled to the surface by a safety rope tied around his body, he was so badly mauled in the process that he died two hours later.

The development of other Flint Ridge caves dates from 1895,

when Lute and Henry Lee opened up a sinkhole on the south flank and named their discovery Colossal Cavern. Officials of the Louisville & Nashville Railroad immediately began legal maneuvering to acquire it and finally succeeded. Afterward, they blasted an opening into the cavern only a mile and a half from the entrance to Mammoth. Their purpose was not so much to exploit Colossal as to find if it connected with Mammoth, since many people had come to suspect that some of Mammoth, as explored by Stephen Bishop and later guides, lay outside land owned by the Croghan estate. When L&N officials failed to discover such a connection, they developed Colossal on its own, but by 1920 it was only a modest operation with relatively few tourists and 2.5 miles of passages. Unknown Cave, which was discovered only a mile and a half north of Colossal, was also found to have no connection with Mammoth and remained of marginal commercial value.

With the Flint Ridge caves attracting only a trickle of tourists, Mammoth continued on its way. In 1908, a twenty-three-year-old German engineer named Max E. Kaemper visited the cave expecting to stay a week. He remained eight months. During that time, he made an accurate map with a surveyor's compass and discovered additional halls and chambers, definitely pushing the limits of the cave off tract land. So anxious were the Croghan heirs to keep the true extent of the cave a secret that they refused to publish Kaemper's findings or to circulate his map. Once, in opening up new passages, Kaemper probed so far from the entrance that his charge of dynamite lifted leaves and sent smoke up through the ground in H.C. Ganter's backyard. Ganter, who happened to be watching at the moment, would remember this incident.

Throughout the decade 1910–20, speculation persisted that Mammoth, Salts, Colossal, and Unknown might be one big cave, perhaps having as many as a hundred and fifty miles of underground passages. One person who firmly believed this and who had a consuming passion for underground exploration was Edmund Turner, a young civil engineer. A small man with long sideburns and a handsome mustache, Turner came to the Mammoth region in 1912 escaping, so people said, from an unhappy marriage. He immediately sought someone to show him around and was directed to another young man, Floyd Collins, who at twenty-five was one of those natives who had virtually given up farming for caving. With Collins, Turner examined Salts Cave in detail, finding some new leads to unexplored passages but not uncovering any connection with Mammoth.

Turner was an insatiable caver who, according to the natives, "dug holes everywhere." At one point he came very close to discovering what later became the Frozen Niagara entrance to Mammoth before he ran out of dynamite and moved on to another location. While pursuing his explorations, he boarded with various families in the area—the Vances, the Cutliffs, the Collinses, and the Edwardses. While at the home of L.P. Edwards, he became convinced that a sizable cavern lay under Edwards's Flint Ridge farm, so he entered into a verbal agreement with him to receive one-half of anything he found. Edwards was a preacher and Turner believed he could be trusted.

The result was the discovery of Great Onyx Cave in 1915. Turner gave it its name, helped to construct its entrance, and developed its trails. Because the cave possessed the finest onyx columns in the region, Reverend Edwards quickly sought to commercialize the venture. He also took advantage of their verbal agreement to cheat Turner out of his half, claiming it all for himself. Less than a year later Turner died of pneumonia, a pauper. A small purse, raised mainly by the guides at Mammoth, made possible a decent burial. Most natives agreed that Edwards's treatment of Turner "was a crime, especially him being a preacher and all." But this did not bother Edwards. When asked to contribute to Turner's burial fund, he angrily replied, "I won't give a dime, I won't give a dime!" Turner's simple coffin was placed in the Mammoth Cave Baptist Church cemetery, with small uncarved sandstone rocks at its head and foot. The grave and the rocks are still there.

Because of subsequent confusion over Great Onyx's precise boundaries and the extent of its passages, adjoining neighbors brought a number of lawsuits against Edwards, who persisted in claiming all parts of the cavern no matter under whose land they lay. Although Edwards lost these suits, he retained the main portion of the cave and later passed it on to his daughter, Lucy Cox. Under the Edwards-Cox management, Great Onyx became one of the more successful Flint Ridge commercial operations. By

1926 the Great Onyx Hotel housed twenty-five persons at the cave site and served delicious meals.

Not long after Great Onyx was discovered by Edmund Turner, another character with an inordinate interest in caving appeared in the central Kentucky region. Known only as Old Man Hackett, he was the kind about whom myths are made. For the first two years he lived in the mouth of Long Cave, refusing to have much to do with anyone, but finally he rented a house in Cave City. People whispered that he was shipping rocks out of Long Cave in trunks. No one knew why, but the speculation was that he was prospecting for rare minerals. One story claimed that he lived like a hermit because he hated women, having been jilted by one as a young man. Hackett was no Beau Brummell. He wore ragged clothes. His hair hung down to his hips when he did not keep it rolled up under a ten-gallon hat. He scared some locals so badly by his peculiar habits that they asked the law to investigate him. Two FBI agents checked him out and discovered that he was a retired postmaster and tavern owner from Texas.

Like Turner, Hackett had a penchant for "digging holes every-where." From time to time he hired crews of local men to help him. He never explained what he was looking for, although the locations of his excavations pointed toward finding a new entrance into Mammoth. On one of these "digs" a tragedy occurred when Harrison Logsdon, one of Hackett's local helpers, was crushed to death by a two-ton rock that fell on him while he was drilling. This brought an abrupt end to Hackett's exploring career in central Kentucky and he migrated back to Texas. There, at age ninety, he accidentally slipped and fell, broke his hip, and in a fit of despondency shot himself.

While Old Man Hackett was still pursuing his mysterious Kentucky underground activities, yet another caving enthusiast, George D. Morrison, turned up in the cave country. A Louisville mining engineer and oil prospector, he was fascinated by the possibility of cave interconnections and new entrances into Mammoth. After talking with natives, among them H.C. Ganter who at the time was no longer in the employ of Mammoth Cave, Morrison formed the Mammoth Cave Development Company and took out subsoil options on land just southeast of the Mammoth tract on

Mammoth Cave Ridge. Starting with Ganter's recollection of what he had seen in his backyard several years earlier, Morrison ran illegal surveys into the southern reaches of Mammoth, trying to determine if its passageways went under land he had recently leased. He even sent hirelings into Mammoth to listen for his drills and to set off small charges of dynamite so that he could watch above for signs of displaced ground and curling smoke. Once he detected some, but they occurred on Mammoth ground. Another time, Mammoth Cave officials caught him, had him arrested, and forced him to pay a fine of seventy-five dollars for trespassing. On still another occasion, his probings came out on that part of Colossal Cave property that extended onto Mammoth Cave Ridge. All this time Morrison maintained the fiction that he was prospecting for oil, and a common joke in the cave region was to ask him, "Found any oil yet?" Of course, everyone, including the Mammoth Cave people, knew precisely what he was doing.

After a number of false starts, Morrison left the cave country to raise additional money for his underground ventures, but World War I intervened and he did not return until 1921. This time he found what he was looking for—a backdoor to Mammoth residing on his own land. Not only that, but he discovered through his new entrance sections of the cave that were, in many ways, more beautiful than anything known in the older part. More important, Morrison's entrance was farther up the road toward Cave City and Glasgow Junction than the original one and thus stood between the old entrance and the primary tourist access route. Morrison quickly improved his entrance and constructed a twenty-five-room hotel, which he named the New Entrance Hotel. He even laid plans to install a $20,000 elevator in the lobby to whisk patrons to the marvelous formations below.

The Mammoth Cave management was furious, especially when Morrison set up road signs calling attention to "The New Entrance to Mammoth Cave" and began selling tickets with "Mammoth Cave" printed on them. Having an entrance closer to town on the main road, he naturally siphoned off large numbers of tourists. The Croghan estate understandably sued for an injunction to block him from using the words "Mammoth Cave." But when Morrison showed the jury his maps and proved that it was all the same cavern—visitors could enter the historic entrance and emerge at his new one—the court found in his favor. The Croghan estate appealed the verdict but the higher court also supported Morrison's position. It did direct him, however, to be more precise in his advertising. He was ordered to add to his literature the phrase, "We do not show any part of the cave which prior to 1907 was generally known as Mammoth Cave; that portion of the cave can be seen only through the old entrance."

Morrison's success was electrifying and spurred further cave exploration and development in the Mammoth region. So did an influx of tourists caused by the greater number of paved roads and an increase in the use of the automobile, especially the Model T. Further, the post–World War I agricultural depression prompted farmers throughout the nation to seek additional sources of income—and in the Kentucky cave country that meant to dig. For many central Kentuckians, caves were like the sea for New Englanders. In time of trouble they looked to them for economic salvation. Those who could not find a cave on their own land did the next best thing—they went into the souvenir business. By 1925, the road to Mammoth was lined with shacks and junky stands selling all sorts of cave merchandise. Ashtrays, bookends, paperweights—all made from polished cave onyx—were stocked. Enterprising peddlers stole much of this onyx from surrounding caves in the dead of night. Aside from the moral question involved, the damage done by such vandalism to fragile and exquisite cave formations was staggering. As one cave-country native recently said, "People didn't care what they done in them days."

By the mid 1920s Kentucky cavers acted ruthlessly and in highly competitive ways. The subsurface geography of the Edmonson, Hart, and Barren counties region, as well as the personality of its natives, promoted aggressive activity. Differing from their Bluegrass neighbors, the residents of this area more resembled the horse-trading Yankee, known for his shrewdness, cynical humor, and wily methods. Here feuds and factional feelings abounded and cave wars were a natural outlet. In order to cut into Mammoth's business, the major local rivals excessively lauded their caverns and from time to time spread false rumors that Mammoth was flooded or that the Mammoth Cave Hotel was closed and falling down. As more caves were discovered and developed, the competition for tourists became even keener. Those who found a cave on their own land, even a modest one, borrowed heavily from caving bankers to build a ticket office and curio shop. Then they roamed the countryside looking for tourists. In warm weather, they herded those they could find into their caverns, down makeshift stairways and past misspelled signs. In cold weather, they hunted more caves.

In this predominantly Baptist region, shooting and knifing were taboo, but virtually anything else was allowed—harassment, lying, and tricks of all kinds. Some natives estimated that by 1925 as many as a third of all visitors to the Mammoth area were diverted to the smaller, private caves by nefarious means. Mammoth's managers went to court several times to prevent such competitive cave-huckstering and to seek injunctions blocking use of the county roads for this purpose. But all their attempts failed.

To capture their share of the Mammoth trade, the private cave owners relied primarily on solicitors (later called cappers because they wore visored caps) who were paid by the head to deliver rerouted tourists to their doors. Rival cappers sometimes engaged in rock throwing at choice locations where arriving tourists had to pass. One old-timer remembered this competition as being so grim "you had to stand there and fight for your life." Some cappers would flag down motorists as if wishing a ride, then jump on the running board and begin their sales pitch. Some played the role of visitors, frequenting local hotels where they ran down Mammoth. One of their ploys was to pretend that they had just come from there and had found the walls smoked up by kerosene fumes and the walk too strenuous for the elderly. Another ruse was to contend that all the caves in the area were interconnected and therefore it made no difference which one you entered—you saw the same thing.

As a practitioner of cave warfare, however, George Morrison remained the most successful. He cut deepest into Mammoth's clientele by aggressive and innovative action. A hero to the other cave entrepreneurs, Morrison served as the example to emulate. All of them, after all, shared the common goal of siphoning off the lucrative Mammoth trade. In achieving this, the beauty of a cave was of course important. But it was not the most critical factor.

Location made a cave pay. If it had direct access to the Cave City
highway, or if its entrance was ahead of Mammoth's, it would do
well. If it was away from the highway, or beyond Mammoth, it
would have a difficult struggle to survive. Obviously, by the middle
of the 1920s, the best strategy in Kentucky's cave warfare was to
find another opening into Mammoth even farther up the road than
Morrison's—or discover a beautiful new cave there altogether.

Floyd Collins was born April 20, 1887, and lived all of his life in the
Mammoth Cave region of Kentucky. The original settlers who
populated this area were Anglo-Saxons. They arrived in the late
1700s, bringing with them Scotch-Irish prejudices and ways. Most
of these people came into Kentucky by way of Virginia and filled
the area with such family names as Estes, Doyle, Hanson, Cutliff,
Cox, Logsdon, Edwards, Houchins—and Collins. Neither the
coming of the stagecoach, the steamboat, nor even the Louisville &
Nashville Railroad altered their folkways much. Residents rarely
traveled outside their immediate neighborhoods, largely confining
their trips to the three surrounding county seats of Brownsville
(Edmonson), Munfordville (Hart), and Glasgow (Barren). As late
as World War II, a local boy who suddenly found himself in Japan
might never have been farther away than Elizabethtown to the
north or Bowling Green to the south. In the mid 1920s, a trip to
Louisville was still an "occasion."
    Most people in this cave country had sided with the Union in the
Civil War, and veterans of the Grand Army of the Republic were
still numerous at the time of Floyd's birth. The war had invaded the
area through Morgan's Raiders and the burning of nearby Dennison's Ferry. Also, the South's repeated attempts to capture the
L&N Railroad had resulted in some destruction of property and
loss of life. But slavery had been relatively rare in this section of
Kentucky and the region escaped the worst excesses of Reconstruction. Actually, the relationship between whites and blacks in the
area was usually good. Segregation existed, to be sure, and blacks
were referred to as niggers. But the caves had provided a strange
and interesting bond between the two races. Beginning with
Stephen Bishop, a series of Negro guides had been used in
Mammoth, passing on this heritage from slave father to freed son.

Black families—such as the Livelys, Woodsons, Browns, Bransfords, and Garvins—had worked for Mammoth for several generations. Over the years, they built up their own black community along the Crystal Cave and Great Onyx Cave roads. They had their own school and their own church, and some of them became well-to-do entrepreneurs. Henry Bransford, for example, controlled six hundred acres of land. Matt Bransford and his wife ran a profitable hotel with twenty rooms, catering to black Mammoth Cave tourists.

White or black, the majority of the inhabitants of the Kentucky Cave country were simple, honest God-fearing folk. Most of them could quote freely from the Bible, especially those who adhered to fundamentalist faith. All but one of the churches in the area were Baptist, or some variation thereof, and they possessed such picturesque names as Joppa, Little Hope, Little Jordan, Temple Hill, Silent Grove, and Dry Branch. Their ministers included in their sermons liberal doses of hell-fire and damnation, and front-row worshippers enthusiastically urged them on with shouts of "Amen, God give him breath!" The faithful packed missionary society and Wednesday night prayer meetings.

This is not to say that the daily language was pure, that drunkenness did not exist, or that marital infidelity was unknown. Woman-chasing was tolerated in the men, if not actually condoned. However, divorces were rare, broken homes virtually unheard of, and the average family was large. Men distilled whiskey and consumed it in considerable quantity although the Baptist Church and its leaders waged a vigorous campaign against it. When Prohibition was proclaimed in 1920, most natives obeyed it, but moonshine making continued. Obscenities studded normal male speech, with the oaths being both sacrilegious and scatological. The straitlaced settled for such exclamations as "Gosh durn," "Jeeminy Crickets," and "Good Granny."

Superstitions and myths were common in the cave country and played a large role in people's daily lives. Everyone knew that blue racer snakes could milk cows, that spit on a worm encouraged fish to bite, that cornshuck tea made a good tonic, and that a knife placed under the bed cut pain. Certain words and pronunciations, which if spoken in other parts of the nation would elicit a quizzical look, were universally understood here. A *gully-washer* was a downpour; a *box* was a guitar; a *dab* was a small amount; a *goner* was a hopeless case; and *coal-oil* was kerosene. Words like *rinse, boil,* and *ask* came out *rinch, bile,* and *ast.* There was always something interesting to do, although life was relatively uncomplicated and unsophisticated. Bean-hullings, pea-shellings, candy-breakings, hog-killings, wheat-threshings, shivarees, and revivals produced excitement and camaraderie. The year's biggest happening by far was the local July Fourth picnic and fireworks display at Mammoth Cave. "Everyone lived for that day," recalled one oldster recently, as youngsters and adults alike clambered aboard the "Hercules," which increased its trips from two to six for that one twenty-four-hour period.

The region's inhabitants, of course, spent most of their time on more mundane matters. During the growing season the men worked in the fields while the women kept house. Children alternated between going to school and helping out with the chores. Education was very primitive and few youngsters earned a high school diploma. It was unusual to complete even the eighth grade. One-room schoolhouses were all that existed, and their academic sessions lasted only from July 1 to Christmas. Teachers and older students taught reading, spelling, arithmetic, history, and geography. For punishment there was the customary dunce bench, and canings by the teacher were frequent. Pupils supplied wood for the cast-iron stoves, the only source of warmth in the wintertime.

To survive the winters, the average family would butcher its own meat and can several hundred jars of fruits and vegetables. Inhabitants traded at locally run general stores for dry goods, sugar, coffee, candy, and the like. During cold weather, the women would sew or make quilts while many of the men would trap or hack ties for the L&N Railroad. The Kentucky cave region was an excellent tie-hacking area and an expert wielding a broadax could hew twenty to twenty-five per day. The splinters made good firewood and were called juggles.

The Collinses were a typical cave country family. Leonidas (Lee), the father, was born in Franklin, Kentucky, in May 1858. A Baptist fundamentalist and teetotaler, he had resided in Hart County since he was twenty-two, except for one year spent in

Oklahoma. His wife, Martha, came from the Burnett family of Barren County and bore him eight children, five boys and three girls. Elizabeth, the oldest (born in 1883), died at the age of three months. James (Jim), the eldest son, was born next (1885). Then, in line, came Floyd (1887), Annie (1890), Andy Lee (1895), Marshall (1897), Nellie (1900), and Homer (1903). Martha died in 1915 of tuberculosis after her family was mainly grown, and Lee married for a second time—a Mammoth Cave guide's widow named Sarilda Jane Buckingham. She, like Martha before her, was deeply religious. Since Sarilda was a difficult name to handle, she was simply called Miss Jane by all those who knew her.

The Collins farm was on Flint Ridge near the Hart-Edmonson county line and, like most farms in the area, was marginally productive. The Collins house was a one-floor rectangular frame building with a high-pitched tar-paper roof and an L-shaped addition on the back. Resting on stones at its corners instead of concrete footers, it resembled hundreds of other Kentucky hill farm homes built in the early twentieth century, and both living space and privacy were at a minimum. To make ends meet, familial cooperation was necessary and Lee relied on his sons and daughters to help him scratch a living out of the soil as well as engage in other activities to bring in cash. Compared with other families in the neighborhood, the Collinses did rather well. On their two hundred acres of land, they raised corn, oats, a little wheat, cane (for sorghum), and garden fruits and vegetables, most of which they sold to neighbors. They ground their corn into meal at Joe Sells's mill on Flint Ridge but took their wheat to Horse Cave to be made into flour. During the cave tourist season, the women baked fried pies, which were sold to the Mammoth Cave Hotel and to customers in Horse Cave and Cave City. Long before dawn, Lee would hitch up a horse to his huckster wagon and would return at night with a pocketful of money. In cold weather, the men trapped for furs, felled timber, and cut ties for the L&N Railroad.

Floyd contributed his share to this joint family enterprise, but he also developed an early interest in caves. Buzzard Cave, in a bluff about a thousand feet north of the Collins house, was where all the Collins youngsters cut their caving teeth. According to Homer, Floyd began to investigate caves seriously at age six when he wandered alone into Salts Cave only a mile from the Collins home. As a boy, Floyd poked into every crevice he could find, and even in the dead of winter he would stop to examine "breathing holes" and watch as they blew a column of "smoke" into the chill air. Four miles away was the little one-room Mammoth Cave School, which the Collins children attended. Floyd often straggled in late or was absent altogether because of his caving activities. Even at this young age, he possessed a phlegmatic personality that was well adapted to cave work. He remained unruffled in the midst of crisis and seemed totally unconcerned by danger. His contemporaries remembered him as a daredevil, climbing trees like a monkey, taking spectacular risks, and not always exercising sound judgment. Mrs. Katie Pace, who grew up with him, recalled him laughing whenever one of his companions suggested that what he was doing was risky. His love for caves, she later asserted, bordered on a mania. Floyd, it seems, was more at home beneath the ground than above it.

Throughout his adolescence and early adulthood, Floyd explored caves for fun only. Caves were his recreation not his vocation. He continued to work hard at his family chores and, stingy to the point of being a neighborhood joke, saved enough money by age twenty-three to buy thirty acres of his own land adjoining his father's. Much to his delight, he discovered a small cave on it, which he called Floyd's Cave, and he built a shack directly over the entrance. Normally a tenant occupied this building and worked the land for shares, but from time to time Floyd also "batched" it there when he was not at his father's house. Lyman Cutliff, one of Floyd's neighbors, recalled staying overnight with him once and entering Floyd's Cave through a trapdoor in the floor of the cabin. The cave was eight hundred feet long, rather damp, and not very beautiful. But it gave Floyd the itch to find a commercial-sized cavern. Also it contained some onyx draperies and stalactites, pieces of which Floyd sold to tourists himself or peddled to the souvenir stands along the Mammoth Cave road.

Floyd's life as a professional caver blossomed when he met Edmund Turner in 1912. Part of the time that Turner stayed in the cave country he made his home with the Collinses, paying them three dollars a week for room and part board. Periodically, he hired

Floyd as a Salts Cave guide for one dollar per day. But Turner gave Floyd more than money by imparting to him some knowledge of geology and other scientific cave information. Although not a dullard, Floyd was remembered by those who knew him as being "not the brightest fella in the world." Certainly he did not have much "book larnin'," completing only the fifth grade. Prior to meeting Turner, all Floyd knew about caves he had gained from practical experience. Even some of that rested on superstition. He claimed, for example, that his body enjoyed an innate magnetism that gave him no need for a compass. One day a friend tested him when Floyd said he was facing north. He wasn't, but his companion did not have the heart to tell him. Once Floyd took a needle from a broken compass and put it in his pocket, carrying it with him thereafter to add to his "body magnetism."

Floyd's explorations in Salts Cave with Turner, and Turner's later discovery of Great Onyx, heightened Floyd's own caving aspirations. Great Onyx lay just west, down the ridge line from the Collins farm, and Floyd surmised that there were other such caverns in the area. Indeed, for a while the whole Collins family experienced "cave fever." All the Collins males at one time or another crept into small passages on their own land to see where they went or to mine cave onyx—crack off stalagmites and stalactites—which they sold to souvenir-hunting tourists.

By World War I, Floyd, in particular, was spending most of his time mining onyx or exploring caves. Yet his great discovery occurred by accident. The winter of 1916–17 was long and severe and the Collinses, like others, trapped more intensively than usual. While tracing a trapline near the house in December, Floyd noticed that one of the traps had disappeared in a depression, having been dragged there by a captured animal. Upon poking around, Floyd uncovered a crevice that, because of the way it was "breathing," made him confident that it connected with a big cave.

Ignoring the lost trap, Floyd returned to the house and casually asked his father whether he could have half the profits if he found a commercial cave on the family property. Floyd and his father were not close. Although Lee later liked to claim that he, too, was a caver and Floyd was therefore "born to it . . . it's in the blood," Lee never considered caving to be a worthwhile occupation. He

often castigated Floyd for the time he "wasted" crawling around
under the ground. Lee did not mind the extra money that could be
made from onyx mining, but he considered that only a sideline at
best. For Floyd's part, it was not that he actively distrusted his
father, but he had seen what the cave wars had done to relationships in some families, and he believed it was wise to get the record
straight at the outset. Besides, his father was growing old and Floyd
knew that much of the exploration and development of any cavern
would fall to him.

After sleeping on the proposition, Lee agreed in writing. Floyd
went back to his exploring. First, he uncovered a crawlway two feet
in diameter. Then, after two weeks' hard labor, he came into a
room sixty-five feet high with walls encrusted by hundreds of white
and cream-colored gypsum flowers, some of them eighteen inches
long. Delirious with excitement, Floyd rushed back into the house
even though it was past midnight, awakened everyone there, and
urged them to come see what he had found. Still in their
nightclothes and carrying kerosene lanterns, Marshall, Marshall's
wife Anna, Annie, Nellie, Homer, and Andy Lee crept into the
narrow entrance behind their brother. Only Lee and Miss Jane did
not go; they were too old and too large. The bedazzled cave visitors
did not emerge until dawn.

Floyd first called his discovery Wonder Cave, but William Travis
Blair, the Collins's next-door neighbor, suggested he name it
Crystal after its gorgeous gypsum flowers. Now the whole family
pitched in to develop it. Lee and Floyd's brothers helped enlarge
the entrance. They smoothed the floor and made trails. At the
expense of their farming, they moved rocks, filled holes, constructed stairways, and, after twelve months' back-breaking work,
set up signs along the road to Mammoth announcing that Crystal
was open for business. Floyd, meanwhile, explored new passages
and chambers, and assigned them intriguing names like Grand
Canyon Avenue and the Valley of Decision. The result was one of
the most beautiful caves in the area, filled with interesting helictites, gypsum crusts and draperies, but most of all with delicate
gypsum crystals that resembled asters, marigolds, larkspur, and
lilies.

With the opening of Crystal and the hiring of a manager, the

Collins family formally entered the cave wars. Unfortunately, Crystal was far off the beaten track, reached only by an almost impassable dirt road, and was four and a half miles down the highway beyond Mammoth. Moreover, the opening of Crystal in the spring of 1918 came at a bad time. World War I had curtailed travel and there were fewer than usual tourists to go around. Floyd and his family fought vigorously for their share, taking turns prowling the Cave City highway in search of customers. But the odds were against them. Solicitors of other caves had a relatively easy time discouraging visitors to go to Crystal. The Collinses had the unenviable task of luring sated tourists to a cave which, although beautiful, had no modern accommodations or conveniences. Crystal was the last stop on the central Kentucky "cave route."

Those few patrons who did dribble in to Crystal received a real treat if Floyd, himself, showed them through. In the largest room of the cavern, he would raise up his lantern on a twenty-foot pipe so that they could see the vastness of the place. His enthusiasm sometimes caused him to break off a gypsum flower and hand it to an astonished guest. His rapture as well as his confidence was captivating. Frequently he would tell visitors about his explorations beyond the tourist trails. "I love to squeeze through those passageways," he would say. Sometimes he would extinguish all lights and then lead them out, giving them a sober, but fascinating, lesson in how to read the signs of the unseen. Yet, even with all this, Crystal did not make much money, certainly not enough to repay Floyd and his family for all their hard work.

In the lulls between tourists from 1918 on, Floyd relentlessly explored Crystal. Sometimes his brother, Homer, and a few caving companions such as Lyman Cutliff, John Vance, Arthur Adwell, Elkanah Klein, Harrison Dennison, or Johnnie Gerald went with him. Mostly he went alone. Floyd considered caving as recreation after a day of farming or guiding guests over the same old tourist trails. He was the first to admit that he wanted to attract more visitors to Crystal. But his basic interest in exploring the cave further was not mercenary. He loved the cave; he loved its beauty; and he was excited by the prospect of probing its deepest mysteries. For Floyd, caving was like a religion. It spoke to his soul and provided him a contact with the mystery of the unknown which he evidently needed. Moreover, caving was high adventure. A cave, after all, does represent a unique challenge. Its routes are hidden in inky blackness, and although a caver may know where he wants to go, he cannot see or plan in advance how to get there. Also, unlike other sporting activities, once a caver plunges underground, he is out of contact and out of sight. The cave swallows him. Within moments, his starting point—the basic reference for proper orientation—is lost. The walls and passages twist in a confusing and bewildering manner and are confining. The caver can never look out from a vista as a mountain climber can—cave distances are usually measured only in feet. Yet a cave, unlike a mountain with its peak, just seems to go on and on.

To the average person, a cave is foreboding, making him feel uneasy and apprehensive. For those who are claustrophobic, it is the ultimate hell, causing shortness of breath, panic, mind-numbing fear—all heightened by the darkness, the closeness of the walls and ceiling, the threat of falling earth and rock, and the nameless dread of being buried alive. For a caver like Floyd, of course, caves were not hostile at all. He saw the subtle differences in the walls and ceilings, felt the air move and heard the cave "murmur," and detected clues in the trickling water, the humidity, the stone texture and temperature, the shifting of the mud, and the scurrying of the salamanders and cave crickets. To experience such joys, Floyd Collins would set off in the darkness, with a coal-oil lantern in his hand and a can of beans in his pocket, humming to himself as he went and disappearing for a day at a time. As a result of such journeys, he found numerous new passageways in Crystal such as the fabulous Big Room, a vast gallery over a mile long, which was not rediscovered until 1940 when modern cavers found his bean cans there.

Floyd's explorations in Crystal were always filled with chances. He seemed to relish risks and at times acted downright foolhardy. He would go into places where rocks were still falling, and if warned by others would merely reply, "I don't care, I ain't afraid." While caving alone, something no sensible person would ever do, Floyd edged through compression squeezes, chimneyed up sheer walls, climbed down vertical drop-offs, pushed for hours out endless crawlways, and worked for days at dangerous breakdowns. Once, in the far reaches of Crystal, his lantern went out and after eighteen frightening hours he finally stumbled outside. At another time he was trapped by a rockfall but ultimately dug himself out, commenting later that "it wa'n't nothin'." His family got used to these scrapes and his long absences. As for Floyd, such experiences merely made him more reckless and added to his confidence. After several years of exploring in Crystal, he had done it all—worked muddy drains that threatened to siphon, traveled through crawl-ways that ripped his knees, negotiated passages too low for standing and too narrow for stooping, passed through squeezes too small for his build, and squirmed hundreds of feet down tubes where only an idiot—or caver—would go. For eight, ten, fourteen hours he would explore, leaving a trail of empty bean cans and wall autographs behind, and then emerge soaking wet, with clothes shredded, and with steam rising from his body.

Although Floyd could become talkative on the thrills of caving, he was normally silent and placed little trust in others. Withdrawn, even aloof, he was often accused of being selfish. But he was merely a loner. He neither smoked nor chewed, rarely swore, had no intimate friends, and even the few caving companions he had were not close to him. Caving with Floyd could be more like work than pleasure because he usually wore out those who accompanied him. Following his solitary expeditions, Floyd never revealed their true extent nor where he had been. More than once he "popped out of a field like a groundhog" several miles from his starting point, encouraging the belief that many of Crystal's passages, like Mammoth's, extended far beyond owned land. Some of Floyd's neighbors claimed that in the dead of night he gathered up boulders and debris to plug up holes he feared might lead others in.

Floyd Collins's caving prowess did not alter the poor tourist situation at Crystal, and from 1918 to 1924 the cave was only intermittently profitable. The Collins family was forced to rely on farming and their other activities to remain solvent. In 1920 Floyd even invested in a still, and for a short time prior to Prohibition made legal whiskey to supplement his income. It was said that after the passage of the Volstead Act he continued to make moonshine, much to the disgust of his abstemious father. Throughout this whole period the Collins family was gradually breaking up and circumstances at the Flint Ridge homestead were changing. Jim, the eldest son, died of typhoid in 1922. Andy Lee migrated to southern Illinois to try his fortune there. Annie also left for that same state to start her family. Marshall married and moved onto a farm of his own adjoining his father's property. By 1924–25, only Homer, Nellie, and Floyd remained at home.

Lee, who watched this family disintegration with mixed emotions, gradually grew tired of investing more time and money in Crystal and began agitating to sell. Floyd disagreed, but finally late in 1924 entered into a sales contract with his father and Johnnie Gerald, one of his sometime caving confederates. Under terms of the agreement, Gerald was to buy himself, or try to sell, Lee's half for $4500 and Floyd's for $8500. The higher price that Floyd demanded for his share underscored his reluctance to part with the cavern. Drawn to run until January 1, 1925, this sales option was renewable at the initiation of the two owners.

When January 1 came Floyd refused to renew. Lee, who continued his part of the option for four more months, was furious and threatened to sue his son. By this time Floyd had developed a deep distrust of his father and believed he was turning senile. Moreover, Floyd had never given up hope that Crystal could be made into a highly profitable cavern. It was still one of the most beautiful and extensive caves in the region. Besides, there was already talk about Congress converting the whole Mammoth area into a national park. In that event Crystal would bring a better price from the government than from any private buyer.

Differences with his father over Crystal stiffened a resolve that Floyd had carried in his mind for some time. All his life he had watched or had heard about the area's chief cave developers and explorers—Bishop, the Lee brothers, Kaemper, Turner, Old Man Hackett, and George Morrison. Of them all, Floyd desired to be another Morrison. He had long been convinced that Crystal's many passages led to connections with surrounding caves. Unknown to anyone, Floyd had already explored five or six miles of passageways in Crystal's depths and in the process had uncovered many potential leads, some of which ran toward Mammoth. The trick, of course, was to find a commercially exploitable outside opening. If he could discover one in the proper place he could leapfrog them all, including Morrison's New Entrance. He could be the first, not the last, on the tourist access route.

Floyd planned his moves carefully. He talked with old-timers and other cavers about their various experiences. He consulted charts and old maps. He looked over the entire area in detail, following contour and ridge lines. From all this, he concluded that the most likely spot for a new opening was just over the line in Barren County on the narrow bridge of upland connecting Mammoth Cave Ridge with Flint Ridge at the latter's extreme southeast corner. There both the geologic and logistical conditions were right. Approximately four miles from the Collins home on the upper end of Flint Ridge, this land bridge was only six miles northwest of Cave City, was intersected by the main highway, and was ahead of Morrison's New Entrance. An opening there might connect both ways—into Mammoth and into Crystal.

Floyd knew from his past explorations on this upland that a sandhole existed on the farm of Beesley Doyle, only three hundred yards off the Cave City highway. Since Doyle's was only one of three farms controlling the upland area, Floyd began negotiations not only with him but with Edward Estes and Jesse Lee, the other landowners. Of the three, only Estes was a caver, sometimes raiding surrounding caves for onyx stalactites and cave rock which he sold to passing motorists. Floyd offered to search their land for a cavern in return for one-half the profits. The three farmers were to split the remaining half between them. Floyd would conduct the exploration; while he worked they were to give him room and board on a "week-about" basis. When capital was necessary, all four would supply it in proportion to their profits. Estes thought Floyd's bargain was a hard one, but Doyle and Jesse Lee were eager to let him begin. They feared that if they did not, a caver of Floyd's reputation would easily get others to sponsor him. Besides, Floyd promised that he was going to find something "new and big." Estes, prodded by the others, finally also agreed.

Starting with the hole on Doyle's farm, Floyd began to probe. Later called Sand Cave by the press, the name was actually a misnomer. It was not a cave but a narrow twisting crack of a passage leading downward. Situated at one end of an elongated depression caused by the collapse of a large cavern ages ago, this passageway skirted the base of an overhanging shelter's back wall, which was cluttered with sandstone debris. By choosing this route, Floyd hoped to save himself time—he was following a shortcut to what he hoped would be solid limestone below. Where this passage might lead was problematical—another entrance to Mammoth, a back door to Crystal, or a new cave altogether were possibilities.

Floyd lived at Doyle's for the first two weeks while he dug out the entrance and began his descent through the crumbling passageway. Doyle had recently butchered and had plenty of meat on hand, so Floyd remained there a second week, even though according to the agreement he was supposed to move on. Both weekends Floyd returned to his father's house on Flint Ridge. While at home on the second weekend he had another row with Lee over Crystal and over his current explorations.

"If you're so all-fired interested in Crystal," shouted Lee, "what're you a-diggin' around on Doyle's property for?"

"Ain't none of your business," replied Floyd.

Homer, who was shaking his head, interjected, "Ya know, Floyd, that hole's a bad un. You'll get caught in there. Floyd you're gonna get hung up!"

Miss Jane, his stepmother, was especially upset. That same weekend he had confided to her a dream in which he had been trapped by a rockfall and was finally rescued by angels. Superstitious and religious at the same time, she was convinced that this was a warning from God. "Don't go back in there, Floyd," she pleaded. "I wish you'd quit diggin' in them awful places." Tearfully, she appealed to Homer to reason with him and then to Lee, who only scowled and turned away.

On Monday, at the beginning of his third week of work at Sand Cave, Floyd moved over to Edward Estes's place to sleep but left his work clothes at Doyle's because it was closer to the cave. He also continued to take his meals at Doyle's because of the latter's well-stocked larder. Floyd's progress in the cave that week was rapid, especially after his use of dynamite on Monday. On Thursday he brought out a few stalactites to show to Doyle and Estes, telling them that they were proof of the great wonders lying farther below. The next morning, as he ate breakfast with Doyle, he chided him for any lingering doubts or fears.

"Don't you worry none," he said when Doyle complained about the risk and suggested that maybe they ought to give up the project. "This thing'll turn out. I jes' know it." Then he put on his jumper and coat, inserted a new globe in his lamp, picked up his climbing rope, and left for the cave.

That was Friday morning, January 30, 1925.

# 2

## Friends and Relatives

"Did Floyd come in?" It was Saturday morning and Bee Doyle looked worried as he talked to his neighbor, Edward Estes.

"Naw," replied Ed. "Figured he was over at your place." Rubbing his fingers over his chin, Estes added, "Guess we'd better see about him."

Doyle nodded as their eyes met. They knew what they had to do. They had to go to Sand Cave.

Both men had been uneasy about Floyd since the previous evening. Floyd should have returned to Doyle's house to remove his cave clothes at the end of the day's work, but he had not. Nor had he shown up at Estes's place to sleep. That night the Community Club had gathered for its regular monthly meeting at the Estes home and talk had touched on Floyd. Someone asked where he was, and Estes jokingly remarked that he was probably stuck in the sandhole.

Nobody yet took Floyd's absence seriously. But when Floyd did not return by the time the Community Club adjourned, Estes had gone over to Doyle's to inquire about him. Doyle was not at home; however, his twelve-year-old son informed Estes that his father had not seen Floyd. Told of Estes's visit after arriving a short time later, Doyle hurried to the mouth of the cave and called for Floyd, but got no answer. Returning home to bed, Doyle was awakened in the middle of the night by thunder and lightning and got up to see if Floyd had come in. Discovering that he had not, Doyle considered going to the cave once more, but a driving rain washed away his determination. He justified his inaction by assuming that Floyd had probably gone straight on to Estes's without stopping in. He would check with Ed first thing in the morning.

This Doyle had done—and as the two men now left for Sand Cave, Estes called to his seventeen-year-old son, Jewell, to accompany them. Slogging through puddles of icy water left from the previous night's downpour, they were prepared to be angry at a false alarm. But as they neared the entrance, Jewell, who had forged ahead, saw Floyd's coat hanging on a rock. The three yelled anxiously into the opening. There was no answer. They lighted a lantern and cautiously started in.

Doyle and Estes crept as far as the first squeeze and gave up. Jewell continued. A clean-cut young man with prominent ears and hair brushed straight back, Jewell was not a caver. However, he was slender and strong.

"Floyd! Floyd!" he called as he groped his way ahead. He was about to turn around when he heard a faint rasping reply.

"Come to me. I'm hung up."

Angling and twisting along toward the final squeeze, Jewell answered back, "That you, Floyd?"

Relieved at being found, Floyd coaxed his failing voice along. "Yep. Bring some tools." As calmly as he could, he assured Jewell that although a rock held his foot, he was mainly cold and hungry, and again requested that the young man come on down.

Jewell, who had managed well up to this point, could not force himself through the final squeeze. Besides, he was sickeningly afraid and admitted as much to Floyd. The trapped man betrayed a momentary impatience, then said, "Go get Johnnie Gerald."

"I don't know where he is," answered Jewell nervously. "My pa's here, though, and so's Mr. Doyle, and we can probably get some others."

"Well, go, boy, and hurry! Get Homer and Marshall and anyone else that'll come."

Jewell scrambled out of the cave. He was wet, muddy, and thoroughly frightened. "Floyd's hung up," he breathlessly told Doyle and Estes, "and wants us to get tools to get a rock off his foot." He also told them that Floyd wanted his two brothers, Homer and Marshall, to come to the cave at once.

The three men hurried back to Estes's, where the two older ones mounted a horse for the four-mile ride to the Collins home. They arrived about noon, just as Lee was getting ready to eat.

"What's up, Ed?" Lee asked when he saw them.

"Floyd's hung up in the cave and needs help," exclaimed Estes, jumping down from his horse.

As Estes described the situation and repeated Floyd's request for his two brothers, Lee listened in silence. Referred to by the neighbors as Old Man Lee to distinguish him from his sons, the sixty-five-year-old Collins could be a formidable figure. Stocky in build, he had suffered recently from a touch of rheumatism, which caused him to walk with a limp. His close-cropped, frizzled beard contrasted sharply with his dark bushy eyebrows. His most striking feature, however, was his deep-set gray eyes which, although beginning to lose their visual acuity, could shift from being haunting to piercing, depending on his mood. Normally a mild-mannered man, Lee was now angry, and when Estes finished he bitterly lashed out: "I knowed somethin' like this was gonna happen. That Floyd—always crawlin' around in some hole. 'N' you two eggin' him on a-hopin' to make some money. Wal, I reckon you boys who have him in there can get him out."

Lee had just recovered from the flu and had no desire to go outside in the cold. He also was currently preoccupied with his youngest daughter, Nellie, who had a history of mental illness and whom he had just brought home from a six-month stay in an asylum in Hopkinsville. Marshall, on the other hand, was anxious to go. Living in his own house only a stone's throw from the family homestead, he had first observed the commotion at Lee's through a window and, after learning of Floyd's plight, raced to the stable, climbed on a mule, and followed Doyle and Estes back to Sand Cave. Homer, who normally would have been at home, had gone to Louisville earlier in the week to visit friends and buy a car. He was not expected to return until later that day or on Sunday.

Marshall was the smallest of the Collins brothers and possessed the softest features. His face had a pouty look that was reinforced by a prominent Adam's apple. Although a strong champion of his caving brother, Marshall was not much of a caver himself. He had never ventured, for example, into any of Crystal's lower levels. However, he had been underground numerous times and knew basically what was required. Upon reaching the cave, he immediately organized a rescue party from among the twenty-five or so persons standing about in the wind and the cold. News of Floyd's plight had obviously already spread through the local telephone party line, and representatives of many of the neighborhood families, both black and white, were there. Of the first five men who accompanied Marshall into the cave, only one remained with him all the way. The others either became frightened or stuck. That one, Lewis Brown, was a black "trailer" at Mammoth Cave—a person who followed behind the tours to prevent stragglers from being separated from the rest of the group.

When Marshall got within twenty feet of Floyd, he heard his voice but could not find him.

"I don't see no hole," Marshall said when Floyd told him to look around for the chute opening.

"You're in the wrong place," admonished Floyd. "Come back to this end 'n' look for a hole jes' over my head. It's a little pit ten feet deep." When Marshall found it at last, Floyd cautioned, "Be careful—don't knock no rocks down on me."

Marshall adjusted his lantern and peered into the chute. He still could not see Floyd, who was off to one side in the crevice and shielded from view.

"How 'n hell did you get down there?" Marshall gasped. No matter how Marshall tried he could not force his body through. "Looks to me like this thing's caved in some, Floyd," he finally said.

Marshall began to dig. Jabbing with a crowbar and scooping up dirt with his bare hands, the younger Collins attempted to enlarge the chute opening. But Marshall had also recently suffered from the flu and his stamina quickly faded. Because the passageway at that point would accommodate only one man, Lewis Brown was unable to offer much assistance. Nor could two other black men, Clifton Bransford and Van Smith, who ultimately managed to catch up with Marshall and Brown after squirming past the final squeeze. Two white neighbors, Oscar Logsdon and Lewis Davis, found that they, too, could accomplish little once they got there. In such manner, three futile hours passed and still no one had reached the trapped victim.

Homer first heard about Floyd on Saturday afternoon at 3:30 P.M. He was driving back from Louisville in a Model T when he stopped for gas at a station near his home. The attendant innocently asked him if they had gotten his brother out yet. Homer was surprised at the news but not stunned. He was well acquainted with Floyd's peculiar caving habits.

Homer was by far the handsomest of the Collins boys. Curly-headed and possessing sharply etched features, he could have passed for a movie star. If he had any physical flaw, it was a long narrow nose, which was characteristic of all Collins males. Taller and lankier than Marshall, he was also much more at home in caves. At twenty-two he had more caving experience than anyone else in the family except Floyd. Often he had accompanied Floyd on deep explorations in Crystal.

Arriving at the site about four o'clock, Homer parked his car and ran across the field to the cave. His first impression was one of campfires burning and people moving aimlessly about. One fire was located on the bluff directly above the cave's entrance and was causing melting ice water to run down over the edge of the shelter overhang. Homer asked those standing by if Floyd was free and was told that he was not but that rescuers were talking to him. Without stopping to change clothes, Homer grabbed a lantern and went in.

The entrance passage was muddy and he half slid ahead. As he moved toward the first squeeze, he edged past several men who seemed to be doing nothing. Asked if they had been down to Floyd, they shook their heads. When Homer at last arrived near the top of the chute, he found Marshall and Oscar Logsdon there. They backed up to make way for him.

"Floyd, you all right?" called Homer.

"That's my ol' buddy Homer," Floyd cried. "I knowed you'd be comin' down to help me!"

Homer, who like Floyd weighed about a hundred and sixty pounds, tried to squeeze through the opening into the chute but failed. "You're never gonna make it with those city clothes on," observed Logsdon. Homer retreated to the turnaround chamber where he stripped to his underwear and removed his shoes before starting down again. He was cut and bruised by the time he wiggled through the chute opening and worked his way down the sharp slope. He shuddered when he realized that there was barely room to crouch in the cubbyhole at the bottom.

After the men lowered his lantern to him, Homer saw for the first time his brother's terrible plight. Surveying the tragic scene in front of him, his eye settled on Floyd's lamp, which was tipped over and its globe broken. His first question was perceptive.

"How come your lantern's up here and your hands are at your side that way?"

"I shoved it through first," answered Floyd. Recounting briefly the main facts of his entrapment, he informed Homer, "It's my left foot that's caught and it's stuck fast. Once I get it free I can get outa here."

A problem immediately confronted Homer that frustrated every subsequent rescuer. If a person came into the chute headfirst, he was forced to work upside down and was compelled upon leaving to push himself feetfirst up the sharp slant and then backpedal twenty feet more before he could turn around. If he dropped in feetfirst, as Homer had just done, he could not bring the upper part of his body down to Floyd's level without contorting himself into almost impossible positions.

As Homer twisted down he tried to scrape away some of the gravel as best he could from around Floyd's shoulders. Then he yelled for a small bucket. While this was being sought, Floyd told Homer that he was starving, and Homer ordered Logsdon to send out for some food. When it came, Homer had to feed Floyd like a baby since the trapped man could not raise his hands. It was pitiful, yet Floyd did not complain. He hungrily consumed nine sausage sandwiches and a pint of coffee before he stopped. Between bites, he told Homer exactly how he had been caught and what he had discovered. "There's a big pit down there, Homer, and I know it leads to a big cave. There's openings in 'n' out. But I got to find me a better way down to it." With a grimace, he added, "I'll shore never come this way again."

Both before and after the feeding, Homer worked, using a No. 10 syrup can to pass up to those above him what he dug out. Rocks tore at his hands and soon they were raw, making the digging agony. Also, as fast as he removed some gravel, more came sliding in. In frustration, Homer ranted at the situation. Floyd, however, remained remarkably calm. Finally, Homer, who was still in his underwear, began to shiver. Floyd noticed it and told him to leave.

"See if you can't get Johnnie Gerald to come help," said Floyd to his weary brother. "And when you come back bring an oilcloth to keep this here water from drippin' on me."

"Wait a minute," replied Homer, "let's try these." He took some burlap bags, which Floyd had used earlier in the week to remove rock in the passageway, and stuffed them around Floyd's body and over his face.

Floyd was relieved to be free of the dripping, even temporarily. "Where's all this water a-comin' from?" he asked. Homer told him it was from the rain and melting snow outside. Apprehensively, Floyd turned his eyes upward and remarked to Homer as he left, "If this keeps up, you'll have to timber the passageway to keep it from cavin' in."

Oscar Logsdon helped Homer out of the pit. Covered with perspiration, yet chilled by the dampness, Homer put on his clothes and stumbled out of the cave. Although shaken by his experience, he minimized the seriousness of Floyd's situation as he warmed himself at one of the fires. There was no cause for alarm, he said; Floyd would soon be free. Others, meanwhile, went in the cave, ostensibly to keep Floyd company. Some wore puttees and coveralls and cloth hats that held carbide lamps. Some were garbed in farm work clothes, and carried coal-oil lanterns and flashlights. All were made miserable by the mud, the icy water, the clammy chill, and the passage's close quarters. Most of them, overcome by fright, stopped somewhere along the way. Only a few got to the final squeeze, and none of these actually reached Floyd's side. Oscar Logsdon, Ellis Jones, Lewis Davis, and Carl Hanson crawled close enough to talk with him, but that was all. After coming out, none of them wanted to try again. Following his last trip in on Saturday evening, Ellis Jones, foreman of the Dixie Garage in Cave City, declared, "I wouldn't go back in there for a cold thousand, bad as I need money."

From eight o'clock to midnight on Saturday such ineffectual comings and goings continued. Then Homer went in again. This time he took a piece of oilcloth with him and rigged it over Floyd's head to intercept the leaking ground water. Again, the syrup bucket was passed up and down. With a short crowbar Homer picked furiously at the gravel and scooped away the sifting dirt and rocks. Progress was unbelievably slow. After three hours of exhausting labor, he had removed no more than two bushels of debris. Although this was sufficient to uncover the buried man's torso and upper arms, it still left his legs and thighs covered. While Homer labored and fumed, Floyd tried to help. Homer, however, cautioned him against moving unnecessarily and wasting his energy. At one point, Homer stopped working long enough to feed his brother some coffee and milk. He also placed a blanket on top of the wet burlap bags surrounding Floyd's body. Homer hoped that this additional covering would keep Floyd warm even though he was soaking wet.

Toward Sunday morning, as the hours passed and Homer's energy waned, Floyd complained that he was beginning to feel numb. Homer noticed with alarm that his brother suddenly seemed much weaker. "I'm awful cold, Homer," murmured Floyd through chattering teeth. "I got to get warm. Maybe a whiskey toddy like mother used to make would help me out."

"I'll go mix one for you," said Homer, seizing the opportunity to leave and get a brief rest himself. His mind, however, was racing ahead to what he might try next. He realized that what he had accomplished after eight hours of strenuous labor was not enough. Still buried to his waist, Floyd remained immobilized, and Homer had not yet hit upon a satisfactory plan to release his foot. What had begun as a simple rescue effort was turning into a nightmare.

As he rearranged Floyd's covers before leaving, Homer's eyes filled with tears. It was Floyd who broke the tension. "Now don't you get me no moonshine," he smiled, "I want some good stuff."

As Homer emerged on Sunday morning at six o'clock, many bystanders were already expressing doubts about a successful rescue. Homer himself was filled with apprehension. Old Man Lee had just arrived, dressed in an army coat and a bright red sweater. He sensed Homer's panicky feeling. So did Marshall, who tried to keep things moving while Homer rested. However, nobody had any new ideas and nobody offered to go in all the way. As the crowd expanded on Sunday morning, an increasing number were there who were neither friends nor neighbors of Floyd and did not care about him personally. They were merely curious. Drinking, which had been rare, now became commonplace.

Although a few potential rescuers continued to go in and out of the entrance, only one group mounted a serious attempt on Sunday morning to reach the trapped man. About nine o'clock, a team composed of Ish Lancaster, Columbus ("Lum") Doyle, and Van Smith entered the cave. Lancaster was the same age as Floyd and a friend. He had first gone in the cave on Sunday at 2:00 A.M. but had failed to get through the second squeeze. Lum Doyle, a forty-nine-year-old Baptist minister and the brother of Bee Doyle, had arrived at his small church on Flint Ridge that Sabbath morning only to find that most of his congregation had deserted to Sand Cave. He had hurried after them. Van Smith had already been down in the passageway with Marshall on Saturday afternoon.

When these three men crawled to the top of the chute, they found that Floyd was cold and wanted more covers. Doyle relayed this message to the mouth of the cave and then carried a quilt back down the crawlway. Lancaster crammed it down the chute and stuffed it around Floyd's body with his feet. But more than this the men were unable to do. After Lancaster and Doyle left, Van Smith stayed behind for a moment to talk with the imprisoned victim.

"Floyd," he said, "can't you help yourself?"

"No," came the reply.

"Can't you wiggle your foot and pull it out? Try, Floyd, try."

"I can't, I tell you. I jes' can't. I'm trapped, and trapped for life."

Not knowing what else to say, the black man scurried after the others out of the cave.

Following this midmorning attempt, only two other groups, variously composed of Lyman Cutliff, Lincoln Wells, Oscar Logsdon, Milton E. ("Casey") Jones, and, again, Van Smith, got as far as the lower passageway prior to Sunday dinnertime. And none of these men actually reached Floyd's side. Cutliff, who had to remove most of his clothing to wriggle even to the top of the chute, once talked with Floyd, urging him to keep his spirits up. Understandably impatient at the many delays, Floyd was testy.

"Why don't you come down here and help me, Lyman?" he complained. "Why does everybody jes' stay up there and talk?"

"The hole's too damned tight, that's why, Floyd," replied Cutliff.

"Wal, what're you doin', then, to get me out?" Floyd shot back.

With considerable exaggeration Cutliff answered, "Everything we can."

"You'd better hurry!" admonished the trapped man.

By Sunday dinnertime over a hundred persons were milling around the entrance to Sand Cave. Many argued about what should be done and loud profanity peppered their advice. All sorts of proposals, many of them halfbaked, were offered by persons who had never been inside the cave. Those few would-be rescuers who were still going in emerged shaking their heads. When Carl Hanson, an experienced Mammoth Cave guide, came out, he declared, "I been a-caving for twenty-eight years and never seen anything like it. How Floyd come to get back in there I'll never know." Lincoln Wells, who went in with the intention of easily saving Floyd, gave up when he saw the final squeeze and all the mud and water. Floyd, said Wells, must have worked his way down there "like a rat going through a corn pile." When Dr. H.P. Honaker, a physician from Horse Cave, asked one of the rescuers what a doctor might do to help, he was told the situation was hopeless and was warned against doing anything. Indeed, his question caused so much shouting and swearing among the bystanders that a thoroughly frightened Dr. Honaker, fearing things were getting out of hand, hastily departed.

Homer, who all this while was trying to recover his strength, sought several times to organize a new rescue party. Meeting with increasing indifference, he ultimately wheedled a few teenage boys to take some food in to his brother. They disappeared inside and then emerged quickly, telling tales of how they had held the trapped man's head, fed him, and comforted him. Homer knew they were lying and, disheartened and discouraged, finally prepared to go in the cave again himself.

In answer to Floyd's earlier plea for a toddy made with "good stuff," Homer had obtained some prescription whiskey from a druggist friend which he now carried in a bottle toward the entrance. Clay Turner, the Cave City magistrate, noticed it and immediately ordered it confiscated. A man of muscle, with squinty eyes and a square protruding jaw, Turner resembled a typical western marshal. He had recently arrived on the scene in answer to complaints that drinking was taking place. Ironically, Homer was his first victim.

"Gimme that bottle, son," exclaimed Turner. "There's not gonna be any whiskey down there."

Homer was incensed. "Why're you stoppin' me when there's all this other drinkin' around?"

"Don't give me no trouble. You know likker's against the law."

"Dammit," cried Homer, "my brother's down there in the mud and water. He ast for this 'n' he's gonna get it!"

Turner glowered. "Not while I'm here he ain't."

Continuing to argue about the whiskey and also about the growing crowds, Homer at last yelled, "If you wanta do somethin' why 'n hell don't you get these people away from here?"

"Now, calm down, boy, calm down," Turner advised and, pulling on the brim of his hat, walked off with the bottle.

Accompanied by Oscar Logsdon and seething with rage, Homer moved down the passageway at five o'clock. He noticed with concern that some rocks had been knocked loose from the ceiling by the futile rescue traffic. What disturbed him more were the abandoned food and blankets he saw stuck in the cracks along the way. When he reached Floyd, he ascertained what he already suspected. Nobody had been down to feed or work around his brother since he had left early that morning. Nevertheless, Floyd's spirits at the moment were good and, with hope returning, Homer began to dig around Floyd's left arm and hand. Even when these were uncovered, they remained confined to his side by the surrounding rock. Still, the moment they were usable at all, Floyd suggested, "If you'll slide that crowbar into my hand, I believe I can get my foot loose." Homer stuck the bar alongside his body. Floyd, however, was too weak to do much with it.

While the trapped man tried unsuccessfully to use the crowbar, Homer assaulted the limestone block overhead. He had brought with him a ball peen hammer, several cold chisels, and a gasoline blowtorch. He hoped that he could widen the space above Floyd's body so that he could crawl over top of him and reach his legs. But this was solid limestone, and Homer's puny tools were no match for it. He could not get a proper swing with his hammer and only tiny chips rewarded his most vigorous efforts. It was exasperating; but before long, Floyd stopped him anyway. He was afraid that Homer's hammering might crack the boulder, prompting the whole ceiling to collapse. Besides, such activity was again causing debris to filter down and threatening to undo the progress already made. So Homer turned to the blowtorch. Earlier he had tested it on the sandstone ledge outside the cave and had found that the heat made the rock more brittle. Crouching in the cubbyhole beside Floyd's head, he now attempted to light it. He failed. He tried again, and then again. Finally, fearful of an explosion in the confined space, he gave up. "This damned thing jes' won't work," he said. "We'll have to dig."

Back to the syrup bucket. Homer tried this time to uncover his brother's lower body. He worked desperately. As he dug one load after another, Oscar Logsdon dumped them up the passageway. Floyd said nothing. Slowly Homer made progress—enough gravel was removed from under and around Floyd's waist and hips that Homer was finally able to push in part way over top of him. Also, Homer could at last see both of Floyd's hands. They were dark brown from dried blood and matted dirt, the flesh having been torn from his fingers by his earlier clawing at the rock. The younger Collins paled and turned his eyes away.

After four hours of exhausting labor, Homer had to quit. Helped from the cave by Logsdon, he sank down at the nearest fire while Marshall, who anxiously had awaited his return, asked him what else they could do. Homer shook his head. Both brothers were close to hysteria. Old Man Lee began to prattle that Floyd's entrapment was God's will; Floyd might never get out. This provoked the three Collinses into a violent argument. Marshall ordered Lee to shut up and Homer bitterly charged their father with not caring whether Floyd lived or died. At his wit's end, Marshall suddenly offered $500 to anyone who would go in and bring Floyd out. The crowd, which at 9:00 P.M. still numbered over a hundred, buzzed with excitement at this family quarrel and at Marshall's offer. But there was no rush of volunteers. Finally, Clyde Hester, a local neighborhood man who was about Marshall's age, stepped forward. After shaking hands with Marshall to seal the bargain, he disappeared into the cave with a hastily assembled crew, most of whom seemed none too steady on their legs. They were gone only a moment. Then Hester reappeared and announced that Floyd was dead.

Homer was stunned. Marshall began to cry. Lee started to pray. Clay Turner, who not only was the Cave City magistrate but also the town's acting coroner, began to assemble a coroner's jury. "I need someone to check this story," he declared, and asked for a volunteer. This request was met with silence until one lone voice said, "I'll go." It belonged to L.B. Hooper, a twenty-year-old electrician's helper in the Radnor (Tennessee) yards of the L&N Railroad. Known as "Tennessee" to his friends, he had been on his way to visit a brother when he had heard of Floyd's accident and made a detour past Sand Cave. Arriving at 1:00 A.M. Sunday morning, he had entered the cave and crawled as far as the section leading to the final squeeze when he became so frightened that he had turned around. He had never been in a cave before and upon emerging remarked that he would never go in another one. On Sunday afternoon, however, he had steeled himself to try again. This time Hooper entered with a crew, whose members did not get past the first squeeze. When one of them said, "Let's get the hell outa here," they had all stampeded for the surface.

Hooper harbored few illusions about this third attempt. When he told Turner that he would volunteer, he added that he was a goddamned fool for doing so. To keep him company, Hooper asked a young black, named Horace Boatley, to go with him. But they were barely inside when Boatley announced, "I don't reckon I'll go." Wearing an unfamiliar miner's hat, Hooper continued alone, bumping into the ceiling every couple of feet. After twenty-five minutes of fearful suspense, he arrived at the top of the chute and called down to Collins.

"Hey, Floyd. You there?"

For an agonized moment there was no reply. Then a weak voice said, "I'm hungry. Bring me somethin' to eat." Excited by the fact that Floyd was still alive, Hooper momentarily forgot his fright, dropped into the pit, and gave Floyd some coffee from a quart bottle he had brought with him.

At first Floyd thought that Hooper was Johnnie Gerald. Hooper's light was in his eyes and Floyd's mind was also beginning to play tricks on him. "That you, Johnnie? Thank God you've come!"

"I'm not Johnnie, but I came to help," answered Hooper. As the young man looked around, Floyd's predicament almost overpowered him. "Jee-sus!" he exclaimed, and, fighting down an aching desire to flee, added quickly, "What can I do?" It was more a cry of desperation than an invitation to command.

"You know somethin' about caves?" Floyd asked.

"No," admitted Hooper.

"Wal," Floyd rolled his eyes, "this 'n's a bad un."

"You're sure as hell right about that," Hooper mumbled. Then he asked, "Is there another way in or out?"

"Naw, only the way you came."

Awkwardly, Hooper fussed with Floyd's covers. Finally, he blurted out, "Clyde Hester been here?"

Floyd looked at him, puzzled, then said, "I ain't seen Clyde Hester."

Hooper made a fast retreat. Anger up, he emerged from the mouth of the cave at eleven o'clock, yelling, "Where's Hester? He's a goddamned liar!" Hooper quickly recounted to Turner and to Floyd's brothers what he had found. Of course, Hester was nowhere to be seen, and Turner hastily abandoned the coroner's inquest.

False though Hester's death report proved to be, rescue hopes did not rebound. For almost two days, rescuers had been going in and out of Sand Cave to no avail. These early rescue efforts had been sincere. But they had also been disorganized and chaotic. They had involved much wasted effort and a lack of intelligent planning and leadership. People on the scene had spent too much time in argument and recriminations. Many who claimed to have reached Floyd never did. Food and drink that were intended for the trapped man had been abandoned along the way. There was something truly fearful about Sand Cave that had brought out the worst in men, and for the past two days cowardice had clearly outstripped bravery. Undoubtedly the cave seemed all the worse because only one man could reach or work at Floyd's side at a time. The cave had literally divided and then conquered Floyd's would-be rescuers one by one.

Sunday night, February 1, presented a dismal scene. A cold rain fell. The crowd, which still numbered in excess of a hundred, stood around in puddles, discussing rescue prospects and trying to ward off the wet and the chill. Lanterns glowed from the branches of trees or cast light out from stone ledges to illuminate the cave area while sputtering campfires barely stayed alive. Moonshine, which earlier in the day had been kept out of sight, once again made an appearance. Although the liquor unquestionably helped many in the crowd to keep warm, it did not add to their reason or enhance their dispositions. Scuffling matches erupted, loud arguments occurred, and profanity split the air. From time to time, a drunk would reel toward the cave's entrance only to stop short of going in. The few who did disappear inside came out quickly, using the occasion as a reason for taking another drink.

By Sunday midnight all rescue efforts had stalled. The falling rain gurgled in rivulets down the crevices and between rocks, making descent into the cave even more miserable. Water now stood two to three inches deep in some sections of the passageway. No one wanted to enter, drunk or sober. Most of Floyd's relatives and friends were exhausted, dispirited, and scared. Neighbors like Oscar Logsdon, Ish Lancaster, and Lyman Cutliff publicly expressed a willingness to continue but privately confided their lack of spirit. As one of them said, "Any man with brains a-tall wouldn't go in there." Marshall, meanwhile, was starting to cough and was not well. Lee was currently paying less attention to the rescue than to the drinking and swearing, which offended his Baptist soul.

Only Homer remained active. His energetic efforts had been the spark plug of all the early rescue attempts. Now, even though his confidence was shaken and his energy depleted, he refused to give up. Hester's report of his brother's death had frightened him. And his discovery of abandoned food and blankets in the passageway had convinced him that there was nobody except himself on whom he could rely. Frustrated and feeling isolated, he wearily reentered the underground quagmire of Sand Cave at 2:30 A.M.

What Homer found dismayed him. His brother was again cold and shaky and complained of numbness in his extremities. Floyd's body temperature was obviously sinking in the fifty-four-degree chill of the cave and his thinking process and other functions were slowing down. A normal-sized man immersed in fifty-four-degree water will die of hypothermia in a little over four hours. Floyd had been trapped in Sand Cave for two and one-half days. As a result, he was beginning to alternate between wakefulness and sleep, between being lucid and being in a stupor. Sometimes, for example, he thought he heard people talking and would call out to them but receive no answer. At other times, he would hear voices shouting to him but could not understand what they said.

When Homer visited him early Monday morning, Floyd's dreams and reality were finally becoming hopelessly mixed. For a time he and Homer conversed rationally, even debating various rescue possibilities. At one point, Floyd suggested that they try to pull him out using a harness placed around his body. At another point, he even broached the grisly subject of amputation. But as the hours dragged on, he faded in and out. . . .

. . . White angels came riding by in white chariots drawn by white horses. They were so beautiful. One more beautiful than the rest, with flaming hair, pointed a finger at him. . . . "Take me, take me," the trapped man cried as they sped away. Jerking suddenly awake, he found himself praying over and over, "God, help me, oh, God help me." Then, seeing Homer, he murmured, "Oh, Homer, oh, Homer." . . . Sandwiches, trays and trays of chicken sandwiches . . . How he loved them. And liver and onions . . . It

smelled like liver and onions—and fresh milk, gallons of milk. . . .
Floyd turned his half-open, clouded eyes toward his brother. "Save
me some liver and onions, Homer," he said. . . . The feather
mattress was soft and it felt so good to be in his own bed where he
could stretch out his legs and roll over on his stomach. . . . He
raised his head. "Oh, God, Homer," he moaned, "please take me
home to bed."

At first Homer tried to ignore these murmurings and concentrated on his digging, but the imprisoned man's anguish ultimately
prevented him from doing his work. Finally, Homer abandoned it
altogether, made himself as comfortable as possible, and maintained a silent vigil beside his tormented, hallucinating brother.
Dozing himself from time to time, he rested his hand on Floyd's
shoulder, a constant touch. Together, they suffered through the
remainder of a cold, wet night.

# 3

## *The Outside World Intrudes*

Louisville, Kentucky, was a city of four newspapers in 1925. The *Herald* and the *Courier-Journal* competed for the attention of the reading public in the morning. The *Evening Post* and the *Times* did the same at night. The *Herald* and the *Post* were owned together, as were the *Courier-Journal* and the *Times*. On weekdays, all four of these papers were on the street. On Sundays, there were only two—the *Herald-Post* and the *Courier-Journal and Times*.

Such rivalry helped create, and at the same time fed on, that style of sensational journalism identified with the 1920s. Some of this sensationalism followed naturally in the wake of the recent stirring events surrounding World War I; but its taproot actually lay in the yellow journalism of the late nineteenth century. By the decade of the twenties, however, competing for readers and exposing them to all sorts of exciting "news" had reached a high art. Already, in the summer of 1924, the public had been given a sample of what the press could do in the way of carnivalistic reporting by its frenetic handling of the Loeb-Leopold murder case.

Following this sensational event, a relatively slow news period had set in that, except for the presidential election in November 1924, lasted well into January 1925. The major national news at that time was President Coolidge's economizing in the White House, the pending trial of Harding's corrupt Veterans' Bureau chief, Charles Forbes, and a big jump in stock prices. Only the emergence of the Nome diphtheria epidemic late in the month held out a promise of more interesting material. Even sports news was in the doldrums. There was talk of Jack Dempsey's possible retirement, and numerous articles appeared on the indoor track exploits of Paavo Nurmi, the "Flying Finn." It was January, after all; the football season was over and the baseball season had not yet begun. As a result, newspaper readers had to content themselves by spending more time perusing the movie ads (Rudolph Valentino in "A Sainted Devil," Noah Beery in "The Spoilers," and Bessie Love and Roy Stewart in "Sundown"), reading descriptions of what the new Essex 6 ($895) could do, or puzzling out the advantages of a Crosley Trirdyn ($85) over the latest Atwater Kent with separate speaker ($128).

In Louisville, as in other areas of the country, hometown or regional happenings were called upon to fill some of this news gap. Here, also, the fare was meager. On January 15, the *Evening Post* was reduced to using this headline: "MOTHER IS KILLED BY DAUGHTER." Four days later it ran one, "FOUR TOTS DIE AS KIN LISTEN TO THE RADIO." To get even this marginal material before Louisville readers, the town's two newspaper combinations and their four journals raced with each other to hit the streets first. The losers compensated by making their stories fuller and more intriguing. In presenting such news, each of the Louisville papers used every kind of gimmick and technique: eyewitness accounts, in-depth analyses, artists' drawings, and personal interviews. Sometimes, when interesting or sensational news did not exist, they invented it. Colorful and aggressive reporting, of course, was the basis upon which this whole competitive system rested, and, to aid in this enterprise, each of these papers not only employed a stable of reporters but also retained an intricate network of local informants.

On Saturday night, January 31, after Floyd Collins had been trapped in Sand Cave about thirty-six hours, rural correspondents of the Louisville papers began phoning in their accounts. Both the *Herald-Post* and the *Courier-Journal and Times* were notified. The story created no sensation because these papers had received such reports from the cave country before. The cave wars had lent themselves to a variety of hoaxes involving lost and trapped persons, and Louisville editors had to be careful. Still, even if the story proved to be false, a man caught in a cave had some news value, and both papers ran a brief account of it in their Sunday morning editions.

The main national story that particular weekend was the Nome diphtheria epidemic and the dramatic attempt to supply that isolated Alaskan community with lifesaving serum. The second lead related to the conviction of Charles Forbes for conspiracy and fraud. The primary local news story described a Ku Klux Klan shooting in nearby Herrin, Illinois. Although the Floyd Collins item appeared on the front page on Sunday, February 1, it was small and carried only a modest caption. The *Courier-Journal and Times*, whose circulation of ninety thousand made it Kentucky's largest newspaper, reported: "Cave-in Pins Man Supine in Cavern." The *Herald-Post* ran a small headline: "Kentuckian Rescued from Cave." Hoping to outflank its opposition, this paper had altered the information it received from its Cave City informant, Mrs. Ira D. Withers, and claimed in a subheading, "Collins Free—Says Never Again." The accompanying article told of a wholly fictitious rescue centering around Jewell Estes, whom it called Jewell Ester.

After reading the *Herald-Post* account, Neil Dalton, city editor of the *Courier-Journal,* called his local correspondent in Cave City to complain about being scooped. The correspondent replied that Collins was not free. Dalton immediately ordered one of his reporters, William Miller, to go to the cave country to investigate, but only if he could get the special rescue squad of the Louisville police and fire departments to accompany him. Dalton believed it would be an excellent promotion scheme for the *Courier-Journal* to sponsor a cave rescue. But when Miller contacted the police and fire authorities, they absolutely refused to send the rescue squad, claiming it would be a waste of Louisville taxpayers' money. Miller, however, still wanted to go, and Dalton finally decided to send him on alone.

William B. Miller was a thin-faced, sandy-haired twenty-one-year-old who weighed a hundred and seventeen pounds and was five feet five inches tall. Called "Skeets" because he was "no bigger than a mosquito," he hailed originally from Parkland, Kentucky. After graduating from the local high school there, he had entered the newspaper game. Skeets, who had a fine voice and aspired to be an operatic baritone, considered his career in journalism only a temporary thing. Employed first by the *Evening Post* as a police reporter, in late 1924 he moved over to the *Courier-Journal* into a slightly better job. In January 1925, he was not yet a seasoned reporter and was making only twenty-five dollars a week.

Miller caught a train late on Sunday night from Louisville to Glasgow Junction. There he hired a car to take him the rest of the way to Cave City and arrived in that small town at 7:00 A.M. Monday morning. He went directly to the Dixie Hotel, where he inquired about Collins. He was informed that Floyd was still trapped but that his brothers and friends were trying to get him out. After pausing briefly to eat breakfast, he made a deal with a local taxi driver to take him the remaining six miles to Sand Cave.

On the way, Miller stared out the window at a dreary scene. Here and there an occasional farmhouse broke the monotonous landscape. For the final three miles only empty fields with their ghostly cornstalks could be seen. A purple haze covered the ground when the taxi approached the rescue site shortly after 9:00 A.M. The sun, not yet high, was hidden by a gray sky, and a few isolated patches of snow still lay on the ground. Alighting from the taxi, Miller was told that Sand Cave was just beyond a field of low brush bordering on the right edge of the road. For three hundred yards, the young newsman followed a broken path that twisted through foliage and led around the left side of a slope. The trail then dropped away into a natural amphitheater, fronted by an overhang of stone in the shape of a crescent. Immediately in front of this brow of rock stood a prominent swell of earth that masked a darker recess beyond. Extending in the opposite direction was a sparsely timbered ravine. To the left of the earth mound, Miller saw a campfire over which hung a five-gallon coffeepot. About fifty men were sitting around the fire or standing in several inches of muck off to the side. The rain of the night before had stopped, but now it was growing colder. The temperature stood at twenty-four degrees.

Miller was not the first newspaperman to witness this scene. William S. Howland of the *Nashville Tennessean* had arrived that same morning at seven o'clock. After talking to some of the bystanders, he had tried to enter the cave's passage but gave up after going no more than thirty feet. Similarly, A.W. Nichols of the *Evening Post* had arrived before Miller, dressed in a suit, overcoat, brimmed hat, striped tie, and looking every inch the city news-paperman. He later claimed that he went into the tunnel to within "ten or twelve" feet of Floyd and shouted words of encouragement to him. This is highly doubtful. A.D. Manning of the *Louisville Herald* was also there before Miller showed up, but made no claim of trying to enter the cave at all.

At the moment Miller arrived, Homer had just emerged wet and tired from his Sunday all-night vigil. He was warming himself by the fire and agonizing with Marshall over Floyd's deteriorating con-dition as Miller strode up. Homer had come to hate all curiosity seekers, and newspaper reporters incensed him most of all.

"I hear you're the brother of the fellow who's trapped in the cave," began Skeets.

Homer ignored him at first. Then, looking him up and down dourly, he snorted, "I judge you're another reporter."

"Yes. I'm from the *Courier-Journal* in Louisville. Is your brother still alive?"

"Humpf," Homer snorted antagonistically.

"Are you going to get him out?" asked Miller.

Homer frowned, then snapped. "If you want information, there's the hole right over there. You can go down and find out for yourself."

That should have ended it, but to Homer's amazement his challenge was accepted. Asked later why he agreed to go in, Miller said, "I guess I was ashamed not to." Dressed in an overcoat and a

khaki-colored gabardine suit, he quickly changed into coveralls
and, with Homer and Estes leading the way, entered Sand Cave.

When Skeets Miller started down he was a rank amateur with
respect to caves. He slid along headfirst as Homer directed him
which way to go. All the while he fought back a wildly growing
fear. Rocks of various sizes hung down from the ceiling, giving him
the impression that they were ready to fall. At the first squeeze, his
two companions stopped, and Miller's lonely ordeal began. Clutching a flashlight Homer had pressed into his hand, the young
reporter moved ahead. Grit from above funneled down his neck.
His hands and knees plowed through cold mud. When he crawled
on his belly, ice water slushed down his front. His teeth chattered
and he had the shivers. An awful feeling of aloneness enveloped
him; it was so cramped and so still.

To soothe himself as much as to elicit an answer, he began to
call, "Floyd? Floyd?" At first there was no reply, then an
unintelligible response. Miller elbowed his way forward, slid down
a sharp drop, and fell against a wet mass. It groaned and moved.
Petrified, he tried to push away but was prevented from doing so by
the steepness of the incline. Another groan, "Oh-h-h . . . you're
hurting me." Sanity returned as Miller realized it was Collins.

Working his way back up to the top of the chute where he could
turn around, Miller descended again, this time feetfirst. He was in
the dark, having dropped his flashlight, which went out when he
fell. Fumbling around, his hand touched a lantern Homer had left
there and which Skeets had overturned when he bumped into
Floyd. He tried to light it. At the same time, he inadvertently
moved some of the wet covers from around Floyd's face. The
trapped man moaned, "Put it back, the water—" Floyd also
mumbled something about not wanting the lantern lit because it
would hurt his eyes. Miller hastily abandoned the lamp and
recovered his muddy flashlight, which he used sparingly to see
where he was.

He was appalled. He could not imagine a more terrifying place.
As he looked around he was overcome with nausea. His survival
instinct told him to flee, but the reporter in him forced him to
remain. Collins seemed drugged and was not too communicative.
Learning only that Floyd's left leg was pinned and that he felt cold,

Miller managed a few words of encouragement before he scrambled out. The newsman had stayed in the pit something less than ten minutes.

The passage in had been all downhill. The way out demanded more effort, and Miller had to stop twice from fatigue. His heart pounded in terror. Time stood still as he crawled and inched his way upward. More than once he told himself to relax, but the thought kept recurring that he, too, might be caught in this horrible cave. Even his meeting Ed Estes halfway up did not allay his fear. Finally, exhausted, shivering, and covered with mud from head to foot, he stumbled out into the light and sank down with his head between his knees. By now he had forgotten all about his paper, and he was crying.

It was an experience Skeets Miller would never forget. He had entered Sand Cave at about 10:00 A.M. and reappeared at 11:15. These seventy-five minutes altered his life. His relief at his own deliverance was matched by an intense pity for the trapped man. Collins was obviously weak, he could not gain his own release, and his position was such that perhaps no one else could help him either. Miller had never seen Floyd Collins before, yet he was impressed by the man. Floyd had touched a deep nerve in the young reporter who so feared this hole but empathized so strongly with the victim lying in it. Thereafter, William Miller's existence and Floyd Collins's fate were inextricably bound together.

Lieutenant Robert Burdon arrived in Cave City sometime before noon on Monday, February 2. He anticipated that his job was going to be an easy one. A member of Truck Company No. 1 of the Louisville Fire Department, he also belonged to the city's special police-fire rescue team and had volunteered to accompany a compressed-air drill to a place called Sand Cave where a rescue effort for a trapped caver was under way. Thirty-three years old and a seven-and-a-half-year veteran of the fire-fighting force, Burdon was a tall, lean, aggressive extrovert who exhibited considerable ambition. He had seized this occasion to enhance his future prospects because the Louisville Fire Department promoted men partly on merits given for rescue work. "Captain" Burdon sounded better to his ear than "Lieutenant" Burdon.

After an early lunch, he obtained a ride from Cave City to the rescue site. There he found a large gathering of men, none of whom seemed to know who was in charge or what was being planned. He was told that a young reporter from Louisville had just come out of the cave and that the trapped man's brother had gone back inside. Many in the crowd asserted that they, too, had been in the cave, had talked with the prisoner, and had fed him. The thought crossed Burdon's mind that if half of what they said was true, the entombed man's ears must be ringing and his stomach bloated. Burdon could not help but notice a strong smell of liquor on the breaths of many.

Dissatisfied with secondhand impressions, the Louisville fireman decided to investigate for himself and, despite protests, entered the cave's mouth and started down. After a short distance he met Homer, who was crouching in the upper passageway. The younger Collins ordered him out, grumbling that if he continued there would be another fool caught down there. But Burdon, a direct and blustery man, indicated that he had no intention of stopping and, focusing his flashlight ahead of him, crawled on to the top of the chute. Along the way he saw the bottles of milk and food abandoned in the cracks. He speculated to himself that not one in ten of those who had claimed to have done so had actually seen or reached Floyd Collins.

Although six feet tall, Burdon weighed only a hundred and forty pounds and easily entered the chute. Twisting down beside the trapped man, he was stunned by Floyd's situation. Never had he seen anyone caught like this. Whenever the breeze through the cave lessened, a fearful stench assaulted his nose. With a shudder, he guessed it was from Floyd's excreta over the past three days. Nearly gagging, the fireman asked Floyd how he had gotten in this fix and if many persons had been down to see him. At the moment Floyd was in control of all his faculties and answered Burdon's questions succinctly. Only his brother Homer and one or two others had been close enough to touch or feed him, Floyd said. Burdon then asked if there was another way in or out of the cave. Floyd shook his head.

Finally, just before leaving and after shining his flashlight around the hole once more, Burdon commented, "We got a hellava problem here, but I think we can get you out with a rope."

"I've thought some about that myself," remarked Floyd.

Burdon reflected for a moment and then, looking along the trapped man's body, said, "We might pull your foot off."

"Pull my foot off, but get me out."

"I'll do that, partner."

With that, Burdon left. Like Skeets Miller, he had been with Collins no longer than ten minutes.

Burdon's emergence early on Monday afternoon immediately intensified discussions about what direction the rescue should take. Skeets, who had gone to file a personal account of his morning trip in the cave with the *Courier-Journal,* had just returned. Lee, Homer, and Marshall were there, too. Also joining the discussion was a newcomer, Johnnie Gerald. Gerald had not yet crawled into the cave but was already regarded, especially by Floyd's relatives and friends, as a key rescuer.

Lieutenant Burdon dominated the conversation, his voice exuding authority, his language peppery. Having come here to earn easy merit points, he had temporarily forgotten about them in the glow of his flashlight when he had first observed Floyd's terrible predicament. Like Miller, he had been impressed by the trapped man's dignity and patience. Now he sincerely wanted to get Collins out and believed that he could show the others the proper way. The air drill, which he had been asked to accompany, had just arrived by truck from the Cave City freight station, but Burdon knew that its use was impossible. There was too little room inside the cave. Homer also agreed that the drill should not be used, although for different reasons. His experience with the sifting gravel and loose rock told him that a drill would produce disaster. The fragile passageway walls and ceiling would not stand the jarring.

Burdon claimed that the surest way of rescuing Floyd was by sinking a shaft. He admitted, however, that this approach was impractical since there was neither the equipment nor the skilled manpower present to handle such a project. Homer, supported by Gerald and Marshall, rejected this idea anyway. Homer maintained that the geologic formation of the hillside was not suited for shaft sinking. More important, he feared that Floyd's physical and mental condition was deteriorating so rapidly that he could not last that long. Enlargement of the hole where Floyd lay was a better possibility, although Homer realized that such digging would require constant relays of very small men to work there. Moreover, there was always the danger that the accompanying traffic might cause cave-ins in the less stable portions of the passageway. Amputation of Floyd's leg was also an option, but for the time being neither Lee, Homer, nor Marshall were willing to consider it.

According to Lieutenant Burdon, the best alternative was to pull, and he argued aggressively for it. Skeets Miller agreed. The Collinses were not so sure. Johnnie Gerald was vehement in his opposition and was joined by native bystanders, some of whom could remember the fate of Pike Chapman who had died in 1897 while being pulled out of a rock slide in Salts Cave. Floyd's foot would be torn off, said Gerald, and he would bleed to death before he could be brought to the surface. Two local doctors, who were listening to this argument, admitted that the trapped man's leg might rend at the ankle or the knee, but more likely his shoulder and chest muscles and some of his internal organs would tear first. In either case, they said, Floyd would die. Burdon countered by agreeing that pulling represented only "one chance in a thousand" and that Floyd's vital organs might rupture. But if this did not happen, and if he could be moved just far enough to get someone behind him, he might be brought out alive. "That boy is gonna die for sure in that goddamn hole unless we drag him out," contended Burdon.

Johnnie Gerald remained unconvinced. But Homer and Lee finally agreed. Marshall found this entire discussion so unnerving that he had a fainting spell and had to lie down under the shelter of the cave's overhanging ledge. Homer, who the previous night had discussed just such a rescue possibility with Floyd, immediately left for Cave City to find someone to fabricate a pulling harness that could be strapped on his imprisoned brother. Burdon, meanwhile, organized a clearing party, which, for the remainder of the afternoon, removed loose rock from the passageway and maintained intermittent voice contact with Floyd. Johnnie Gerald, in turn, stood silently by—and waited.

About five o'clock, Homer returned with a harness designed to fit around Floyd's shoulders and chest. It resembled a Sam Browne belt with two straps instead of one and with a ring attached on the back. Before descending, Homer packed two ham sandwiches, some hot coffee, a sedative pill from one of the doctors, and a little whiskey. Clay Turner was not there at the moment to protest. Homer entered the cave first, followed by Skeets Miller, who, despite his earlier scare, was again anxious to help. Then came Lieutenant Burdon and five others. When Homer reached Floyd, he began to feed him while Miller remained at the top of the chute peering in. Burdon lay on his belly behind Miller, waiting, as did the others who were strung out up the passageway.

Floyd was in a daze when they arrived and his face was lined with pain. In a lucid moment earlier that afternoon, he had tried once again to work with the crowbar Homer had placed next to his left hand the previous evening. He had exhausted himself in this futile effort, leaving him shaky and badly depressed. But now the food, whiskey, medicine, coffee, and human companionship made him feel better. The hot liquid, in particular, helped restore some of his body heat and sharpen his faculties. Newsman Miller seized the occasion to talk with Floyd as Homer fed him slowly. During the ensuing conversation, in which Floyd repeatedly called the young reporter "fella," he explained how he had been exploring Sand Cave when he was caught, how he had discovered a "beautiful cavern" on down below, and how Jewell Estes had finally found him. It was essentially the same story he had told Homer on Saturday, except for the "beautiful cavern" part. Homer was surprised at this addition and assumed that his brother was only imagining it, but he could not be sure.

All this time Lieutenant Burdon and the others were growing impatient and cold in the breezy crawlway, and he yelled down to Homer and Miller to hurry up. Homer quickly explained to Floyd what they intended to do and struggled to get the harness on him. It was a difficult task and took a long time to work the straps under his back and down to his waist. The tolerances were small and Floyd could offer little help.

As the preparations neared completion, Floyd became ambivalent about the whole project. He began to talk rapidly. "Homer, you won't pull my foot off, will you? Oh, God, you can't pull my foot off?"

"Now, Floyd, we won't even try if you say so," soothed his brother.

"Sweet Jesus, don't leave me here again, Homer. Pull me out

then!" Pleas and moans spilled simultaneously from the trapped man. None of this helped bolster Homer's morale. He was unnerved before the pulling even began.

Homer tied a hundred-foot rope to the harness ring and fed the other end up the passageway to Miller, who handed it on to Burdon. The other men in the line grabbed hold of it. Haltingly, Homer gave the signal to begin.

As the tension on the rope tightened and his body straightened five or six inches, Floyd began to cry out, "You fellas can't do it! Don't do it!"

"Keep going! Keep going!" Burdon bellowed in the passageway.

"Stop! I can't stand it! It's pullin' me in two!" shrieked Floyd.

Homer, seeing the agony on his brother's face, blanched and began to haul in the opposite direction. But his tugs were no match for those who were still pulling above. They strained all the harder, thinking the rope had caught on a snag.

"It's breaking my back—stop them, oh, God, stop them!" gasped Floyd.

In a frenzy, Homer jerked the rope violently. "Stop it! Stop it! You'll kill him!"

The rope fell slack. Homer was sweating. Floyd slumped back in to his old position, whimpering. Miller, who had been scrabbling for footholds in the ooze at the top of the chute, was relieved because Floyd's cries had terrified him. Even Burdon was shaken, although he believed they should not have stopped. He immediately wanted to try again, but Homer said no. When Floyd realized that they were preparing to depart, he once more began to beg, "Don't leave me. Please, don't leave me. Dope me and pull me out. Oh, God, please!" As the others dejectedly left, Homer remained behind temporarily to soothe his hysterical brother while his own fear and anxiety rapidly mounted.

The harness attempt had failed. A crowd of about two hundred saw it written on the faces of the rescuers as they began to emerge at 7:30 P.M. On the way up, both Burdon's and Miller's flashlights winked out, causing the two men to panic. They quickly expended what little energy they had left by crawling feverishly toward the surface. Burdon collapsed at the mouth of the cave and had to be carried away. Miller was also dragged from the entrance. Homer was so exhausted that as soon as he emerged he fell to the ground in a stupor.

A car picked up Homer and Marshall within the hour and drove them to the Dixie Hotel in Cave City, where they were put to bed. Marshall had not yet recovered from his fainting spell earlier in the afternoon and was already under the care of a physician. Just before they left, Homer tearfully offered $500 to any doctor who would go in and amputate Floyd's left leg. It was a final, desperate sign that he was ready to give up. Lieutenant Burdon was also taken to Cave City and put to bed. Skeets Miller sat by the fire for a while, then went off to file an eyewitness account of the harness attempt with the *Courier-Journal.* Saddened by the failure, the young reporter wondered what would now happen to the trapped man.

Marshall proved to be so ill that he was incapacitated for three days and participated in no further rescue attempts. Homer, however, did not remain away from Sand Cave very long. After only several hours' rest he returned to the site because he heard a rumor that his brother was free. Burdon, meanwhile, tossed fitfully in his bed, mulling over in his mind how he might still rescue Floyd with a rope. He vowed not to make the same mistake again of wasting time feeding Floyd before the pulling began. And he certainly would not take Homer along. A thought suddenly occurred to him: What he needed was a fire-hose hoist. He got up, sent a wire to his fire company in Louisville, and then fell into a deep sleep.

John B. Gerald was a short, moon-faced, serious man whose personality was placid and whose reactions were normally low-keyed. Except for his darting eyes, he could appear at times almost lifeless. Older-looking than his thirty-two years, Gerald was a resident of Cave City and during cold weather, like the present, was easily recognizable on its streets by his button-down billed cap and his leather mackinaw with a lamb's wool collar.

Gerald had grown up in the cave country and had lived near Sand Cave earlier in his life. Yet he was not acquainted with it, although he knew considerable about the other caves in the area, many of which he had explored personally. As a real estate agent and sometime auto salesman, Gerald was mainly interested in the profits to be made from caves and in putting together financial deals concerning them. It was in this latter capacity that he had recently negotiated a price for the sale of Crystal with Floyd and his father. Gerald had known the Collinses for a long time; he and Floyd had grown up together. Sometimes they had joined forces in caving expeditions, and Gerald was one of the few who had gone with Floyd into the lower levels of Crystal. Once when Floyd got stuck there Gerald had helped him get loose, while two others who were along were too afraid to do anything.

Little wonder, then, that Johnnie Gerald was one of the first persons Floyd had asked for when Jewell found him trapped in Sand Cave. Gerald, however, was enigmatic, and his early actions with respect to Floyd's rescue proved it. On Saturday afternoon, January 31, he was on his way from Horse Cave to Cave City when he stopped to see Wood Ford, a neighbor. Ford asked him if he had heard about Floyd's being caught in a cave. Replying that he had not, Gerald drove his car to a Cave City garage for minor repairs and while there asked one of the mechanics if he knew anything about Floyd. The mechanic said he didn't. Walking over to Johnson's restaurant, where he ordered a cup of coffee, Gerald again inquired about Floyd. Told that Floyd was caught in a hole on Flint Ridge but would probably be out by dark, Gerald thought little more about it. That evening he chauffeured the local basketball team to Munfordville.

Gerald slept most of Sunday, but at 4:30 P.M. went back to Johnson's restaurant to ask what had happened to Floyd. Told that Floyd was still trapped, he set out in his car for Sand Cave after picking up several friends. They arrived about dinnertime and found nearly a hundred people present. Here, for the first time, Gerald learned that Floyd had been asking for him. Warned, however, that he was too stocky to get past the squeezes, he remained outside. After about an hour of listening as some of the men described exactly how Collins was caught, he drove back to his home in Cave City and went to bed.

Sometime that night Floyd's plight caused Gerald to begin formulating his own rescue plans. On Monday morning he contacted a friend, Clarence Owens, and borrowed an air drill. He also stopped by Walker Stewart's supply store and bought three hundred feet of air hose. Next, he hired a small truck to haul this equipment to Sand Cave. Arriving in his own car a short time later, he found Lieutenant Burdon already there with an air drill from Louisville. The time was early Monday morning and a discussion was under way about the most practical rescue approach. Lieutenant Burdon had just crawled out of the cave and was voicing his views on the advantages of pulling.

Gerald's opposition to Burdon's pulling scheme made the two men antagonists from the start. Gerald stood sullenly by while the Louisville fireman organized the Monday midafternoon rock-clearing party. He also remained on the surface while the harness attempt was made. But when the latter failed, and Burdon, Homer, and Marshall were taken away to Cave City, Gerald became the rescue leader by default. Even before the harness attempt, most natives had begun to gather around him for advice. Old Man Lee, in particular, regarded him as *the* person to rescue Floyd and centered the family's waning hopes on him. More important, Floyd himself, by repeatedly asking for Gerald, obviously had great faith in him.

Gerald held definite opinions about the proper direction of the rescue work. Although he had brought an air drill, he rapidly concluded, like Burdon, that it was useless. The sinking of a shaft, he believed, would take too long and would run into difficult engineering problems. To pull Floyd out by a rope was both dangerous and inhumane. The only solution was to protect the stability of the existing passageway, maintain Floyd's body heat and energy levels by dry covers and hot food and drink, and dig around and over top of him. This would be laborious, but it was the best way to proceed.

Early on Monday evening Gerald began to implement his beliefs. Convinced that outsiders—"outlanders," the natives called them— were uninformed and reckless in their behavior, Gerald first sought to restrict their access to the cave. He wanted only those to go in who knew something about central Kentucky caves and their peculiarities. According to his view, rescue crews were to be

selected for their caving knowledge and be few in number. The
more persons who were allowed to go in and out, the more likely
that wall and ceiling damage would cause a collapse.

At 8:00 P.M., a half hour after the harness attempt had failed,
Gerald entered the cave with a personally selected crew for the first
time. Since he had been told that he might not make it through the
squeezes, he let Lieutenant Ben L. Wells lead the way. Gerald
came second, followed by Charles Whittle, and two others.
Lieutenant Wells was a recent graduate of West Point and currently
a math instructor at Ogden College in Bowling Green. Whittle,
although only twenty-five years old, was president of Ogden. These
two men knew the local caves and had driven over late that
afternoon to inquire if they could be of help. Gerald had co-opted
them immediately.

Lieutenant Wells took the lead through the first squeeze. As they
reached the small turnaround chamber, Gerald yelled for Wells to
let him pass. His voice carried down the passageway, and Floyd,
who was in the depths of despair as a result of the harness ordeal,
heard it. "That you, Johnnie?" It was a plea more than a question.

Gerald did not answer immediately because he was busy calling
at the same time, "Floyd, Floyd! Do you know who this is?"

Again Floyd asked, "Is that you, Johnnie?"

"You betcha! I come to get you out."

Floyd's hopes were rekindled immediately, and he excitedly
exclaimed, "That's Johnnie Gerald; he's my friend. Let him down
here! Let him down here!"

By now Gerald had arrived at the top of the chute and was
peering in. "Is there another way in there?" he asked.

"No. Come on down, Johnnie."

"Did you go through this hole?"

"Yep."

Gerald eyed the opening. "I don't see how ya done it."

"Wal, I done it, but it was awful tight."

Gerald knew that he would never make it without some digging.
Suddenly Floyd interjected, "I'm thirsty, Johnnie. Got somethin'
to drink?"

Lieutenant Wells had brought a bottle of milk along and Gerald
yelled to him to hand it forward. Then he remembered that he had

not yet reached Floyd and asked Wells for a piece of string. Gerald tied this onto the bottle and lowered it into the pit before realizing that Floyd could not move to reach it. Wrapping the string's loose end around a rock, he mumbled, "That's the best I can do now," and left the milk dangling.

Gerald's immediate problem was how to widen the chute's mouth so he could get in. He first thought that if he removed two of the largest rocks forming the lip of the pit he might force his body through. These two stones he passed back to Wells, but still he could not squeeze in. He wrestled more rocks out, followed again by failure. Finally, after a discussion about what to do next, the entire group began to crawl to the surface. "I'll be right back, Floyd," called Gerald, "I've got to get me some gloves and tools."

As he stepped from the entrance shortly after nine o'clock, Gerald noticed a growing rowdiness among the hundred and fifty or so persons who were still gathered at the cave. The crowd had seemed restless earlier in the evening, but nothing like now. Men lurched and reeled unsteadily. Voices were louder. There had been an increase in drinking. Gerald also noticed that two tents had sprung up at the cave's entrance—one to provide snacks and hot coffee to potential rescuers and the other to serve as a first-aid station. Other newcomers had also appeared, some of them workers from the Kentucky Rock Asphalt Company in nearby Kyrock. They were beginning to shore up the cave's entrance, but by whose authority nobody seemed to know.

The outside world was crowding in, and this intrusion added to the general confusion. Johnnie Gerald frowned. Goddamn, he thought. None of these people could help the situation where it mattered most—at Floyd's side. From any vantage point, they were useless. Worse, they were dangerous. Their tramping around might set up vibrations that would trigger rockfalls in the passageway. If these outlanders would only leave, thought Gerald, it would be better for everyone. Most of the natives at the cave obviously felt the same way, and profane shouting matches were already developing between them and some of the newcomers. These quarrels, when added to the antics and carousing of the merely curious, threatened to change a deteriorating situation into a melee.

At ten o'clock Gerald turned his back on this churning mob and descended into the cave for a second time, again followed by Lieutenant Wells, Whittle, and several others. Arriving at the pit, Gerald asked Wells to hold on to his feet while he reached down and pulled out some of the larger rocks that lay on the bottom. One was over thirty pounds and he almost ripped out his insides wrestling it up. A second one, weighing at least sixty pounds, required a rope before it could be hauled to the top of the chute and passed back to the other crew members above. Several smaller rocks were also removed from the pit and the chute opening itself was enlarged. At last Gerald could drop in.

While assessing Floyd's desperate situation, Gerald gave him the milk he had earlier dangled in on a string. He tried to hold on to his flashlight and feed Floyd at the same time, causing some of the milk to spill and Floyd to gag. Cursing himself loudly, Gerald shifted to a new position, after which the feeding went much better. Floyd was relieved to have Johnnie back and between swallows told him the now-familiar story of how he had been caught. He did not mention to Gerald anything about finding a "beautiful cavern."

Taking up where Homer left off, Gerald began the slow process of digging out gravel and dirt from around Floyd's body. His plan was to try to wedge in over the top of Floyd after all loose gravel was taken away from his upper thighs and from under his back and buttocks. In this position Gerald hoped to be able to remove the rest of the gravel from around Floyd's knees and lower legs. With a short crowbar, the offending rock could then be lifted off and Floyd's left foot freed.

Gerald worked patiently and, for the most part, silently. By now several syrup cans were making their way up and down the chute. After two and a half hours, he was exhausted and the men behind him were stiff from the cold breeze and miserable from the wet. Yet progress was being made. Not only was the space enlarged between the limestone ceiling and Floyd's chest, but Floyd was again able to move his upper right leg. Hopes were growing. However, Wells, looking in from the top of the chute, could see that Gerald's efficiency was declining and suggested that they all go to the surface to rest for a while. Gerald reluctantly agreed, and before leaving placed a rolled up blanket under Floyd's head and covered him with a dry quilt. Floyd was mercifully asleep when they left.

Once outside the cave, Gerald flopped down at the nearest fire. Conditions on the surface had not changed. Although some in the crowd had left, those who remained were still arguing, drinking, brawling, and milling about. Clay Turner, who earlier had attempted to restrict the drinking and maintain some kind of order, had given up in disgust. Now, standing by the same fire as Gerald, Turner asked him if there was anything he could do. "Shit yes," Johnnie replied. "Keep those damned drunks out of the cave!"

As soon as the natives saw Gerald emerge, they quickly surrounded him, asking if there was any chance for Floyd. Gerald described his plan to them and asked them to help keep unauthorized persons out of the cave as a way of aiding his rescue effort. Such a request naturally conformed to their parochial views and drew an immediate favorable response. Conversely, it did nothing to reverse the deepening animosity between the locals and the outlanders. Quarreling, shouting matches, and near fistfights continued to erupt, and only the advancing lateness of the hour prevented things from getting completely out of hand.

Around 3:00 A.M. Johnnie Gerald went in for the third time, again accompanied by Wells, Whittle, and three others. Floyd was awake when Gerald arrived and they talked briefly about what he hoped to accomplish. Then Gerald reached down and around Floyd's lower waist, and began removing gravel and loose dirt handful by handful. It was a time-consuming process. Impatiently, Gerald tried a number of times to crawl over Floyd, to wedge his head and shoulders into the space above Floyd's chest, but his bulk always prevented it. Throughout he kept reassuring Floyd that his rescue was near: "It's workin', Floyd. It's comin'. Yessuh! Ain't nothin' gonna stop us, Floyd. You're shore hung up, but by God we'll get you free."

As the hours passed without success, however, Floyd became torn by doubt and began to show it. His buoyant "How's it comin', Johnnie? How's it comin'?" gradually changed to "What's the matter. What's wrong?" Finally, he began to complain cantankerously that Gerald was hurting him. The smallest stone falling on him caused him to moan pitiably. At one point he said his gold tooth was throbbing—a strange trifle to worry about, thought Gerald, in view of his overall situation. At another time Floyd began to sob and Gerald immediately sent up for some coffee to calm him down. Once, Gerald washed Floyd's face with a wet handkerchief in an effort to make him feel better.

Wells, Whittle, and the others, meanwhile, continued to grub out rock from the lower passageway. Lieutenant Wells estimated that by the end of three and one-half hours, they had moved half a ton of rubble and transported it up the crawlway. During this same time Gerald succeeded in cleaning debris away from Floyd's thighs and was now scraping rocks from around his legs. Floyd could move his right leg some, but his left remained immobilized, and no matter how Gerald tried, he could not squeeze in far enough to work below the trapped man's knees. Although he was perspiring profusely, Gerald was cold. His hands trembled and his body shook. Floyd finally noticed this.

"Johnnie, why don't you go out and rest a minute and then come back?"

"I reckon I'd better," Gerald wearily replied. As he turned to leave, he knelt close to Floyd. "Floyd," he confided, "I don't want others a-comin' in here. They'll destroy what I've done. I wanta keep them out."

"Ya know, Johnnie," said Floyd looking at him, "I'd druther you got me out than anyone else in the world."

Gerald patted his shoulder. "Don't you worry. I'll get you out."

"Wrap me up afore you go."

Gerald pulled the quilt into place and readjusted the oilcloth. "Will that smother you?" Floyd shook his head. "I won't be back for a spell," Gerald said. "I'm really tired." Then, observing the trapped man carefully, he asked, "You gonna be all right?"

Floyd managed a wan smile. "I can live here two weeks if someone'll jes' feed me."

Gerald and the others moved out. It was 6:30 A.M., Tuesday morning, February 3.

"CAVE VICTIM NEAR RELEASE," "KENTUCKIAN TRAPPED ALIVE BY 7-TON BOULDER," "MAN UNDERGROUND 80 HOURS, STILL LIVES." These were some of the headlines that greeted Americans in such cities as Chicago, Washington, and New York when they read their newspapers on Tuesday morning, February 3.

Yet, as late as Monday afternoon, the Floyd Collins story was still a local cave country and Kentucky happening. The Glasgow and Bowling Green papers reported the incident on Monday with front-page coverage. The press in Danville and Lexington on that same day also told their readers of the events at Sand Cave by front-page headlines. Following their Sunday accounts, all four Louisville newspapers continued to develop the story both for its intrinsic value and as a weapon in their war of competition. In the process, only the barest truth was preserved. The *Courier-Journal* and the *Times* were generally more accurate than the *Herald* or the *Evening Post*, but all of them at one time or another violated the canons of good journalism.

Beginning with the original circumstances surrounding Floyd's entrapment, the local Kentucky press unfolded a suspenseful tale of tragedy. These early accounts asserted that a seven-ton boulder had fallen on Floyd's foot, that both feet were swollen twice their normal size, and that only a boy named "Esters" had been able to feed him even though there were "over five hundred persons" at the site. Continuing in the fanciful pattern of its Sunday article, which had claimed Floyd was free, the *Louisville Herald* maintained in its Monday edition that Floyd was separated from his rescuers "by more than eight feet of solid rock" through which only an eighteen-by-twelve-inch tunnel remained open. Brother Homer, the paper said, had tried unsuccessfully to squeeze through this passage and was rescued himself only "after several large pieces of skin had been torn from his body by the jagged rocks."

The arrival of reporters on the scene on Monday morning and the trips into the cave by Lieutenant Burdon and Skeets Miller greatly intensified press interest. They also temporarily resulted in more accurate coverage. Miller was the main reason. Homer later remarked that one of the primary benefits of Miller's entering the cave was as an antidote to the wild rumors and fictitious stories circulating about Floyd and his condition.

If Skeets Miller supplied a needed remedy to some of the falsehoods, he also popularized Floyd's plight. Following his traumatic first trip on Monday morning, the young reporter filed an eyewitness account with his Louisville office sometime around noon. The staff of the morning *Courier-Journal* had not yet come on duty, and Miller asked to be switched to the *Times* desk, which took his account and printed it on page one of its Monday evening edition along with an eight-column headline. *Courier-Journal* editor Neil Dalton was furious at losing this story to the *Times,* and he told Miller so. Miller replied that he thought it was better to give his account to the *Courier-Journal's* sister paper than risk being scooped by a wire service. Anyway, to prevent a recurrence, Skeets was ordered to send all his subsequent cave stories directly to Dalton. Accordingly, after the harness attempt that same evening, the young reporter phoned Dalton, who, after sharpening and revising parts of Miller's account, put it in the *Courier-Journal's* Tuesday morning edition under the banner headline "C-J REPORTER, 3 OTHERS MAKE FIRST GAIN IN EFFORT TO SAVE VICTIM." That same morning, the opposition *Herald* also described the harness attempt but emphasized the role of Lieutenant Burdon and hardly mentioned Miller at all.

Miller's first two eyewitness reports marked a turning point in press coverage of the Collins episode. The Associated Press pounced on his accounts and began distributing them with lavish fanfare to all its member newspapers. Simultaneously, city editors of large eastern and midwestern papers assigned their own reporters to Sand Cave in order to cash in on the burgeoning publicity. The L&N Railroad suddenly became a major communication and news artery. Both reporters and information started to flow in and out of central Kentucky by rail. Cities along its route immediately began to draw in news from Sand Cave, and their inhabitants got heavy daily doses of Floyd Collins thereafter.

On Monday, February 2, many big-city newspapers were printing stories about Floyd, but the accounts were relatively short and garbled. Receiving much of their information secondhand from the Louisville press, these urban papers repeated the same mistakes and passed along the same distortions. The *New York Times,* for example, in its early Monday morning edition had a special insert near the top of its front page under a small headline: "Landslide Traps a Kentucky Cave Owner; 200 Men Work Vainly 36 Hours to Free Him." In its later morning edition, it reported him freed. The *Nashville Tennessean* began its account of the Collins saga on the same day with the sentence "Moaning and begging for a knife with which to cut off his left foot, Floyd Collins. . . ." Similar inaccuracies or distortions abounded in other papers: Floyd's age was variously reported as twenty-one, twenty-eight, and thirty-five; Homer's was twenty-two, twenty-eight, thirty; Floyd was trapped in Crystal Cave "which he owned"; an explosion from Floyd's lantern had caused "the cave-in"; Floyd was caught face down and was suffocating; "hundreds" of workers were desperately tunneling to him; and the temperature in the cave was a numbing sixteen degrees.

On Tuesday morning, February 3, the tragedy of Floyd Collins suddenly pushed Nome's diphtheria epidemic into second place in the nation's press—a story that since January 27 had been holding the lead in all major newspapers. This epic of the frozen northland had teamed intrepid sled dogs and brave drivers in a race against the elements and had immortalized such names as Gunnar Kaasen, one of the sled masters, and Balto, an Alaskan Malamute dog. Now a lone Kentuckian grabbed top attention. The capital's main newspaper, the *Washington Post,* accorded Floyd full front-page treatment on Tuesday, a position he would not relinquish in that paper to any other foreign or domestic event for the next two weeks. The *New York Times* carried Collins's entrapment as one of its lead stories on February 3 and every day thereafter. Beginning on that same date, other metropolitan newspapers, such as the *Philadelphia Inquirer,* the *Atlanta Constitution,* and the *Los Angeles Times,* also devoted their lead columns to the Collins affair. But no paper was more complete or detailed in its accounts than the *Chicago Tribune.* Its February 3 front-page story was the beginning of a coverage that subsequently expanded to embrace wartime headlines eight columns long and two inches high.

Clearly, by Tuesday, February 3, the plight and ultimate fate of a Kentucky caver was *big* national news. Collins no longer belonged merely to Cave City, the Mammoth cave country, or even the Commonwealth of Kentucky. At the very moment that Johnnie Gerald was emerging from Sand Cave on the morning of February 3, still hoping to keep Floyd's rescue a local matter, the name of Floyd Collins was becoming an American household word.

# 4

## *Human Chains and High Hopes*

Lying wearily on an army cot at seven o'clock Tuesday morning, an exhausted Johnnie Gerald stared vacantly ahead. With Lieutenant Wells on one side and Charles Whittle on the other, he had just been helped up the last incline of the cave's entrance and into the recently pitched first-aid tent. Through a cloud of fatigue, he was confident that success was near and that Floyd's release was inevitable. Only his own failing stamina prevented it from being achieved at once. Also, he was now more convinced than ever that final success depended on keeping excess traffic out of the cave. Nobody must be permitted to enter.

Immediately new controversies concerning Floyd's rescue arose. One was a holdover from the day before. At 6:30 P.M. on the previous evening, Isaac F. Woodson and Fred and Ernest Kratch of the Woodson and Kratch Monument Company of Louisville had arrived at the cave with two of their expert stonecutters. For five hours they had attempted to find someone who was in charge and with whom they could discuss rescue procedures. Failing to do so, they had stayed in Cave City overnight and had returned to the site at 5:30 that morning to try again. They were still waiting outside when Gerald and his crew emerged.

Fred Kratch immediately sought Gerald's ear and explained to him as he rested on his cot what they proposed to do. The Kratch and Woodson men would dress in thin garments to get through the squeezes. They would first run a survey and then they would chisel away the limestone rock over Floyd's head. Kratch asked in return that no one be allowed to enter the cave or interfere with them until they were finished. Lee, who was standing by Gerald's cot at the moment, quickly agreed. Ed Estes, who was also listening, assented vigorously. But Gerald said no. Weary and anxious to rest, he was in no mood to argue with outlanders. These Louisville men knew nothing about caves or their characteristics. To Gerald they were merely do-gooders who, with their pounding and amateur ways, would again fill up the crevice around Floyd's body and make his extrication more difficult.

Woodson, the two Kratches, and their colleagues continued to press their case. Finally, in the face of Gerald's steadfast refusal, they left in a huff, charging him with gross incompetence. This blowup particularly perturbed Ed Estes, who feared that a real rescue opportunity was being lost. Subsequently, he drove to Cave City to try to bring the stonecutters back. But by the time he reached town they had already departed for Louisville. When Marshall later learned of this incident, he railed at Gerald and blamed him for an unforgivable mistake. Homer, however, saw Gerald's side of it and refused to condemn him.

No sooner had the monument men stormed away and Gerald again lain down on his cot than another controversy erupted. This was also an extension of one that had begun the day before. Lieutenant Burdon suddenly reappeared at the cave ready to initiate a new pulling scheme. In response to his previous night's telegram, a fire-hose hoist had been delivered to the rescue site, and he was busily moving it into place. He intended to put it in the mouth of the cave, attach a long rope to it, and winch Floyd out, with or without his foot.

Old Man Lee was aghast. Many of the natives screamed loudly. Gerald, unable to sleep because of the noise, got up to see what the commotion was about and then joined in the argument. The Louisville fireman defended himself by claiming that Gerald was not being aggressive enough in his plan of action. Gerald countered that Burdon was crazy to propose such a dangerous rescue method. Floyd will come out *with* his foot, Gerald claimed, if others, like Burdon, would stay away. Burdon again vividly painted the alternatives of leaving Floyd to die where he was or taking a chance on dragging him out. His blunt language so upset Lee that he was reduced to tears. At last the fireman abandoned his hose-hoist plan, but not before he had generated more ill will between himself and the natives and markedly strengthened their inclination not to tolerate any further outside interference. Gerald, meanwhile, concluded that it was impossible for him to enjoy any rest at the rescue site and left for Cave City where he got a shave and a meal before going to bed.

With Gerald's departure at approximately 10:30 A.M., the rescue work at Sand Cave virtually halted. A few persons continued to remove some rocks out of the upper passageway. The Kentucky Rock Asphalt volunteers were still propping up the cave entrance ceiling, but without direction. No work at all was being undertaken farther down the passageway. Worse, nobody was paying the least bit of attention to the most obvious need—maintaining communication with Floyd and getting warm food and hot drink to him.

This was the situation when Henry St. George Tucker Carmichael, a fortyish, thin-faced man with crinkly eyes and unruly gray hair, arrived on the scene shortly before noon. Carmichael was general superintendent of the Kentucky Rock Asphalt Company (locally known as Kyroc), a firm employing over a thousand persons, which mined black sandstone containing natural asphalt and sold it for road surfacing. Its main headquarters was in nearby Kyrock, Kentucky—a town in which everything was owned by the company. It was there that Carmichael had first learned of the Floyd Collins tragedy while reading the Louisville *Courier-Journal* after dinner on Monday evening. Intrigued by the trapped man's unusual predicament, he had ordered ten Kyroc volunteers under the direction of Thomas Smith to go to the cave and help. These volunteers had arrived sometime before midnight on Monday and had begun to shore the entrance, not knowing what else to do. Indeed, circumstances at the cave proved so confusing that Smith called Carmichael early Tuesday morning and asked him to come to the site personally to supervise further Kyroc activities.

A graduate of Washington and Lee and a licensed civil engineer, Carmichael had come prepared to work and was dressed in a well-worn sheepskin coat, high top boots, and an old felt hat. He quickly ascertained that no one was actually in charge of the rescue and that previous attempts had been unstructured, desultory, ineffectual, and chaotic. Such confusion and lack of direction offended his engineering sense of efficiency and orderliness. Consulting with Smith and others in the Kyroc crew, he learned that the trapped man was in about a hundred and fifty feet and down approximately sixty feet and that the upper part of the passageway was accessible but that the lower reaches were extremely tight and dangerous. He was also told that Collins was buried in rubble to his waist with his left foot caught by a rock, and that many rescue parties had gone in but only a few persons had actually reached him.

Carmichael immediately set about to organize a systematic and coordinated operation. He first issued a call for more Kyroc volunteers, raising the total number to twenty. Next, he ordered a list made of crew members who could relieve each other in making deep trips into the cave. Finally, he assigned gangs of men to work in the upper reaches of the passageway, handing out rock and gravel. Carmichael's objective was to use people efficiently. After the rock-clearing activity got under way, he ordered other Kyroc men to shore the entrance room of the cave, then move on down the passageway. Meanwhile, Carmichael himself scouted the area for a possible rescue shaft site.

Throughout the rest of Tuesday afternoon, the Carmichael plan was implemented. By midafternoon, the Kyroc superintendent had found a likely spot for a shaft, and seven Kyroc drillers prepared to drill. This produced a storm of protest from the natives. Homer, who was again back at the cave, absolutely forbade Carmichael to begin. Homer claimed that the jarring would weaken the roof of the passageway, causing it to collapse and destroying any further chance of rescue. Using the same argument he had employed

against Lieutenant Burdon on Monday, Homer prophesied that
even if a shaft were begun, Floyd would not live long enough to
benefit from it. Reluctantly, Carmichael agreed to concentrate all
rescue efforts through the existing passageway.

The Carmichael scheme for propping up the entrance and
clearing the upper reaches of the cave was followed. Many of the
natives at first opposed even this conservative action because of
their continuing desire to keep strangers out. But most of them
finally dropped their criticism for lack of a better alternative. As a
result, beginning just before noon, designated clearing crews, some
of them composed of Kyroc men and others of natives, passed back
rock and debris. In all, some fifteen to twenty men labored in this
project. Most of the clearing was concentrated in the area above
the first squeeze. A few rescuers worked farther down, and two
eventually reached Floyd. One was Casey Jones who fed him a pint
of coffee and potato soup from a bottle sometime between noon
and one o'clock. Jones remained with Collins about thirty minutes
and did most of the talking. He later said, "I had to keep talking to
forget where I was and to keep up my nerve, for I didn't like the
situation at all." Sometime after Jones departed, John I. Gerard, a
practical engineer from Bowling Green, wriggled to the top of the
chute and spoke with Floyd for about five minutes. Gerard told
those at the mouth of the cave when he emerged that he had been
petrified all the time he was there and had no ideas at all about how
to get Floyd out. Gerard described the lower passageway as "a
death trap" and told reporters that Floyd's section of it was "sheer
hell."

The most daring foray of Tuesday afternoon was undertaken by a
team whose members were Everett Maddox (a miner), J.C.
Anderson (a dairyman from Glasgow), J.O. Horning (Barren
County agent), and Tennessee Hooper. Hooper had been at the
cave since Sunday when he had proved Clyde Hester a liar.
Anderson had first arrived Monday noon just as Lieutenant Burdon
was going in. He had subsequently entered the cave twice with
different crews but had never gone down all the way. Horning had
been at the cave since Sunday and had not gotten beyond the
second squeeze until Monday night when he had talked with Floyd

briefly from the top of the chute. Maddox, like Anderson, had been at the cave since Monday afternoon, but had not descended to the trapped man's chamber before.

Entering the cave between 2:30 and 3:00 P.M., these men worked their way down to the chute's opening. Maddox, who was in the lead, dropped in and twisted his body down to Floyd's level. Being an experienced miner, Maddox was at home underground but he was not prepared for what he found. He tried to mask his consternation by being flip.

"What 'n hell you doin' in this hole in this fix?" he asked Floyd.

Anderson, who remained at the top of the chute and was also shocked by the evil-looking surroundings, chided Maddox for his apparently insensitive manner. "Dammit, Maddox, why'd you say that?"

Before Maddox could reply, Collins, nettled by this exchange, broke in angrily, "I wish you'd do less jawin' and more workin'." For the moment, Floyd was again in complete control of himself and, nodding toward his feet, demanded, "Move that there rock jes' three inches and I'll be free."

Experiencing difficulty with his lantern, Maddox could not see very well and mistook Floyd's remarks to refer to the big limestone rock over his chest. "Shit, no!" Maddox replied. "You move that rock and it'll all come down on us. We'll have to get you out another way." Too weak to argue, Floyd merely groaned.

"What else can we do for you?" Maddox asked quickly.

"I want some warm water and some milk and a damp warm rag and a pair of gloves."

Floyd found it difficult to swallow the warm water when it arrived. When the gloves were slow in coming Anderson took off his own and handed them down to Maddox who gave them to Collins. Floyd insisted on putting them on himself, holding each one close to his side while he wriggled his fingers in. Finally, he displayed his gloved hands and like a small child sought Maddox's approval.

"See that?" his eyes searched Maddox's face. "I got pretty good nerves, haven't I, fella?"

"You sure have."

"This isn't hard on me like it is on you all," bragged Floyd. "Ya know, in my own Crystal Cave I was hung up once for twenty-four hours and freed myself."

Maddox began removing gravel from around Floyd's thighs while the imprisoned man continued to talk. Floyd related again how he had been caught, what a beautiful cavern he had found, and how Jewell had first discovered him. His brother Homer and Johnnie Gerald, he said, had done most of the work uncovering his body although others whose names he could not recall had talked to him from time to time. The milk Floyd had requested suddenly arrived and Maddox stopped working to feed him. But Floyd said he didn't want it and continued to rattle on. He was afraid his new visitor might leave. All at once Maddox's lantern began to flicker. Anderson shined a flashlight down from above and beckoned Maddox to come on out. The latter paused, his pity now fully aroused by the desperate loneliness of this man. Then he patted Floyd on the shoulder and heaved himself out of the pit. Floyd was still prattling as he left. Hooper, who was farther up the passageway, let the others pass, after which he crawled to the top of the chute and yelled in, "Good-bye, Floyd."

"Good-bye," answered the despondent man when he finally realized they were all leaving. "I'll see you in heaven."

Skeets Miller was standing at the mouth of the cave when the members of Maddox's crew dribbled out at 5:00 P.M. During the course of Tuesday afternoon, the young newsman had been formulating his own plans for a new assault on Floyd's prison chamber. While clearing crews worked at the loose rock and Carmichael attempted to organize other aspects of the rescue effort, Miller and Ellis Jones, the Cave City garageman, had rigged up an electric drop cord with several light bulbs pigtaled along it. Miller hoped to string these lights in the passageway. The cave entrance end was to be wired into a thirty-two-volt generator supplied by Grover Lane, the Delco agency manager in Munfordville. Also, with Lieutenant Burdon's assistance, Miller had gathered together an assortment of jacks, crowbars, and tools to be used to enlarge the opening around Floyd and to pry the rock off his foot.

Miller had come to the cave on Tuesday with the announced intention of either getting Collins out or staying in with him. Although he dreaded the prospect of going back in, he was no longer the amateur he had been when he had first entered. This time he wore gloves, heavy shoes, leggings, warm clothes covered by overalls, and a wool hat which he pulled down over his ears. At precisely 5:30 P.M., he disappeared into the cave as the lead man of a large crew. Lieutenant Burdon was second. The two of them were the first links in a chain of ten men that extended from Floyd almost to the surface.

Dragging the terminal bulb of the light cord with him, Miller could now see the details of the passageway clearly. The light dispelled some of the terror. Aside from the jumble of rocks, there was an amazing amount of debris everywhere—loose boards, broken glass, cigarette butts, spent chewing tobacco, clothes, blankets, and food. Arriving at the top of the chute, Miller dropped the light in and followed quickly behind. To his surprise, he found the pit clean with all the rubble gone, making it much easier for him to move around. Floyd was still in the same impossible position but progress had been made even there. The trapped man was able to twist his body laterally from side to side and he could use his hands and arms within the limits permitted by the surrounding rock.

Miller felt a surge of hope. He talked excitedly with Lieutenant Burdon, who remained at the chute opening above. Burdon, too, was impressed by the quantity of work that had been done since he had last been there. Miller immediately turned his attention to clearing away more gravel from around Floyd's legs and trying out a new digging technique. He put his left foot over the top of Collins's head and maneuvered it down along Floyd's right side until Floyd's head was at his belt. Then he shifted weight to his left knee, moving his right leg along Collins's left side and sliding his lower body horizontally in on top of Floyd. Ducking his head down and to the right and reaching back with his right hand, Miller could pull handfuls of gravel up from around Floyd's left leg. The width in which Miller had to work was about that of an ordinary dining room chair. The vertical distance above Floyd's body was no more than five to six inches. As Johnnie Gerald had already discovered, it was impossible to push in headfirst over Floyd's torso—and this awkward position was Miller's alternative.

Working slowly and deliberately, the young newsman managed to free Floyd's left knee. But try as he might, he could not reach down farther than Floyd's left calf. The work was agony and Miller was soon drenched in sweat. Every minute seemed like an hour and the sharp shards of rock penetrated his gloves like a knife. Finally, he could do no more and sat panting in the bottom of the pit while those above him, numbed by the wet and by the cold breeze, moved back up to the entrance to get warm.

Before this human chain disbanded, it passed down a quart of coffee, a pint of milk, and a half pint of whiskey for Miller to give to Floyd. Now all alone with the trapped man, Miller fought down his weariness and frustration. The electric bulb glared harshly in the muddy enclosure, sending sparkles of reflected light off the dripping walls, exaggerating the closeness of the place. Yet, the light was a comfort to the prisoner and his visitor alike; it gave them a sense of companionship, a close bond. Skeets could see clearly Floyd's four-day-old whiskers and the pain lines etched in his face. In the dazzling light his deep-set eyes seemed all the more sunken in the sharp shadows cast by his facial bones. Although it was still difficult to feed Floyd, the light was a boon because it permitted Miller to use both hands. First, he arranged himself so that Floyd's head rested on his knee. Then he gave him the whiskey. Next, holding the milk bottle in one hand and a soda straw in the other, he regulated the flow into Floyd's mouth by pinching the straw shut when the trapped man needed to swallow.

As the two sat there—one sucking in life-giving liquid, the other risking his own death—the most unusual interview in the history of American journalism was held. Never before had a newspaper reporter been able to touch and talk with a man who was so hopelessly buried alive. The two of them now conversed, not in frenzied bursts under the pressure of an impending crisis, but leisurely and reflectively. Perhaps it was the light, or Miller's sincerity, or the whiskey, but Floyd was more lucid and composed than he had been for some time. "I was mighty weak a few hours ago—mighty weak," he began, "but now I feel better." Encouraging him to talk, Skeets read to him the contents of several telegrams and assured him that thousands of prayers were being said for him all over the nation. "It's mighty fine to know so many people are pullin' for me." Floyd smiled. "Tell 'em I love 'em all."

Once more Floyd began to recount how he had been caught, mentioning again the beautiful cave that he had found. All this Skeets had heard before. Then Collins began to describe what it was like to be trapped and unable to move, how his spirits had risen and fallen with each rescue attempt, what he thought about in the dark, and how he begged the Almighty for deliverance. He told Miller that he had yelled on Friday night until his voice gave out. "I knew my chance was slim," he admitted, "but I couldn't give up without doing somethin'." Later, he had prayed. "I prayed as hard's I could. I begged God to send help to me." He related how relieved he was when young Estes found him on Saturday morning but how discouraged he became when his brothers failed to free him. On Sunday night, he said, he lapsed into a stupor and was unable to separate reality from his dreams. "I saw white angels and trays of chicken sandwiches and smelled fried onions," he recalled.

Monday was a day of hope, he continued. For the first time, strangers came down to him and he felt somewhat better. In between the times when rescuers were with him, he tried to help himself. He would marshal all his strength for each attempt, grab at the ground, hunch his shoulders and draw up the muscles of his abdomen in an effort to free his left leg. But it was to no avail. Sometimes he would hear stones rolling down the incline and plunging into the large abyss behind him. What, he thought, would happen if the limestone rock above him were to fall? "I kept tryin' to drive my mind to somethin' else, but it wa'nt much use. How could I?" he asked Miller. "You been here and you know—you know why."

Monday night had been a time of agony. Floyd told Miller that his foot had pained terribly and felt like it was going to break off. He remembered Homer bringing him food and admitted that he sometimes cried unconsolably. As one attempt after another failed, he began to pray almost all the time. Fortunately, he said, he would often become unconscious or fall asleep. On Tuesday morning, his first thought was: *Four days down here and no nearer freedom than I was the first day. How will it end? Will I get out, or—?* Floyd said he could not bear to think of it. "I've faced death afore," he confided to Miller, "it don't frighten me none. But it's so long—so long."

As the suppertime interview neared an end, Floyd declared, "I'm achin' all over, but my head's clearer now than at any time since I been here. I'm still a-prayin' all the time—prayin' that God's will be done. I believe in heaven. But I know I'm gonna get out. I feel it. Somethin' tells me to be brave, and I'm gonna be."

The young reporter had long since fallen silent. After his first few opening queries, it was no longer necessary to prime this conversation with questions. Floyd's words came spilling out, easily and naturally. In utter fascination, Skeets Miller listened as the trapped man expressed his hopes and his fears.

It was almost eight o'clock when helping hands hauled Miller out of the cave's mouth. Once again he experienced an overwhelming sense of personal relief at being outside. Yet the memory of Floyd's face during the just concluded interview drew him back. With resignation he stripped off his mud and water-soaked overalls, gulped down several cups of coffee, and discussed with Lieutenant Burdon their next rescue steps.

They agreed that the time had come to try the jacks. Several different sizes had been rounded up to fill their anticipated needs. The plan was to remove more dirt from around Floyd's left leg, then insert a crowbar against the offending stone and jack it up. They hoped the rock would topple back into the deep pit behind Floyd, freeing his left foot. As the jacks and the crowbars of different lengths were carried to the mouth of the crawlway, a new human chain formed. The men adjusted their hats, gloves, leggings, and coveralls. At nine o'clock they began to disappear one at a time into the cave's entrance. Miller again led, Burdon was second, and eleven men followed. It was the longest chain of the rescue.

Arriving at Collins's side, Miller attempted one last time to crawl in headfirst over Floyd's body. He hoped to push his head past Floyd's crotch and up beyond the limestone ledge in order to get a look at the rock that had trapped the man. He knew it was a risky maneuver because in this position he, too, could be caught by new falling debris. Pushing and grunting, Skeets succeeded only in rubbing the skin off his temples before Floyd cautioned, "They'll be sending in for two of us if you don't stop."

Stymied in this approach, Miller again bent himself into his feetfirst position and reached back as far as he could with his right hand to pull out gravel. Floyd, meanwhile, stretched his own hand down his leg and grasped a few loose stones which he passed up to the newsman. By the end of a half hour of painfully slow scratching, they had almost reached Floyd's ankle. Collins was excited. Skeets dripped with sweat and shook with anticipation. Conversely, the men up in the passageway were numb with inactivity. They kept hoping that Miller would hurry up. While waiting there they had at first talked to each other in low tones. Then, individually, they had fallen silent as misery forced each into a private hell. The ooze in many portions of the cave was several inches deep. Lying flat on their backs or bellies these rescuers had become soaked in minutes and were thoroughly chilled by the wind sweeping up the passageway.

After what seemed an eternity, Skeets called for a jack. The chain returned to life and passed one along as Miller worked a crowbar in beside Floyd to the spot where Floyd's ankle disappeared into the last of the rubble. Skeets tried to put some downward leverage on the bar but failed. At that moment a Chandler automobile jack arrived and Miller tried to wrestle it into position. He quickly discovered that it was much too big to fit between the ceiling and the crowbar. Also, the jack was too heavy for Miller to hold with one hand while he applied the proper tension with the other. He yelled for a smaller jack. Shortly, another was dropped down the chute. Miller maneuvered this one around, but it, too, would not fit in the available space. A jack was required that was smaller still and, frustrated and angry, he scratched a mark on the one he had to show how short it should be. Lieutenant Burdon, who was looking in at the top of the chute, suggested that the newsman himself tell those on the surface what was needed since it was not size alone that made a jack suitable.

Again the human chain inched its way to the surface. Those who had been in the passageway were delighted for the opportunity to escape the mud and the chill even temporarily. One man, however, remained behind—Ben G. Fishback—to talk to Floyd while they were gone. A Barren County farmer who lived only two miles from Sand Cave, Fishback waited until the others passed and then crawled down toward the chute.

"Can I get in there to you?" he yelled as he approached the opening.

"Shore," came the answer.

"Is there a hole I can fall in?"

"Naw." Perceiving that a new rescuer had arrived, Floyd began to beg, "Please get these rocks off my feet and catch my shoulders and lift me out."

Eyeing the chute opening, the hundred-and-sixty-four-pound Fishback replied, "I don't believe I can make it in."

"Who're you? Hanson?"

"No. I'm Fishback."

At this moment, a sizable rock fell from the ceiling, scaring the local farmer so badly that he panicked and churned his way toward the turnaround room. Floyd heard the commotion and called after him, "What's the matter? Come back! Come back to me!" But it was no use. Moving headfirst toward the cave's mouth, Fishback plunged on until he reached the first squeeze. There he got caught and remained immobilized in a state of nervous exhaustion until Miller and Lieutenant Burdon, returning for the third jack attempt, set him free.

While Fishback was experiencing this terror, those in the human chain who had left the cave were excitedly preparing for the final jack assault. Full of high hopes, they warmed themselves at the various fires and speculated about how long it would be before Floyd was on the surface. They all believed that his release was imminent. Miller, meanwhile, carefully explained to several mechanics the kind of jack that he needed to finish the rescue job. They suggested he go to Cave City to one of the garages or to the hardware store to see if they might have one. This Miller did and promptly returned to the cave with a small screw jack whose lift was four inches but whose body would fit between the crowbar and the cave ceiling.

At 10:30 P.M. the human chain re-formed. Again, the first two in the line were Miller and Burdon. For the third time in five hours the young newsman was at Floyd's side. In consternation he discovered that the jack he now possessed was too small. The toe of the crowbar had shifted while he was gone, changing the angle of its other end in relation to the ceiling. Anxiously, Miller requested that some wood blocks be sent down. These he gingerly piled between the crowbar handle and the jack, which he held against the ceiling. Clutching the blocks with one hand, he slowly turned the jack screw with the other, but the crowbar twisted and the blocks fell out. Patiently he repeated the process, wishing he had at least another hand. Then Miller saw the crowbar move. Floyd saw it too. "Keep turnin', keep turnin', fella, it's comin' off!" yelled Collins. Lieutenant Burdon, waiting above, later said that he had never heard such joyous words. Miller continued turning with care. The crowbar moved some more. But just as their hopes were soaring, the blocks again began to slip and finally tumbled down. Throughout this entire operation Miller's position was extremely awkward and his back and shoulders ached. Yet he had no choice but to remain where he was. While the men in the chain in the passage above asked repeatedly, "How's it going? How's it going?" and Floyd pleaded, "Try it again, try it again," Miller once more piled the blocks in position and once more they slipped out of place.

When the news of this last failure was relayed up the passageway Burdon said they all felt like crying. Some of the men were again cold and uncomfortable, and Burdon suggested that they go out and warm themselves. But the members of the chain said no, that they would stay until Miller also decided to come out. The newsman, meanwhile, was resting in the bottom of the pit, wondering what to do next. Later he would berate himself for not thinking of using either wire or tape to hold the blocks together. Floyd, in turn, seemed more alert than ever. The electric light, the covers, the heat of others working around him, the hot drinks and the excitement stimulated his senses. At the same time, the alcohol acted as a mild sedative that assuaged any rising disappointment. Incredibly, it was Floyd who now spoke words of encouragement to Miller: "Try it again, fella. You can do it, I jes' know you can do it."

Grimly Skeets went back to his task. For another tantalizing hour he attempted to wed crowbar and jack in such a way that the stone on Floyd's left foot could be lifted. Three more times he inserted various combinations of blocks. Three more times his attempts ended in failure. His hands bruised, sweat blinding his eyes, and tears of frustration rolling down his cheeks, Miller finally collapsed on his back, exhausted and panting. Through it all, Collins remained unbelievably patient, making the situation all the more maddening. Finally, in a quiet voice, he said, "Fella, you get out of here and rest a bit and get warm. Then come back 'n' try again. You're small and I believe you're gonna get me out. You'll make it next time."

Miller did not want to quit but his reeling senses told him that he should. Just before the newsman left, Floyd requested that some burlap be put over the cave's entrance to cut down the wind sweeping through the passageway. Miller promised to ask that this be done. Then, as a final gesture, Skeets asked Floyd if he wanted something to drink. When Collins said no, the reporter took a bottle half full of milk and stuck it in a crack above Floyd's head. He also adjusted Floyd's covers and looped the electric light cord around his neck, wrapping the bulb in burlap and resting it on his chest so that Floyd would have heat as well as light.

Promising to be back shortly, Miller discovered that he was almost paralyzed as he crawled up the chute. He had worked beyond his endurance and at first thought he might have to remain in the cave all night. At the small turnaround chamber he had to stop and rest. Aching in every muscle, he finally made it to the upper passageway before crumpling in a heap. The chain ahead of him was also experiencing difficulty in getting out. At the upper squeeze Burdon had to be hauled through and he, in turn, had to help drag Miller to the entrance. It was slightly before one o'clock, Wednesday morning, when they stumbled out of Sand Cave together.

The jack attempt had failed. But neither Lieutenant Burdon nor Skeets Miller were ready to admit defeat. A crowd of reporters and inquisitive bystanders surrounded them as soon as they emerged from the cave. Miller hardly had time to catch his breath before he became the main center of attention. Talking freely and openly, he claimed that Floyd was stronger than he had been earlier, that he now had heat and light, that his spirits were good, and that he was almost free. Although the attempt to rescue Floyd with jacks was off to a poor start, Miller asserted that it would ultimately succeed. Floyd's courageous, lonely battle simply had to be rewarded with victory. His patience, his perseverance, and his faith, said Miller, were incredible. Floyd may not have been religious earlier in his life, continued Miller, but he was now uttering some powerful prayers and certainly knew how to plead with his God. When asked by reporters if he had anything to say about his own role in this affair, the young newsman merely requested that someone notify his mother that he wasn't in any real danger. He knew she would be worried.

Lieutenant Burdon, meanwhile, held his own press conference. In his blunt way, he flatly predicted that Floyd would be out shortly. At the same time he warned all other would-be rescuers to stay away. More crawling around in the cave was both unnecessary and potentially dangerous, he claimed. The ceiling was showing signs of crumbling and the passageway was becoming unstable. Success was so near, asserted the Louisville fireman, that it would be a crime if anyone detracted from it. Floyd would only need to be checked on once or twice during the night; then, in the morning, he—and Miller—would complete the rescue task.

Lieutenant Burdon's comments and warnings were aimed primarily at Johnnie Gerald and signaled the fact that not only did sincere differences continue to exist over proper rescue procedures but that competition and personal vanity had begun seriously to permeate the rescue effort. Although Gerald was not currently present, he had been there. Following his last trip in on Tuesday morning, he had slept all day and then had returned to the cave at 5:30 P.M. expecting to rescue Floyd himself. Instead, he found Burdon and Miller had just gone in. Gerald basically approved of Miller's plan to release Floyd's leg by levering the rock; however, he was fearful of a ceiling collapse in the vicinity of Floyd because of the growing moisture in the cave, the constant human rubbing of the wet walls, and the rising temperature in the passageway.

After Miller had emerged from the suppertime interview and just before the thirteen-man human chain went in at 9:00 P.M., Gerald had argued with him and Burdon about the large number of men being used. Gerald claimed that a smaller crew would cause less cave damage, reduce the wall rubbing, and radiate less body heat. Besides, he contended, only one man could work at Floyd's side at a time anyway. Burdon and Miller tried to assure him that there was no cause for alarm. The chain, they claimed, would facilitate the passing down of materials and help speed the rescue effort. Still doubting the cave wisdom of these outlanders, Gerald did not wait around for the results of the jack attempt and drove back to Cave City in an angry mood.

This running conflict with Gerald over rescue operations was only the first of a number of controversies that caused trouble on Tuesday night. The most serious involved a Louisville builder, Samuel H. Matlack. Matlack had come to Sand Cave late on Tuesday afternoon bringing with him an oxyacetylene torch. Lieutenant Burdon and Miller had just disappeared into the cave, so Matlack spoke with Johnnie Gerald. He told him that he was confident he could burn away the limestone rock over Floyd's head. Gerald refused to take him seriously. First of all, Gerald could see that Matlack was much too large to make it through the squeezes. Further, to heat the rock to the 6000°F that Matlack proposed would pose a grave danger to Floyd in his tightly enclosed chamber. Moreover, such intense heat escaping into the passageway would encourage the walls to collapse, burying prisoner and rescuers alike. For all such reasons, Gerald regarded Matlack as just another impractical dreamer and walked away, shaking his head.

Matlack persisted in urging his approach on anyone who would listen. Most of the natives, taking their cue from Gerald, poked fun at the builder and his fiery torch. Matlack ultimately concentrated his efforts on Lee and Homer Collins, both of whom were at the cave anxiously awaiting the outcome of the jack attempt by Miller and Burdon. Lee was skeptical of Matlack's plan, fearing his boy would be "burned alive." Homer, on the other hand, was attracted to it, and Matlack in a practical demonstration melted away two inches of the sandstone ledge outside the cave in an attempt to win him over. However, the heat radiating from the spot was intense and the question remained of the torch's effect on solid limestone. Throughout this demonstration, rowdies in the crowd hooted at

Matlack that he wanted to convert Floyd into a cinder. Then it would be easy, they shouted, to get him out. Visibly affected by such raucous opinions, Homer finally also backed away from the project.

Matlack still refused to give up and continued pushing his scheme when Skeets Miller and Lieutenant Burdon emerged after the final jack attempt about 1:00 A.M. The Louisville builder tried to convince them that his torch was the only solution and offered to stage another demonstration for their benefit. Lieutenant Burdon immediately pointed out the possibility of an accidental explosion in the tight passageway and the problem of getting the torch and its oxygen and acetylene bottles, hoses, and regulators down to Floyd. Miller, who remained convinced that the best way was to jack the rock off Floyd's foot, paid no attention to Matlack at all. He curtly told him that he would consider the matter later if it became necessary.

As Miller and Burdon were bundled into cars early on Wednesday morning and driven into Cave City for some rest, an unhealthy competitive thrust had indeed begun to intrude into the Collins rescue. Chauvinism was beginning to affect all the major participants. The key personalities and their associated crews were now vying openly with each other for the honor connected with final success. Each of them sincerely believed that what he was doing was right and that if left alone he and his crew would achieve the desired goal. Yet their rescue efforts, undertaken originally because of their concern and pity for the trapped man, were also turning into a contest of wills, vanity, and personal pride. Such partisanship served to increase the animosity at the cave's mouth, causing sides to be drawn even more sharply and lessening the chances for a unified approach. Arguments, name-calling, obscenities, and near fisticuffs continued. By early Wednesday morning, some bystanders were placing their bets on Miller and Burdon. Others were certain that Gerald and his friends would get Floyd out. Still others were impressed by Carmichael and his Kyroc crews. Even Matlack and the departed Louisville monument carvers had their champions.

The basic division, of course, continued to be between natives and outlanders. Between these two, the conflict was not simply how to rescue Floyd. Deeply rooted cultural, social, and economic differences also shaped their attitudes. Natives, like Gerald, were rural and small-town folk, poorly educated, superstitious, clannish, and parochial. Outsiders, such as Miller, Burdon, and Carmichael, were professional men, connected with the city, generally well paid by local standards, and possessing technical skills. Such individuals and their ideas were automatically suspected by the natives. Outsiders, in turn, viewed the natives with condescension, hostility, and even contempt. Of course, the real tragedy was that regardless of their reasons, neither of these groups, by attempting to monopolize the rescue or by withholding their full cooperation, was helping to alleviate Floyd's desperate situation. He continued to suffer while they indulged their petty gamesmanship.

By Wednesday morning, February 4, Floyd Collins was not only the paramount national news story; he was also becoming a publicity phenomenon. Had Floyd been killed outright or had he been rescued quickly, few Americans would have known or cared. But for four days he had been trapped underground while all efforts to free him had failed. Citizens everywhere were now beginning to ask about him and to volunteer their services.

Floyd's plight elicited a strange sort of universal response. The *Wichita Eagle* (Kansas) claimed: "The public's first reaction to the predicament of Floyd Collins is a restless squirm." One gas station attendant in Cave City remarked, "People are funny. Fellas that wouldn't have lent Floyd fifty cents are pert near killin' themselves goin' down that hole to pull him out." Almost everywhere there was evidence of a mounting genuine concern. A special interdenominational unity prayer service was held for Floyd on February 3 in the Central Christian Church of Battle Creek, Michigan, followed by an emotional all-night vigil. A similar service occurred in Chicago, arranged by the Bethel African Methodist Episcopal Church. Race, color, creed, or geographic location seemingly made no difference in the outpouring of empathy and sympathy for this trapped man.

Newspapers both fanned and fed on this public interest. Following their early garbled accounts of February 1 and 2, many newspapers began to sort out some of the fiction by February 3.

Even so, managing editors, as well as most readers, continued to be confused about Floyd's exact situation. They were used to thinking in mine accident terms—of shafts, tunnels, bad air, and heavy drilling equipment. To them, a passageway was like a pipe, a smooth-bore tube, small, to be sure, but easily traversed. They could not understand why a drill could not be used to dig under or around Floyd. Also, it seemed inconceivable that he could be talked to and fed but could not be brought to the surface. Those who had never experienced the feeling of being in a contorted position in a tiny earthen space easily misunderstood Sand Cave's particular rescue problems. Readers could not comprehend the scene all at once: the icy water, the mud, the tight squeezes, the twists and turns, the collapsing walls, the protruding rocks, the shifting gravel, the soggy clothes, the clammy numbness, the formidable barrier of the massive limestone block above the victim's chest, and the inaccessibility of the small rock that held his foot. Gradually, however, the message began to seep through. Something was extremely bad here. Strong men collapsed. Rescuers came out exhausted, broken down, their nerves shattered, even sobbing. This was not hysterics or merely press sensationalism. This was real.

By February 3, most newspapers were carrying not only front-page headlines and stories about Floyd, but also a full layout of pictures showing the various rescue parties, Homer and Lee Collins, and Skeets Miller. Even the West Coast press was infected, the *Los Angeles Times* running a February 3 headline: "DEATH RACE ON IN CAVE." All sorts of new information was now reported. Some of it was again garbled or erroneous. A Cave City "sportsman" by the name of "George Geralds" (Johnnie Gerald) was quoted as promising to have Floyd out in twenty-four hours. A tunnel was allegedly being started around the rock that had trapped Collins, and hundreds of buckets of gravel were being carried from the cave. Floyd supposedly was helping in his own release by using a hoe given him by one of the rescue leaders, "Al Mattox" (Everett Maddox). The harness attempt was recounted with fair accuracy and Homer's and Marshall's collapse on Monday night was covered in detail. Also by February 3, some newspapers were mentioning the growing friction at the cave and the increasing competition between the rescue crews. This latter condition was viewed at first as beneficial, but by February 4, the press was giving off vague hints that such competition might be hampering the rescue effort. Especially advancing this view were Howard Hartley of the *Evening Post* and A.W. Nichols and A.D. Manning of the *Louisville Herald*. Constantly striving to outflank the *Courier-Journal,* these men seized upon the competitive issue as a way to cast doubt on the motives of Skeets Miller, the *Courier-Journal's* reporter and a chief rescuer.

With respect to Miller, his rivals were waging a losing battle. His underground activities, his various press interviews, and the publication of his own conversations with Collins continued to create a journalistic sensation. Through the auspices of the AP, papers from New York to California carried full reports of his Monday and Tuesday exploits along with his talks with the trapped man. The *New York Times* published them on the front page on both February 4 and 5. So did the *Los Angeles Times.* Conversely, the *Louisville Herald* on February 4 and 5 barely mentioned Skeets at all while the *Nashville Tennessean,* which continued to get its reports from its own on-the-scene reporter, William Howland, described the events of Tuesday night without even mentioning Miller's name.

Such a slight was more than compensated for by the *Courier-Journal,* which used screaming headlines to announce to its readers on the morning of February 4: "C-J MAN LEADS 3 RESCUE ATTEMPTS." The rest of its front page was devoted to Miller's firsthand accounts of the Tuesday night rescue activities. These reports showed signs of patchwork composition by both Miller and editor Dalton, but the sincerity of the young newsman and the terrible plight of the prisoner came through. For the first time readers got a sharp picture of the situation in the depths of Sand Cave and learned of the agony going on in the trapped man's mind. As a result, Floyd Collins was no longer a nobody caught under the ground, but a warm, courageous human being who clearly articulated and communicated his feelings and fears. Skeets Miller suddenly became the contact between Collins and the American people. He was Floyd's interpreter to them and their messenger to him. In more ways than one, he was the trapped man's psychological as well as his physical lifeline.

In the process, Miller became a national hero. By February 5, the *Courier-Journal* was spilling as much ink about him as about Floyd. A front-page feature article, for example, was headlined: "'Skeets the First' is Cave City Ruler." This account claimed that "Cave City is 'Skeets' Crazy" and that if the village were a kingdom, Skeets would be the reigning monarch. One of Miller's fellow *Courier-Journal* reporters wrote of him unabashedly, "He took off his coat and rolled up his sleeves [and] got a talk, that's what they call it on the papers, with the imprisoned man. Helped him. Obeyed the orders of others. Tried to get him out. Worked night and day. Risked his life. Risked pneumonia. Went on exhausted but determined, rescuing with one hand and reporting the story with the other."

It was to Miller's credit that he did not succumb to all this flattery. He gained personal satisfaction from the attention, but he did not let it throw him. Hardened newspapermen, who in increasing numbers were flocking to the cave, liked Miller all the more for his modesty and his unassuming ways. Gradually a kind of Miller cult developed, especially among newspapermen from the big cities, who themselves were vicariously flattered to push one of their own profession. They boosted Miller's stock, sending their newspapers interviews with him and stories about his bravery. By doing so, they inflated the role of newspapermen and newspapers everywhere. It was an orgy of self-adulation and the press reveled in it. William C. Eickenberg of the *New York Times* called Miller's feat "The finest thing done in a long time." Dave Austin of the *Cincinnati Post* asserted that Miller's interviews with Collins were journalism at its best. Said Tom Killian of the *Chicago Tribune:* "The kid has guts!"

Fittingly, in the midst of all this personal praise, it was Miller's interviews with Collins more than anything else that continued to remind everyone that the man with the most guts was not a young newspaperman nor any other rescuer, but the hapless victim who still lay trapped and buried after four horrible days. *He* was still the central figure in the story emanating from Sand Cave.

# 5

## *Final Contact*

The failure of the jack attempt at one o'clock Wednesday morning was a crushing blow for Floyd Collins. Throughout his long ordeal since Friday, January 30, he had experienced a number of emotional lows, but he had remained convinced that ultimately he would be freed. On Tuesday night, while Skeets Miller was working with the jacks, he had believed that his release was only minutes away. Now he was unsure and extremely fearful. Despite the added comfort of the electric light, the departure of the young newsman had heightened Floyd's feeling of apprehension and loneliness. An overpowering sense of helplessness flooded over him. His left foot was numb; perhaps it was dead. Other parts of his body screamed in pain. Not since those early panic-stricken moments on Friday afternoon had his situation seemed so hopeless. Floyd began to cry.

Suddenly Everett Maddox's face appeared in the cubbyhole. He had elected to stay behind while Miller and Burdon and members of their chain worked their way to the surface. Accompanying him was Ben Fishback, who had recovered from his earlier scare and was again trying to help. While Fishback remained at the top, Maddox dropped into the pit and began to talk.

"How the hell's it goin', Floyd?"

Collins was obviously very upset, his face contorted and his voice trembling. "Won't you get me outa here?" he sobbed. "You can get me out if you'll only try."

Made to feel guilty by Floyd's pleas and by the tears staining his cheeks, Maddox replied defensively, "We're doin' what we can."

Looking at the crowbar and along Floyd's body to the still-trapped left foot, the miner was tempted to try something new—just anything; but, instead, he grabbed the bottle of milk Miller left behind and encouraged Floyd to drink, hoping to spare himself further entreaties. Then he rearranged Floyd's covers, pulling off one of the outside quilts that was soaking wet. "There," he said, "that's better."

"Where's Johnnie Gerald got to?" whimpered Floyd.

"He'll be back," answered Maddox. "He's gone home to rest." Not knowing what else to say or do, Maddox prepared to leave. "I'll tell Gerald you want him."

"Wait," said Floyd, believing his chances for ultimate rescue were now growing dim. "Kiss me good-bye."

Embarrassed, Maddox leaned over and while kissing him noticed how brightly the light from the bulb on his chest reflected off his gold tooth. Then he yelled to Fishback, "Help me up!" and scrambled out of the pit. Floyd again began to cry.

As Maddox and Fishback wormed their way to the surface, they observed that the ceiling at the top of the chute and for several feet up the passageway was developing large cracks. Sizable rocks were beginning to slump downward and some debris was falling. They reported this weakening to Carmichael as soon as they reached the mouth of the cave about 2:00 A.M. The Kyroc superintendent was again nominally in charge since Burdon and Miller had left for Cave City and Johnnie Gerald was also absent. Homer and Lee were at the cave but neither was effective. Lee did nothing more than meet each emerging crew with the plaintive query, "How's my boy, how's my boy?" Homer had a deep wracking cough—some claimed he was also drinking—and was unable to assume any serious rescue responsibilities.

Alarmed by the Maddox-Fishback report, Carmichael asked John Gerard if he would go down and evaluate the situation. Gerard, who on Tuesday afternoon had been to the top of the chute and had reported it to be hell, frankly told Carmichael that he did not want to go but that he would if given an expert crew. Carmichael selected Casey Jones to go with him. The Gerard-Jones team started down about 2:30 A.M. Cautiously they crawled past the final squeeze and toward the chute opening. Gerard was petrified, and when they reached the small turnaround chamber Jones took the lead. Rocks in the ceiling were loosening and Gerard wanted to go back, but Jones pushed ahead. About six feet this side of the chute, a bulge in the ceiling had dropped so low that Jones had to wriggle to pass under it. Finally, he reached the top of the chute as Gerard, nauseous and nearly fainting, remained back in the passageway. There, while waiting, Gerard thought he heard the settling of the earth above him and yelled in terror for his companion to come back.

Jones, meanwhile, was talking to Floyd from the top of the chute. The trapped man obviously did not know what was happening in the passageway above, and Jones spoke rapidly to allay his own mounting concern.

"You all right, Floyd?" Jones asked. "We're gonna get you out. Don't worry. We'll get you out." When Floyd appealed to him to come on down, however, Jones hedged. "Can't now, Floyd, but I will when I come back. I'll be back, I promise."

As a ploy to keep Jones from leaving, Floyd suddenly asked for a drink. Torn between his own safety and Collins's request, Jones hurriedly moved headfirst down into the space beside him. Offering Floyd some coffee, Jones spilled half of it before realizing that the trapped man was far more interested in his company than in the liquid. While pondering how to deal with this stalling tactic, he heard Gerard's near-hysterical shouts, "For God's sake, Jones, come on! Come out! You'll get us killed!"

Fearful that the ceiling was collapsing in the passage above, Jones dropped the remainder of the coffee and hastily crawfished back up the chute. Floyd begged him not to go and then pleaded for him to bring back a physician. "Get a doctor. For the love of God, get a doctor and have him come in here and cut off my leg," were Floyd's parting words.

By now, Gerard was in a paroxysm of fear and was already scrambling up the passageway toward the squeeze. "I'm getting out," he yelled over his shoulder to Jones, who was almost too late to wiggle under the still-descending ceiling rock. At the turnaround room, Jones paused to look back. "Christ," he mumbled as he saw the small opening through which he had just squirmed continue to close. Nearby more rocks were tumbling down and still others were hanging ominously. The worst area was a ten foot section just this side of the drooping ceiling. It appeared as if the whole thing was about to collapse. For a brief moment Jones attempted to clear out some of the nearest debris but soon concluded that no one could any longer work his way down to the chute. Dimly, he could see the glow from Floyd's light shining through the tiny aperture that was left. He called to Floyd in desperation but could hear only his continuing plea, "Stay with me, oh, please don't leave me! Stay with me!" Sick at heart, Jones fled up the passageway, catching up to Gerard just as he emerged on the surface. The two of them, scared and shaken, reported their findings to Carmichael and declared that the situation was hopeless.

It was now 4:00 A.M., Wednesday morning, and after an unbelievable four and a half days Floyd Collins lay trapped worse than ever.

Lieutenant Robert Burdon slept fitfully in his Cave City hotel room from 3:00 A.M. to 8:00 A.M. on Wednesday morning. Then he got up, dressed, grabbed a bite to eat, and immediately headed back to Sand Cave. Unfortunately, the taxi he hired to take him there developed engine trouble and sputtered to a stop several miles before the rescue site.

Johnnie Gerald also awoke at 8:00 A.M. and, after a quick breakfast, he, too, prepared to return to the cave. Before leaving, he encountered Everett Maddox on the street and received a glowing progress report. Maddox, who had been in the last human chain with Burdon and Miller the night before, said that Floyd was in excellent spirits, his left leg was exposed almost to the ankle, and

Miller was gradually working in over top of him. Maddox guessed that it would take only two more trips to free him. Hitching a ride from Gerald to the cave, Maddox was still describing in detail the events of the last jack attempt when they came across Lieutenant Burdon sitting by the side of the road. The two picked him up and they arrived at Sand Cave at 9:30 A.M. The three of them received the bad news of the early-morning cave-in together.

Skeets Miller climbed out of bed in his Cave City room also about eight o'clock. He was full of plans for the day. On his way to bed he had been informed that a portion of the passageway was closing, but he assumed that it would still be passable in the morning for a small man like himself. Also before going to sleep he had reconsidered the matter of Matlack's torch and had decided to ask the Louisville builder to show him how to use it. With the torch he might be able to reduce just enough of the overhead rock to allow him to slip in over top of Floyd's body.

Skeets left his hotel at 9:00 A.M. and was immediately mobbed by well-wishers who wanted to hear more about his previous night's exploits. As he talked, a sort of informal bodyguard grouped around him, escorting him to where he wanted to go. His first stop was to buy new overalls and gloves. Then he ate a quick breakfast and hired a taxi to take him to the cave. He arrived at ten o'clock, one half hour after Gerald, Burdon, and Maddox.

Skeets refused to accept the news about the cave-in and wanted to investigate for himself. Carmichael sought to stop him, believing the passageway was now too dangerous for amateurs like Miller to venture in. Homer, however, rushed to Miller's defense and said that he would go with him if necessary. Knowing Homer's weakened condition, Maddox quickly offered to accompany the newsman instead, and the two of them descended rapidly to the breakdown. The passage at that point was only eighteen inches high and two feet wide. The two men estimated that the cave-in was about four feet thick, had occurred just in front of the opening into the chute, and was approximately twelve to fourteen feet from the victim. Although it definitely blocked any access to the trapped man, the debris was not yet packed and they could still hear Floyd and he could hear them through the cracks.

Miller called. "Floyd, Floyd?" No answer. Then again, "Floyd, are you there?"

There was a faint reply. "Come on down, I'm free."

Maddox gave a low whistle. Miller was stunned. "Are you sure? Are you sure, Floyd?" he yelled.

"Come down 'n' see."

Incredible! For almost five days they had been working to release this man. Now, free at last, he was cut off from them by a cave-in. Miller could not believe the irony. Trying to keep knowledge of the collapse from him, the newsman quickly replied, "We can't make it right now, Floyd, but if you're hungry, do you see that bottle of milk above your head?"

"Yes."

"Well, reach up and get it, it's half full." There was no response. Miller called again, "Floyd, can you reach the bottle?"

Still there was no answer. Miller and Maddox held their breath. Finally, the voice behind the barrier said, "I can't."

Realization of what this meant broke the suspense. "Goddamn!" sputtered Maddox. Miller dropped his head on his arm. Evidently Floyd had been afraid that unless he said something sensational, they would leave him. At last the newsman said evenly, "You're not free, are you, Floyd?"

A moment of silence. Then came the expected reply. "Naw-w. I'm not free."

Sorrowfully, Maddox and Miller began to move out when suddenly they were met by Homer coming in. Angered and frustrated by the confusion and inaction on the surface, he had decided to see for himself what was going on below. Maddox, fearful that a new ceiling collapse was imminent, urged Miller to use his "Irish guile" to get Homer to back up. Skeets pacified the younger Collins by promising him that upon reaching the surface he, personally, would ask Carmichael to speed up the rescue process. Homer reluctantly turned around and preceded them out.

In his report to Carmichael, Maddox said that he thought further efforts to save Floyd by way of the Sand Cave passageway were useless. To dig through the breakdown would only cause more of the ceiling to collapse. Although he, too, feared that the situation was hopeless, Miller could not bring himself to say it. The young reporter had too much of himself invested in a successful outcome to give up now. After resting a short time, he begged for permission to go in the cave again, this time to carry down a field telephone so that volunteers who might be recruited to work at the breakdown could use it. It was strange that no one had thought of a field telephone before. At any time during the past four days rescuers could have placed one with an open circuit by Floyd's head so that he could have maintained constant contact with the surface. Also, at any time prior to the Wednesday cave-in, a feeding tube could have been rigged near Floyd's mouth and run up the passageway past the danger spots so that the imprisoned man could have continued to be fed. With light, heat, communication, and food, Floyd's chances for survival and ultimate rescue would have remained good. Now it seemed too late.

About 11:30 A.M. Miller again crawled into Sand Cave, dragging a telephone behind him. This was the newsman's seventh and last trip. He moved to the breakdown, deposited the telephone, and yelled some words of encouragement to Floyd. He then began to pluck gingerly at the face of the collapse until some rocks and mud fell across his legs, scaring him badly. He lunged back, turned around, and squirmed his way to the surface, emerging about 12:15 P.M. There, in spite of what he had just experienced, he told reporters that he still believed a rescue was possible. He claimed that he would lead another human chain in to Floyd if someone would clear out the cave-in. In the meantime, he was going to return to town to await developments. Arriving in Cave City shortly thereafter, he told those who gathered about him that if the collapse were cleared by nightfall, he would take an oxyacetylene torch in with him and also pull the phone on down to Floyd. Asked if he might not be trapped alive with the victim, Miller admitted that that was a possibility. He might have to stay with Floyd for some time, he said, but ultimately they would come out together.

During the remainder of Wednesday afternoon, several others went in to examine the breakdown. Lieutenant Burdon wanted to be the first, but Gerald's antagonism prevented him from going down until four o'clock. Even then, a crew of natives was detailed to accompany him and he was not pleased, later claiming that most of them reeked of whiskey. Burdon crawled to the cave-in and estimated it to be forty feet from Floyd, disputing the contention of all others that it was much closer. He also claimed that he heard Floyd screaming for help and praying wildly. Burdon concluded that Floyd's mind had finally snapped. Following this trip, he declared to Carmichael that the breakdown was too treacherous to handle and that even a shaft sunk from the surface would not save the trapped man now. For the Louisville fireman, the attempt to rescue Floyd Collins was over.

Johnnie Gerald did not reenter Sand Cave until Wednesday afternoon at 5:00 P.M. He listened impassively to various descriptions of the cave-in before deciding to see for himself. But inside he was fuming. He had often warned of such a disaster and believed that the amateurish activities of outlanders such as Skeets Miller and Lieutenant Burdon had contributed heavily to it. With a handpicked crew, composed of Maddox, Wells, and Norwood K. Ford, he worked his way in slowly to the breakdown and estimated it to be fourteen to eighteen feet from Floyd. Encouraged by the fact that it was not tightly packed, he discussed with Maddox, the man immediately behind him, how it might be removed. Maddox, who had already told Carmichael that he thought the collapse was impassable, remained dubious that anything could be done. Gerald disagreed, although he admitted that it would be very difficult to prevent new material from falling down as the old was removed. As the two men talked, Floyd faintly heard them.

"Johnnie, Johnnie, is that you? I knowed it was you! Come to me. Why don't someone come to me?"

Gerald stalled. "Some rocks have fallen, and we will, Floyd, we will. First, we got to dig 'em out."

"Johnnie . . . Oh, God . . . help me. . . ." Sobs, racking and uncontrolled, came fast. "O Lord, dear Lord, Jesus all powerful . . . save me . . . Johnnie . . . Johnnie. . . ." Gerald finally could stand it no longer and left.

Emerging about 6:00 P.M., Gerald sought out Carmichael. He had no love for the Kyroc man, believing that he, too, was partially responsible for the collapse. But now he needed him since Carmichael and his Kyroc crews had experience in shoring.

Carmichael, in turn, had closely observed the various rescue attempts for the past two days and had come to the conclusion that of all the rescuers, Gerald made the most sense. The Kyroc man admired young Miller for his courage, but not for his cave experience. He regarded Lieutenant Burdon as sincere but too erratic and hot-tempered. Of them all, Carmichael believed that Gerald was probably the man to get Floyd out—if anyone could.

Gerald outlined his plan to the Kyroc superintendent. Kyroc crews would undertake shoring in the passageway wherever possible. Gerald and others selected by him would work at the face of the breakdown. Gerald hoped that enough of the cave-in could be removed so that a small man could finally wriggle past. It was a race against time, emphasized Gerald. The rain of the past several days, the rubbing of the walls, the midwinter thaw, and the dripping ground water were all conspiring to make the cave structure deteriorate rapidly.

Carmichael immediately issued a call for volunteers, coupling it with a warning: "Boys, we're going down into that hole and we're going to start shoring. There's death down there. The walls and ceiling are crumbling. Unless you are determined to take the biggest chance you ever took in your life, tell me now and stay outside." To those who accepted, Carmichael said, "It's the last try. The boy can't live much longer. He's been in that slime for five days. His vitality must be gone. And if we can't free him from that rock when we do shore, he's a goner."

As winter dusk fell and flickering fires and lanterns etched the drawn faces of muddy and exhausted men, the battle to remove Floyd Collins through the Sand Cave passageway reached a climax. For four hours shoring parties worked diligently, clearing out debris and propping up every rock and ledge under which they could wedge a piece of wood. On the hillside other men cut timber and sawed it into short logs for shoring purposes. However, because of the narrowness of the passageway at the face of the collapse, shoring at that point was virtually impossible. Gerald, Maddox, and Wells alternately worked there and rock by rock the cave-in was reduced. At the same time, Kyroc workers managed to break up and remove most of the rocks restricting the passageway at the end of the cave's entrance room. Here there was enough space to swing a sledgehammer, and the Kyroc men passed the rock fragments out the entrance.

During this period no one was allowed in the passageway except for the Kyroc volunteers and Gerald's men. For the first time in the rescue effort there was an orderly command system operating. Gerald was in charge of all caving activities and the Kyroc superintendent oversaw everything else. Natives at the site served as a police force. Ed Estes, Bee Doyle, and Clay Turner prevented anyone not screened by Gerald or Carmichael from going in. When Skeets Miller returned to the cave at 7:00 P.M. with plans for crawling down with Matlack's torch, Carmichael told him no. Waiting until Gerald came out from one of his trips, Miller asked his permission, but Gerald brushed him aside by telling him that he would not be able to go in before morning. If he tried before that, warned Gerald, he probably would not come out alive. Miller wondered whether this was meant as advice or a threat. A colleague standing nearby and hearing Gerald's words said softly to the young newsman, "Your worst enemy down here is provincialism. Better stay out." Miller took the hint.

Matlack, meanwhile, had also returned and in the confusion surrounding a Kyroc crew change surreptitiously entered the cave around 7:00 P.M. Accompanied by George Morrison, the owner of the New Entrance to Mammoth Cave, he crawled unnoticed past the first squeeze before being stopped by J.O. Horning, one of Gerald's men. Horning ordered them back, but Matlack stood his ground, arguing that if given a chance he and his torch could get Floyd out. Morrison also remonstrated with Horning, claiming that if the torch didn't work only a vertical shaft could save Floyd now. Horning was unimpressed. He only scowled and prodded them toward the cave's mouth.

On Wednesday evening at eight o'clock a final desperate assault on the cave-in was mounted. Gerald, followed by Maddox and Wells, entered with cold chisels and a grease gun. They hoped to squirm past the remaining breakdown to Floyd and squirt Vaseline around his foot in an attempt to slide it out. Working feverishly, they struggled to remove the last of the debris and keep ahead of what kept falling in. Finally, they cleared an opening just big enough for a small man to slip through. They quickly discovered, however, that any rubbing of the walls prompted new slides and concluded that it was too dangerous to crawl past without some shoring. The cleared opening did afford easier voice communication with Floyd, and Gerald yelled to him that they were coming.

Floyd had not seen anyone since Casey Jones at three o'clock that morning. Since that time he had experienced indescribable terror and despair. Through it all, Johnnie Gerald had remained his one final hope.

"Get me out, Johnnie, ol' pal," Floyd cried. "For God's sake, get me out 'n' you 'n' Oscar Logsdon take me back to Cave City. My God, Johnnie, we was boys together. You can't fail me now!" These words, interspersed with sobs and moans, flowed faintly out of the unplugged opening.

"I won't, Floyd, I won't," said Gerald.

Leaving the grease gun and the other tools there, Gerald quickly returned to the surface and requested a final shoring effort at the cleared-out collapse. Gerald's own crew was momentarily useless. Maddox was so exhausted that he had to be taken to the home of Bee Doyle and put to bed. Carmichael immediately called a Kyroc conference and two shoring volunteers were selected, Edward Williams and William Lemay. They were gone only a brief time and reemerged shortly after 10:00 P.M. Although they were unable to do much shoring, they maintained that with luck and plenty of guts someone might now get past. Skeets Miller, who was standing by, offered to try. But Gerald, ignoring Miller and buttoning on a dry pair of overalls, moved back toward the entrance. He had been in Sand Cave five times that day and this rescue effort was still his. He would bring Floyd out.

Gerald reentered the cave at 10:30 P.M. Behind him were Lieutenant Wells and four other men. Gerald's last words before going in was a promise that he would have Floyd on the surface within the hour. Down past the first squeeze, out through the turnaround chamber, and into the passage beyond he went. Suddenly he came upon a new collapse. This cave-in was in front of the old one but close enough to be a part of it. When Gerald saw it he was at a loss what to do. For five minutes he lay there collecting his thoughts. Finally, wearily, he began to dig. A small rock fell from the ceiling and hit him on the head. He stopped and rested for a moment. Then he tried calling Floyd.

"Floyd? Floyd?" There was no answer. At the top of his voice he yelled, "Floyd?" There was only a groan. "Floyd, hold on!" he pleaded.

"Don't bother me," came a tired voice from behind the new barrier. "I've gone home to bed and I'm going to sleep."

His emotions cruelly whipsawed between hope and despair and his body tortured beyond endurance, Floyd had at last fallen into a permanent stupor. Gerald desperately turned back to his digging. All at once a rock weighing about forty pounds fell and struck him on the spine. At first he was startled; then came the pain; finally terror engulfed him.

"What's the matter, Johnnie?" asked Wells.

"You got to get another man, lieutenant. I'm done. My nerve's gone."

Wells backed up so that Gerald could get to the turnaround room and sit down. Upon reaching it, Gerald calmed himself, and then he and the others slowly made their way up as rumors raged on the surface. Clusters of men stood around campfires and speculated. Some claimed that at that very moment Floyd was being released. But as the minutes passed and Gerald's crew did not return, some expressed fears that the entire group had been swallowed by a new cave-in. At last the men began to emerge. Gerald's face, in particular, telegraphed a message of failure.

It was 11:45 P.M., Wednesday, February 4. Homer was there. So was Lee. So were Lieutenant Burdon and Skeets Miller. Before Gerald could speak, Homer tried to rush into the entrance, but restraining hands held him back. Lee begged his son not to be foolish and resignedly muttered, "It must be the Lord's will." All the rescuers now were defeated. Bravery and courage had not been enough. The entire passageway seemed to be crumbling. Gerald admitted to reporters that he would not go back in there if he were deeded the whole state of Kentucky. It was suicide to try to do anything more.

Superintendent Carmichael later stated that when news of the second collapse became known "our hopes dropped from one hundred to nothing." He immediately announced that he would not ask for any more volunteers because the risk was too great. Yet there were still those who wanted to try something. Standing around the entrance to the cave was a group of striking miners from Muhlenberg County, headed by Darrell E. Bennett, chief of police of Drakesboro, Kentucky. They offered to go down to appraise the latest situation. Claiming to have surmounted similar obstacles before, they were insistent on helping. After conferring with Carmichael, they agreed to send in their best man, Roy Hyde, to have a look.

Thirty-three years old and weighing about a hundred pounds, Hyde was a minister in the Christian Church as well as a miner. Lieutenant Wells accompanied him past the first squeeze and then sent him on alone. After some moments, Hyde returned claiming that a rescue might still be effected. As a result, a Muhlenberg rescue party was organized and entered the cave about 2:00 A.M. to work at the face of the new breakdown. Hyde later compared it to digging in a barrel of apples—remove one and others fall in. For two hours the men labored, relieving each other after short intervals so each could go out, rest, and get warm. As they worked, they constantly called to Floyd but received little intelligible response. Amid his groans, they sometimes could hear him mumbling over and over the names of his brothers and his dead mother, and once they heard him yell out, "Oh, God, help me, help me!"

No matter what they attempted, the Muhlenberg miners achieved no success. As Reverend Hyde emerged from the cave's mouth at 4:00 A.M., he declared, "That's it. That's my last trip. I'd never come out alive if I tried it again." Hyde admitted that he had never seen anything as difficult as this and that nothing more could be done. He also told Carmichael that a "tunnel squeeze" was developing, that the cave's walls were weakening and hydraulic pressure was forcing the floor up to the ceiling. Not only was Floyd beyond reach, said Hyde, but he soon would be crushed to death.

While "tunnel squeeze" is possible in mines where openings have recently been blasted and the stresses have not yet reached equilibrium, such a squeeze is not possible in limestone cave passages. Nevertheless, the majority of those at the entrance to Sand Cave accepted the Muhlenberg miner's observations without question and shook their heads over Floyd's impending doom. All hope was clearly gone.

Wednesday, February 4, which supposedly was to have seen Floyd rescued, had been a day of disaster. For the first time in almost a week the sun had shone brightly, but this had brought no end to the tragedy at Sand Cave. After five and one-half agonizing days of working and worrying, Floyd's relatives and friends were either ill or exhausted. Lieutenant Burdon of the Louisville Fire Department had failed. Newsman William Miller had failed. Johnnie Gerald, and now the Muhlenberg miners, had also failed. For all of them, Floyd's last intelligible words carried a shattering meaning. Before leaving the face of the second breakdown for the last time just before 4:00 A.M., Reverend Hyde had called in, "Don't give up, Floyd, don't give up. We're coming!"

"You're too slow . . . too slow," said the voice from below.

# 6

## The State Takes Over

Cave City magistrate Clay Turner was a worried man. Since Sunday, February 1, events at Sand Cave had been growing beyond his control, and he was under increasing pressure to do something about them. William Hanson, the town marshall, who was saddled with the specific responsibility of enforcing the law, had been no more effective than Turner in maintaining order. By Tuesday, February 3, their ban on drinking was being openly flaunted and the mounting altercations and controversies at the rescue site were too much for them to handle.

Reporter A.W. Nichols of the *Evening Post* suggested to Hanson on Tuesday afternoon that he request state aid. Nichols even drafted a telegram addressed to Kentucky governor William J. Fields and gave it to Hanson, who, in turn, showed it to Turner and Sam H. Caldwell, president of the Cave City People's Bank. They advised him to send it at once, and Hanson did. The telegram's most important section read: ". . . I feel the situation is such as to need the assistance of state troops to aid in more effective rescue work." When Governor Fields received this request, he forwarded it to Adjutant General James A. Kehoe. In response, at 4:30 P.M., Kehoe ordered a small contingent of National Guardsmen from Smiths Grove to proceed to the rescue site "to harmonize the work to rescue Floyd Collins."

There were thirty-three guardsmen and three officers stationed at Smiths Grove, which was only a half hour's auto ride from Sand Cave. At 6:30 P.M. a special volunteer group of ten men was mustered under the command of Lieutenant Edgar E. Cross. They were the smallest men in Headquarters Company, Third Battalion, 149th Infantry, and all of them agreed to work underground if necessary. After several delays, they arrived at the cave shortly before ten o'clock, just as Skeets Miller was heading in for the final jack attempt. Turner and Hanson welcomed the uniformed men and expressed great relief at their arrival. The guardsmen pitched their tents on the bluff above the cave and began to patrol the area. Although the presence of these soldiers temporarily caused the moonshiners to vanish, it did not restore peace among the squabbling rescue factions nor give a unified direction to the rescue efforts.

By Wednesday noon, February 4, it was clear that this small contingent from Smiths Grove was not enough. The crowd at the cave currently exceeded two hundred fifty and more were coming. When M.E.S. Posey, executive secretary of the Kentucky Highway Commission and a representative of the governor's, arrived early on Wednesday afternoon, he was disturbed by the continuing chaos and telegraphed Governor Fields to send more guardsmen and appoint someone to coordinate the rescue work.

Upon receipt of Posey's telegram, Governor Fields again contacted Adjutant General Kehoe, who early on Wednesday evening ordered twenty-five guardsmen in Service Company, 149th Infantry, stationed at Bowling Green, to leave for Sand Cave. Under the command of Captain Julius L. Topmiller, a Bowling Green businessman, the first truckload arrived late on Wednesday night. The last group did not get there until Thursday morning. In the meantime, Governor Fields met with Kehoe in a midnight con-

ference in Frankfort to decide who should be placed in overall
command. They wanted someone who would wield strong authority
and finally settled on Lieutenant Governor Henry H. Denhardt.

A brigadier general in the National Guard, Denhardt received
his orders from Fields at 1:15 A.M. on Thursday morning. Within
fifteen minutes he left his Bowling Green home for Sand Cave with
aides, Captain Alex M. Chaney and Major William Cherry. They
arrived at the cave at 2:15 A.M. as the last group of Muhlenberg
miners was going in. During the guard's stay at Sand Cave, General
Denhardt remained its commanding officer, but his actual military
operational responsibilities were taken over by Captain Topmiller.
This freed Denhardt to concentrate solely on the supervision and
coordination of the rescue work.

Denhardt proved to be a controversial selection. He was a tall,
bald, heavily built man who in private life was a lawyer, banker,
and newspaper publisher in Bowling Green. He had been a
lieutenant colonel with the field artillery in World War I and had
been cited for bravery in the St. Mihiel and Meuse-Argonne
offensives. As head of the Kentucky guard he had quelled riots in
Newport in 1921–22 and had been the lieutenant governor of the
state since 1923. A bombastic figure who was curt in his personal
relationships, Denhardt was known for his aggressive action rather
than for his sagacity. He commanded more fear than respect.

The natives at the cave did not like Denhardt from the beginning.
To them he was "that martinet army officer," even though he took
pains to play down the military aspects. His firmness and disinclina-
tion to "jaw" over rescue matters especially antagonized the local
people, and he showed little sensitivity in dealing with their pride.
Inevitably he came to symbolize all outside intrusion, and everything of an unfortunate nature that happened thereafter was laid on
his shoulders. With the natives, Brigadier General Denhardt could
never win.

Nevertheless, the general's appearance at the cave had its
salutary side. There was both authority and control in the rescue
operation after his arrival. The rowdiness at the cave disappeared,
pickpockets were forced to abandon their trade, the moonshiners
rapidly cleared out, and the drinking stopped. By Thursday
morning, February 5, the state of Kentucky had taken over, the

most visible indication of that fact being the army tents that dotted the landscape. By that time, bonfires were burning on the hillsides at a dozen sentry posts, the flames forming a loosely joined circle.

The arrival of General Denhardt and the National Guard was not the only factor that drastically altered the rescue situation by Thursday morning. The second cave-in, the failure of the Muhlenberg miners, and the withdrawal of the local champion, Johnnie Gerald, opened the way for outside experts and engineers to dominate. These had been congregating for several days. Kyroc superintendent Carmichael had been the first. Shortly thereafter came B.C. Owens, an engineer from the state highway commission operating out of Bowling Green. Later, on Wednesday, C.A. Herbert and Joseph Davies, members of a U.S. mine rescue team stationed at Vincennes, Indiana, also showed up at the cave.

The most important arrivals, however, were two personal representatives of Governor William Fields—Highway Commissioner M.E.S. Posey and Professor William D. Funkhouser. Posey arrived at the site on Wednesday at 3:30 P.M. and set the wheels in motion that eventually brought General Denhardt there. Funkhouser was head of the zoology department of the University of Kentucky at Lexington and was regionally well known for his zoological work in Kentucky caverns. Governor Fields believed that Funkhouser's expertise on the Kentucky cave country might prove useful, so he had asked the professor on Tuesday night to go to Sand Cave. Funkhouser arrived on Wednesday at the same time as Posey and immediately helped Carmichael inject some order into the rescue effort by organizing and keeping track of compatible rescue teams.

By the time of the second collapse, most of these experts had become convinced that the release of Floyd Collins was no longer a caving problem but an engineering one, and even before General Denhardt arrived early Thursday morning they had started to run an engineering survey of the Sand Cave passageway. Unbelievably, no such survey had yet been made. Now it had to rest on incomplete data because Floyd's exact location could not be pinpointed due to the cave-ins. The first survey was begun as soon as the last of the Muhlenberg miners emerged warning of an impending "tunnel squeeze." Several survey teams simultaneously swung into action, the major participants being Gerard, Wells, Ford, and Edward Williams, with Roy B. Anderson in charge. Anderson was a graduate civil engineer of the Pennsylvania State University who had been working in the area for the Louisville Gas and Electric Company. He reduced the findings of the various teams to a composite map which showed twelve survey stations and indicated that Floyd was located in a surprising place. Because of the passage's many twists and turns, the trapped man was about fifteen feet northeast of the mouth of the cave and straight down fifty-five to sixty feet below that spot. On this basis, a general area was designated where a shaft should go and Posey and Major Cherry were sent into Cave City to begin rounding up materials for shaft-sinking and drilling.

On Thursday morning final discussions concerning the advisability of a shaft were held. General Denhardt strongly favored this course of action. Professor Funkhouser, Posey, Anderson, and the other surveyors and engineers also supported the idea. Superintendent Carmichael, who had advocated a shaft from the start, heartily agreed. Hence, at 8:30 A.M., General Denhardt officially announced that a shaft would be sunk. He placed Carmichael in charge of the digging and told the volunteer crews, "It is now up to you men to drill through the ground directly to Collins's side. Spare no expenses. The purse strings of Kentucky are open."

In announcing the sinking of the shaft, General Denhardt also ordered that all further work in the Sand Cave passageway be abandoned. *No one* was to enter it thereafter without his permission. Homer, who had just arrived back at the cave, was shocked. He angrily protested to the general, saying that closing the passageway would doom Floyd to death, that before the proposed shaft could reach him he would be gone. Homer also warned that sinking a shaft in this particular hillside would be extremely difficult, if not impossible. Dismissing as fallacious the Muhlenberg miners' theory about a "tunnel squeeze," he told Denhardt, "We've got to timber up all the bad places inside the passage and get all these damn fools away from here." Homer was especially vitriolic toward Carmichael, whom he regarded as the primary shaft proponent, and loudly complained that the rescue operation was falling into the hands of "armchair" superintendents who knew nothing about caves. Denhardt, who did not like being crossed, fidgeted impatiently while Homer talked and finally cut him off. "Practical men have had their way," said the general curtly. "It takes men with brains to get him out. We'll sink a shaft."

"This pitting of the puny strength of man against the mighty forces of nature and the onward rush of precious time is one of the most thrilling spectacles ever given man to witness." So commented one reporter in describing the beginning of the Collins rescue shaft. Those who were engaged in sinking it, however, had no time to thrill to the spectacle. Their problems were complicated and their decisions fraught with error.

Their first puzzle involved the exact place to start, and it required several hours to reach agreement. After considering the logistics problem, the slope of the hillside, and the best location for installing a hoist, Funkhouser, Posey, Denhardt, Carmichael, and Anderson finally decided on a spot no more than twenty feet from the cave entrance and just under the lip of the sandstone overhang. They estimated that if they dug there they would arrive within three feet of Floyd, intersecting the passageway at a point behind his trapped left leg and just at the edge of the deep cavern he had found.

Because of these lengthy deliberations, it was not until 1:30 P.M. that the outline of the shaft's six-foot-square mouth began to appear. The surface rocks and adjoining land were cleared and trees were cut down. Wooden runways were constructed from the shaft head to a dumping site a hundred feet away. A power shovel, which had been acquired by Superintendent Carmichael, was hauled down the bluff and put in place. However, it was abandoned when it was discovered that the exhaust from its engine was sometimes drawn into the cave. Similarly, the use of dynamite and pneumatic drills was excluded for fear they might cause Floyd's prison chamber to collapse. From the beginning, the only tools employed were picks and shovels. Throughout the remainder of the rescue, man's most modern digging equipment lay idle and off to one side because of safety considerations for the victim.

During the first twenty-four hours, Superintendent Carmichael assembled a large force of skilled people. His own Kyroc men served as a nucleus and the L&N Railroad contributed both common laborers and professional help. L&N track supervisor R.W. White headed a volunteer contingent of bridge and section gangs who were experts in drilling and blasting. But many others whom Carmichael put to work were merely individual volunteers who had heard of Floyd's plight and had turned up at Sand Cave to help—men such as Albert B. Marshall (who was knowledgeable about mine shafts), Edward Brenner (a professional miner from Cincinnati), and Albert Blevins (an ace timberman and shoring foreman). By nightfall on Thursday, the Kyroc superintendent had experts such as these to supervise every line of activity, and he commanded a total work force of over seventy-five men.

Not only talent but also supplies and machinery rapidly flowed into the cave area. By the late afternoon of February 5, a steady stream of equipment was moving over the road from Cave City— hoisting derricks, railroad ties, drum drills, wheelbarrows, pick- axes. Motor trucks careened through the mire, stopped at the cave to disgorge their contents, and then churned back toward town. Posey's and Major Cherry's early-morning requests for aid were obviously being filled. At the site itself, six-mule teams were used to maneuver the heaviest equipment into place. On Thursday afternoon, two Fordson tractors arrived, sent with the compliments of the tractor division of the Bowling Green Ford franchise. One was used to haul dirt from the shaft to the dumping site, the other to notch seven-by-nine-inch railroad ties for shoring. A complete Delco lighting system also arrived on Thursday and was imme- diately installed so that the digging could continue around the clock. Meanwhile, the L&N attached special cars to all its trains running to and through Cave City, expediting the arrival of all sorts of material.

When the digging of the shaft began shortly after lunch on Thursday, Floyd Collins had been trapped for a hundred and forty- four hours and had not had anything to eat or drink for over thirty- six hours. Speed was therefore essential. As the first shovelful of dirt was dug, Carmichael predicted that it would take thirty hours to reach Floyd's level. That meant a digging rate of two feet an hour. If they were lucky, added Carmichael, they would break in just behind him; if not, several more hours would be required to probe. The Kyroc superintendent admitted that digging the final ten feet would be tricky because of the deep pit near the trapped man. The workers might have to be suspended in cradles to protect them from falling through the shaft's floor. General Denhardt, in making his assessment, claimed that the shaft would reach Floyd in "about thirty-six hours" and told reporters that Collins would be brought to the surface shortly thereafter. Conversely, the U.S. mine experts from Vincennes, Indiana, maintained that such predictions were too optimistic. They claimed that on the basis of their experience, it would take at least seventy-two hours to reach the trapped man. Volunteer workers at the site did not know what to predict but agreed among themselves that if it took as long as the U.S. mine experts said, they were probably digging for a corpse.

The work started rapidly. For the first four or five feet diggers struck nothing but muck and this was hauled away quickly. Then the problems began. Below five feet, shoring was needed to hold back the shaft's lengthening sides. For the next several feet mixed rock was encountered and, as the shaft deepened, only three persons were able to work in it at a time. At 7:00 P.M. the shaft was down only seven feet, representing a digging speed of only a foot an hour. Carmichael's timetable was already off. The Kyroc superintendent was disappointed and briefly considered using dynamite. "It's the only thing we can do," he wailed. "If we don't hurry, he'll die anyway." But his fear of cave-ins ultimately won out, and he ordered the men to continue digging by hand.

As campfires twinkled on the hillsides on the night of February 5–6, the work proceeded at a snail's pace. Reporters pestered everyone about Floyd's chances under these circumstances. To one such query, Lieutenant Wells replied: "We do not know whether Collins is alive or dead, but as far as we are concerned he is alive until we reach him and a physician officially pronounces him dead." All the shaft workers shared this viewpoint, although their mounting concern was difficult to hide. It was backbreaking, monotonous work and morale sagged as the night wore on. Indeed, just before dawn Carmichael barely rousted out enough volunteers to keep the operation going.

With the arrival of the sun on Friday morning, the tempo of the work as well as hopes for Floyd's rescue picked up. At 10:00 A.M.

—the same time Floyd had disappeared into Sand Cave exactly one week before—S.H. Lane, who was in charge of all rescue lighting, conducted a bizarre experiment. Electric current was still being sent into the cave on wires. Skeets Miller's primitive shop cord of Tuesday had since been replaced with heavier gauge material, and presumably the bulb he had placed on Floyd's chest was still burning. Lane connected a radio amplifier across these wires on the off chance that any movement by Collins would produce vibrations that could be picked up as sound. To encourage Floyd to move around, Lane alternately switched the light on and off. After listening closely, he claimed that he heard clicks and crackles in his earphones. Lane speculated that Floyd's bulb had loosened in its socket and his movements were now alternately closing and opening the contact. After reproducing this condition with another bulb on the surface and comparing the noises, Lane flatly declared that Floyd was still alive. Although this conclusion was disputed by some sound experts who tried to duplicate his experiment in laboratories across the country, Lane's assurances lifted the spirits of those working at Sand Cave and for the rest of Friday gave a large boost to the rescue effort.

Doctors who were present at the site also claimed that Floyd could still be alive and, if he could maneuver his mouth to catch dripping ground water, might survive for several more days. One of those holding this opinion was Dr. William H. Hazlett who had been at Sand Cave since Wednesday afternoon. A surgeon on the staff of St. Luke's Hospital in Chicago, he had first become interested in the Floyd Collins tragedy when a patient of his, Mrs. Emmons Blaine, offered to send him with all expenses paid to Cave City. Mrs. Blaine, wife of a prominent Chicago lawyer, was also the daughter of the inventor of the reaper, Cyrus McCormick, and a daughter-in-law of the well-known politician James G. Blaine. She had read of the need for a doctor to amputate Collins's leg and wanted to supply her own physician.

Accompanied by another colleague from St. Luke's, Dr. Harold Jones, Dr. Hazlett left Chicago for Louisville by train on the night of February 3. Before embarking, he discussed the possibility of an amputation with reporters. "The operation would be unprecedented if successful," he remarked. "It would have to be performed under a local anesthetic and, because of the impossibility of obtaining freedom in which to work, it would be extremely difficult." Moreover, the doctor added, the light would be poor and the amputation would involve the femur, nearly waist high, occasioning great loss of blood. For that reason, he said, he was taking along the most advanced hemostats and hemostatic forceps to retard the flow from severed veins and arteries.

When the news of the two doctors' departure reached Kentucky, the *Louisville Herald* immediately arranged to fly them to Cave City. But Dr. Jones went on by train so that, as Dr. Hazlett put it, "at least one of us will get there safely." Dr. Hazlett had never been in the air before and was scared. He told reporters later, "I just resigned myself to fate. I thought that if I must die I might as well meet death in an airplane." The fifty-seven minute flight was made in a two-seater open-cockpit biplane. Clouds were thick and heavy, limiting the flight altitude to about four hundred feet, until at last the plane was forced to land in a cornfield some six miles from its Cave City destination. A second plane was to have accompanied Dr. Hazlett's from Louisville, but it had to abandon the trip when the pilot warmed up the engine too much and was badly burned when he removed the radiator cap.

Dr. Hazlett arrived at the cave on Wednesday afternoon, still wearing his aviator's togs. Told that there was nothing he could do because of the cave-in, he nevertheless remained at the entrance talking with various people. At dinnertime he was still wearing his flying clothes. Part of the time he spent arguing with Lee and Homer about the feasibility of amputation. Old Man Lee had greeted the doctor when he first arrived with a hearty, "May God bless you," but left little doubt that he opposed such a drastic procedure. Homer, too, remained unpersuaded despite his tearful $500 offer of Monday night. Even without Lee's and Homer's objections, there were other detracting considerations. Dr. Hazlett was rather large and it was doubtful whether he could get down to Floyd. Also, it was difficult to reach to Floyd's thighs to dig, let alone to make a series of delicate surgical cuts. Floyd's bleeding to death on the way out was a distinct probability. Moreover, in his weakened condition the trapped man might not survive the shock of the operation. Dr. Hazlett recognized these dire possibilities and frankly admitted to reporters on Wednesday night that although amputation might save Floyd's life, it also might not.

When the passageway was abandoned and the shaft begun, Dr. Hazlett stayed on while Dr. Jones returned to Chicago. Hazlett soon became an indispensable figure in the rescue work. By Thursday night he had organized and staffed a small but well-equipped field hospital in a tent on the bluff overlooking the shaft. Complete with bandages, medicines, drugs, surgical instruments, a pulmotor, and even an ambulance, this hospital served not only as a standby emergency room for Floyd, but as a superb first-aid facility for the rescue workers. During the ensuing days, Dr. Hazlett treated many of them for cuts, colds, contusions, bruises, and physical exhaustion, and acted as their guardian against diphtheria and pneumonia. On Friday morning two Red Cross nurses, Rubel Lawrence and Fay Lewis, arrived from Louisville and thereafter served on Dr. Hazlett's growing staff. By Friday night he had seventeen volunteer doctors under his jurisdiction either at the cave or on call.

Besides medical services and supplies, more talent and material arrived at the site on Friday. If Thursday's flow was a stream, Friday's was a flood. Inexplicable things happened. Trucks and vans suddenly appeared and dumped machinery of all shapes and descriptions over the hillsides. Who ordered it and what it was for was a matter for conjecture. Wire, cable, sledgehammers, picks, logs, cots, blankets, coffeepots, and a host of other items both large and small were unloaded and left lying about. The Louisville Gas and Electric Company sent so much equipment that it required five trucks to haul it in. By Friday night the rescue site looked like one huge chaotic salvage yard. Although a testimony to the concern of the public and its desire to help, much of this material was unusable or inapplicable to the Sand Cave situation.

Offers to provide additional personnel continued to arrive. The Louisville Board of Public Safety, Captain Jack Loran of the Louisville Police Rescue Squad, and Chief Alex Bache of the Louisville Fire Department promised to send whatever manpower was necessary. Similar offers were made by the officials of the surrounding communities—Glasgow, Brownsville, Bowling Green. Individual volunteers also continued to show up at the site. These

newcomers added to the already crowded conditions and placed a
serious strain on the operation's shaky financial structure. Prior to
Thursday the Collins family itself bore the responsibility for
whatever cash outlays were necessary. On Thursday, Sam Caldwell
of the People's Bank was named treasurer of a small group that
began to solicit funds to shift the economic burden away from the
Collinses. By Friday, however, it was clear that the rescue was
going beyond anything this group could handle, and on Saturday
the National Red Cross stepped in. The Cave City chapter had
already set up a coffee and sandwich canteen at the cave on
Wednesday. By Friday it was feeding almost two hundred persons
per meal and the chapter was broke. Late on Friday an emergency
financial appeal by the Kentucky headquarters of the Red Cross
was sent out over the air and was carried in all the major state
newspapers. The following morning Red Cross headquarters in
Washington announced that it was assuming the responsibility for
defraying all day-to-day operational expenses at Sand Cave. Now
that the National Red Cross was feeding the men, commented one
paper, they would no longer have to survive "on black coffee,
crackers, and moonshine whiskey."

If only the digging could have kept pace with this outpouring of
support for the rescue effort. Instead, that process remained slow.
By Friday afternoon the work at the shaft was well organized,
coordinated, and efficiently managed. Hoisting machinery for
removing dirt from the pit had been installed and long flues were
attached to the exhausts of gas engines to carry the fumes over the
bluff above the cave. Yet, ankle-deep in mud, the men continued
to dig laboriously with picks and shovels as the huge mining
machinery and air drills that had been brought in over the gumbo
roads still stood mute and unused. As the shaft dropped below ten
feet only two men, instead of three, could work with ease. Big
boulders had to be pried out separately and removed. Because the
sides fell in constantly, workers were forced to excavate much more
than the volume of the shaft itself. The material they removed was
shoveled into a metal hoisting bucket which was hauled up to the
surface by a gas engine. This bucket was emptied into a small cart
which was pulled along the track to the dumping site by a cable
attached to a Fordson tractor. Every three feet a shoring crew had

to replace the diggers in the pit and install railroad ties to prevent further cave-ins and keep the shaft's sides square and in place.

All day Friday Carmichael frantically sought ways to speed up this process, but he was stymied by the difficult jumble of boulders, muck, large blocks, and gravel through which they were digging. To provide him with accurate information about the formations lying below, he asked R.C. Flaherty, who was thirty-five miles away in Kyroc, to bring a one-inch diamond drill to the site. Within hours, this rig, located just to the side of the shaft, was probing the ground for hidden voids and providing constant core samples. At 2:00 P.M., when the shaft was at fifteen feet, the drill indicated that a layer of limestone lay ahead. Time was fleeing and Carmichael felt the pressure. He told reporters, "We'll have to shoot the rock if it is solid and thick." Once again the decision to use dynamite was abandoned when it was discovered that the formation was not solid but only large boulders clumped together.

By late Friday afternoon another concern developed—the weather. Temperatures had moderated considerably since Tuesday, the thermometer hovering in the forties and fifties. Those who had to live in tents at the rescue site welcomed the warmer weather, but it slowed the digging. Ground water, held immobile during freezing weather, now ran freely and made the deepening of the shaft more difficult. As Friday night approached, rain threatened to complicate matters further by making it more miserable to work in the shaft and by markedly increasing the danger of cave-ins.

On Friday night heavy gloom settled over the site. The shaft was down only seventeen feet and the most arduous digging was yet to come. Progress had been less than one-half foot an hour. Superintendent Carmichael could only shake his head. His new estimate for reaching Floyd was Sunday at the earliest. Despondently, he told reporters that the odds were now heavy against Floyd's rescue and the possibilities for his death many. Collins might have been crushed by cave-ins; he might have died of shock and despair when he realized communication was cut off; he might be a victim of thirst, starvation, or pneumonia. "There isn't a chance," said the Kyroc superintendent, "but we're going to keep on digging until we find the body."

Some still refused to give in to pessimism—and General Denhardt was one. Normally carefully attired and groomed, on Friday night he was covered with mud from the waist down, and he was ebullient. To Adjutant General Kehoe at Frankfort, he sent this telegram:

WORK PROGRESSING WONDERFULLY WELL. EVERYTHING MOVES SMOOTHLY. CONFIDENT COLLINS IS ALIVE AND THAT WE WILL SAVE HIM.

Denhardt's enthusiasm was certainly not shared by the natives watching the shaft operation from the hillsides. They muttered resentfully. For the past two days Bee Doyle's farm had been transformed into a highly disciplined beehive of activity, but without local approval or local help. Beginning on Thursday afternoon, natives were eased out of the action area. No one but officials, designated digging and shoring workmen, engineers, surveyors, and newspapermen were allowed at or around the shaft. The "system," with its centralizing procedures, had taken over. Local control and individual initiative were being forced out.

Throughout Thursday and Friday, local scorn for the outlanders reached new heights. Not happy about the decision to sink a shaft anyway, natives clustered in small groups, blocking the way of those arriving with shoring and other materials. They complained constantly about where the shaft was being dug. Many were convinced that it would end up nowhere near Floyd; it was much too close to the mouth of the cave. Some openly feuded with the experts and the engineers; others stood sullenly off to one side. All of them were particularly incensed by the string of outside volunteers who kept arriving and were put to work by Carmichael even though they "didn't know nothin' about caves."

The Collins family reacted to this new order in various ways. Old Man Lee was a picture of confusion. The last several days had taken their toll. His limp was more apparent and he seemed unsteady and weak. Under the mounting tension, his mental aberrations also grew more pronounced. His hand now quivered as he ran it across his eyes. On Thursday afternoon he stumbled around the rim of the pit, appearing haunted and forlorn. He had already spent all his available money on rescue food and clothing and he fretted about how the remaining expenses were going to be paid. His touch with reality was obviously becoming tenuous. For example, he disclosed to reporters that he had received a proposal from a Chicago booking agent offering Floyd a salary of $350 a week for a vaudeville tour, then added sorrowfully, "I don't know whether that boy of mine will take it seriously, though."

Although confused and in despair, by Friday morning Lee Collins had clearly not given up hope. He comforted himself by claiming that "The Lord's able to give my boy strength to last till the new shaft reaches him." God's will might have led Floyd into the cave, reasoned Lee, but intercessory prayer might yet get him out. To one Chicago reporter, he pleaded, "Ast the country to pray for my boy." "I know the Lord'll save him," he would exclaim to anyone who would listen and then declare, "If we only pray enough my son'll come out alive." Sometimes he would demand that they offer a prayer for Floyd on the spot. By Friday afternoon, a cold Lee had contracted earlier in the week was growing worse, and he hacked constantly as he talked. This was of deep concern to his relatives and friends because of his recent bout with the flu. Several times Dr. Hazlett ordered him home to bed and tried to give him some medication, but he refused. Lee said that as long as Floyd was trapped he was going to remain at the site "even if this cold kills me." With tears in his eyes, he stated, "I reckon God wants me and my boy. Wal, I'm ready, but I fear Floyd is not."

This latter possibility particularly worried Lee and, as hope for Floyd's rescue dwindled on Friday night, he began to rationalize his son's tragic situation. He finally concluded that Floyd's death would be all right because Floyd was "saved." Floyd's lack of religious zeal had often been a source of friction between the two men. Floyd, like others in the family, had attended the Mammoth Cave (Baptist) Church, where he could be seen almost every Sunday. But Floyd wore his religion lightly the other days in the week. Even a promise at his mother's deathbed to be baptized had not led him into more holy paths. Now Lee wanted to believe that the Sand Cave experience had changed his son and, after hearing Skeets Miller and others talk about the prayers Floyd had uttered, Lee became certain of it. For Lee, Floyd's impending death was final proof that a transformation had taken place. "Down there almost a hundred feet under the ground, Floyd's been converted," declared the old man. "God's worked His will, and it may be for the best. . . . Floyd's going to his mother in heaven."

Floyd's stepmother, Miss Jane, arrived at Sand Cave for the first time on Friday afternoon. Sixty-five years old and suffering from asthma and heart trouble, she leaned heavily on Homer's arm as she looked into the murky depths of the cave's opening. Upon seeing it, she collapsed and had to be carried into Dr. Hazlett's hospital tent. After being revived, she was escorted to the edge of the rescue shaft on the arm of Lieutenant Cross so that she could see what was being done there. Halting at the edge, she muttered a little prayer and tottered backward. Dr. Hazlett quickly grabbed her other arm and, together, he and Lieutenant Cross drew her away. Floyd's younger sister, Nellie, was also there for the first time, her face white as she clung fiercely onto Miss Jane's hand. For the major part of Friday afternoon she and Miss Jane sat on a log on the hillside silently watching the proceedings, lost in their thoughts.

Another family member at the cave on Friday was Floyd's remaining brother, Andy Lee. With several days' growth of beard on his chin and his hat slouched down over one eye, he had arrived that morning with his wife and three children, having driven in a mad dash from Kewanee, Illinois. On the way they had had two car accidents, but fortunately no one was hurt. Upon viewing the mouth of the shaft for the first time, Andy Lee fainted and, like Miss Jane, had to be revived in the hospital tent. Dr. Hazlett suspected, and some observers claimed, that Andy Lee's real trouble was too much liquor. In any case, he continued to be so distraught that friends eventually took him to Cave City and away from the tension of the rescue scene altogether. Before leaving, however, he leveled charges left and right, primarily blaming Johnnie Gerald and his own father for Floyd's plight.

Andy Lee was not the only one who was hurling loud accusations by Friday afternoon. Lieutenant Burdon was also being extremely vocal. The Louisville fireman had never stopped sulking over being excluded from the cave by Johnnie Gerald on Wednesday, nor had he forgiven Homer for thwarting his various pulling schemes. On

Friday morning, immediately after S.H. Lane stated that Floyd was still alive, Burdon had set up a small steam engine at the mouth of Sand Cave to blow hot air down to the trapped man through a seventy-five-foot hose. After receiving General Denhardt's permission to enter the passageway to position the hose, Burdon had seized the opportunity to go on down and examine the second collapse. Upon seeing it, he thought that it looked suspiciously like the first one he had seen at 4:00 P.M. on Wednesday afternoon. The Louisville fireman therefore emerged asking several pointed questions: Was it possible that Gerald had been lying, that there had been only one cave-in instead of two, and that it had never been reduced? For his part, Gerald ridiculed Burdon's attempt to "heat" Sand Cave and said that it further demonstrated the stupidity of outlanders about Kentucky caverns. Scientists later confirmed what Gerald already knew—that the hot air pumped into the cave dissipated into the surrounding rock and soil as soon as it was released, making the heated area more susceptible to collapse.

Homer Collins, meanwhile, became a highly volatile and unpredictable factor in the continuing rescue. Dismayed by the decision to sink the shaft, he spent most of his time on Thursday complaining. He especially raged at General Denhardt's order placing Sand Cave off limits. He told newsmen that he would still gladly risk his life for his brother, but that he was being prevented from doing so by "that military bastard." At one point on Thursday, he attempted to steal back into the passageway but two guards stopped him with the warning, "Don't try to go into that cave!" Homer argued with them: "My brother's in there. You can't keep me out." But they did, and he retreated to the hillside where he continued to protest.

On Friday morning and early afternoon Homer stayed close to Andy Lee, Miss Jane, and Nellie. Generally, Homer shunned Old Man Lee and, although he did not support Andy Lee's emotional charges against their father, he was nonetheless increasingly embarrassed by Lee's actions. Also, unlike Andy Lee, Homer did not attack the motives of Johnnie Gerald. Homer's targets remained the state officials and engineers who had closed the cave and started the shaft. Sometime in midafternoon on Friday, he slipped away from his relatives and again attempted to sneak into Sand Cave. This time he succeeded. Crawling to the second breakdown, he found that the electric light there was still burning. It offered him hope that his brother's light was working, too. He called and called but received no answer. How long he remained inside is not clear, but it was long enough that he was missed on the surface. Those who knew he had returned to the cave finally became fearful that he had become trapped and leaked word to Denhardt where he was. The general was furious. So was Carmichael, since it forced him to divert his efforts to assembling a new cave rescue team. Carmichael was just beginning to select its members when Homer suddenly reappeared and sobbed to reporters that he now believed his brother was dead. Andy Lee, who was in the process of being bundled off to Cave City following his earlier fainting spell, collapsed again when he saw Homer crying and covered with mud.

Unwittingly Homer emerged in the middle of a bitter altercation among Carmichael, Denhardt, and Johnnie Gerald. After his failure to free Floyd on Wednesday night, Gerald had gone home to rest and had slept around the clock until Friday morning. At 9:00 A.M., on his way to get a shave, he ran into Lee and Marshall. Marshall had recovered from his illness of Tuesday and was again taking an interest in rescue matters. The two Collinses begged Gerald to accompany them to the cave and talk with state officials. They were dissatisfied with the shaft's location and with the speed of the digging. Gerald, however, made no promises, and after arriving at the site first searched the surrounding area for an alternate route into Sand Cave. Discovering none, he spent early Friday afternoon watching the rescue operation from a point on the bluff directly overlooking the shaft. In midafternoon, he was joined by Lieutenant Wells, who asked him if he was going to try to get back into the cave. Gerald admitted that he would like to make another trip in to see if the passageway had changed any.

The problem was how to get past the guards. Lieutenant Wells suggested that Gerald ask Carmichael to intercede for him with General Denhardt. When Carmichael was approached, however, he flatly refused. Irritated by this refusal, Gerald *demanded* to be allowed back in the cave and charged that the shaft was murdering Floyd. Frustrated and worried about the slowness of the digging anyway, the Kyroc superintendent lost his temper. He angrily told Gerald that they had done all that was possible through the old passageway and that if Floyd was to be saved it would be as a result of the engineering knowledge of men like himself and not the hit-or-miss work of the natives.

Gerald retreated to the hillside where he attracted a large group of local people who were already grousing about the slow progress and the possibility that the shaft was mislocated. They were still grumbling to one another when the flap arose concerning Homer's absence. As Carmichael set about organizing a rescue party, Gerald rushed up insisting that he be included. At that precise moment Homer reappeared. Gerald immediately switched to again demanding permission to enter the cave to reexamine the second breakdown.

"Shit," shouted Gerald to Carmichael, "the shaft's no damned good. We got to go back in the passageway!"

Carmichael was about to answer when General Denhardt came striding up and brusquely interjected, "Gerald, you can't go in. My God, man, do you want to commit suicide?"

"Hell, no," came Gerald's hot reply, "but goddamnit, you're killin' Floyd—you and all these other dumb sonsabitches!"

Denhardt turned white with rage. Already furious at Homer, he now snarled at Gerald, "Goddamn you—you're the cause of most of our trouble," and, motioning for a guard, commanded, "Get him the hell out of here!" Homer, too, was summarily ejected from the shaft area, but before a guard could hustle him away, he collapsed and had to be carried into the hospital tent.

Not long afterward, both Homer and Gerald were again on the hillside voicing their discontent to disgruntled natives. Gerald told his listeners that he had been maligned and that he had done nothing to deserve General Denhardt's ire. He only wanted to help Floyd. Homer was vituperative. In the heat of the moment he forgot all about his earlier failures in Sand Cave and spoke only of how near he had been to saving Floyd before the shaft was begun. Lieutenant Burdon, who was preparing to return to his home in Louisville, added to the turmoil by loudly proclaiming to reporters that the natives were stupid and incompetent. In response, some local hotheads began to talk of using their squirrel rifles to run off the state authorities and outlanders such as Burdon. Word of this quickly passed to Denhardt, who had been warily watching hillside developments out of the corner of his eye. Still believing Gerald to be the primary instigator of the continuing trouble, the general, flanked by two officers, marched up to him and ordered him out of the cave area completely. One of the officers grabbed Gerald by the arm and led him to a waiting car which deposited him in Cave City.

Gerald's banishment at about 5:00 P.M. on Friday was only one of several actions Denhardt took that day to advertise his authority and assure the maintenance of order. Earlier, as the crowds increased and the digging continued slowly, Denhardt notified Adjutant General Kehoe that "an ugly situation might be imminent," and suggested that they hold a conference. Also, earlier on Friday, he had stationed a few plainclothesmen among the various groups on the hillside to report to him on crowd attitudes. By midafternoon they all were recommending that he act vigorously to forestall violence. While Denhardt was pondering exactly what to do, Kehoe appeared at the cave, having been flown in by a chartered plane. The two men agreed that twenty-five more guardsmen should be rushed to the scene and an additional eight hundred rounds of ammunition be sent from Frankfort.

By dinnertime on Friday, February 6, although the state remained firmly in control, nerves were frayed, tempers were short, and a bitter three-way struggle raged at the Collins rescue site. Natives were convinced that neither the experts nor the outside amateurs were needed—the amateurs had prevented success through the Sand Cave passageway and the experts were wrong in sinking the shaft. Outlanders like Burdon believed that they could have saved the trapped man if they had been left alone by the natives, and neither the military nor a shaft would have been necessary. The experts and engineers believed that both of these groups had been in error, that they had wasted much valuable time, and that their rescue efforts had been unavailing and primitive.

But by Friday night, the engineers and the experts were not doing too well either. Their shaft-sinking was slow and there was no assurance that they were headed in the direction of Floyd. Using only picks and shovels, their methods, too, remained unsophisticated and time-consuming. Little wonder that despondency set in as darkness fell. Anything could have happened to Floyd by now—even electrocution, since once during the evening the higher

voltage wires carrying power to workers in the shaft accidentally fell
across the lower voltage pair going to Floyd in the cave.

Toward dinnertime, as rain threatened, the Friday afternoon
crowd of five hundred began to thin out. But friends of Floyd and
his family continued their vigil. Old Man Lee, Miss Jane, and Nellie
did not leave until 8:00 P.M. Marshall stayed until midnight. Homer
slept on a cot in the hospital tent. It was a time of despair, and of
contrasts. One wrinkled old crone watching above the shaft area
whispered to a hillside companion, "Prayer'll now do more for
Floyd Collins than all the shovels in the world." Looking down at
the same scene, a well-dressed urban newsman turned to a
colleague and asked, "Did system and proper authority arrive in
time? One wonders and hopes."

Saturday, February 7, was a day of reassurance. Urged by
Professor Funkhouser to adopt a more conciliatory attitude toward
the local people, both General Denhardt and Superintendent
Carmichael tried to convince them that everything possible was
being done to rescue Floyd and that the present plan was best.
Early Saturday morning a procedure was inaugurated of notifying
Floyd by periodic but steady blinks on his light bulb that help was
on the way. Simultaneously, a light was rigged in parallel on the
same wires going to Floyd in the cave and placed on the bluff above
the entrance. Bystanders were told that as long as Floyd's bulb was
burning this one would remain lit as well, offering visual proof to
everyone in the cave area that Floyd was still receiving light and
heat.

To quiet native doubts about the shaft's going in the right
direction, Carmichael approved a series of elaborate sound tests.
At 2:15 P.M., Anderson, Ford, Gerard, and Lieutenant Wells were
sent back into the Sand Cave passageway roped together and
carrying microphones and other sensitive acoustical equipment.
They hoped to pick up Floyd's heartbeat as well as surface drilling
noises. Thirty minutes after they disappeared the diamond-core
drill was run for two minutes, then there was five minutes of silence
followed by another five minutes of drilling. This sequence was
repeated several times. All machinery and above ground noises
were stilled during the silent periods. Even the crowd on the

hillside was requested to remain quiet. Once a baby cried, causing a nearby guardsman to frown. At another point a spectator laughed and got a whispered order to leave. Two hours passed as these tests continued. When at last the listening group emerged from the cave, they reported that although they could not detect any signs of life in the passageway, they had been able to ascertain that the shaft would come within ten feet of Floyd. Naturally, the natives were immediately told of this latter fact.

Officials at the rescue site on Saturday also encouraged a search for alternate routes into Sand Cave. Gerald had told Denhardt on Friday that Floyd believed all the caves in the area were connected and that it was shortsighted not to explore this possibility more fully. Funkhouser had agreed with Gerald, and on Saturday the professor spent much of his time looking for new approaches. But he met with no success and, after observing the area's water drainage and rock strata, finally concluded that there was no relationship between Sand Cave and any other cavern in the surrounding region. If there was such a connection, he speculated that it would have to be on a much deeper level and not accessible from the surface.

While Funkhouser was arriving at this conclusion, Homer was also searching. Such activity gave him a constructive outlet for his frustrations. Although less scientific in his approach than the professor, he was more aggressive in his probing and on Saturday afternoon discovered a small sinkhole some two hundred yards from the Sand Cave entrance. After crawling down into it by means of a ladder, he was able to move laterally for about seventy feet before coming to the edge of a chamber he estimated to be at least sixty feet deep. On the way he found two unburned matches with blue heads and red tips—the same kind that Floyd regularly used. With rising hope, he returned to the surface for a rope and a flashlight. There it was pointed out to him that the crawlway he had just discovered went *away* from Sand Cave and not toward it. Further, the intervening rock formations precluded any connection between them. Reluctantly, Homer had to agree and assumed that Floyd had come to that same conclusion when he had been there.

While the natives were being placated by sound tests or were having their energies drawn off by searching for alternate routes,

newly arriving members of the Kentucky National Guard unob-
trusively took up their stations. By Saturday night a total of fifty
were present along with a nine-man contingent of the Tennessee
National Guard under the command of Captain Clyde H. Hall of
Company A, 146th Engineers. They had been sent by Tennessee
Governor Austin Peay as a goodwill gesture. Now, more than ever,
a tinge of the army camp permeated the rescue amphitheater. One
could hear the echoing voices of challenging sentries on all the
surrounding paths, and bivouacs dotted the sides and tops of the
hills. The extra ammunition that had been requisitioned from
Frankfort was quietly stockpiled at the site. A five-strand barbed-
wire fence was stapled in place on trees, providing an enclosure for
the entire rescue area. Starting at the left side of the ledge, where
the path led in from the Cave City road, this fence ran forty feet
back from the top of the overhang, down along both sides of the
slope, and cut across the ravine at a point over three hundred feet
from the shaft itself. General Denhardt had good reason to believe
that by nightfall on Saturday continuing order was assured and
security achieved.

Carmichael, meanwhile, strove for greater efficiency in the
rescue operation and for increased speed in the digging. By
Saturday afternoon almost all rescuers were housed in tents on the
site. Only a few still boarded in neighborhood farmhouses. Also on
Saturday signed meal tickets were issued to the workers to prevent
panhandlers from clogging the mess lines at the Red Cross canteen.
In order to prevent the work from being impeded by rain, a canvas
fly of twenty-four hundred square feet was strung over the shaft
entrance and an elaborate system of drains for the rock overhang
was installed. Although the expected rain of Friday night had not
materialized, its threat continued and Carmichael wanted to be
prepared. To provide a more equitable distribution of tasks and a
higher degree of worker efficiency, each rescuer was assigned to a
specific shift and to a designated crew. The crews were changed at
least every two hours. But even this was not sufficient to stave off
fatigue. The men, especially those working in the shaft, were
covered with mud and almost unrecognizable at the end of their
particular stint. They flopped down on their cots from sheer

exhaustion, not caring to clean up nor even bothering to take off their shoes.

Still, the shaft only crept down. For a time on Saturday morning the progress was 7.3 inches per hour but fell off sharply as the diggers encountered another layer of limestone boulders. By Saturday night the depth of the pit was twenty feet, with two-thirds of the way yet to go. Probing ahead, the diamond drill indicated that solid limestone would be encountered at the forty-eight-foot level and would continue for at least six feet. Somewhere at about fifty-five feet they could expect to find Floyd's prison chamber. Slow progress, rocks, solid limestone—all this was discouraging, and Carmichael was loathe to make new predictions. Late Saturday night he glumly told a group of inquiring reporters, "I cannot say just when a shaft will reach Floyd. But I will tell you this. If we get Collins out of there by Tuesday, I will stand up and sing the doxology."

The real action on Saturday did not take place in the rescue pit, in the Sand Cave passageway, or in the activities of various persons searching for alternate routes. It occurred among the crowd on the hillside, in Cave City, and in the nation at large. Already by Friday the rescue site was clogged with people. On that day over four hundred automobiles jammed the road at Sand Cave, and approximately fifteen hundred persons were there at one time or another. Usually the crowd numbered about five hundred. On Saturday the numbers shot up. Bee Doyle soon found his corncrib depleted by visitors' horses, his pump torn out by those who were thirsty, and his fields churned into quagmires. It was estimated that by early Saturday afternoon cars were coming and going at the rate of 120 an hour. By three o'clock, two thousand people watched the sinking of the shaft. Milder temperatures unquestionably helped attract this flood of observers; in late afternoon the thermometer stood at a balmy sixty degrees. Instead of sticking together in small whispering groups as on Friday, people wandered about without purpose except to satisfy their curiosity. Undoubtedly, the increased number of guardsmen had a pacifying effect.

Cave City was drastically affected by this sudden influx of

visitors. A relatively young town, it had for some time aspired to great things. Its history had begun in 1853, long after many neighboring communities had been settled. In that year a group of Louisville men, known as the Knob City Land Company, bought the town site for $6850. They hoped to build a resort community near Mammoth Cave. The company surveyed streets and offered residential lots for sale even before the Louisville & Nashville Railroad was built in 1859. Thereafter, not only did the L&N run through the town but so did the Louisville and Nashville stage. A feeder stageline also connected the village with Mammoth Cave.

By 1860 Cave City boasted a post office, but only a few families actually resided within the town's limits. During the Civil War and post–Civil War period its growth was much slower than planned. In general, its progress and economic health were directly affected by the fortunes of the surrounding caves. Unfortunately, in 1870, Cave City was hit by a severe tornado that cost fifteen lives and left the village a shambles. Its black section was wiped out and the white community's lone church building, school building, and Masonic Lodge were lost.

The most publicized event in the life of the town prior to 1900 was not the 1870 windstorm but the 1880 holdup of two stages halfway between Mammoth Cave and Cave City by Jesse James. James and his men got $1000, several gold watches, and a diamond ring in these robberies. When a confederate later shot Jesse, the famous outlaw had in his pocket the gold watch that he had lifted from Judge R.H. Roundtree, an occupant of one of these stages. For years afterward, those who claimed to have intimate knowledge of this matter told many a tall tale about it at Oscar's Blacksmith Shop, Cave City's best-known loafing spot.

With the coming of the twentieth century and the ensuing cave wars, Cave City experienced a new birth of enthusiasm and entered into vigorous competition with surrounding villages for a share of the cave business. Local boosterism encouraged Cave City dwellers to think in expansive terms. Unexpectedly, the Collins tragedy immediately fulfilled some of their wildest dreams. A community of 680 persons in 1925, the town's population by Saturday, February 7, instantly quadrupled, prompting one reporter to comment, "Not since the gold rush into Alaska has such a scene been duplicated."

Cave City did resemble a boom town. Every automobile was pressed into service, stocks of merchandise were quickly depleted, and both hotels were overflowing. By Saturday night, those townspeople who temporarily became taxi drivers were making more money than they thought possible by charging a fare to Sand Cave of a dollar and a half each way. Beds and cots stood in the hallways of the hotels. Hungry visitors were paying extra money for spaces at tables in their dining rooms. Rooming houses were full and a normal seventy-five-cent overnight stay zoomed to two dollars, causing the *New York Times* to prophesy, "Many a moss-covered mortgage will be lifted if Collins is not rescued soon." Latecomers to Cave City were forced to sleep in any place they could find. By the weekend as many as five persons were sharing a room and sleeping in relays. When Neil Dalton, Skeets Miller's editor, arrived on Saturday, he had to sleep in a bathtub with a leaky faucet. The lobbies of the hotels became oration pits for those who were expounding their own theories on how to set Floyd free, or trading centers where rides were purchased and meal and room privileges were swapped. It was said that by Saturday night newsmen were offering ridiculous bribes and resorting to naked threats to get even bathtub accommodations.

This influx of people with money proved costly for some Cave City residents. Property suffered considerable wear and some actual destruction. Although merchants were making a profit from most of the visitors, they were also carrying thousands of dollars in credit for Sand Cave workers, engineers, and experts. Cave City also experienced a crime wave and a marked increase in public drunkenness. One old-timer later commented that the town was suddenly "just as alive at night as in the daytime" and that "nobody got very thirsty for quite a while." Pickpockets seemed to be everywhere and thievery skyrocketed. This criminal activity so worried the town fathers that in order to combat it Magistrate Turner deputized twenty-five residents who began to patrol the streets. White ribbons bearing the word "Police" were used for badges.

Of all the visitors to Cave City, none were more prominent than those from the news media. Being the nearest town to the rescue site, Cave City inevitably became the hub of the information-gathering and reporting activities relating to Floyd Collins. News-men were present from almost every state in the union, and even a few were there from foreign countries. An English correspondent made the first trans-Atlantic phone call ever handled from Cave City. Representatives were in attendance from sixteen big-city newspapers and from six motion picture studios. The Chicago papers had more than a dozen men there. The New York press had ten. Special writers, photographers, and sketch artists swelled the total number of media people to almost a hundred and fifty. Reporters alone outnumbered the guards at Sand Cave.

Such concentration of news talent naturally placed extremely heavy pressure on the communication lines running out of the community. The Tucker Telephone Company was the only voice link to the outside world for the first several days, and it was swamped. Newsmen waited as long as two hours to send their stories out, while the operators on duty barely had time to sleep. The postal telegraph office was likewise overwhelmed, its only telegrapher having to work day and night. Later, to supplement this telegraphic service, a 500-watt radio transmitter, using dry batteries and having the call sign 9-BRK, was set up at Sand Cave. Another radio, designated 9-CHG, did the receiving at the Cave City telegraph office. Under the direction of H.E. Ogden, this circuit remained in operation for several days before it was commandeered by the military. Belatedly, Western Union installed a telegraphic branch office at the cave itself with more than a dozen operators to handle both incoming messages and outgoing news stories.

All of this was symptomatic of the nation's growing insatiability for news about Floyd. Following publication of Skeets Miller's interviews on Wednesday and Thursday, February 4 and 5, the public's preoccupation with Collins was amazing, and the media rushed to supply additional information and to analyze every nuance of the Sand Cave tragedy. The circumstances were just right for the development of a sustained national interest. The Collins affair occurred in the dead of winter when the public was shut in and could concentrate on its newspapers and radios. The story itself was dramatic, sensational—involving physical and mental torture, danger and exhaustion, unbearable tension, rivalry, heroism, and an uncertain outcome. It concerned a lone victim whose suffering was indescribable but whose thoughts and feelings were clearly known. The average citizen is seldom affected by the raw statistics of a disaster—a hundred persons lost in a flood or a hundred thousand starving in a famine. But when a single dying man such as Floyd Collins lies at his doorstep, he can be profoundly moved.

Yet something more subtle and deeply psychological was at work here. The public has always evidenced a morbid fascination with death and dying—and the possibility of a slow, agonizing death made the Floyd Collins story even more perversely attractive. Too, Floyd's plight touched in every person a fear of darkness and isolation, a primordial cave fear that stirred a feeling akin to nothing else in the human experience. Suddenly, millions of Americans were vicariously trapped alive with Collins in a way that these same millions could not fly the Atlantic with Lindbergh or fight in the boxing ring with Dempsey. This "buried alive" fantasy had always called forth the wildest imaginings of writers and had provided the foundation for the tragic fate of several mythical personages. The press could therefore be forgiven for claiming that nothing more awful had ever been chronicled. As one paper editorialized:

> A hundred deaths the victim of this accident has died. . . . Fiction has nothing comparable to the horror of this scene which makes one quail and shudder. Poe and "The Pit and the Pendulum" . . . Conan Doyle and his story of the engineer trapped in a room, the floors and ceiling of which [were] closing . . . neither is comparable to the throes of agony tearing the spirit of Floyd Collins.

The Collins affair was the first sustained nonpolitical event in which the radio played a major role. The misfortune of this helpless man became an important part of every newscast, beginning on Wednesday, February 4. By Thursday, announcers were not only providing listeners with capsule news from Cave City but were breaking in on scheduled programs to bring it up to date. Starting on Saturday, February 7, San Francisco station KPO began its broadcast day, and every day thereafter, with an appeal for its listeners to join in a prayer for Collins. Beginning on Wednesday,

WHAS in Louisville carried eight bulletins a day about Floyd. Other stations quickly followed. No news event prior to this time had been accorded such treatment. So interested was the public in acquiring the most recent rescue information that if news bulletins were the slightest bit late, the offending stations would be swamped with phone calls. Station owners soon realized that a rapidly expanding listening audience was available to them because of mounting public concern for Floyd, and they sought to capitalize on it. Competition picked up among advertisers for the sponsorship of newscasts. Clearly, the motive behind continued widespread radio coverage was both public spirited *and* economically oriented.

The motion pictures also found the Collins entrapment a highly reportable event. By Friday, February 6, several motion picture crews were operating at the rescue site. To capture a record of the story from the very beginning, they engaged in some deceit. They staged shots of Johnnie Gerald pretending he was coming out of the cave exhausted. Homer was filmed as if he were going in to see his brother. Skeets Miller was photographed dressed in his caving gear, supposedly just after his famous Tuesday dinnertime interview.

The most inventive motion picture photographer at the scene was a twenty-year-old cameraman of the Louisville Film Company, Cliff Roney. Beginning on Thursday afternoon, Roney worked without regular sleep for four days and nights, boarding a train for the cave each morning and returning to Louisville each night to develop the day's takes. His films were first shown in Louisville. Afterward, they were released nationally. By Monday, February 9, other movies of the rescue operation were being shown in public theaters throughout the nation, first in the East and then across the country. Millions watching the silent screen were captivated by scenes of the rescue site, the Kentucky cave country, the shaft digging, and by pictures of Skeets Miller, Johnnie Gerald, members of the Collins family, and the official directors of the rescue.

Important as the movies and the radio were to the unfolding of the Floyd Collins drama, the daily newspaper remained the primary source of information and the chief exploiter of the event. Newspapers naturally reinforced listener and viewer interest in the radio and the movies. Radio and film, in turn, enhanced reader interest in the newspapers. And Americans snapped them up.

Issues sold out at once and extra editions had to be printed. One New York paper claimed that it sold an extra sixty to a hundred thousand copies daily from February 7 on. Big-city newspaper circulations were not the only ones that were up. Village and small-town weekly papers were also affected since they, too, carried details of the Collins story for readers in their areas. Even in the Kentucky and Tennessee mountain country, articles about Floyd were passed from hand to hand and were perused by people who usually never saw a newspaper.

Although Floyd remained the focal point of all this press coverage, newspapers really had so little news to report about him after the second cave-in that they turned increasingly to other aspects of the tragedy. Almost anything became grist for their reporting mill. Providing the most colorful copy were the various members of the Collins family. Portrayed as typical Kentucky backwoodsmen who possessed strange and fascinating ways, the Collinses emerged as stereotyped figures for millions of Americans. Lee was seen as a Bible-quoting, poverty-stricken hill farmer; Homer a roughhewn, good-natured, loyal frontier brother; Nellie, a shy, unsophisticated, virginal sister; Miss Jane, a bent, shawl-covered, tired old mother. The *Chicago Tribune,* for example, said that Miss Jane had "sagged shoulders that years behind the plow on the rocky Kentucky hillsides gives its women." The *San Francisco Chronicle* introduced its readers to Miss Jane on February 6 with this unusual (and wholly fictitious) interview:

An' Floyd said to me: "Lor', Ma, I got three days more work in that cave, and Lor' how I wish it was over. I been a-dreamin' of bein' caught in some rocks and some men a-clawin' at me." An' I sez to him: "You stay home here today. We ain't got no wood chopped, and we need you here." Well suh, that boy he went down behind the house and chopped up a whole pile of wood. But at 10 o'clock he went away. That night he didn't come back.

By all odds, Old Man Lee was the reporters' favorite. His idiosyncrasies, biblical quotations, and quixotic actions made a great story in itself. His angry arguments with his sons and his

questionable monetary motives drew reporters to him. At their
hands he almost became a caricature. They loved to talk with him
and quoted him extensively. The press especially played up his
greater concern for Floyd's soul than for Floyd's physical welfare,
and exhaustively interviewed him about his belief that his son had
"found salvation" in the cave.

Whenever colorful and interesting material was not available
from the Collinses themselves, newsmen sought it elsewhere. Late
on Thursday they allegedly discovered a young woman standing
alone near the rescue shaft with tears on her cheeks, and they
immediately proceeded to manufacture one of the great love stories
of all time. Her name, according to reporters, was Alma Clark, age
twenty-two, and she and Floyd were to have eloped and been
married that very day. Since Alma lived eight miles from Sand
Cave, some newspapers said that she walked, some that she rode a
mule, and others that she was driven in a cab to her lover's rescue
site. Upon arriving at the cave, she ran to the entrance, peered into
the opening while calling out, "Floyd, my husband," and then
fainted away.

Of course, this sweetheart angle had tremendous reader appeal,
particularly to women, and newspapers played it up big. Between
February 6 and February 9, pictures of Alma, one of which showed
her dressed demurely in calico milking a cow, appeared in virtually
every American newspaper. In trying to find out more about Floyd
and Alma, reporters were aided by Mrs. Wade Highbaugh, wife of
a Cave City photographer who at the moment was working for the
*Evening Post*. She claimed that she had been a "mother confessor"
to Floyd, and she fed newsmen many interesting romantic tidbits.
"Floyd was going to steal Alma," she claimed, "Yes, sir. He was
going to steal Alma and bring her back here as Mrs. Floyd Collins."
To underscore the seriousness of their relationship, Mrs. Highbaugh said that Floyd had sent all the way to Louisville for a box of
chocolate-covered cherries for Alma for Christmas.

The *Evening Post*, which naturally got this story first, claimed
that Floyd obviously dreamed of other things besides caves: "He
yearned for a home and fireside, a loving wife and babies, and the
country Miss he hoped to enshrine as queen of his rural cas-
tle. . . ." Not to be outdone, the *New York Times* told its readers

on February 6: "In a log cabin behind Floyd Collins's prison, a mountain woman waits for him. No roads run to her home and muleback is the only transportation. The girl, Miss Alma Clark, was his sweetheart, and they planned to wed as soon as Floyd had won his fortune by his cave discoveries." Other newspapers voiced similar opinions, some, like the *Atlanta Constitution*, seeing in Alma a deep significance:

> . . . this may be why Floyd Collins wouldn't give up in his fight for life when he knew the fight seemed lost. It may explain why Collins kept courage when rescuers and friends were downcast. It may reveal how Collins endured torture with a smile at times through six days in the grip of a stone in the cave, and it may show the power that kept alive that spark of faith he cherished.

All this was interesting but hardly factual. The Clarks did live eight miles from Sand Cave and had a daughter, Alma, who was seventeen and not twenty-two. Floyd had visited the Clark family many times, had often talked with Alma, and on several occasions snapped her picture with a Kodak. She thought of him as an "old man" like her own father and never as a sweetheart. Once, when he brought her some candy from Munfordville, she refused to accept it so as not to be embarrassed by friends her own age. Whatever Floyd may have thought about Alma or told Mrs. Highbaugh about her, he certainly did not communicate it to Alma herself. More significant, at no time did Alma appear at the Sand Cave rescue site. Her activities there were entirely figments of journalistic imaginations.

As for Floyd's interest in the opposite sex in general, the record remains unclear. William Travis Blair, who had known Floyd all his life, said Floyd never went with any girls or kept their company. Homer later claimed that Floyd was acquainted and talked with many women but never squired any of them around. Marshall, too, asserted that as far as he knew there was nothing between his brother and any of the local females. Old Man Lee flatly denied the possibility of Floyd's ever marrying because he was simply not interested in the fairer sex.

Whether this lack of interest indicated a latent homosexuality or sexual incapacity on Floyd's part was never discussed by any of his relatives or contemporaries. The only concrete statement his father ever made was: "Floyd never had much use for girls. He never stayed out of a cave long enough to get well acquainted with one." Some psychiatrists would claim to see a significant connection between these two facts. A Freudian explanation is possible. Conceivably, caving may have been not only an adventurous and even religious experience for Floyd, but a sexual one as well. Floyd's antipathy to his father and lack of close male friends is suggestive. As indicated by his rapport with Miss Jane, Floyd was far more sensitive to the females in his family than the males. Yet he felt uncomfortable around other women and did not relate to them easily. If Floyd was indeed sexually immature and repressed, caving may have provided him with sexual sublimation or substitution. Freudians would certainly find deep meaning in the slippery and wet passageways down which Floyd loved to crawl and twist. Such places can be symbolic of vaginal vaults. Squeezes, in turn, are restrictive orifices which, upon opening into larger rooms, act like the mouth of a womb. Struggling through these, Floyd may have found a subconscious comfort and security in the uterinelike chambers beyond, and there, crouched in a fetal position and resting in the glow of his lantern, he subliminally fought against the moment when he had to begin his return journey (be "reborn") into the real world. It is also possible that actual sexual stimulation and self-gratification may have accompanied these underground adventures. But whatever Floyd's sexual orientation, the Alma Clark story was certainly fictitious, and even it lost its uniqueness when, not long afterward, three publicity-seeking women from other areas came forward to claim that Floyd really intended to marry them.

A similar mountain out of a factual molehill was made about Floyd's dog. On February 6, several reporters claimed to have found the trapped man's faithful companion, whom they variously named Chinee Chow or Tray, wandering around the rescue site, staying near the mouth of the shaft and howling mournfully. Sometimes, wrote these reporters, he would lie down with his head between his paws, forcing workers to walk around him. On

Floyd Collins about 1924.
*Wade Highbaugh*

Sand Cave in the summer of
1925 after Floyd's body was
removed. *R. T. Neville*

Sand Cave rescue site. Canvas flies protect against rain. Track is for dump car. Note pile of shoring timbers for rescue shaft. *Ernst Kastning Collection*

Top of the rescue shaft. Skeets Miller is fourth from the left. *Ernst Kastning Collection*

Henry S. Carmichael, in charge of the rescue, shaft superintendent Henretta, and Professor Funkhouser at the rescue shaft. *Ernst Kastning Collection*

Kentucky National Guard officers at Sand Cave. *Ernst Kastning Collection*

Magistrate Clay Turner and Johnnie Gerald at Sand Cave. Turner tried vainly to banish drinking from the rescue scene before the National Guard arrived. Gerald was a rescue leader. *Ernst Kastning Collection*

Homer Collins and Marshall Collins, brothers of Floyd Collins, during the rescue attempt at Sand Cave. *Ernst Kastning Collection*

Bee Doyle operated Sand Cave as a tourist attraction for about a year following Floyd Collins' entrapment. Visitors pose with the 26 pound rock that trapped Floyd. Building is the Sand Cave ticket office. *R.T. Neville*

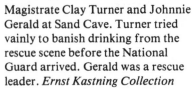

The body of Floyd Collins just after being removed from Sand Cave in April, 1925. *Wade Highbaugh*

The body of Floyd Collins in the undertaker's workroom. *Wade Highbaugh*

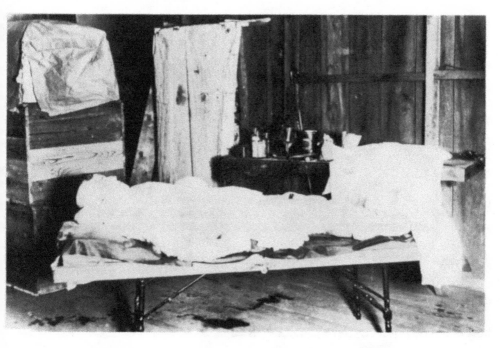

Today Sand Cave's entrance is blocked by a welded gate. The authors obtained permission to enter and survey. This view is looking up at the first squeeze inside the gate. *R. Pete Lindsley*

South end of the largest room in Sand Cave, at the bottom of the first squeeze. *R. Pete Lindsley*

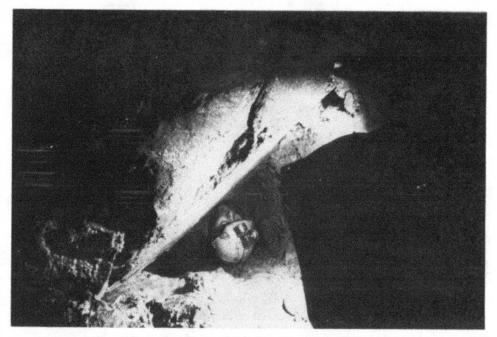

After digging away the seal at the bottom of the Volkswagen-shaped room, (below the large room), the investigating cavers squeezed through bodysize passages. (Several inches of ooze coat the bottom of this triangular-shaped squeeze.) This part of Sand Cave has not been seen since the rescue workers left in 1925. *R. Pete Lindsley*

1925 artifacts in the Turnaround Room. *Roger W. Brucker*

The collapse in Sand Cave and the 9″ crack that was found to by-pass it. This discovery demonstrated that rescuers could have continued to feed Floyd Collins and to work to free him from inside the cave. *Roger W. Brucker*

The tube in which Floyd Collins was trapped. Note the electric wires that disappear in layered gravel. They supplied current to the light bulb that warmed Floyd. Further efforts to follow the wire would require digging upside down. *Don Coons*

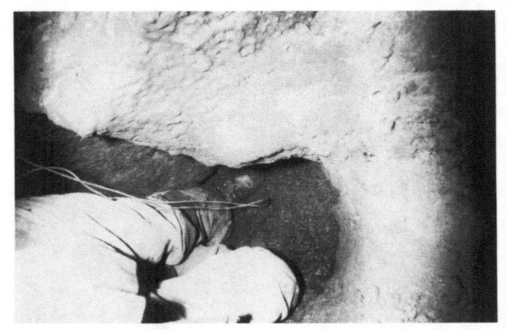

February 7, the name of this dog was changed to Old Shep. Old Shep, it seems, had been at the mouth of the cave when Jewell Estes first arrived and had not moved since. "There he has remained," wrote one reporter, "motionless save for an occasional twitching of a body wracked with the torture of hunger and thirst. Food has been placed before him, but he has scorned it." Obviously, Old Shep was dying of a broken heart. This had considerable reader appeal since contemporary interest in a man and his dog was already keen because of the recent Alaskan exploits of Gunnar Kaasen and the malamute Balto. As the *Evening Post* reporter feelingly told it: "Floyd and Shep have been buddies for two years. The friendship began when Shep first blinked friendly eyes at a wonderful world, sniffed for the first time the bracing Barren County ozone, and decided that life was sweet."

All this was fascinating but not quite true. There was a Collins dog at the site from time to time. He was a Chinese Chow named Obie. Obie did remain near the entrance to the cave while part of the rescue work was going on. During the first several days, Homer had to warn people not to pet him because he was excitable and had a tendency to bite. It was true that Homer could not get him to eat nor could he chase him away, so Obie roamed at will until he was finally chained up. It really made little difference what his name was, why he would not eat, or whether he was actually "waiting" for Floyd. If such a dog had not existed, the press would have invented him.

This press practice of altering the truth to conform to what it wanted to report was particularly evident during the height of the Collins struggle. At the beginning, facts were confused, mainly because of a lack of information, and some of this type of garbling continued. But gradually the truth was twisted because of the necessity to add something novel to the mass of information already known. Reporters pirated material, rewrote and changed each other's stories, used "purple prose," and conjured up fake interviews. The pressure on them to supply new information was intense, and the actions of some of them were unbelievable. One local observer, who spoke for many natives in their distress at the inaccurate reporting, later commented that reporters "dug up anything they wanted to and put it in the papers." Natives were especially incensed at news stories that poked fun at their folkways and depicted them as unintelligent and inbred hillbillies. One woman reporter for a Chicago paper was particularly detested because she evidenced surprise that Cave City's citizens wore shoes. "She was really snooty, and looked down her nose at us," exclaimed one resident with feeling, as late as 1964.

The net result of all this press competition was column after column of sensational reporting about the various happenings in Cave City and at Sand Cave. Some of the writing was good, some bad, and some truly ingenious. In trying to explain to bewildered New Yorkers what the Sand Cave situation was like, the *New York Times* asked them to visualize a cave opening at the subway kiosk at the north end of the Times Building. Then they were to imagine crawling from Broadway and 43rd Street diagonally across Times Square to 46th Street, then west-to-east back across the Square, and finally diagonally from Broadway and 46th Street to 7th Avenue and 43rd. At that precise spot, said the *Times* writer, Floyd Collins lay trapped. Scale problems aside, it was a vivid picture.

It is no exaggeration to say that in reporting the Collins story the Louisville papers, and not the metropolitan ones, set the tone and the pace. These Kentucky newspapers and their staffs proved more adept than their big-city counterparts in ferreting out news both at the beginning of the rescue and as time passed. Accounts first published in these Kentucky papers rapidly appeared in metropolitan newspapers as well. Many urban reporters merely elaborated on them for their own editors. Besides Skeets Miller, the most important reporters at the scene were A.W. Nichols *(Louisville Herald)* and Howard Hartley *(Evening Post)*. Their knowledge of Kentucky and its people helped them immensely. But they also had a nose for news and for sensationalizing it. They, for example, not the reporters of the *New York Times* or *Chicago Tribune,* uncovered Alma Clark and Old Shep.

Skeets Miller remained the primary cog in the machinery grinding out stories from Sand Cave. Even after metropolitan dailies had their own reporters at the site, they still relied heavily on Miller's briefings and on the information he supplied to the Louisville *Courier-Journal.* No other newspaperman had seen Collins or talked with him and no one knew more about the affair.

Miller continued to be interviewed almost as often as the members of the Collins family. The Associated Press later congratulated the young reporter and the *Courier-Journal* on the fact that their news articles were used by over twelve hundred other newspapers. These articles, along with others sent out over AP wires, often caused the same words to be read about the Collins tragedy from one end of the nation to the other. In this respect, too, the Floyd Collins rescue attempt was one of the first truly *national* media events.

Whatever the story's journalistic significance, both the press and the reading public reveled in it. Every incident or rumor became a reason for a special edition or extensive analytical comment. The Muhlenberg miner "tunnel squeeze" theory was accompanied by such scary headlines as "CAVE'S FLOOR RISES; VICTIM HELD IN VISE," and "DEATH IN FOUR FORMS FACES COLLINS IN CAVE." The *Washington Post* flatly declared that "all trace of the cave" was being obliterated; other papers asserted that Floyd "will soon be crushed." Even the most hair-brained ideas or rescue schemes were reported. When one man turned up at Sand Cave with a bloodhound named Joe Wheeler and offered to send him in with provisions tied around his neck, the *Nashville Tennessean* ran an eight-column headline: "DOG TO BE SENT WITH FOOD TO COLLINS IN CAVE." The paper did not bother to explain how Floyd was supposed to get the provisions off the dog's neck, assuming the animal could even get to him. This scheme, of course, was never tried. Yet on February 7, the *Atlanta Constitution* reported the project as fact and claimed that the dog crept into the tunnel a few feet, "found an old bone which he began to chew on, and refused to go further."

Always, the press sought to sustain maximum tension and suspense—even at the expense of truth. Newspapers on Wednesday had Floyd alternately trapped by cave-ins and freed. Some said he was hopelessly caught but was being fed through a tube. Another said he was gulping down eggnog, while still another claimed he was so weak that he was taking nourishment only "one drop at a time." When Homer sneaked back into the cave on Friday and heard no sounds from Floyd's prison vault, the *Chicago Tribune* baldly reported that Floyd had talked with him: "Homer, if the men don't get me out of here, the angels will. Yes, the angels will get me out if the men don't, so don't you worry." On that same day, the *Los Angeles Times* was telling its readers that Floyd was "doubtless dead," but if he was not "he will be a hopeless, helpless lunatic for life." According to this paper, Johnnie Gerald had left him "gibbering like an idiot," and to drive home the point, added, "As the wiry little product of the hills of old Kentucky slowly inched his way from his friend, in his ears rang the horrible laughter of a maniac."

The depth of the shaft and predictions about when Floyd would be reached were handled by the press in a totally confusing manner. Some of this was not the newsmen's fault, in view of the confusion among officials themselves. On Thursday, February 5, papers reported that Floyd would be out by Saturday (February 7). On Saturday morning some papers were still telling their readers that Floyd would be reached by noon. By that time, however, most papers had shifted the day of rescue to Monday or Tuesday. Simultaneously, the exact depth and size of the shaft were being consistently garbled. Some newspapers said the shaft was eight foot square, others five foot square, still others four foot square. Only a few used the correct six-foot-square figure. The speed of the digging was variously reported as a foot and a half an hour, a foot an hour, and ten inches an hour. The same paper that told its readers the shaft was twenty-five feet deep at 9:00 P.M. on Friday night stated that it was twenty-four feet deep at 11:00 P.M. on Saturday night. From Thursday afternoon on, most papers had the shaft at least ten feet deeper than it actually was.

Regardless of the inaccuracy of much of this reporting, or maybe partly because of it, the Collins tragedy by February 7–8 had transcended that of a news story and had become a social and cultural event of considerable significance. Contributing to this fact was the new and expanding communication technology. Not only the newspapers, radio, and film, but the telegraph, the long-distance telephone, the wirephoto facsimile machine, the fast train, and the motorized newspaper delivery truck helped expand and intensify the impact of the Collins story. In the process Americans were brought psychologically closer together because of the misery of this one man, and their reaction was remarkable. As the *Omaha World-Herald* said: "One of the great stories connected with the drama enacted in Sand Cave, Kentucky, can scarcely be told. Fragments of it can be collected and placed together, but the whole thing is too big for one man to handle. That is the story of the concern of millions of people who never heard of Floyd Collins before."

It is indeed impossible to catalog the various expressions of public sympathy and interest in Floyd's rescue. The most direct evidence appeared in the small Kentucky town of Cave City. Here, telegrams, phone calls, and letters of every kind poured in. Offers of help arrived from more than two hundred companies which promised to make and rush special equipment to the cave if only someone would tell them what was needed. The local telephone office was unable to keep up with the incoming calls, some of which came from overseas. Every sort of suggestion was made on how to extricate Floyd from his underground prison. Even a number of marriage proposals were sent in, one by a woman who offered to crawl down in the passageway for an on-the-spot wedding ceremony. Carmichael's mail was such that he could not read it all, and General Denhardt's was so heavy that he considered bringing in a secretary from Frankfort to handle it for him.

Through it all, the American public steadfastly refused to give up hope for Floyd even though logic demanded otherwise. By Saturday, February 6, no physician and no knowledgeable commentator believed in a successful rescue any longer. Dr. Hazlett's colleague, Dr. Jones, arrived back in Chicago on that day and told reporters that there was no conceivable chance that Floyd was still alive. Even Skeets Miller was telling his readers on Saturday that all hope for Floyd was gone. Yet, at the very time headlines were reading, "COLLINS' CHANCE ONE IN A MILLION" and "HOPE GIVEN UP FOR MAN SEALED-IN," editorials were saying, "millions stand by helpless and pray that some way may yet be found to raise Collins from his living grave." Readers were reminded that trapped men had lived underground for long periods before. A Hazleton, Pennsylvania, miner named "Big Joe" Matuskowitch had been buried for twenty-one days in 1891. In 1906, Lindsay B. Hicks, a Bakersfield, California, miner had been caught in a cave-in in the Kern River Canyon for eleven days, and ninety-seven feet of digging had been required to free him. Unlike in Floyd's case, however, these men had had ample food and water and neither of them was held immobilized. Still, in spite of such critical differences, readers took heart from these examples. If newspapers correctly reflected their readers' opinions, the public persisted in believing that the American genius for organization and engineering that had recently helped win World War I would win in the end at Sand Cave. To the average newspaper reader, Homer and Marshall seemed sincere but inept. Skeets Miller was courageous but inexperienced. Johnnie Gerald was cantankerous and pigheaded. But Carmichael and Denhardt represented a winning engineering-military team. "If he only knew," wrote one paper, "that here at last on the outside was order where order was not before . . . Floyd Collins might yet nurse the spark of life."

But even this underlying public optimism could not obliterate the somber fact that the race against death *might* ultimately be lost. The possibility of failure loomed larger with each passing day and caused newspapers and commentators to search for ever greater meaning in the Collins tragedy. That tragedy had begun with a lone man trapped in a cave by his own folly. Next, it had evolved into high drama replete with heroes, an impossible rescue situation, and a stoic prisoner. Now it was assigned epic significance. At the hands of the press, the Collins story was at last seen as the perpetual struggle of fragile man against the brutal forces of nature. Carried away by the symbolism of it all, the press by February 7–8 transformed the Collins affair into a colossal cosmic play entitled "The Prisoner of Sand Cave." It was said to be a tragedy in several acts in which the master playwright was Fate and the leading character was Man. And the audience? The audience was the entire American nation.

# 7

## *Carnival Sunday*

Sunday, February 8, dawned cloudy and mild. The warming trend that had set in at midweek continued. The overnight low had been in the high forties and by noon the temperature again stood at sixty degrees. Intermittent patches of blue sky were seen throughout the day and an occasional burst of sunshine flooded the rescue area.

Unfortunately, the diggers' problems in the shaft remained the same. The constant thawing added to their woes and emergency shoring was necessary to maintain the integrity of the shaft's sides. At one point on Sunday they ran into a tough stretch of rock and progress was virtually halted. Superintendent Carmichael grew impatient and for the first, and only, time in the rescue operation ordered blasting to be done. It was handled very delicately. Two charges of dynamite two inches long and seven-eighths inch in diameter, composed of forty percent gelatin, were employed. After the detonation, workers used an air hose at the mouth of Sand

Cave to blow away any fumes that might otherwise creep down to Floyd. Even so, some of the natives complained bitterly, not about the fumes but about the possibility of the dynamite causing a new collapse. They could have saved their breath. The charges were not strong enough to cause any damage—least of all to the rock in the shaft. Laboriously, it had to be pounded to pieces and dug out by hand anyway.

By 1:00 P.M. on Sunday the depth of the shaft was twenty-three feet ten inches. M.E.S. Posey took the measurement and reported it to Carmichael and Denhardt. Now even the general was discouraged. Carmichael had long since given up hope, but Denhardt had clung to the belief that rescue was still possible. However, with progress slowed to four inches an hour, or only eight feet a day, they could not possibly reach Floyd before late Tuesday night or early Wednesday morning. Such official doubts, of course, were kept hidden from the rescue workers and, although they knew the long odds, they continued their work with considerable enthusiasm. New schemes and experiments were constantly tried; most failed, but a few were successful. Just after the blasting on Sunday morning, Lane initiated a new series of radio and circuit tests that lasted over two hours. By shutting down the power to all outlets except into Sand Cave and then measuring the current flow, Lane ascertained that the bulb on Floyd's chest was still burning. By switching the power on and off, he also determined that there were no shorts in the circuit and that the wire had not been damaged by dampness or by the collapse of jagged rocks. Moreover, the fact that the filament in Floyd's bulb was still working proved that there had been no surge of current when the high-voltage wire had fallen across the line into the cave on Friday night. Lane alo picked up a few intermittent clicks and crackles in a three-stage audio amplifier that he said might indicate Floyd was still alive, but he was not sure.

Late on Sunday afternoon another novel experiment was carried out—this one with banana oil fumes. Before returning to their Indiana headquarters, the experts from the U.S. Bureau of Mines had suggested that a mixture of amyl acetate and ether—banana gas—be used to check for another opening into Sand Cave. Adjutant General Kehoe immediately ordered a supply of the gas and it arrived at the site on Sunday afternoon. By dinnertime, "sniffers" under the direction of Professor Funkhouser were stationed in Mammoth Cave and at all the other known cave and sinkhole openings in the area. At a signal, D.I. Elder and B.A. Carleton of the Pittsburgh laboratory of the Kentucky Rock Asphalt Company released the gas into Sand Cave Supposedly a downdraft would carry it into all openings or crevices and the fumes would reveal where they were. Since banana gas is harmless to humans, Floyd would not be hurt if he were still alive. The "sniffers" waited patiently and sniffed, but without success. Funkhouser's own party remained in Mammoth Cave until 11:45 P.M. but detected nothing.

Again, as on Saturday, Sunday's main story was not to be found in the shaft nor among the rescue workers, but with the crowds along the roads and up on the hillsides. From the first light of day an endless stream of humanity moved toward Sand Cave. They came by car, train, taxicab, carts, springwagon, buggy, horseback, and mule. There was no excuse for not knowing the way since for the past two days the Louisville Automobile Club had been distributing flyers showing the recommended routes. Also, the Louisville *Courier-Journal* and the *Times* had set up a phone service to tell callers precisely how to get there. On Sunday morning, the rival *Louisville Herald-Post* devoted a whole column to the best itinerary from Louisville to Sand Cave. The most publicized trip involved using the Dixie Highway to Horse Cave, then a somewhat poorer road to Cave City, and finally the six-mile spring-buster to the rescue site. The one-way distance for Louisville residents was eighty-nine miles.

In addition to hundreds of animal-drawn conveyances, by night-fall on Sunday an estimated forty-five hundred automobiles had been in and out of the Sand Cave area. They bore license plates from twenty different states. By 11:00 A.M. there were two solid lines of cars on the road from Cave City. For the last three miles they touched fender to fender. By late afternoon state troopers halted the cave-bound traffic because of the crush, and hundreds were forced to park their cars and walk, often as much as two miles, to the site. Trucks carrying food and supplies were caught in this monstrous tie-up and Sunday dinner for the rescue workers was over an hour late. Farm yards and open fields became parking lots for the estimated peak load of three thousand automobiles. For this one day the L&N Railroad added four coaches to its morning Louisville-to-Cave City train, then picked them up on the return trip that evening. During the whole weekend the railroad sold an extra twenty-five hundred passenger tickets. On Sunday morning Cave City taxicabs made the run to Sand Cave for a shocking three dollars a head and were consistently packed. By late afternoon, taxis were trapped in the traffic jam like everyone else and were left abandoned by the wayside.

The actual number of individuals attending the site on Sunday was a matter of conjecture. The low estimate was ten thousand and the high fifty thousand. The *Chicago Tribune* was responsible for the latter figure. L&N Railroad officials set the crowd at twenty thousand. Magistrate Clay Turner guessed "thirty or forty thousand." Howard Hartley of the *Evening Post* claimed there were fifteen thousand there at 3:00 P.M. Natives agreed that more people were present than they had seen in their entire lives. The confusion, the poor access, and the constant milling about probably made the rescue area seem more populated than it really was. In any case, the presence of so many people at so remote a spot stretched the credulity of even the most unimpressionable observer and easily made Sand Cave, Kentucky, the most popular and best-known place in America on Sunday, February 8.

It was like a country fair, with a religious revival thrown in. Women in poke bonnets were there, sitting astride long-eared mules. Bewhiskered men wearing Confederate slouch hats, and even coonskin caps, stood or walked beside them. Families arrived in flivvers, clutching supplies of corn pone. Children spilled out and raced away as frantic mothers called for them to come back. Cityfolk gingerly stepped through the mud and mire, hoping to salvage their shoes and finally abandoning the struggle. Young girls on the arms of their beaus coquettishly allowed themselves to be helped over the fences and across the ruts. Here and there a "flapper" appeared, attracting the eye of attached and unattached males alike. Frisky adolescents razzed each other and stole one another's hats, throwing them in the air. Mothers carried small babies in their arms and nursed them with breasts modestly hidden by shawls. At the dry spots on the hillsides men, women, and children sat in family groups and ate the contents of picnic baskets. Tree stumps, boulders, and low bushes served as emergency comfort stations.

Many of these people came through Cave City, which reaped a rich harvest on that balmy Sunday. Virtually everything edible was gobbled up. By noon, the only two restaurants in the town hung out Bread and Water Only signs. As one visitor later said, "We ate every old rooster in that part of the country." With an eye for business, some enterprising citizens set up concessions at the cave and gouged the visitors unmercifully. Newspapers describing the scene later claimed that the crowd "ate enough sandwiches to appease an army division and drank sufficient soda water to float a dreadnought." Lunch wagons appeared as if by magic, selling hot dogs, hamburgers, popcorn, pie, and apples. A tiny hamburger cost twenty-five cents—five times the normal amount in 1925. Soon there were no hamburgers to be bought at any price. Even homemade ham sandwiches, peddled from the surrounding farm-houses at an outrageous cost, were purchased and bolted down as soon as they appeared. Professional hawkers, meanwhile, offered all sorts of merchandise for sale—camp chairs, games, artificial flowers, cave onyx. They came from as far away as Louisville to huckster their wares. A favorite souvenir was a blue balloon on which was printed the words SAND CAVE. Hardly a child went home without one.

For those at the other end of the age scale, there were elixirs—one being offered by an old-fashioned medicine man who dispensed it from a covered wagon. Claiming to have discovered an all-purpose sassafras remedy for indigestion, dizziness, and the ague, he did a land-office business. Soda pop and Coca-Cola vendors avidly hawked their products to young and old alike, and as the temperature rose so did their sales. By late afternoon, the dis-carded stubby Coke bottle, so familiar to past generations, could be seen everywhere. Moonshiners, in turn, circulated furtively through the crowd selling another kind of "tonic" whenever the military was not looking. They also had some takers.

There was so much to see, so many different things to watch, that most people stayed on for hours, thereby adding to the congestion. And the more who came and remained, the more fascinating became the spectacle. In the process, the majority forgot about the imprisoned man underground. To entertain the crowd, two jugglers put on an act, moving constantly about the hillsides, passing the hat and quickly pocketing the money. Mountebanks and con artists abounded, prying nickels and dimes out of the onlookers for one cause o another. Their favorite ploy was to take up collections to buy food and supplies for the volunteer rescue teams. Through it all, families strode back and forth as at a carnival midway—dad up ahead, mother next, and the rest of the brood trailing along behind. The trick was to keep moving in order to be always where the most interesting action or entertainment was. If one happened to be in the vicinity of Lee Collins, he was certainly not disappointed. Lee talked to everyone. Reporters who observed him believed that the strain had at last proven too much and that he was now mentally unbalanced. He spoke constantly of Floyd as if he were dead. "The Lord giveth and the Lord taketh away," he would say, and then add, "Blessed be the name of the Lord." Sometimes he would follow this with a little laugh. On Saturday he began passing out circulars to Crystal Cave and giving a spiel about it. He willingly accepted all monetary gifts from the crowd and always urged his listeners to take the two-dollar tour through Crystal before going home. By Sunday noon he had run out of circulars, so he began selling photographs of Floyd for a dollar apiece, telling the crowd stories about his son's caving adventures. Lee's interest in making money caused him on Sunday to refuse to pose for any more newspaper pictures unless he was paid. Red Cross representatives on Sunday night had trouble getting him to sign over contribution checks that had his name on them.

Sunday was still the Lord's day and not the concessionaires' or Lee's, and many of the activities were religiously oriented. Actually, Floyd Collins was a special concern of most church people on that Sunday both at Sand Cave and throughout the nation. Unity services were held and prayers for his release were offered. Church collections were set aside for the rescue work and many ministers used Floyd's plight as the text for their sermons. All clergymen in the Mammoth Cave region and in the Kentucky and Tennessee hill country did so. Sermon titles of "Caught in a Cave," "Finding Salvation," and "Repent, Before It's Too Late" were commonplace. In these addresses, Floyd's entrapment was seen as punishment for his sins, his travail in Sand Cave as his Gethsamane, and his prayers for deliverance as guaranteeing him eternal life. He was a tailor-made object lesson. Floyd Collins—sin-cursed man— was trapped by the rock of evil, but was finally freed in spirit if not in body by the liberating influence of prayer.

At Sand Cave itself, the morning began with an impromptu church service held by a small group to the northwest of the cave entrance. They sang and prayed unbothered by others milling about. Numerous free-lance prayers were offered elsewhere for Floyd and now and again a hymn was begun. The early verses attracted quite a following with the later less-known ones petering out. At one point, Reverend Lum Doyle arrived and began an emotional preaching service, which was punctuated by energetic cries: "Praise the Lord!" and "Amen!" Here and there families held their own prayer sessions, bowing their heads while the eldest in the group voiced what was in their collective hearts and minds. It did not seem to matter that vendors and con artists moved about freely while this praying was going on.

The climax came at 3:30 P.M. Earlier in the week, religious leaders had asked General Denhardt for permission to hold a special unity service at the cave on Sunday afternoon. The general granted their request and authorized the Reverend James A. Hamilton, a circuit-riding minister from Louisville, to conduct it. Shortly before the appointed time, Parson Jim, as he was affectionately called, arrived straddling a sleepy mule and looking like the reincarnation of Ichabod Crane. Tall and lean, he wore an old homespun coat and preached with arms flung high, his blue eyes alive in his wrinkled face. Billed by the press as "America's most dramatic sermon of the day," his words were heard by an estimated five thousand while another five thousand milled about. Hamilton's address was not flowery nor especially filled with evangelical intonations or Bible thumping. Still, it was effective. With characteristic hyperbole, reporters told their readers on Monday, "The shrill screams of the steel drills in the pit below were his commas, the roaring concussion of dynamite made his periods." More important, Hamilton's sermon was laden with the symbolism and the fatalistic dogma common to all Kentucky hill country fundamentalist sects, and the message neatly dove-tailed with the beliefs of his native listeners. The hymns that were sung, like "Lead Kindly Light" and "Nearer, My God to Thee," carried a special meaning for most of those who were at Sand Cave that Sunday.

The high point in these climactic religious proceedings came at the end of Reverend Hamilton's address when he maintained, "Some have said that the rescue of Collins will be a miracle. We find in the Bible that all things are possible through prayer. If God wills, the mountains may be moved and the seas dried up. If it be His will, Floyd Collins will be brought back to his loved ones alive. And if we appeal to Him on bended knee and with reverent hearts, He will hear us." Reverend Hamilton then intoned a concluding prayer, his cheeks glistening with tears: "O Lord God, who turned back the tide at Galilee, have pity on this, your child imprisoned in your earth. Give him back to them who treasure him upon this soil. And if, Lord, it be Thy will that he shall not return to them, then, Lord, Thy will be done. Amen." Men, women, and children knelt, weeping in the common bond. Lee, who already had fallen to his knees several times in private prayer, was down again, this time accompanied by Miss Jane. Both were crying softly. In describing this scene to his readers the next day, reporter Howard Hartley wrote that a skylark just then "trilled its song of gladness, wheeling through the hazy air on wings pulsating with sheer joy of freedom. Down there a man, master of the earth, lay dying, held fast in the cruel jaws of a rock trap. Perhaps the skylark was God's messenger. The bird climbed higher until at last it disappeared. Man's plea to God was on its way."

After the service, the crowd began to disperse. People slowly returned the way they came, suffering through more traffic jams and enduring the bad roads. Most of the fields where the cars were parked had long since been whipped into seas of mud, and motorists had to help one another get out of the axle-deep mire. Many were unable to leave until long after dark, and highway 31W was lit up most of the night by departing automobiles.

All of these visitors returned home without catching a glimpse of the man they had come to see. Many undoubtedly had arrived expecting to pass by and gaze in upon a human being in death's throes. Some of them had not even been able to spy the rescue shaft. The five-strand barbed-wire fence placed around the cave area kept the crowds at least one hundred yards away from that point. Even so, thousands clung to this fence all day and stared. Ironically, the hottest selling items at Sand Cave on this Sunday were the Louisville newspapers, which were eagerly read for information about a man whose fate hung in the balance only three hundred feet away.

Or was he three hundred feet away? Incredibly, by Sunday night, February 8, there were growing doubts about it. The ingredients for such a bizarre circumstance were the hoaxes used during the cave wars, the mutual suspicions existing between outlanders and natives, and the continuing journalistic battle between competing local newspapers. The immediate catalyst was the repeated charges of skulduggery and fraud made by some of those who had been involved in the rescue earlier.

Already on February 4 (Wednesday) both the *Louisville Herald* and the *Evening Post* had published interviews with the Woodson and Kratch monument men who claimed that Johnnie Gerald held the members of the Collins family under his control and was blocking Floyd's rescue by his arbitrary decisions. These two papers also printed the opinions of several individual miners who asserted that Floyd could have been freed on Monday, or at the very latest on Tuesday, if Homer's and Gerald's opposition had not prevented it. On February 5, the *Evening Post* carried the headline "COLLINS MARTYR TO DESPICABLE GREED FOR FAME" and under Howard Hartley's by-line offered the theory that many skilled rescuers had been purposely excluded by "certain persons" who possessed a "lust for glory." Hartley's obvious target was Skeets Miller. Helping this "lust for glory" theme along was Edward Williams, one of the surveyors, who was pounced on by *Herald* and *Evening Post* reporters when he returned to his home in Louisville on Friday night. In an interview published by both these papers on Saturday, February 7, Williams cast doubts on the rescue attempts of Miller and Gerald and left the impression that Floyd, if he should die, was not a victim of nature but of cowardice and the desire for publicity.

The key figure, however, was Lieutenant Burdon. After arriving in Louisville following his condemnation of Johnnie Gerald and the locals on Friday afternoon, he gave an exclusive interview to *Herald* and *Evening Post* reporters. It was published on Sunday morning by the *Evening Herald-Post* under the banner headline "FLOYD COLLINS VICTIM OF BUNGLING RESCUE ATTEMPTS." Burdon's interview was inaccurate and self-serving. He garbled his activities, placed himself at the scene earlier than he had actually arrived, and took most of the credit for the various attempts to release Floyd. He referred to the harness-pulling team as his and said the party consisted of himself, Homer Collins, and "another small man." The small man, of course, was Skeets Miller. He also took credit for the jack attempts, again largely ignoring Miller.

Burdon's attack on Gerald was especially bitter. He suggested that Gerald was a liar and that his rescue motives were impure. He even questioned whether Gerald had actually ever reached Floyd. Burdon was convinced that the local man was not telling the truth about the cave-ins. Floyd Collins's life, he said, was being forfeited because of a "desire for individual glory and professional jealousy over the discovery of a colossal subterranean chamber which, if developed, [might] exceed Mammoth Cave in dazzling beauty." The Louisville fireman concluded, "I think that there are two or three men down there that are guilty of nothing short of murder. I won't tell you their names because I haven't got anything to prove it with, but I guess you know who I mean."

While such sensational accusations were being spread, the Collins family itself added to the growing suspicions. Marshall had long since raised questions about Lee's motives and had attacked him openly in front of reporters. Marshall's animosity toward Johnnie Gerald was also well known. After his arrival on Friday, Andy Lee had been equally outspoken and had complained loudly about the activities of both Gerald and his own father. He told boggle-eyed reporters that the two of them had joined forces to cheat Floyd out of Crystal Cave. Gerald, he said, was no friend of Floyd's but actually an enemy. Certainly Lee's own behavior on Saturday and Sunday did little to allay rising doubts. His habit of praying to the Lord while simultaneously seeking the Almighty Dollar jarred many observers and encouraged them to believe the worst about him.

Prior to Sunday, these matters were mentioned only in passing by the press outside of Kentucky. Dissension among the competing rescue crews and arguments between outlanders and natives had been reported, but malevolent motivations or improper actions by the main rescuers had been kept muted. However, with the appearance of the Burdon interview on Sunday morning, it was no longer possible to ignore them. Moreover, the attitudes of the people at the cave on Sunday forced a general reevaluation. Gouged by the local citizenry, conned by itinerant mountebanks, and unable to see Floyd or, indeed, much of anything relating to the rescue, many visitors left convinced that Floyd was not even there. It was an unconscionable farce, they said, and rumors spread that the whole affair was another cave-war hoax to drum up business.

Some observers, closely watching Lee's antics on the weekend, suspected that it was merely a plan to advertise Crystal Cave. One story made the rounds that Floyd had closed off the Sand Cave passageway to block potential rescuers and then slipped out another way. He allegedly crawled out of the cave each night and returned each morning. Homer's Saturday afternoon discovery of a nearby sinkhole in which two of Floyd's matches were found was offered as proof of Floyd's secret escapes. Other rumors circulated. One claimed that the Louisville *Courier-Journal,* with the cooperation of Floyd Collins and Skeets Miller, dreamed up the entrapment to stimulate sales of that paper. Another rumor maintained that Floyd's drawn-out rescue was a scheme concocted by the L&N Railroad to increase its passenger traffic. Still another was that Lee, Johnnie Gerald, and Floyd, together, had created the disaster to bilk money out of a gullible public. The darkest rumor hinted that Lee and Johnnie, because of their business connections, did not want Floyd rescued and had left him in the cave to die.

Few natives and no rescuers working in the shaft ever doubted that Floyd was there. This rumor was spread by transients who returned home to repeat it over and over. On the other hand, local people, knowing that the cave wars could produce almost anything, did not completely discount some of the other allegations. Running out of both local color and new rescue developments to report, newsmen were naturally intrigued by all these suspicious reports.

Learning in advance of the Sunday morning publication of the
Burdon interview, editors of metropolitan newspapers, such as the
*Chicago Tribune, Philadelphia Inquirer,* and *Atlanta Constitution,*
obtained copies of it beforehand and published it in their own
papers on Sunday under huge headlines. The night before—
Saturday—reporters from Cincinnati, Chicago, Nashville, and Atlanta met in the Dixie Hotel with correspondents from the
*Louisville Herald* and the *Evening Post* to discuss all the various
rumors, and they agreed that jealousy, personal enmity, and
commercial strife, some of which Floyd himself had participated in,
were far greater factors in his imprisonment and impending death
than "the forces of nature."

By Sunday night, the whole question of rescue motivation, blame
for possible failure, and accuracy in press reporting came to a head.
Late that afternoon, Thomas Killian, chief reporter for the *Chicago
Tribune,* filed a story that was sent out as an AP dispatch from Cave
City, detailing the various rumors and containing the statement
"Many of the cave country folk long accustomed to the cave
obsession of Floyd Collins were more pronounced today in asserting their doubts that Collins really is trapped in Sand Cave."
Containing a germ of truth, yet technically inaccurate with respect
to the opinion of most local natives, this dispatch created a furor
and prompted two simultaneous but separate reactions. Barren
County attorney J. Lewis Williams immediately met with reporters
of the *Louisville Herald,* the *Evening Post,* the *Chicago Tribune,*
the *Cincinnati Post,* and the *Nashville Tennessean* and demanded
that they turn over to him any information of a criminal nature that
they possessed that could be of value in a grand jury investigation.
General Denhardt, in turn, set the wheels in motion for a thorough
military probe.

Denhardt was particularly infuriated by the Killian article. Since
Friday, he had been worrying about the growth of the rumors and
about their potential effect on his maintaining order at the cave.
Carmichael, too, had become alarmed about them because of their
impact on worker morale. Early on Sunday afternoon, when
General Denhardt first learned of the Saturday night Dixie Hotel
correspondents' meeting, he talked with Killian about it, lecturing
the *Chicago Tribune* reporter on press responsibility. Hearing later

of Killian's dispatch, Denhardt contacted Governor Fields and suggested that he authorize a military court of inquiry to investigate all the rumors, but especially the charge that Floyd was not there. Fields responded vigorously. The governor was angry because such unfounded accusations were casting reflections on the commonwealth of Kentucky and the intelligence of its officials. Fields not only authorized a military court of inquiry to be convened, but demanded that the AP retract the claim that Floyd was missing and that the *Chicago Tribune* "remove the correspondent who sent it out."

By late Sunday night, February 8, the Collins rescue situation was more confused than ever. Just a week before, on Sunday, February 1, there had been a small group of Floyd's relatives and friends at Sand Cave, with a few rescuers going in and out and drawing coffee from a five-gallon pot suspended over a campfire. Now there were multitudes present, along with derricks, equipment piles, a powder magazine, kitchen and mess halls, a hospital, a blacksmith shop, rest tents, over fifty soldiers, taxis, and lunch and fruit stands. Floyd had gone in alone to explore a cave—and a nation was awaiting his return. Yet his release was not in sight. Although the rescue operation was now orderly, organized, and secure behind its barbed-wire barrier, there were increasing misunderstandings, slanderous charges and countercharges, scapegoating, and the spreading of false information. Meanwhile, the rescue shaft was moving very slowly, and all officials were frustrated and discouraged.

Floyd Collins needed the prayers of the nation as Carnival Sunday ended.

# 8

## *Investigation and Frustration*

Three events hit the public with devastating effect on Monday, February 9. The decision for a military inquiry, the possibility of a grand jury investigation, and the Killian AP dispatch appeared in the press simultaneously. Descriptions of the carnival scenes of Sunday were introduced by headlines that indicated there were new and sensational angles to the tragedy. One read: "MURDER IS HINTED IN CAVE PROBE"; another, "COLLINS NOT IN CAVE." Subheadings went on to say that "Kentucky Natives Think He Found Exit or Has Food Cache," while accompanying articles elaborated on these themes. Angry disputes in the Collins family were highlighted and Johnnie Gerald was singled out for special attention. It was said that to rescue Floyd he was being given $2000, along with a partial interest in Crystal Cave. Andy Lee's and Marshall's charges against Gerald were treated in detail as were Lee's money-grubbing weekend activities. Even Floyd himself was not immune to this sudden muckraking. He was now depicted in some accounts as "a shiftless fellow, supported by his father, although he was thirty-eight years old." Floyd's absence from home "for long periods of time" was said to indicate an irresponsibility that inevitably led him to disaster.

Four new theories were now advanced to help explain the situation at Sand Cave: (1) Floyd Collins was part of a colossal hoax to lure tourists to the Kentucky cave country; (2) Collins was murdered by a person or persons unknown after he entered the cave; (3) food and water had purposely been withheld from him so that he would die; (4) Collins was still alive and went out and back in every night. The *Evening Post* and the *Louisville Herald* took much of the credit in their Monday editions for uncovering the "mysterious circumstances surrounding the entombment of Collins" that required these new conclusions. Howard Hartley, writing for the *Evening Post,* claimed that his paper's activity in this regard represented "the outstanding [journalistic] coup of recent years." The *Herald,* in turn, stepped up its assault on the *Courier-Journal* and Skeets Miller. In a Monday evening front-page insert, entitled "News or Bunk?", it left the clear impression that the *Courier-Journal* and its young reporter had been indulging in lies all along and that for the truth the Louisville public should read only the *Herald.*

Lieutenant Burdon, meanwhile, could not stop talking. Even as Monday's newspapers were still discussing his weekend interviews, he was making new accusations. He referred again and again to his hose-hoist scheme and reiterated that he could have gotten Floyd out if Johnnie Gerald had given him the chance. He also contended that if the state had been invited in immediately, it could have secured Floyd's release. Claiming that he had "positive knowledge that some of the natives put obstacles in the way to keep outsiders from aiding in the rescue work," Burdon said the military probe was a good thing because it would discover that Floyd's rescue was made impossible by "two or three men." He again left no doubt that he thought Johnnie Gerald was the primary culprit and had merely playacted at being Floyd's friend.

Already stung by Burdon's weekend interviews, Gerald spent the better part of Monday defending himself. Normally unruffled by controversy, he was incensed by the slander circulating concerning his rescue activities. On Monday morning he boarded the 10:30 A.M. train from Glasgow Junction to Louisville, grabbed a taxi at the station, and went to the offices of the *Courier-Journal*. There he dictated a lengthy statement that was published in that paper the next morning. He denied Burdon's accusations one by one and declared that no pulling scheme could have rescued Floyd alive. He stated that he had never had any trouble with the Collinses, that Floyd was a friend of long standing, and that his business dealings with the trapped man and his father were legitimate and nonsecretive. He detailed his various trips into the cave and claimed that his sole aim had been to get Floyd out. He said that he was still prepared to help in any way he could and that General Denhardt had had no cause to banish him from the rescue site.

Johnnie was not alone in his anger over the various sensational press revelations of Sunday and Monday. Local people were likewise agitated by suggestions of native culpability in the impending failure at Sand Cave. Cave City residents, in particular, were upset, and knots of them stood around on Monday afternoon at the drugstore and the gas station discussing the situation. They regarded as especially offensive Thomas Killian's assertion in the Monday *Chicago Tribune* that the Collins tragedy was "a blessing to the inhabitants of the little town." This statement may have been true, but it was highly inflammatory in the context in which it was set. Ominously, that evening a threatening note was tossed over the transom of Killian's Cave City hotel room. Illiterately scrawled on a piece of brown wrapping paper, it read: "If you don't quit writing up Jonny Geral we will shoot your head off he never done no one harm take our advice and git out of town or you gong to wake up dead."

Both Gerald and the people of Cave City could have saved their breath—and their threats—as far as the national press was concerned. Long before Tuesday's headlines proclaimed "DEATH THREATS MADE ON EVE OF CAVE CASE QUIZ," the press had come down on the side of the outlanders and viewed Gerald and his local supporters as stubborn and cantankerous parochials whose motives were tainted and whose actions were suspect. Johnnie Gerald now became the chief villain as most newspapers struggled toward a reinterpretation of the Sand Cave affair. By Tuesday, February 10, a new series of press myths began to circulate. The Kentucky cavefolk were not so much colorful, hardworking, and frontierlike as they were prejudiced, petty, suspicious, and spiteful. General Denhardt and the military were needed not only to bring order to the rescue scene but also to teach civilized behavior to an unregenerate section of the nation. If the engineering-military combination present at the cave failed, it would not be because of the natural forces confronting it but because local animosity, corruption, and betrayal had rendered success impossible. For many newspapers, the tragedy at Sand Cave was no longer the noble and epic struggle of Man against Nature but the same old sordid story of human avarice and stupidity, showing the dark and shallow side of man. As for Floyd, although still worthy of public sympathy, he would not have been where he was except for his own folly and greed.

The military court of inquiry was scheduled to convene in Cave City at 10:00 A.M., Tuesday morning, February 10, on the second floor of the Handy Building next to the Dixie Hotel. Plans for it had been laid hastily but nevertheless with care. Late on Sunday night, General Denhardt drove to Frankfort to discuss the nature and organization of the inquiry with Governor Fields. Returning to Cave City early Monday evening, he announced to a press conference that the purpose of the probe was twofold: to clear up all suspicions of criminal efforts to block the rescue work, and to scotch rumors that Floyd Collins's entrapment was not genuine. Following this conference, Thomas Killian drew Denhardt aside and showed him the threatening note he had just received. The general, automatically assuming that Killian would be at the opening of the court of inquiry on Tuesday morning to testify, immediately promised him protection. However, sometime during Monday night, the *Chicago Tribune* reporter left Cave City without warning and never returned. Although he wrote several articles for his paper after leaving the scene, Killian's reporting chores were taken over by Orville Dwyer, whose by-line now appeared on all releases going to that Chicago paper from Sand Cave.

In Frankfort, meanwhile, Governor Fields issued a statement

reiterating that the main reason he had ordered the investigation was to disprove the Killian Sunday night AP dispatch. Simultaneously, he created a stir by asking the Louisville police to "pick up Johnny Gerald." At that moment Gerald was on his way back to Cave City from his visit to the *Courier-Journal*. Unknown to the governor, Gerald had already indicated before leaving Louisville that he would be at the court of inquiry when it convened on Tuesday. Later on Monday evening, when reporters asked Governor Fields if Gerald was still to be placed under arrest, the governor embarrassingly replied that he had merely wanted to make sure that Gerald would attend the investigation and that perhaps his "pick up" order had been premature.

Governor Fields appointed the following to the court of inquiry: Lieutenant Colonel Henry J. Stites (Louisville), Captain John A. Polin (Springfield), Captain Julius L. Topmiller (Smiths Grove), and Captain Alex M. Chaney (Bowling Green). Major William H. Cherry was also named to the court but was unable to serve because he was suddenly taken ill. General Denhardt was designated president and Captain Chaney, a Warren County attorney in private life, acted as chief interrogator. Richard H. Lee, a civilian, was selected as court reporter. All the officers appeared in military uniform, General Denhardt bedecked in full regalia including his campaign ribbons. It was reminiscent of the war and lent authority to the occasion.

Barren County attorney J. Lewis Williams wisely decided to suspend any civil action by his office until after this court completed its examination. Denhardt, in turn, agreed to turn over to Williams whatever information might prove useful to him. Nobody raised the constitutional question whether this military court was valid, since martial law had not been declared in the Cave City area. All witnesses, except Killian, seemed willing to testify, and this made the question of the court's legitimacy academic anyway. Everybody's main concern at the moment was to prove or disprove the rumors.

When the court convened at 10:10 A.M. on February 10, the atmosphere was low-keyed. Cave City accepted the court's presence with a feeling of relief. The room where the court was held could easily accommodate the one hundred and twenty-five spectators who attended the first session. A few onlookers occupied rockers while the rest sat in split-bottom straight chairs. Among the spectators was Johnnie Gerald, who created a brief flurry of excitement when he arrived shortly after 9:30 A.M. Asked by reporters if he was going to testify, he bluntly replied, "Yes, I have nothin' to hide." About fifty of the one hundred twenty-five persons present were newspapermen and photographers. Only three women were there, and two of them represented the press. Some of the court's officers puffed on cigars while flashlights popped, and the flare and smoke threatened from time to time to disrupt the proceedings. The court reporter took down all testimony, and an opportunity was given for questions to be asked by the members of the court even though the normal rules of evidence did not apply.

On this first day the major witnesses were Skeets Miller, Lieutenant Robert Burdon, and Professor Funkhouser. They revealed nothing new. Miller admitted that there were factions among the rescuers and some competition. He denied that there was any jealousy involved or that such competition had been harmful. He also admitted that the rescuers shared little information and did not employ a unified approach. Johnnie Gerald, he said, was suspicious of outsiders and had warned him on several occasions about going into the cave. But Miller refused to attach any sinister motive to those warnings. As for the various rumors, he stated that he had heard them but not from anyone associated with the rescue operation.

When Lieutenant Burdon took the stand, he repeated his now-familiar story, although in softer tones than in his weekend newspaper interviews. While still condemning the natives, he was good-naturedly humorous and extracted several laughs from the audience. Admitting that he clashed frequently with local partisans over rescue methods, he added, "I guess I was wild and hysterical several times myself." He remained harsh, however, with respect to Gerald, believing him to be the primary obstacle to a successful rescue. He still insisted that his pulling methods would have released Floyd, but agreed that the shaft was now the only alternative. He deplored the fact that the digging had not been started sooner. He labeled as "totally ridiculous" all suggestions that Floyd was not in the cave and described the trips on which he had personally seen and talked with the trapped man.

Professor Funkhouser's testimony was what one would expect from a scientist. He was the only one who could reconstruct a detailed chronological account of the rescue operations, basing it on field notes and scribblings he had made since first arriving on the scene. In this recounting he criticized no one. He told how and why he had been called to the site and discussed his particular expertise. He explained how he had helped to determine where the shaft should be sunk and described the failure of the banana gas tests. Asked once by Captain Chaney to define "a squeeze," Professor Funkhouser broke into laughter and the spectators joined in.

The only surprise of the first day's hearings came at the end of Funkhouser's testimony when General Denhardt asked if anyone else had a statement to make. Samuel Matlack rose, identified himself, and stated that he had come to this court from Louisville "at my own expense and in the interest of justice." He informed the court that he was forty-three years old, a builder, and a graduate of the DuPont Manual High School in Louisville. For two years he had worked as a roustabout in the southern Indiana gas fields where he had gained experience in using welding equipment. This experience had prompted him on the previous Tuesday to borrow an oxyacetylene torch and bring it to Sand Cave. He would have freed Floyd, he said, if he had been given the chance because his torch would have "melted" the rock.

Matlack lashed out in all directions with his testimony. He charged that Lieutenant Burdon was interested only in rescue merits and Skeets Miller in newspaper publicity. Both were glory-seekers. Almost all of the others were liars. Strangely, Matlack had a few kind words for Gerald, calling him "a brave man." Claiming to have sneaked into the cave for eighty-four feet after the first collapse, Matlack said he saw no big rocks and nothing to be afraid of. Men were sitting around doing nothing, discussing only how to protect themselves, he declared. He could have gone all the way to Floyd, if "they" had let him. Who were "they"? asked General Denhardt. "Everyone," Matlack spat back vehemently. According to the Louisville builder, *no one* really wanted to save Floyd Collins and, as a result, "a man's life was being sacrificed for the hope of hero worship." At the climax of his testimony, Matlack even attacked Superintendent Carmichael and Professor Funkhouser. At this, Captain Chaney, a stocky, youngish man with a large head and a temper to match, angrily asked Matlack whom the court should believe: "the men who went down and risked their lives to save a man's life, or you, who didn't have the nerve to go down more than eighty-four feet?" Before Matlack could reply, Chaney snarled, "Get out of here!'

In the audience Professor Funkhouser suddenly fainted. General Denhardt quickly adjourned the court until 9:30 A.M. the next day and guardsmen hurried the startled spectators out. The professor was given first aid and was then whisked away to the Dixie Hotel. Johnnie Gerald was seen talking animatedly with Denhardt as the last of the audience disappeared.

The Matlack testimony was an unexpected interruption and caused much comment. Some observers, such as the *Louisville Herald,* were of the opinion that Matlack had not been treated fairly. Indeed, that paper sent a telegram to Denhardt requesting that the Louisville builder be recalled to the stand. Denhardt agreed, and on Wednesday morning a somewhat subdued Matlack testified again. He began by complaining that the question posed to him at the close of the session on Tuesday afternoon was improper since he could not answer it without appearing to be a coward. The remainder of Matlack's testimony came close to being a retraction of what he had said the day before. He claimed that he had not meant to criticize Skeets Miller and Lieutenant Burdon, only to indicate that the publicity had gone to their heads. Further, he had not intended to brand anyone a liar, although he felt some rescuers had bent the truth. He meant only to show that no one would try his torch. In that action, they had been wrong. The torch would not have burned Floyd and would have freed him. Even now he was willing to demonstrate to the court that it would work. When the officers did not take him up on his offer, Matlack relinquished the stand and headed back to Louisville.

A number of other witnesses followed Matlack—William Hanson (marshal of Cave City), J.C. Anderson (an early rescuer), and Dr. H.P. Honaker of Horse Cave. By far the most important of those who testified on Wednesday were Lee Collins and Johnnie Gerald.

Gerald's testimony had been awaited with much anticipation. But if anyone expected fireworks or novel revelations they were disappointed. The only witness to be accompanied by legal counsel, Gerald was neither evasive nor belligerent. When told that he did not have to answer certain questions because his words might later be used against him, he said, "Go ahead and ast me anythin' you like." Such forthrightness served to restore some of his credibility, although there were still those among the press and in the audience who professed to detect improper motives.

Gerald's testimony was slightly jumbled. Once he got confused about which trip he was discussing and had to ask the court reporter, "Which one is it I done been down?" He explained that he had gone in so many times he could not always remember. In general, he repeated the information he had given to the Louisville *Courier-Journal* on Monday morning. No, he had never had any altercations with Floyd. No, he had not been hired by Lee to get his son out. No, he had not been "in charge" of the rescue. His arrangement with the Collinses had been legal and fair. He and Floyd had been together in caves before and his interest in getting Floyd out was purely neighborly. Gerald attacked no one but stated bluntly that the rocks and walls in the passageway, already loosened by the seeping ground water and the thaw, were finally brought down by ignorant, amateurish activity. He admitted that he opposed some of Lieutenant Burdon's rescue schemes: "Floyd was my friend, and I didn't want Lieutenant Burdon to pull him loose 'cause I thought Floyd'd be killed in the attempt." He described his own activities after the second cave-in, explaining that when the big boulder hit him, "that got my nerve." "I would've dragged Floyd out inch by inch," concluded Gerald, "if I could've got him loose."

Lee Collins's testimony was often confused, sometimes contradictory, and anticlimactic. He told the court about his son's obsession with caves, his desire to find a new one in the area, and his dreams about being caught just prior to the Sand Cave tragedy. Lee described his dealings with Floyd and Gerald relating to Crystal, denying that there was anything unusual about them. He also denied that he was making money out of the rescue situation. Asked about the public funds that were being sent to him to defray expenses, he stated that they were not his but were controlled by Sam Caldwell of the Cave City Bank. As a matter of fact, said Lee, he had no money at all and was broke because of the asylum care required by his younger daughter. On the subject of disorders at the cave, Lee became quite animated. There was "a right smart" of confusion in the early days, he stated, and he blamed it on "too much drinkin'." Whiskey, he said, was one of the primary factors contributing to the possible death of his son. When asked to name the bootleggers operating at the cave, however, he gazed squarely at Captain Chaney and declared, "I cannot tell you, suh."

On the question of Johnnie Gerald, Lee was emphatic. Johnnie had never asked him for money nor had he offered him any to rescue Floyd. Johnnie had simply told him, "Lee, I'll go in and get him out." Lee was satisfied that Gerald had done all he could. Yes, Johnnie was all right. "He lay in the water and ice and come out cramped from the cold. I had to rub him," said Lee. As for the shaft, Lee claimed that he had made his peace with it. He expressed confidence in Carmichael and believed that "God Almighty's cooperating in every way" with the Kyroc superintendent. When asked if he was positive his son was in the cave, Lee replied, "I will jes' say that if that boy ain't in there I'll give up all my part of Heaven."

At almost the same moment Lee was making this statement, reporter Skeets Miller received a collect telegram from Haddam, Kansas, which read:

PLEASE CONTRADICT STATEMENTS THAT I AM BURIED ALIVE IN SAND CAVE. TELL MOTHER I AM ALL RIGHT. AM COMING HOME.

FLOYD COLLINS

Shortly thereafter, General Denhardt got one from Mayor F.W. Shearborn of Haddam that said:

FLOYD COLLINS HERE HAS IDENTIFIED HIMSELF BY SCAR ON LEFT OF UMBILICUS ABOUT TWO OR THREE INCHES LONG CAUSED BY GERALD. ALSO AMERICAN FLAG ON RIGHT ARM. WEIGHT 144 POUNDS AND FIVE FEET FIVE INCHES IN

HEIGHT. SAYS MOTHER IS DEAD BUT HAS STEPMOTHER. HE
WIRED REPORTER MILLER. WE ARE HOLDING HIM HERE
UNTIL HEAR FROM YOU. HAS NO MONEY.

Neither did Haddam, evidently. This telegram, too, was sent
collect.

When Miller showed Lee his telegram, the old man only smiled
and said he knew it was a fake because Floyd never called his
stepmother "mother." Gerald was likewise definite. Floyd had no
tattoos and certainly he had no scar caused by him. General
Denhardt assigned his telegram no importance whatsoever, except
that it cost him $3.80. "That's what I object to," he said. In
scattered sections of the country, several other "Floyd Collinses"
now also appeared but they, too, were quickly exposed as frauds.

Although such imposters created further confusion in the public
mind, they had no effect on the continuing investigation in Cave
City. Thursday, February 12, was a busy day for the court of
inquiry as Bryan L. Abernethy (Louisville AP correspondent), Roy
Hyde, John Gerard, Casey Jones, Tennessee Hooper, Clay Turner,
and Homer Collins testified. For the first time, the courtroom was
packed. Many were there because of the news of the Kansas
"Collins," and because Homer was scheduled to take the stand. As
expected, Abernethy defended the AP dispatch, claiming that all
the rumors mentioned in it were already common knowledge in
Cave City. Other reporters besides those associated with the AP
had written similar accounts, complained Abernethy, but they were
not being singled out for examination by the authorities. Next,
Hyde, Gerard, Jones, Hooper, and Turner told of their roles in the
rescue. Jones and Gerard, in particular, took issue with Matlack's
contention that an oxyacetylene torch could have been used in
Floyd's prison chamber. As for Floyd's being trapped there,
Gerard described for the court the foul odor in the cave caused by
Floyd's urine and feces.

Homer was the last witness of the day. With fatigue lining his
face and still clad in overalls stained with cave mud, he elicited
great sympathy and admiration. He declared frankly that he would
never have risked his life in that dreadful hole for anyone except his
brother. He asserted that he and other natives had been concerned

that the constant traffic in the passageway would cause cave-ins and that they had advised outsiders to keep out for their own safety. He denied that anyone had been prevented from entering the cave before the National Guard arrived. He and Johnnie Gerald had never gone in together, he said, not because they were antagonistic to each other, but because it would have been wasteful to use two rescue leaders on the same crew. Floyd and Johnnie had known each other all their lives, stated Homer, and Gerald had not exerted undue pressure on Floyd to sell him his half of Crystal. Homer declared that he had had absolute confidence in Gerald at all times and believed that he had tried "with all his power to get Floyd out."

Friday, February 13, was newsmen and miners day as the inquiry began to wind down. In the morning, a series of correspondents testified—A.D. Manning *(Louisville Herald),* W.S. Howland *(Nashville Tennessean),* and A.H. Kirkland *(Chicago Herald and Examiner).* All agreed that they had been treated courteously by the military and that there had been no censorship of the news. But they also agreed that rumors were a legitimate part of the news, if they were labeled as such, and they saw nothing wrong with the Killian AP dispatch.

On Friday afternoon the court moved to Sand Cave to take the testimony of some of the miners working there and to examine new evidence that Floyd was indeed trapped in the cave. Businesses closed and Cave City became deserted as everyone trooped along— everyone, that is, except Johnnie Gerald, who was still forbidden to appear at the rescue site. He sauntered alone into the lobby of the Dixie Hotel before going home. At the site, diggers Edward Brenner, Albert B. Blevins, William H. Bailey, and William H. Bailey, Jr. were questioned. The court had a special interest in these men because that very morning they had heard coughing in the bottom of the shaft and also a gasp in the Sand Cave passageway. Floyd was in there, they testified, and, in their opinion, he was also alive.

The military inquiry held its final hearings on Saturday, February 14. Testimony from J. Norman Parker (an early rescuer), Lieutenant Ben Wells, Bee Doyle, and Edward Estes added little to what was known, and the court retired shortly after dinnertime to reach

its preliminary conclusions. The evidence before it showed remarkable unanimity. All witnesses had agreed that numerous
rescuers had lied about reaching and feeding Floyd and that only
Homer, Miller, Burdon, and Gerald had spent much time with him.
All agreed that Sand Cave was a terrible place. As Cave City
Marshal Hanson put it: "There was something there that unnerved
the best of men." Also all agreed that liquor, to a greater or lesser
degree, had played a role in the tragedy. Moreover, there was
virtually universal agreement that dissension and bickering had
lessened the chances for rescue and that the introduction of the
military had been necessary if only to bring organization to the
rescue effort. Certainly chaos would have resulted on Carnival
Sunday if the soldiers had not been present. Further, almost all
witnesses supported the shaft as the only remaining rescue alternative.

There were minor differences. Some complained of the odor
where Floyd was; others did not. A few said that they had been
prevented from entering the cave; the majority said that they had
not. Most agreed that neither Matlack's torch nor the Woodson and
Kratch stonecutters could have freed Floyd; but several claimed
that they should have been allowed to try. None, except for Burdon
and Matlack, suggested Machiavellian motives for any rescue
action, and even these two muted their criticism as the investigation
wore on. On one critical point there was complete agreement:
Floyd Collins *was* in Sand Cave and any talk of his slipping out and
in at night was utterly ridiculous.

Despite such general unanimity, the press and the military
remained poles apart on the AP dispatch and the reporting of the
rumors. Although all witnesses indicated that these rumors had
been circulating long before the Killian dispatch was sent out, the
court insisted on saddling Killian with the blame. Indeed, at the
close of the inquiry on Saturday night, General Denhardt issued a
fifteen-hundred-word statement that was given to the press and was
also incorporated in the final record of the court. "I am convinced," said the general, "that if it had not been for Killian's
activities in broadcasting these rumors, the country would never
have gotten the idea, which it held for several days, that the Floyd
Collins tragedy was a joke and a hoax." The general's statement

went on to say that the *Chicago Tribune* reporter had been wanted as a witness but had skipped town to avoid questioning. Moreover, said Denhardt, Killian had been warned on Sunday, February 8, that reporting such rumors would harm the rescue work. But Killian had persisted, and for that reason, if no other, he had to bear the responsibility.

This was not the first, and would not be the last, time in American history that the activities of a free press and the desires of the military would clash.

While the interest of the public and the press temporarily shifted to the court of inquiry in Cave City, the struggle to free Floyd Collins continued unabated at Sand Cave. The court was actually a godsend for newsmen who otherwise would have had to suffer through days and nights of watching the digging without any real news to report. Yet the battle for Floyd was being won or lost in the shaft, and that contest was proving frustrating.

First of all, the weather was uncooperative. About 10:30 P.M. on Sunday, February 8, a light sprinkle began. Throughout that night and into Monday morning the rain continued as temperatures hovered in the high forties. Although the protective canvas above the shaft's mouth helped shield the rain from overhead, it was useless against the water trickling down through cracks and earth. By Monday noon, a foot stood in the bottom of the pit and pumps had to be installed to keep ahead of it.

As if this were not enough, Carmichael suddenly faced a dearth of personnel. As soon as it was announced that a military probe was to be held, some workers quit and went home. They indicated to Carmichael that although they had nothing to hide themselves and did not believe the rumors, they did not want to be hassled by the military. Morale plummeted as the flow of supplies also diminished, donations to the Red Cross fell, and telegrams of encouragement gave way to long-distance phone calls of outrage. Carmichael attempted to plug the gap by requesting more men from the L&N Railroad and from his own company. When asked about this deteriorating situation, he told reporters that he would keep going if only he, one shovel man, and a hoist operator were left.

This troubling drop-off in personnel ironically occurred at a moment when there was renewed evidence that Floyd was still alive. Radio tests on Monday, February 9, were encouraging. Using the same procedures he had employed in his previous experiments, Lane heard a series of repeated clicks and crackles in his earphones which he again said were from the closing and opening of the contact at the base of the bulb on Floyd's chest. After listening to these same noises, Dr. Hazlett contended that they indicated Floyd was breathing twenty to twenty-six times per minute (the normal rate is eighteen) and that he did not yet have pneumonia (which would cause a breathing rate of at least forty times per minute). After crawling in the Sand Cave passageway as far as possible to check the wires running to Floyd for any breaks or shorts, Superintendent Carmichael announced that he, too, believed Floyd Collins was still alive.

Whether rescue officials were really as convinced as all this indicated is arguable. When asked by reporters about the strength of his conviction, Dr. Hazlett replied, "We are going on the assumption that Collins is alive," and then added significantly, "We must keep up the morale of the workers." Any talk of Floyd's being dead was firmly discouraged at the site and every indication that he still lived was given immediate publicity. Some of this "evidence" undoubtedly rested as much on wishful thinking as on hard fact, but under the circumstances that was understandable. Confidence was absolutely necessary to undergird the rescuers' philosophy of "Dig, dump, and pray!"

The opening of the military court of inquiry on Tuesday and the subsequent lack of any startling revelations was reflected in a steady rejuvenation of worker support at the cave. It was also reflected in a return of faith on the part of the public in the nation as a whole. Tuesday's newspaper headlines "COLLINS ALIVE" and "DOCTOR FINDS COLLINS LIVES" added to this feeling as some of the suspicions of the past weekend were swept away. Meanwhile, at the cave site the work and experiments went on. Three times on Tuesday, Lane repeated his radio tests and three times the results were reassuring. At 4:00 P.M., when the last experiment was made, Dr. Hazlett claimed that Floyd was breathing at the rate of twelve times per minute, indicating he was sleeping. Even though engineers and scientists elsewhere in the country continued to cast doubt on the validity of Lane's radio evidence, those at the rescue site accepted it unquestioningly.

As the shaft neared the forty-foot level, there were other encouraging signs. Cave crickets began to appear, suggesting that small openings into surrounding crevices and voids were close by. Simultaneously, banana oil fumes from the gas released earlier in the mouth of Sand Cave were now detected seeping into the rescue pit. When Posey climbed out of the shaft after a personal inspection at 11:00 P.M. Tuesday night, he told waiting newsmen: "We feel certain we are near some one of Sand Cave's barrel-like passageways. Whether or not it will lead directly to Collins is problematical." In subsequent remarks made off the record, Posey said he thought they might be as close as ten feet to the trapped man. Enthusiastic diggers talked of reaching Floyd before the night was over. Dr. Hazlett, who at the moment was resting in Cave City, hurried back to the site in order to be on hand if they suddenly broke through. A harness of rope and leather was rigged to lift Floyd out as soon as they reached him. Wednesday morning's headlines confidently proclaimed: "COLLINS' RELEASE FROM CAVE TRAP PREDICTED TODAY."

Nothing could have been further from the truth. The ordeal of those at the rescue shaft was just beginning, not ending. The intermittent rain of Monday and Tuesday changed to snow flurries early on Wednesday morning as a cold front moved in. Sleet pattered on the canvas over the shaft's mouth and workers huddled around warming fires. By midafternoon on Wednesday the temperature had dropped into the twenties. Flies were attached to all tents in preparation for a cold night and a tarpaulin was stretched along the windy side of the shaft's mouth. More blankets were rushed to the scene from nearby military stores to protect the rescuers against the chill. In the shaft itself, diggers encountered new difficulties, slowing their progress. Beginning at the forty-four-foot level, shoring crews had to work harder and longer. For as many as three and four hours at a time they struggled to keep the sides from buckling. Numbed hands and frigid feet greatly impaired their efficiency.

Far more ominous was the fact that new radio tests on Wednesday failed to detect signs that Floyd was still alive. Moreover, the telltale light above the cave's entrance winked out. Perhaps Collins's bulb was broken or it had shaken loose in its socket. Lane chose to believe that the latter had happened. In any case, there was a noticeable increase in concern as workers and officials alike lost the only audible and visual assurances they had that Floyd still lived.

Thursday, February 12, brought added frustrations and a false alarm. At 3:00 A.M. Dr. Hazlett, Posey, and Funkhouser were rousted from their Cave City beds with the news that Floyd had been found. Hurrying to the cave, they discovered that this report was in error, although the shaft workers were now uncovering small crevices, any one of which might provide a way in. At 5:50 A.M., Carmichael was notified that large limestone blocks were again being struck, and he ordered that the diamond drill be transferred to the bottom of the shaft to continue probing for voids or passages. He also ordered work shifts cut to one half hour so that fresh men were always digging at top speed.

By Thursday noon, nothing new had been uncovered. At that moment Floyd Collins had been trapped for exactly thirteen days. His voice had not been heard in more than five and he had not eaten in over a week. Long faces watched the hours slip by. Discouragement deepened when the entire afternoon on Thursday was lost because one wall of the shaft disintegrated as the shoring was being erected. No one was hurt, but precious time was wasted as the loose rock and dirt had to be scooped out and new timbers set in place. Three more such cave-ins occurred before the shaft reached forty-eight feet, each one causing serious delays. In the fear that the bottom of the shaft itself might collapse, Carmichael ordered the men for a time to work from a suspended platform. Rigging this platform, and shifting it from side to side as the men dug, further slowed the work. When asked by reporters if he might have to abandon the shaft because of these worsening conditions, · Carmichael uttered an emphatic "No. It simply means our task will be more difficult."

Difficult was hardly the word. Yet worker morale remained excellent. Laboring under unbelievably trying circumstances, the men kept at their tasks around the clock, catching rest and sleep as best they could. Carmichael was one reason for the good morale.

He peered down the shaft watching each worker. At the slightest
sign of fatigue, he would bellow, "Get that man out of there. Get
him up here!" His gruffness underscored his concern and the men
knew it. Their welfare was a top priority. Adequate food, clothing
supplies, and medical attention were constantly maintained. As a
result, the accident rate was extremely low and the level of the
health of the workers kept high. The first rescuer to be injured was
twenty-two-year-old Henry Hughes from Louisville, who was
struck by a pick handle while digging in the shaft. The first serious
emergency patient was Casey Jones, who had a pickax driven into
his foot. One worker was treated for septic poisoning, another for a
cut hand, and several others were held for observation for incipient
pneumonia. That no one was killed by cave-ins or died from
overexertion is remarkable.

By Friday, February 13, persons from all types of backgrounds
were involved in the digging effort—professional engineers,
miners, drillers, surveyors, day laborers, college students, even
hobos. Earlier in the week, ten members of the Western Kentucky
Normal football team had showed up, excused from their classes
until the race against death at Sand Cave was finished. They were
put to work dumping dirt. Shortly thereafter, six Vanderbilt
students arrived from Nashville vowing to surpass the Western
Normal football team's record of filling a one-sixth cubic-yard
bucket every two minutes for an hour. At midweek, the Brother-
hood of Hobos sent word that it was coming to Floyd's aid, and the
very next day representatives began arriving. Several were given
jobs on the dumping crews. One colorful addition, appearing on
Thursday, February 12, was Bill Takasy of Dayton, Ohio, who
brought his harmonica with him and whose playing lifted worker
morale immensely. A self-styled soldier of fortune, Bill claimed he
often rode the rails to wherever adventure called. His "My Old
Kentucky Home" became the workers' favorite piece. Another
unusual addition to the work force was "Spark Plug" Eddie Bray,
who, it was said, was a champion welterweight fighter from Hot
Springs, Arkansas. Bray, so the press claimed, was currently in
training for a fight and had decided to keep in shape by wielding a
shovel at Sand Cave. Bray, who was only sixteen years old, actually
had been shining shoes in Hot Springs when he heard of Collins's

plight and had hitchhiked to the scene of the tragedy. His total fighting career had consisted of one round in a sparring ring in place of a fighter who was ill.

Such individuals were the unsung heroes of Sand Cave. As the days and nights lengthened and one frustration piled on another, they continued to work voluntarily and without pay. Most of them remained nameless, living at Sand Cave during this crisis and then silently moving on. With grubby-gray faces and bloodshot eyes, they were personified by the barrel-chested Cincinnatian whose name is not recorded but who answered a reporter's query, "Why do you do it?" by saying, "I'm a miner. I'm going to Floyd Collins because he'd do the same for me." Throughout the cold nights and the damp chilly days they passed the time between shifts amusing themselves in simple ways. Some worked crossword puzzles. Others engaged in swapping tall stories. Still others played cards. The college boys avidly read their school newspapers, which were delivered to them to keep them up on the home news. On Friday, February 13, a number of the crews cut out paper hearts to exchange with each other the next morning. The press duly noted that in trying to help Collins they already were giving the nation a practical demonstration of the true meaning of St. Valentine's Day.

Friday the thirteenth itself was a cruel time of rising hopes and crushing disappointments. At about 10:00 A.M. a four-foot-deep crevice was uncovered in the bottom of the shaft and digger William Bailey and his son heard some coughing. They breathlessly reported this to Carmichael. Carmichael immediately asked two experienced miners, Edward Brenner and Albert Blevins, to go back into the Sand Cave passageway to try to detect any signs of life. These men did as they were told, Brenner leading the way and Blevins remaining at a field telephone in the turnaround room.

Brenner was a native of Bavaria who had migrated to the United States at age fifteen to work on an uncle's farm in Alabama. Somewhat later he took a job as a coal miner and ultimately worked his way through the Alabama, Virginia, and West Virginia coal fields north to Ohio. Currently a steelworker in Cincinnati, he had participated in several mine rescues in which the victims had been saved. Reading in the Cincinnati papers that skilled miners were needed at Sand Cave, he had paid his own way to Kentucky. At the moment, he was one of the main diggers in the bottom of the shaft.

For about an hour Brenner alternately tapped on rock at the face of the second breakdown and listened. Then, just before leaving, he heard a noise. Collins was alive! He knew it. "Floyd!" he yelled, "Hold out. We're coming!" There was no answer. For five minutes more he alternately called and listened, but detected nothing else. Finally, he gave up, bringing with him to the surface not only news of what he had heard but also a used-up lantern and Floyd's harness which he had found.

Rumors about this incident spread rapidly. By the time the story got to Cave City it was claimed not only that Floyd was alive but that he had been rescued. People excitedly rushed about with this information until the somber truth arrived. In Washington, D.C., a similar false report succeeded in impeding government business. Washington newspapers and radio stations were flooded with calls and even the White House tried to run down the details. According to the story in the capital, Floyd was found weighing only eighty pounds. One wild facet of this rumor was that the State Department had somehow effected his release! Before all this nonsense could be corrected, there was so much confusion and so many phone calls between government offices that work was suspended for the day.

As indicated earlier, upon learning of the experiences of the two Baileys and Brenner, the military court of inquiry, which was currently meeting in Cave City, adjourned to the cave. The two Baileys described for the court the coughing they had heard and swore that it could have come only from Floyd. Ed Brenner was more explicit. Asked for his credentials, he told the court, "I'm pretty tough. I raised myself, see." Asked what he did in the shaft, he said, "All we do down there is pound and dig." To a question concerning his importance to the rescue work, Brenner replied, "There's damned sight better men than I am here." Then he detailed his Friday morning trip into the Sand Cave passageway, stating that he had heard a groan "like you hear from a man that gets hurt, in a hospital, ya know." Captain Chaney interjected, "A

gasp?" Brenner shot back, "Now you've got it. It was a gasp."
When asked if this could have been his imagination, Brenner
exclaimed, "No, sir!"

Once again newsmen had a field day. Since early Friday morning
when the first rumors began to circulate that Floyd was still alive,
they had been prowling around Sand Cave, interviewing everyone
they could find. Ultimately they created such confusion in the
rescue work that Captain Topmiller found it necessary to restrict
them from the shaft area. He even ejected two reporters, who were
particularly obnoxious, from the site altogether. The press immediately complained, charging the military with an attempt at
censorship. A compromise was finally reached whereby the shaft
area was to remain closed to newsmen, but they would be allowed
in a special compound created for them only thirty-five feet away.
Here they could interview personnel and observe the arrival and
departure of the various rescue crews. At the same time, it was
agreed that three official bulletins would be issued each day either
by Carmichael, Posey, or Funkhouser—at 9:00 A.M., 2:00 P.M.,
and 10:00 P.M. These bulletins, it was hoped, would eliminate the
current press discrepancies in the direction, nature, and depth of
the shaft, as well as curtail unnecessary speculation about Floyd's
condition.

In the shaft itself, worker morale soared. It had suffered from the
discouragement of the past two days. Now it rebounded and the
work redoubled in the belief that Floyd was indeed alive. But
almost immediately new problems appeared. The diamond drill,
now resting in the bottom of the shaft, showed no more voids until
seventy-one feet. Obviously, the shaft was not going to intersect the
Sand Cave passageway and lateral probing would be necessary.
This would take more time, but it could not be helped.

Carmichael decided to continue to dig to the sixty-foot level
before sending a lateral tunnel off. Reaching sixty feet, however,
was not going to be easy. Beginning at about fifty feet so much
loose material was struck and kept falling in at such a rate that
Carmichael feared the entire structure might collapse. At 8:30 P.M.,
one whole tier of timbering crashed down and required the rest of
the evening to repair. Posey's Friday 10:00 P.M. official announcement stated that the shaft was fifty-two feet deep, that constant

retimbering was necessary, and that the work was taking three times as long as usual. Indeed, nine and one-half hours were required on Friday night and early Saturday morning to complete one small section. Posey's 9:00 A.M. Saturday morning bulletin gave the shaft depth as only fifty-four feet.

On Saturday morning a test was made to discover precisely where the shaft was headed and how a lateral probe should be run. While Albert Marshall and Carmichael stood in the bottom of the shaft, Ed Brenner, Al Blevins, and Simon Johns crawled to the turnaround room in the Sand Cave passageway.

Marshall shouted, "Oh, Ed, you there?"

"Yeah," Brenner's voice replied out of the ground.

They smiled. That was encouraging. But no shouts back and forth by any of them elicited any response from Floyd. Brenner later said, "I lay there in the tunnel for fully half an hour, perfectly quiet, straining every nerve to catch the slightest sound. . . . I heard nothing but the drip of the rock sweat." That was not encouraging, and this failure was not broadcast around.

On Saturday evening, when the shaft stood at exactly fifty-five feet, there was doubt that it could go any deeper. Workmen were risking their lives to dig there because of the constant danger of cave-ins. As one said, the bottom was like "a sticky dish of chocolate ice cream with peanuts." Diggers would register gains of a foot or two only to have slides instantly obliterate their progress. The men worked to exhaustion to save what they could—some lying on their backs in three to four inches of icy water trying to get timbers in place. Worse, one whole side of the shaft was beinning to slump. With apprehension, Carmichael noticed at 9:00 P.M. that it was already nine inches out of plumb. Hastily he ordered the cribbing tied in to four three-quarter-inch steel cables which were anchored to twenty-foot-by-twelve-inch-square timbers laid across the shaft's mouth. Simultaneously, he ordered a lateral tunnel begun. It was now or never.

Again, the weather. On Friday night and early Saturday morning there had been spits of rain. Toward Saturday evening a dense fog settled in, creating eerie effects. Shortly before nine o'clock a light drizzle began. By 9:30 P.M. it was raining hard. Sheets of water poured down as thunder rolled and lightning illuminated the scene.

Pools formed and rivers flowed through the camp. Mud made the road and the paths impassable. One huge truck bringing in four sections of galvanized pipe for the lateral tunnel was forced to stop short of the rescue site. The downpour put out the soldiers' fires and forced all spectators and newsmen to scurry for shelter, leaving only the workers in the shaft and two drenched sentries at the barbed-wire gate. Throughout the storm, the chug-chug-chug of the gas engine furnishing power for the dump car accompanied the whir of the dynamo on the hillside supplying power to the lights. Now and again the lightning betrayed the worried face of Carmichael as rivulets of rainwater streamed off the brim of his hat.

By ten o'clock the storm had passed, although a light rain continued. The problem now was how to keep water out of the shaft. The pumps had been started at the beginning of the downpour and emergency trenches had been dug around the top of the shaft. Even so, the diggers below for a time waded in two feet of water. The struggle to divert the flow continued throughout the night with limited success. When newsmen grew restless about the delays and rumors of trouble, Carmichael invited Skeets Miller into the shaft to inspect it as their representative. It was another trauma for the young reporter. While Carmichael was explaining the situation to him, a small slide occurred and Miller jumped, turning his eyes apprehensively up to the narrow window to the outside world.

"Well, what do you think of it?" asked Carmichael.

"It's five times worse than in the hole," replied Miller, and hastily climbed out to give a sober report to his newsgathering colleagues.

"It's one hell of a place," Carmichael himself had to admit.

As light dawned on February 15, bringing with it another Sunday, the Collins tragedy was entering its third week. Rescue was still hours away. For days newspapers had been telling their readers through wartime headlines: "ONLY FEW FEET FROM COLLINS TRAP" and "COLLINS RESCUE IMMINENT." They had also been warning readers that Floyd would die in a matter of hours unless he were reached. Now editors hardly knew what to say. All hope for Collins should have vanished, yet, incredibly, he might still be alive. Dr. Hazlett said Floyd's chances of survival

remained good because of his upright position—much better than if
he had been prone or lying head down. Funkhouser claimed that it
was quite possible that Floyd still lived, especially if he had any
notion that help was coming. Miners in the shaft stated that they
knew "for a fact" Floyd Collins was alive.

In view of this intense struggle and the continuing suspense,
newspapers again reverted to their earlier theme of Sand Cave's
being a titanic battle of Man against Nature and a heroic race
against time. Superintendent Carmichael, the man who was in
charge of this battle, inevitably became its symbol. The press
increasingly followed his actions and hung on his words. "He's
alive! I know he's alive!" Carmichael would tell his workers. "We
won't fail! We simply can't fail!" he would exclaim to reporters. As
an exponent of all that "Dig, dump, and pray!" stood for during the
frustrating week of February 8–15, Henry St. George Tucker
Carmichael was unsurpassable.

As another Sunday approached, Cave City merchants and businessmen planned not to be caught napping and laid in supplies for an
even larger crowd than on Sunday, February 8. They had ample
reason for their optimism. They had just gone through the best
business week in the town's history. By Wednesday, Cave City's
two banks had had to seek additional help from Louisville to
provide more currency because a money shortage was developing.
All merchants reported booming sales and restaurateurs could
barely keep enough foodstuffs on hand. Remembering the previous
weekend, however, the Saturday and Sunday editions of all the
Louisville papers warned those going to Sand Cave to carry with
them their own necessities, including food and drink, because
supplies might again be tight. Many did, and, as a result, better-
prepared and well-stocked Cave City entrepreneurs took an unexpected economic beating.

The crowd on Sunday, February 15, was less than one-half of
what it had been the week before. Although there were again
license plates from many states and some visitors traveled great
distances, the majority came from Kentucky and nearby regions.
The dismal rain and fog of the previous night held the numbers
down, yet by late Sunday afternoon an estimated five thousand

were there. Unlike on February 8, when a carnival atmosphere had existed, the hot-dog vendors, balloon merchants, and Coca-Cola peddlers were missing. They were forced to hawk their wares along the road and not at the rescue site itself. Even more than on the previous Sunday, the approaches to Sand Cave and the surrounding area were a quagmire. Abandoned cars were everywhere. Every time a driver tried to turn his vehicle around, it sank to its hubcaps in the mud. Whole families, from grown-ups to tots, could barely navigate in the sticky goo.

Many scenes were again the same. High school girls wearing blazers giggled self-consciously as they strutted about. Hill natives in whiskers and overalls watched in silence. Mothers clutched on to the hands of their children as fathers peered intently through the barbed-wire fence at the rescue activities. Here and there a young man, as serious as a Carmichael, explained to his girl friend every detail of Floyd's entrapment and the rescue operation. However, in contrast to those on February 8, these people were subdued, obviously impressed with what they saw and with what was being accomplished. It was an awe-inspiring sight—tents with their tall tin pipes belching smoke, great lights bathing everything in white, a steady flow of water from the pumps in the shaft, and the shouts of miners passing on instructions from the deepening hole in the ground. Everywhere army trucks stood tilted on the rough terrain while material of all kinds lay strewn about. Above on the bluff, as a silent reminder of the seriousness of the situation, stood a Red Cross ambulance, waiting to rush the victim to the hospital eighteen miles away. And below and off to one side was the small opening under an overhanging sandstone ledge that was the cause of it all.

Once again the devout came to sing and pray. All during the past week churches throughout the nation had remembered Floyd in their missionary society and Wednesday night prayer meetings. In such cities as Atlanta, Kansas City, St. Louis, Nashville, and Cincinnati innumerable supplications were sent heavenward on his behalf. Now Reverend Lum Doyle spoke for them all in a brief service overlooking the shaft. Again, here and there small groups held services of their own. Somewhere in the crowd someone would start singing a hymn such as "Jesus, Lover of My Soul" and soon others would join in. From time to time, the diggers in the shaft would pick up the tune and hum along.

During most of Sunday the Collins family was at the site. Homer, who on Thursday had been assigned to one of the work crews, had been replaced that very morning on orders by Carmichael because more experienced men were needed. Angered by his removal, he had to be forcibly restrained on Sunday afternoon from joining squads being lowered in the bucket. Andy Lee circulated around the hillside, talking to visitors about the tragedy and claiming that "the army" would get his brother out. Marshall Collins said little and stayed out of the way. Miss Jane remained unnoticed in one of the tents until the sun came out later in the day. Then, dressed all in black except for a colored scarf at her throat, she sat on a railroad tie with Nellie beside her, occasionally talking with newsmen. When asked about Floyd's chances, she would merely say, "Mr. Carmichael will get Floyd out safe enough."

As on the previous Sunday, Lee was the main show. He had stayed at the cave site from Tuesday through Wednesday night and then had returned again on Friday. On Saturday he had passed the hours in the Red Cross tent reading and showing to everybody the hundreds of letters he was receiving from all over the country. "Look at this!" he would exclaim, "they love Floyd, they love my boy!" On Sunday at 10:00 A.M. he began wandering around the grounds, talking with onlookers. "Prayers'll do much for the work," he would tell them, "because God'll strengthen the miners who are a-diggin' for him." Lee evidently had not given up hope, earlier indications to the contrary. He told one group, "Floyd's alive and he'll be saved." He told another, "Floyd knows caves, lived among 'em all his life." Sunday was the first time Lee had ever seen a radio transmitter and he was intrigued by its possibilities. He lost no time in getting station 9-BRK's operator, Homer Ogden, to send out a message to the nation on his behalf. Said Lee, "I'd like to thank everybody for their prayers 'n' their hopes. I feel as they do—'The prayers of the righteous availeth much.'"

The men in the shaft spent Sunday the same as any other day. Generally nontalkative when at work, the Blevinses, Marshalls, and Brenners while resting in their tents or on their cots regaled each other with past exploits, bandied jokes about, and spat streams of tobacco juice into the tiny openings of their sheet-metal stoves. Many of their stories were hyperbolic, but their aim was rarely amiss. Between expectorations, they argued about when they would reach Collins and took unkindly to any suggestion that he might be dead. Told by a reporter that it would be a miracle if Floyd were still alive, one stocky miner blurted out, "Hell, it wouldn't be no miracle a-tall." Claiming that he had gone without food and water for eight days once himself, he added, "Now it warn't no picnic, but by damn it was done."

All the while, these same workers dug the lateral tunnel under the most adverse conditions. By Sunday at 9:00 A.M. it was four feet long. At 11:00 A.M. it was in five feet, and three feet of it were shored up. It was tedious and dangerous work. Sloping slightly downward, this heading was edging through limestone blocks and loose muck. Whenever the tunnelers encountered large boulders, they left them in place and dug the lateral around them. Carmichael was being very cautious. Said he to reporters, "We are not taking the slightest chance of bringing the whole thing down."

At 3:30 P.M. the lateral tunnel was in seven feet. The core drill now indicated that a void lay about six feet ahead and five feet below the present horizontal. New shouting and sound tests proved to Carmichael that the lateral and the Sand Cave passageway were very close to joining. Unfortunately, the water seeping through the ground from the rainstorm of the previous evening still made cave-ins a constant possibility, and every inch of the new tunnel had to be shored.

As Sunday night descended, a clear moon rose, giving promise of better weather. It was certainly needed. Of the last eight days of digging, four had been in the rain. Once again the temperatures began to fall, but this was welcomed since it stiffened the earth surrounding the lateral tunnel and helped keep it in place. At 9:00 P.M. Posey spoke confidently in his official bulletin of the heading going in the right direction and said that the remaining distance to Floyd was only a scant six or seven feet.

The end was at last in sight, and the media geared for it. More than twenty telegraph circuits were standing by to handle the final news. Special editions were planned by all the major newspapers. It was anticipated that the minute Floyd was reached all records for newsprint devoted to a single story would be broken. Already on that Sunday the rotogravure sections of the nation's press had been filled with rescue photos, and the demand for more was endless. At that moment, seven airplanes stood in a field, dubbed Collins Field, just outside Cave City. Flown in from Chicago, Cincinnati, Dayton, Atlanta, Cleveland, and Louisville, they were waiting to speed the final pictures of the Sand Cave struggle to anxious editors. One had as its pilot a young man named Charles Lindbergh.

Newsmen and photographers at the rescue site, meanwhile, elbowed each other and maneuvered for a better vantage point. Cameramen set up their tripods and a few, taking no chances on missing a shot, put pans of flashpowder in place. A score of recently installed telephones, giving reporters direct lines out, hung on nails hastily driven in nearby trees. The feeling of imminent discovery was reinforced by the sudden appearance at the cave of Adjutant General Kehoe. He was dressed in full military uniform, a shining figure amid all the drab, mud-caked rescuers. Upon spying Carmichael coming out of the shaft shortly before 10:00 P.M., reporters besieged him with queries as to when he expected to break through. He told them that it would be at least twelve hours yet and recommended that they grab some sleep. Few did. They had waited too long for this moment to risk missing it. After sixteen incredible days, they, as much as their readers and editors, wanted to know the answer to the question: Would Floyd Collins come out alive?

# 9

## *The Struggle Ends*

"We're there! We're there!" Shouting, then falling to his knees, Albert Marshall clawed at the small opening. The prominent forelock that hung down over his forehead was shiny with sweat. Al Blevins and Ed Brenner, two paces behind him and covered with mud, were caught by surprise. Simon Johns, enjoying a cigarette farther back in the lateral tunnel, rushed forward.

Since late Sunday evening, these men had been working in shifts in the lengthening heading. Slowly, laboriously, sometimes able to move only one cubic yard of dirt an hour, they had pushed the lateral past the ten-foot mark on Monday morning, February 16. By Monday noon, while anxious officials and an expectant press waited, they reached twelve feet. Believing that they still had a yard or so yet to go, Marshall almost lost his chisel with the last tap of his hammer. The time was 1:30 P.M. The tunnel was exactly twelve-and-one-half feet long.

As Marshall's three associates crowded in behind him, word was relayed to Superintendent Carmichael at the top of the shaft that a breakthrough into Sand Cave had occurred. Marshall continued to dig furiously, pulling away rocks with his bare hands until he was able to stick his head in. Stale air and darkness so thick he "could feel it" met him. Drawing his head back, he removed more dirt. All at once a whole section of the heading gave way, revealing tools, a bottle, and several pieces of rope. The opening was now big enough to admit a small man. Flashing his torch in, Marshall thought he saw the outline of a head, but his batteries were low and he could not be sure. Unable to get his shoulders through without risking a serious collapse, Marshall turned around and gingerly lowered himself in feetfirst by hanging onto a section of the lateral's shoring. He touched something—it was a discarded quilt that had been pulled off Floyd earlier in the rescue.

Since Marshall was not keen about going on, Brenner, who was a head shorter and much smaller, offered to take his place. Clutching a fresh flashlight, he went in headfirst as Blevins and Johns steadied his feet. Casting his light around, Brenner surveyed a grisly scene. He realized with a jolt that Floyd Collins lay six feet below him and that the lateral had intersected the Sand Cave passageway above and ahead of—not behind—Floyd's body. Brenner also noticed that Floyd was again wedged in so tightly that it was barely possible to get a hand between his chest and the limestone ceiling. The bulb, although still in its socket, was not burning. Only Floyd's head and part of his left arm were free. A steady stream of water was running onto his cheek, leaving a red mark. His left eye was closed; his right eye was slightly open. His mouth gaped at least an inch, revealing his gold tooth, and his face was bearded and dirty. Brenner had seen enough and yelled for those holding on to his feet to pull him out. Shaking his head, he uttered only one word. "Dead."

Carmichael, having just arrived in the tunnel, requested that they all stay in the bottom of the shaft while he went back up to confer with Denhardt, Posey, and Funkhouser. He did not want to excite unnecessary speculation by those on the surface. But Denhardt had already telegraphed to most observers that something was afoot by ordering a detail of soldiers with fixed bayonets to the shaft head. As a muddy Carmichael emerged at 2:10 P.M., he was immediately badgered by reporters to whom he said, "I'll have something to give you pretty soon." Hurriedly, he moved off, yelling, "Posey! Where's Posey? Get him down here!" By the time Posey arrived, the Kyroc superintendent was already huddling with Denhardt and Funkhouser. Looking furtively from time to time at the reporters and cameramen standing in their compound, the four men talked. Everyone knew what was coming. The machinery had fallen silent and a hush had descended on the workers. Finally, Funkhouser detached himself from the group, turned toward the press bullpen, and said, "Gentlemen, I have a special bulletin to announce. Collins has been found, apparently dead. . . ." Newsmen streaked for their phones. It was 2:42 P.M.

When Funkhouser made this terse announcement, Miss Jane and Nellie were on the fringes of the crowding reporters. At first they listened without showing emotion, then Nellie burst into tears. Miss Jane went into the Red Cross tent and wept softly, repeating over and over, "I begged him not to go down there. I begged him and begged him. . . ." Homer and Marshall were standing just to the side of the shaft when they heard the news. Marshall shook his head and slumped down in despair, the tears welling in his eyes. Homer bore up stoically. Long drained of emotion, he was restrained in his grief. He had given up hope, he told reporters, the day the shaft was begun. Lee, who was up on the hillside at the moment, was told of his son's death by Dr. Hazlett. He, too, was resigned. "Thank God he's been found," Lee said, and then began shaking hands with all those who had helped. As he did so, he talked incessantly about Floyd and his fate. "It's all been in the hand of God from the beginning," he claimed. "I can't complain of Divine Providence. Floyd ast the boys that got to him to pray for him and he would be taken care of by the Power above. I know Floyd's with the angels. He got converted down in that there hole. God did it. God knows best."

While the news of Floyd's death was being absorbed by all those at the rescue site and was being flashed to the nation at large by excited reporters, Funkhouser again joined Denhardt and Carmichael, who were sitting on a pile of planking. With pencil and paper in hand, the professor began to construct a detailed official bulletin about the precise circumstances of the final discovery. This he gave to newsmen shortly after 3:00 P.M. Simultaneously,

Captain J.F. Francis of the medical detachment of the 149th Infantry volunteered to go into the shaft to make a preliminary medical examination. Dr. Hazlett was assigned to go with him while Dr. C.C. Howard, a Horse Cave physician representing the Collins family, remained at the top of the shaft. Hazlett and Francis donned rubber firemen's hats and oilskins and, accompanied by Brenner, were lowered to the bottom. Hazlett waited in the mouth of the tunnel as Francis crawled toward Floyd's crypt. Too bulky to make it all the way in himself, Francis asked Brenner to take his place while he told him what to do.

"How does he feel?" asked Dr. Francis.

"Cold. He's cold all over," replied Brenner.

"Feel just in front of his ear. Can you feel anything?"

"No, I can't feel anything."

"Try his wrist. Is there any pulse beat in his wrist?"

"No."

"Shine the light in his eyes. Can you shine the light in his eyes?"

Brenner tried, but he could not get at the lids to raise them because the eyes were too sunken. Dr. Francis then asked him to describe Floyd's face and Brenner did, even taking note of the water mark on Floyd's cheek.

Returning to the surface, Drs. Hazlett and Francis were pounced on by reporters and, still clad in their oilskins, they related what they had found. They stated that Floyd's death had been due to a combination of exposure, exhaustion, and starvation. To the question of how long he had been gone, Dr. Hazlett replied, "We have no hesitancy in saying that from the condition of the body, as described by Mr. Brenner, Collins has been dead at least twenty-four hours."

From the moment Floyd Collins was found, Carmichael made plans to bring out his body. The family, too, wanted Floyd's corpse recovered so it could be buried somewhere near Crystal Cave and not remain in that miserable hole. But there was a problem. The diggers were confronted by the same set of circumstances that had faced the original rescuers. Floyd's left foot was still held by the rock, and there was no easy way to free him since the lateral tunnel had emerged at Floyd's head and not at his feet.

All night on Monday the Kyroc superintendent sought a way.

There were really only two alternatives: to continue to shore and dig in the old Sand Cave passageway, or begin a new lateral heading altogether. There was yet another problem. Few workers wanted to risk their lives further and many were already packing for home. As long as there had been a chance that Floyd was alive, they had been willing to remain. Now it was a different matter.

To enlist press appreciation for his difficult position, Carmichael again invited Skeets Miller to the bottom of the shaft and balanced him off with A.W. Nichols of the *Evening Post*. Emerging sometime before midnight, these two newsmen agreed that the removal of Floyd's body would be extremely risky. Carmichael, in turn, sought permission from Lee to have Floyd's left leg amputated as soon as it was reached so that the job of excavation could be abbreviated. This immediately caused another Collins row. Nellie cried that she did not want her dead brother mutilated. Miss Jane blanched at the idea, furiously shaking her head no. Both Homer and Marshall also protested the amputation, but Lee agreed to it as the only way to get Floyd's body out. As a result, Carmichael issued a bulletin that he expected to have Floyd on the surface by 5:00 A.M. Tuesday morning. But the question of amputation again became academic when those diggers who continued to work in the tunnel—Marshall, Blevins, Johns, Maddox, and Brenner—finally decided that it was too dangerous to go on. When by dawn on Tuesday no more had been accomplished than opening up a larger "window" into Floyd's death chamber, Carmichael himself was ready to order a halt.

After conferring with Funkhouser, Denhardt, and Posey, the Kyroc superintendent announced at 8:30 A.M. that Floyd's body would remain where it was and that a coroner's jury would be impaneled to handle the final legal details. Magistrate Turner appointed himself chairman of the jury and selected six others to serve with him—Wallace Page, J. Norman Parker, Ish Lancaster, Claude Monroe, Thomas L. Gorby, and Johnnie Gerald. All these men had known Floyd well. Just before they descended into the shaft to view the body, Everett Maddox took a towel and water, washed Floyd's face, brushed back his hair, and propped up his head on several small stones. While turning the dead man's face so that the jurors could see him clearly, Maddox was surprised at how solidly the debris had again settled around him. The earth simply would not give Floyd Collins up. Maddox also noticed how his death mask had frozen into a tight frown of despair and, again, how brightly the light glanced off his gold tooth. Lingering no longer than was necessary, Maddox hurriedly moved back to the entrance of the tunnel and ushered in the first juror—Johnnie Gerald. For the last time Johnnie looked on Floyd's face. He stared for a moment, then abruptly turned away, making no comment. One by one, Maddox escorted the other jurors in so that they, too, could see. As each one emerged from the shaft, Carmichael, anxious to scotch any doubt, asked in a monotonous litany: "Were you in the cave?" . . . "Did you see anyone?" . . . "Who was it?" . . . and "Is he dead?"

Shortly before noon on Tuesday, as the coroner's jury adjourned to Cave City to complete its formal inquest, Drs. Hazlett and Howard were taken down for a final medical assessment. Maddox again served as guide. Observing Collins at close range at last, Dr. Hazlett was shocked to see a cave cricket perched on Floyd's nose, nibbling at the tip. Floyd appeared very emaciated. Hazlett now believed that he had died as much from starvation as from exposure and that he had been dead no more than three days. Although the exact time of death could not be determined from an examination of the corpse's head alone, Floyd's demise, according to Hazlett, had probably occurred sometime on Friday the thirteenth, which in the cave country was known as "hoodoo day."

Superintendent Carmichael, meanwhile, was still bothered by his inability to show tangible proof that Floyd had been trapped below. He supported the decision to leave Floyd's body there, but he toyed momentarily with the possibility of cutting off a finger, a hand, or even Floyd's head and bringing it to the surface. Posey and Funkhouser were aghast at this idea and urged Carmichael to forget it. They pointed out that although such action would quiet the Doubting Thomases, it would also bring a torrent of protest. When, therefore, the press requested permission to take a final death photo, Carmichael seized upon it as a feasible substitute. The press pool agreed that one man would go down and take a picture which they all would share and which would be flown to Chicago for national distribution

The photographer selected was John W. Steger of the *Chicago Tribune.* Crawling to the "window" in the access tunnel, Steger. stuck his camera in and set off the flash. The plate was then flown to Chicago for pool distribution by Lindbergh, who, along with a handful of other aviators, was patiently waiting at the scene. Lindbergh's trip, however, was for naught—he had been handed a negative that was blank. So cutthroat was the press competition and so lacking in ethics were many of the participants that the pool found itself double-crossed. The actual photo ultimately made its way only to the *Chicago Tribune.* Or did it? The next day a death photo was published by that paper showing a bald head, out-of-focus patches of dark and light, and a round shape that supposedly was the light bulb on Floyd's chest. But Skeets Miller later contended that this blurry photo itself was a fake. He claimed that the rock walls would not have permitted such a photographic angle.

With the taking of the death photo and the final medical assessment, Carmichael wanted to shut down the shaft fast. It was a growing menace and the Kyroc superintendent had become increasingly apprehensive as one viewing after another had taken place. He felt relieved when everyone was out at last and no one had been hurt. In making a concluding tour of the shaft himself, he found the entire structure was settling. The lateral tunnel was giving way, its side supports slowly sinking into the mud. Floyd's prison chamber also revealed signs of continuing disintegration. The earth had already packed tightly around the two electric wires that still protruded from the original cave-in. Commenting later, Carmichael claimed, "I don't believe an angle worm could go through that place, as I last saw it." Mother Nature herself was closing Floyd's tomb.

The coroner's jury wound up its inquest in Cave City later on Tuesday afternoon. Members met in the police court and heard testimony from five witnesses for three and one-half hours. The concluding examination was handled by Barren County attorney J. Lewis Williams. In answer to Williams's queries, Jewell Estes described finding Floyd and trying to get help to him. Lieutenant Ben Wells explained the difficult conditions in Sand Cave. Ed Brenner told of his activities in the lateral tunnel and of discovering Floyd's body. Everett Maddox spoke of the deteriorating situation in the main shaft and in the heading. Finally, Superintendent Carmichael recounted a brief history of the rescue operation and defended the final decision not to move the body. "To remove Floyd from his present position," concluded Carmichael, "would probably result in the death of one or more of the rescue party. The Lord knows I wanted to see that fellow gotten out [but] we decided we had better leave Floyd Collins where he was." The verdict of the coroner's jury was unanimous and was signed by all of them: "We, the jury, find . . . that Floyd Collins is now dead and that he came to his death from exposure caused by being accidentally trapped in what is commonly called Sand Cave."

The official closing act of the drama occurred late on Tuesday evening. General Denhardt reconvened the military court of inquiry at that time for its final session. He inserted the coroner's inquest testimony and the jury verdict into its records. After this was done, the general declared the court's work also completed. His parting comment to reporters was: "Our position has been fully vindicated by the finding of the body. It will keep the name of Kentucky untarnished."

It was a sad sight. The trees were virtually barren of leaves, a few brown lifeless ones still swinging forlornly from denuded limbs. Those that were on the ground, now drying from the recent rains, stirred fitfully in the slight breeze. The air seemed colder than the forty-eight degrees shown on the thermometer, and even frequent bursts of sunshine did not completely dispel a general gloomy cast to the day. Here and there at its tree location a telephone still rang, unanswered, as some editor wished to ask his reporter for additional information. The shaft's sheltering canopy had been folded up and the shaft's maw yawned obscenely a hundred and twenty-five feet away. Sitting disconsolately in a crooked row of six chairs were Miss Jane, Old Man Lee, and Lee's elder brother who had recently arrived from western Kentucky. Three of the chairs were empty—Homer, Andy Lee, and Marshall preferring to stand off to one side rather than sit. To the left, up on boulders overlooking the ravine, were fifteen members of various church choirs hastily recruited from Cave City. Obviously nervous because of the battery of movie and still cameras clicking at them, they rustled the pages of their hymnbooks. Spreading in a semicircle behind the six chairs were about a hundred and fifty people—tired men, rough workers, college youths, natives, and soldiers of adventure. Before them all, using a stump as his platform, was the Reverend Roy H. Biser.

It was 2:30 P.M., Tuesday, February 17, and they had gathered to pay their last respects to Floyd Collins. It was an unusual funeral. There was no corpse, no casket, no flowers, and, technically, no grave. That had not been the intention when the original burial plans were made on Monday afternoon. Floyd was to have lain in state in the Cave City High School gymnasium for two days. All four pastors of the local churches had been invited to participate in a unity funeral service scheduled for Wednesday. Governor Fields had planned to attend to convey "the deep sympathy of Kentucky and the country" to the Collins family. Floyd's body was then to have been buried at the entrance to Crystal Cave. But the impending collapse of the shaft and the decision not to remove the body had changed all that. Makeshift arrangements were substituted, with the Red Cross being responsible for the details.

The Tuesday afternoon service began with the hastily assembled choir singing "Nearer, My God, to Thee." They started tentatively, then hit their stride as miners' caps and battered fedoras came off heads. One by one the onlookers took up the music. At the conclusion, Reverend Biser, who was minister of the First Christian Church of Glasgow, read the scripture while a movie camera whirred only a few feet away. In the middle distance stood a sentinel with a rifle. The Biblical text was taken from the Fifteenth Chapter of First Corinthians and from the Thirty-ninth Psalm: "Lord, make me to know mine end and the measure of my days. . . . O death, where is thy sting? O grave, where is thy victory?" After this scripture reading, another hymn was sung, "Jesus, Lover of My Soul." Then Reverend C.K. Dickey, pastor of the Horse Cave Methodist Church, replaced Reverend Biser on the stump and offered a prayer, asking for Divine strength for Lee and his wife and for all the loved ones Floyd had left behind. Reverend Dickey concluded by hoping that all citizens would use the present tragedy to realize again "the uncertainty of life and to prepare always to travel to that country from whose bourne no traveler ever returns."

Following the Dickey prayer, Mrs. Ira D. Withers, the rural correspondent who had first telephoned the news of Floyd's entrapment to the *Evening Post,* stepped forward to sing a solo, "We'll Understand It Better, By-and-By." When this was completed the two ministers took turns delivering the sermon and the eulogy. Reverend Biser began by saying that the Sand Cave episode was "an unparalleled event in the history of the state and the nation." Why had there been such universal public interest in it? "Because," Biser continued, "the story of Floyd Collins is but the story of the romance of the human race and its great struggle for existence and advancement." Elaborating on this theme for ten minutes, he closed by declaring that it was fitting Floyd should be left where he was. "Floyd Collins's body lies in yonder cave," he said, "but his soul is with God, and he is happy."

In his equally short address, Reverend Dickey concentrated on Floyd's prowess as a caver. "Floyd loved the caverns and the caves," the minister said, "and he was never tired of trying to find one or exploring those already discovered. . . . He liked to crawl in the subterranean passages, and he saw in the gigantic formations and in the fantastic patterns on the walls the traceries of God." Turning to those who had tried to save him, Reverend Dickey stated that this spot would be forever blessed by the demonstration of their loving kindness. "Heroic deeds," he concluded, "have laid a permanent monument for the whole country in the exhibition of courage and stamina revealed for eighteen days at Sand Cave." When Reverend Dickey finished, J.F. Van Cleve of Glasgow rose and also praised the rescue workers in a brief speech. Speaking so softly that the water running on the hillside almost drowned out his words, he claimed that those who had struggled so valiantly to save Floyd had already delivered more eloquent eulogies through their actions than any speaker could now utter.

The remainder of the service was brief. As A.F. Pearson, a Glasgow undertaker, dropped a piece of ash, a tiny fern, and a bit of earth into the shaft's mouth, Reverend Dickey committed Floyd's unseen remains to his Maker. The entire funeral service had taken only fifty-five minutes—the final hour of the 384 that had been spent trying to gain Floyd's freedom. Throughout the proceedings Lee Collins sat motionless, clad in his red sweater covered by the old army overcoat whose collar he kept hunched up about his neck. He fixed his eyes vacantly on the dark entrance to Sand Cave while Miss Jane stared down at the clay soil directly in front of her feet. She swayed several times during the ceremony and once sobbed convulsively. The three Collins brothers remained impassive, standing off to the side.

Following the funeral, Lee and Miss Jane walked slowly up the hill, detached and alone, toward their car. Before entering it, they were handed a personal message that had just arrived from Governor Fields. It expressed sadness at their son's untimely death and admiration for his record as a cave explorer. The message concluded: "May your sorrow be soothed with the consolation that he confessed his faith in his Redeemer, and the well-founded hope that while his body sleeps in its cavern tomb, his soul has returned to the God who gave it." As they drove away, Miss Jane was sobbing and Lee had tears in his eyes. But the governor's reminder of Floyd's salvation had also brought a smile to Lee's lips.

Others began drifting away as soon as the funeral was over. The natives returned to their homes to argue endlessly the details of the rescue operation. The workers, some of whom had already left, went their separate ways, following hardy handshakes and promises to keep in touch. Their departure gained momentum during the afternoon and by nightfall it was virtually complete. By late Tuesday afternoon, even the soldiers were leaving. Striking their tents and loading their gear into two large motor trucks, the troops herded into buses shortly before dinner and returned to their homes in Smiths Grove and Bowling Green. By 9:00 P.M. only three guardsmen, under the command of Warrant Officer Dan W. Cline, remained at their posts. These stayed until 7:00 A.M. Wednesday morning, and then they, too, departed. Posey, Hazlett, and Funkhouser left Cave City for Louisville at 8:45 P.M. on Tuesday in Posey's car. Passing by Sand Cave first, they were surprised at how abandoned it seemed.

By Wednesday morning, February 18, only three newsmen were still at the scene, all of them representing Louisville papers. The big-city reporters and photographers had vanished, spirited away by the trains and planes that had brought them. Carmichael discovered that there were not enough workers left to clean up the site and had to issue an emergency call to Kyroc for help. Ultimately, he rounded up about seventy-five persons to move rocks, dirt, and trees into the shaft. He had announced the day before that concrete would be used to seal in Floyd's body and permanently block the entrance to Sand Cave. "It is a dangerous place and we do not want anyone else trapped in there," he declared. However, when the cement did not arrive by Wednesday morning, hc ordered that debris be used to plug the hole instead, allowing nature to do the rest. During the whole operation, only three autoloads of spectators came to see what was going on. By 5:00 P.M., the shaft was filled, all wires this side of the collapse in Sand Cave were stripped out, the cave itself was sealed, and not one visitor remained on the scene. Accompanied by Carmichael, Bee Doyle made a final inspection trip over his wounded land and declared himself satisfied. That evening a lone wreath, sent by Louisville newsboys, hung above the entrance to Sand Cave.

"FLOYD COLLINS IS FOUND DEAD." "CAVERN GRIPS COLLINS BODY." "CAVE KEEPS ITS VICTIM." "COLLINS GIVEN TO FINAL REST IN SAND CAVE." These and similar headlines told Americans what they expected but did not want to hear. On Tuesday and Wednesday, February 17 and 18, the Floyd Collins story crowded virtually all else out of the nation's news-papers. The *Louisville Times* printed three extras on the day he was found. That same day, the *Philadelphia Inquirer* devoted eight columns to the event and the *Chicago Tribune* nine. The staid *New York Times* carried Floyd's death on page one under a three-column headline. Later in the year, this same paper, announcing the news of two other underground tragedies—fifty-three killed in a North Carolina explosion (May 31), and sixty-one in an Alabama coal mine blast (December 12)—would relegate the first to page seven and the second to page three.

Toward the end, the public was consumed by its interest in the outcome at Sand Cave. Although Floyd Collins was only one out of 120 million Americans, his name was on the tip of everyone's tongue. The single question of overriding importance was "Has Floyd been found yet?" From February 12 on, the *Chicago Tribune* estimated that its telephone service answered four thousand calls about him a day. In New York, large numbers of people crowded around store windows that displayed the latest rescue bulletins. Restaurants, movie houses, and hotels posted "Collins Reports" for their guests on the final weekend. In several instances, theater performances were interrupted for the latest news from Sand Cave. In Washington, the sole topic of conversation was Floyd's rescue, newspapers reporting that "the city's interest in affairs of government was far less compelling than that in the battle for the life of the lone man in the murk of Sand Cave." President Coolidge closely followed developments there, and Secretary of Commerce Herbert Hoover, himself a mining engineer, eagerly read all dispatches from the site. Near the end, representatives and senators left debates on the floor of Congress to rush out and get the latest information from Cave City.

When the result was at last known, the postmortems and interpretations immediately began. Insignificant and unknown in life, Floyd Collins in death was fervently claimed by the nation. All commentators agreed that never had one man found himself in a more horrible situation. His predicament, they said, had caused even the strongest American to blanch. It was beyond comprehension that one man had been made to suffer so. Carried away by the thought of it, one reporter expressed eloquently what was felt by many: "Never was known a doom prepared with such cunning ingenuity of torture. Inhumed on a bed of blackness, in the baleful brooding silence of night, Death was the grisly companion of [his] tantalized spirit, weakened by unendurable oppression of the lungs, shivering with affright. . . ."

Although a few papers persisted in claiming that Floyd was killed by his own folly and by the bickering and parochialism of his friends, the vast majority now asserted that he had been martyred to the Fates. Declared one paper, "The battle of Sand Cave is over and Man has hoisted the white pennant of surrender to Mother Nature. . . ." In this battle Floyd Collins was viewed as a surrogate for all; his was not an isolated tragedy but a universally symbolic event. Said the *Washington Post,* ". . . it concentrated in one agonizing individual case the experience of the human race in its struggle for existence."

Many saw a positive and uplifting side to this struggle. The episode, according to some commentators, demonstrated the concern of people for one another. Collins may have suffered incalculably, but the outpouring of human kindness in reaction to his plight was almost worth it. Man's service to mankind was a particularly prevalent theme. Many took consolation in the fact that the tragedy proved America still had a warm heart despite her wealth and apparent callousness. Editors agreed that the Collins affair caused Americans to realize how impotent and vulnerable they were individually and how much they needed one another in the face of whatever destiny was assigned to them. Superintendent Carmichael declared that this experience had proved to him "that just about ninety-nine percent of the human race is pure gold." The *Cleveland Plain Dealer,* upon learning of Floyd's demise, asked: "Is not Kentucky better, is not mankind better, for the struggle?" The *Chicago Tribune* betrayed the same sentiment in a one-column analysis topped by a headline: "Man Loves His Fellow, Cave Stories Reveal." The *Atlanta Constitution* made the humanitarian significance of Floyd's death paramount by claiming that his fate impressed upon the entire world "the ever-strengthening tie of humanity that binds man to man."

Heroism naturally came in for its share of comment. Never before, claimed many editors, had there been such a sustained display of heroic deeds. Some papers continued to champion their favorite heroes—Miller by the Louisville *Courier-Journal,* and Burdon and Carmichael by the *Louisville Herald*—but there were plenty of others to go around. Most observers saw heroes everywhere. Even Johnnie Gerald was rehabilitated and judged to have taken "heroic" action. In the end, the press lauded all persons involved in the struggle. All were "Sand Cave heroes," including those who tended the tents and served the food. Thomas Killian of the *Chicago Tribune,* a man who but a week before had had serious reservations about the situation, now wrote that "veins of golden heroism" had been discovered by the rescue picks. It was an "epic of sacrifice, valor and toil," he said, in which "a new record of American heroism was etched through the plight of one luckless Kentucky mountaineer." Other writers were quick to point out that this "Kentucky mountaineer" himself was the greatest hero of all. His bravery in the face of such overwhelming odds had been unbelievable.

Other impressions or lessons too many to mention were gleaned from the Sand Cave affair. Every journal, every editor, every interest group saw something in the incident applicable to their particular situation or belief. The general press took the occasion to remind readers once again of its value in bringing such events to the attention of the public. The intrepid reporter and his role were especially lauded. Similarly, prohibitionists seized upon the affair to help promote their attacks on current national enforcement failures. Floyd Collins could have been saved, declared "dry" journals, if it had not been for John Barleycorn's appearance at Sand Cave. Fundamentalists, in turn, whose champion William Jennings Bryan would a few months later be fighting Clarence Darrow in the Scopes "Monkey Trial" in nearby Dayton, Tennessee, used the Collins story as a textbook case of salvation redeeming sinful man. Fundamentalist spokesmen maintained that it was impossible to relate the Sand Cave saga without making Floyd's belief in God the central theme. The key aspect of the story was how "the faith that moves mountains" came to a man "trapped by a mountain of rock." Indeed, Christians everywhere saw much in the event that was meaningful. In a four-minute religious analysis, radio station WHAS of Louisville spoke for many believers when it said that Floyd "by his unswerving faith in God and his resignation to Divine Will has shown others how to live and die."

In the cave country itself, the tragedy was not viewed so idealistically or in such epic terms. There, nerves were still raw and tempers had not yet cooled. Some natives continued to insist that Floyd's rescue had been possible but that the early attempts were bungled. John Vance, one of the older residents of Park City, claimed that if he had been younger at the time, he could have saved him. Certainly the Lee brothers, if they had been alive, said Vance, "would have gotten Floyd out, or trapped themselves, one or the other." Lyman Cutliff, Floyd's neighbor on Flint Ridge, declared that the cave-ins could have been worked out and the trapped man reached "if they had only kept at it." Mrs. Ben Monroe, later a motel owner on the road to Mammoth, asserted that Floyd could have been taken out at any time, "but they was afraid." She contended that the rescuers' own fears prevented them from freeing him.

Other cave country opinion was similarly argumentative or

caustic. Many in the area continued to condemn the military. They castigated Governor Fields and General Denhardt for intervening in a local situation and claimed that the state of Kentucky deserved no credit for its role in the affair. In an editorial on February 18, entitled "Didn't Need the Soldiers," the *Park City Daily News* stated that "the civil authorities could have easily managed the situation without them." The military merely made "confusion more confounded." Although a hero to some, Superintendent Carmichael came in for his share of the blame. Numerous natives believed that he was "too slow and not experienced enough in cave work." Dr. Hazlett also was criticized. Why, some residents asked, was it necessary to have had a high-priced doctor come all the way from Chicago? Were not local physicians good enough? As for the expense entailed in the rescue operation, most cave country inhabitants shook their heads. The total cost was estimated at $200,000. Kentucky's bill for the soldiers was put at $75,000. Carmichael set the price of the shaft at $50,000. Slightly more than $1500 a day was spent on communications, and the fees of the pilots and charges for the airplanes came to over $10,000 alone. To cave country residents, such sums were astronomical.

Further, at the very moment the remainder of the nation was clasping Floyd to its bosom, many in the cave country were being far more objective about him. "It ought never to have happened," said one lanky farmer when quizzed about Floyd's culpability in the tragedy. "Floyd was a caving fool. Not even a varmint would have gone down that hole." Carl Hanson, an experienced Mammoth Cave guide, put it bluntly: "Floyd wasn't too bright. If he'd known anything about caves, he wouldn't have been where he was." All of the region's experienced cavers agreed that Floyd had helped make his own grave by going where it was not within the power of anyone to rescue him. In an editorial entitled "The Reason Why," the *Louisville Herald* on February 18 displayed something of this attitude when it said: "But the plain fact is Floyd Collins, for whom others were willing to risk their lives, [thought] he could win a victory from Nature and paid the price of the foolhardy."

Whatever were the opinions held in the cave country concerning Floyd Collins's errors or of the shortcomings of the rescue attempt, natives as well as outlanders could readily agree on one thing—it had been a truly sensational event. Most claimed that it had no equal in their lifetimes. More than one newspaper maintained that it was "the most remarkable news story of this, or any other age." The impact of that story and the reasons for all the public interest naturally remained major subjects for analysis and debate. The Louisville *Courier-Journal,* itself one of the prime movers in stimulating that public interest, explained it best in writing its own epitaph to the Collins story:

> . . . It is not that news of the day has not revealed many tragedies of far greater peril and destruction of human life. Peopled ships have been swallowed up by the sea. Miners by the scores and hundreds have been imprisoned in the bowels of the earth. Fires and floods have swept populated areas. Volcanoes have blighted countrysides and cities. Earthquakes have devastated miles of inhabited territory. But none of these calamities has so riveted and held poignant a universal interest as the fight for this single life in a Kentucky cave.
>
> . . . [the outcome] was so awaited and watched because the world is a world of human beings and every fellow-being with a spark of imagination could and did put himself in that man's place. . . . That is why millions day after day hung upon the reports from the scene of the horror; why the newspapers far and wide were alert to present all tidings about it that could be obtained; why thousands of miles away they issued extras to keep their readers posted as to what was going on in a remote spot in Kentucky which they had never before heard of. That is why the story of Floyd Collins as unfolded for seventeen days in the press of the country was a continued news serial of the most sustained enthrallment of any story ever printed.

# 10

## Making of a Legend

In an editorial on February 18, 1925, the *Park City Daily News* said of the Collins tragedy: "In a few weeks the people will stop talking about it. We are prone to forget the dead. . . . So it will be with Floyd Collins."

The *Daily News*'s prophecy quickly rang true. On February 18, Cave City was almost deserted. The exciting days were over as well as the profits that had accompanied them. As one citizen remarked, "Back to the dullness of the daily round." Taxi drivers and their cabs were missing from the streets. At the L & N depot, the Pan American and other trains that had been stopping for two weeks now rocketed through. Of the many visitors who had roamed the halls of the Dixie Hotel, only one outsider remained—a theatrical producer who hoped to sign Alma Clark to a stage contract. The telegraph instruments that rattled away in the lobby were gone. The stairway that sagged under the traffic was empty. The extra

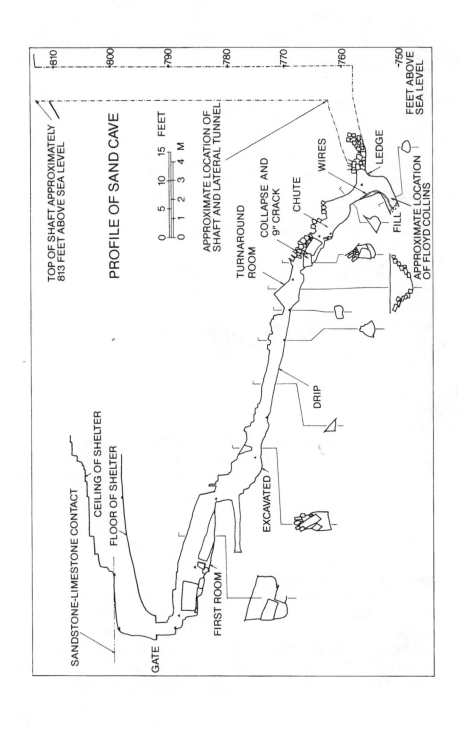

PROFILE OF SAND CAVE

TOP OF SHAFT APPROXIMATELY
813 FEET ABOVE SEA LEVEL

FEET

0     5     10     15
M
0   1   2   3   4

SANDSTONE-LIMESTONE CONTACT

CEILING OF SHELTER

FLOOR OF SHELTER

GATE

FIRST ROOM

EXCAVATED

DRIP

TURNAROUND
ROOM

COLLAPSE AND
9" CRACK

CHUTE

WIRES

LEDGE

FILL

APPROXIMATE LOCATION OF
SHAFT AND LATERAL TUNNEL

APPROXIMATE LOCATION
OF FLOYD COLLINS

FEET ABOVE
SEA LEVEL

810
800
790
780
770
760
750

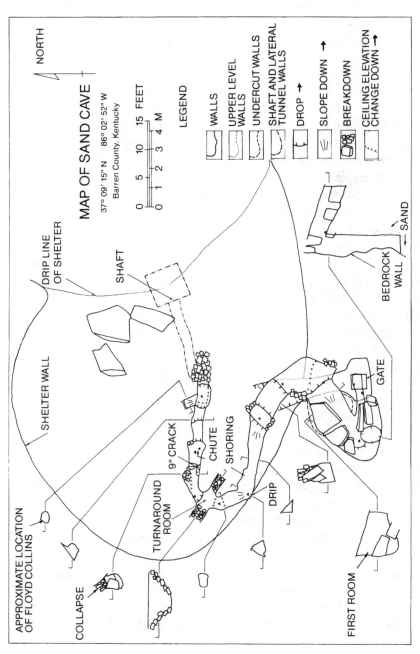

Plan and profile views of Sand Cave. The profile shows vertical relationships by stretching out the cave. Horizontal and vertical distances are accurate. The plan and vertical profile together provide a three-dimensional description of Sand Cave.

wires running across the ceiling were down. Standing on a clock behind the desk in full view was a small placard on which some sentimental newsman had printed the copy finish symbol: *-30-*.

The Collins story was finished. As the *Louisville Herald* phrased it on the day after Floyd's body was found, "Ring down the curtain! Bring on the next article. That is the way of the world." The press did drop the subject abruptly. On February 19, the *Chicago Tribune*'s headline read, "AIR CHIEF ON CARPET TODAY," referring to General William L. Mitchell's running argument with the navy over the effectiveness of airplanes versus battleships. This significant struggle had been pushed off the front pages by the Sand Cave tragedy but was now making its way back. On this same day, February 19, the Louisville *Courier-Journal* carried barely a word about Floyd on its front page. Already the *Evening Post* had returned to its habitual headlines, the top two on that Thursday being: "'LOST LOVE' SUIT FOUND AFTER KICK" and "POWELL DIES VICTIM OF A BOOZE ROW." The first involved a juicy love triangle and the second a bootleg scandal. As a matter of fact, only infrequently did any of the nation's newspapers further mention Floyd's name, and then primarily in connection with some other freak underground accident when the victim was said to be "doing a Floyd Collins."

America's greatest rescue story had indeed ended, but the legend of Floyd Collins had just begun. His name may not have continued in the press, but it was kept alive elsewhere and by other means. Immediately following his death, the citizens of Cave City pledged $1000 to erect "some kind of suitable memorial" to his memory. Edward Estes vowed to construct a Floyd Collins shrine somewhere on his property that people could come and see. If he charged a fee, Estes said, it would be for a Floyd Collins memorial fund. Less than a week after Floyd's death, Bee Doyle offered an option on his farm to two Owensboro tobacco dealers who wanted to find a new way into Floyd's tomb, rediscover his "fabulous cavern," and open it to the public. Their plans called for a tourist camp and the erection of a hotel. However, when the Owensboro men got ready to close the deal, they found that the Doyle deed could not be cleared because of several infant heirs. Undaunted, Doyle decided to capitalize on Sand Cave himself, charging visiting tourists a fee for treading on his land. He erected a ticket office—one room encircled by a veranda—just off the road near Sand Cave. Sitting there, he collected fifty cents from each person who wished to see where Collins had lost his life. Near the office he placed a large sign: "200 YARDS AWAY THE BODY OF FLOYD COLLINS IS IMPRISONED IN SAND CAVE." When asked by reporters in mid-April how he was doing, Doyle said, "Not so bad." Actually, his business was never too brisk, although some in the cave country claimed that he made $7000 showing the site.

The immediate aftermath of the Collins tragedy affected other rescue participants in a variety of ways. General Denhardt returned to his duties as Kentucky's lieutenant governor but was sufficiently proud of his Sand Cave work to include in his 1926 biography in *Who's Who in America* the phrase: "Had charge of rescue of Floyd Collins, cave explorer, 1925." Professor Funkhouser went back to the University of Kentucky, where later in 1925 he became dean of the graduate school. Occasionally called upon to make a speech on the Sand Cave affair, he always emphasized the hopes and fears of those working at the rescue site and the heartbreaking nature of their task. Superintendent Carmichael left Sand Cave in February 1925 a weary man, frustrated that a successful rescue had not been achieved. Resuming his job at Kyroc, he was much in demand as an after-dinner speaker and used a blackboard and a clay model of the shaft, with a little derrick and bucket attached, to explain to audiences the difficult rescue problems involved.

More than any other person, Skeets Miller had his life altered by what had happened at Sand Cave. Returning to Louisville after the tragedy, he turned down a $50,000 offer to join the Chautauqua lecture circuit, electing instead to remain with the *Courier-Journal*. In appreciation for his work at the cave, and for staying with the paper, it ultimately gave him a testimonial dinner and a $1000 check. Then on May 4, 1926, Miller won the Pulitzer Prize for the best reporting of the previous year. One of the youngest Pulitzer winners in history, he immediately became a marked man, his future in American journalism assured.

Not all rescue participants exercised as much restraint as Miller when it came to making money out of their Sand Cave experiences. A number of rescue workers, such as Albert Marshall (the ex-

miner), Bill Takasy (the Dayton harmonica player), and Eddie
Bray (the "fighter"), quickly set off on vaudeville tours. Displaying
hammers, spades, flashlights, and jacks they claimed had been used
in the rescue work, they made the rounds of small movie houses in
Kentucky, Tennessee, Indiana, Illinois, and Ohio, elaborating on
their rescue activities. Most of them flopped after only a few weeks
and the remainder saw their bookings steadily decline as public
interest in the tragedy flagged.

The days and months immediately following the Sand Cave affair
were difficult ones for the Collins family. From the beginning,
Homer disagreed with Lee's decision to leave Floyd's body in the
cave and announced shortly after the site was closed that he
intended to raise money to bring it to the surface. To secure the
necessary funds, Homer appeared before theater audiences all over
the nation for the next eight months, telling them of his life in the
cave country, the entrapment of his brother, and his attempt to free
him. His talk was accompanied by stereopticon slides and a film of
the rescue which, according to one publicity flyer, brought home to
his listeners "all the horrifying experiences endured during that
frightening cave imprisonment." For these appearances Homer was
paid $500 per week. Actually, he cleared far less than that,
sometimes only $50 and expenses. Still, his savings slowly mounted.

If Homer's immediate post–Sand Cave activities were moderately
successful, Lee's were a disaster. The Collins Rescue Fund, which
banker Sam Caldwell had supervised, amounted to $3756.91. Most
of this was spent for rescue clothing and operational costs. The
remainder was gobbled up by the final site-clearing expenses. To
Lee's dismay, there was nothing left. Two days after the last worker
and soldier had gone, he was seen roaming the rescue area picking
up pop bottles to redeem for cash. Simultaneously, he began
advertising Crystal Cave as "Floyd Collins Crystal Cave" in the
hope of attracting more visitors to it. Then, in the first week of
March, Lee, too, went on the stage.

Lee's vaudeville act was short-lived. Opening at Louisville's
Gayety Theater, where he told his story for one week, he
subsequently had few other engagements. Marshall later claimed
that agents "made a monkey" out of his father and that the old man
was losing his grip on reality. One observer who saw his perfor-

mance recalled that Lee came out, "gawked at the audience, and the audience gawked back. . . . A sad thing." During his vaudeville career, Lee's path crossed once with Homer's and intensified the growing feud between them. When the Indiana State Fair opened in Indianapolis in September 1925 Lee was there as one of the attractions in a sideshow. Arriving in the same town shortly afterward to appear at a movie theater, Homer attempted to have the old man's act closed down because, he said, Lee was soliciting money under false pretenses. Lee was currently asking for contributions to pay off a mortgage on the Collins house that he claimed he had taken to raise funds for the rescue effort. His father was a disgrace and a liar, said Homer, because there was no such mortgage.

Long before September, the Collinses had already begun a round-robin series of squabbles and family lawsuits that threatened to convert Floyd's death into an opera bouffe. On February 25, scarcely a week after the funeral, the three brothers, Marshall, Homer, and Andy Lee, filed petitions in the Hart County court to have their father disqualified as administrator of Floyd's estate. In the ensuing hearings, they claimed that Lee was *non compos mentis* and could not act wisely in managing Floyd's half of Crystal, which had automatically reverted to him. The main reason for their concern was Lee's continued desire to sell the cave. The three brothers wanted him to retain it, convinced that the publicity surrounding Floyd's entrapment and death would now make it profitable. Whatever the reasons, Judge C.E. Nichols, after taking testimony from eight witnesses, ordered that Lee be removed temporarily as estate administrator and the Union Trust Company of Glasgow be substituted.

Acting on his earlier promise, Homer negotiated on March 11, 1925, a contract with W.H. Hunt, a miner from Central City, to remove Floyd's body from Sand Cave. Aided by six other miners, Hunt began digging on April 4 and rapidly worked his way down into the old Carmichael shaft. He found the first twenty feet of timbering in good condition, and even below that level only minor repairs were necessary. The sinking had ceased; the rocks and logs that had been thrown in had apparently prevented the shaft's sides from buckling further. On April 10, Hunt hit the bottom, but then the recovery work slowed when he discovered that the lateral tunnel had collapsed completely. Hunt finally decided to dig the main shaft ten feet deeper and send off a new lateral to intersect below and behind Floyd's body.

On April 17, at the sixty-four-foot level, Hunt's miners came to the edge of the deep cavern that Floyd had found. No one climbed down into it, but enough was seen by probing flashlights to indicate there was no "beautiful cave" here. Shortly thereafter, the men came upon Floyd's corpse. They found that the rock trapping Floyd's left ankle was shaped like a leg of lamb and was broken on its smaller end where it had been attached to the crevice ceiling. Estimated at first to weigh between fifty and seventy-five pounds, when placed on the scales it actually weighed only twenty-seven. Bee Doyle immediately claimed it as part of his "property" and began displaying it, along with Floyd's left shoe, as an additional tourist attraction at his Sand Cave ticket office.

When Floyd's body was raised to the surface on April 23, a tearless group watched. Spending emotion on Collins was no longer in style. Only twenty-five cars were present and about a hundred people. Wrapped in a cloth, the body was hoisted to the surface by a hook and lowered onto a stretcher made by two poles run through the sleeves of a miner's blue-denim jacket. To record the event, Hunt and his workmen gathered around it for photographs. "I hope I parted my hair," quipped one of the latter, uncovering his bald head at the suggestion that he remove his hat. Then, before the body was carried away, Hunt exclaimed, "Wait a minute. I don't want anybody to leave saying we brought up a chunk wrapped in rags and called it Collins." Two men quickly stepped forward with pen knives and slit the dirty cloth to reveal Floyd's face. All who were present were requested to file past and look at it. For those who knew Floyd, the gold tooth was identification enough.

After this viewing, the corpse was placed in a wicker basket and taken to Cave City for embalming. The undertaker in charge was J.T. Geralds, Johnnie's uncle, who, unlike his nephew, spelled his last name with an "s." It was a delicate operation. Although the conditions in Sand Cave had helped preserve the body, it was beginning to decompose. Cave crickets had eaten off the ears and part of the face. Three days were required to perform a reasonable restoration. Undertaker Geralds later said that he found only one small turd in Floyd's pants, casting doubt on the testimony of those rescuers who had maintained that there was a foul stench in Floyd's prison chamber. Geralds also discovered on Floyd's person the compass needle that he habitually carried to enhance his "body magnetism," and a bank book showing he had $1900 in a Cave City bank. The latter smelled like a dead body and, even after being kept for two months in the bank's vault, still had not lost its odor when it was finally presented for payment.

On Sunday, April 26, 1925, after having already spent three months in the ground, Floyd Collins received a second, and proper, burial. This time there was both a casket and a corpse. Six pallbearers wore elaborate sashes on their arms emblazoned with the words SAND CAVE. An estimated four hundred persons gathered in the rain on a small knoll overlooking Crystal Cave to hear the brief funeral service. Placed in a grave beside the Flint Ridge family homestead and near the path to Crystal, Floyd's body at last lay where his brothers wanted it to be. The spot was marked by a splendid huge stalagmite.

Although the Collins tragedy brought national attention to the Kentucky cave country, it also created an interesting backlash. The question was inevitably asked: Were the Kentucky caves really safe? Mammoth and other commercial cave interests in the area spent much of their time during the Collins affair asserting that the Sand Cave incident was a "freak" and that the average American would be safer in Kentucky's caves "than on the main street of his hometown."

Despite such efforts, the tourist trade was temporarily adversely affected, with the smaller commercial caves suffering the most. Lacking the resiliency or the reputation of Mammoth, they found it increasingly difficult to attract patrons to their sites. By 1926, Bee Doyle no longer sat in his chair in his ticket booth at Sand Cave— there were too few visitors to bother about. Even Crystal, now widely advertised as Floyd Collins Crystal Cave, was hurt by the post-rescue slump. As a result, Lee, who had never given up wanting to sell the cave, by late 1926 was anxious to unload it for almost any price.

Lee's mind at the moment was on other things anyway. On February 13, 1926, exactly one year to the day after Floyd had allegedly died, Miss Jane passed away. Known for his roving eye and his interest in the ladies, particularly younger ladies, Lee did not seem too grieved. Indeed, less than three months later he announced that he was going to marry again—this time a forty-year-old woman, the "widow Ebinger," whose first name he could not recall. Inviting everyone he knew to the wedding, Lee was pleased when a large crowd of curiosity seekers jammed the Jefferson County Courthouse in Louisville to see the knot tied in late May. "Crowds don't embarrass me," he commented to reporters afterward. "All these people were welcome to watch my wedding. Now they can all come to Crystal Cave and I'll show them through."

In 1927, Lee accepted an offer from Dr. Harry B. Thomas, a dentist in Horse Cave, to take Crystal off his hands for $10,000. Dr. Thomas already owned two other commercial caves in the region—Hidden River Cave and Mammoth Onyx Cave. In the transfer, Dr. Thomas was authorized to move Floyd's body into Crystal if he wished, giving it a new resting place. Lee, who later claimed that his only aim was to get enough money to keep him out of the county home, made this deal without consulting his children or seeking legal advice. The Collins's neighbors, among them William Travis Blair, subsequently maintained that Dr. Thomas took advantage of Lee's advancing senility to trick this arrangement out of him.

Dr. Thomas's motives were certainly clear. An innovator who had pioneered the electrification of the local commercial caves, he calculated that the combination of the light bulb and the showing of Floyd's casket would make Crystal a real moneymaker. Never, however, did Dr. Thomas admit that the removal of Floyd's body to the cave was for commercial purposes. Rather it was to place it where Floyd would have wanted it—inside Floyd's own cave. All the dentist would ever say was, "It's there if anybody wants to see it."

Dr. Thomas made it easy. After poor Floyd was again dug up, he was put in a glass-covered bronzed metal coffin. Again, considerable remedial work was necessary to make his corpse presentable.

Then, on June 13, 1927, with suitable publicity, Floyd's new casket was plunked down in the middle of the tourist trail in Crystal's main concourse where visitors could pass by and look in at him. Placed at his head was a large red granite tombstone which read:

WILLIAM FLOYD COLLINS
born July 20, 1887
buried April 26, 1925
Trapped in Sand Cave Jan. 30, 1925
Discovered Crystal Cave Jan. 18, 1917
Greatest Cave Explorer Ever Known

It was ghoulish, but it was effective. Hundreds now flocked to see Floyd, and in death he became his cave's most successful solicitor. Guides lectured solemnly about the exploits of the "world's greatest cave explorer" as their listeners stared at the white waxed face, the black-suited body, and the glove-encased hands.

Floyd's three brothers were dismayed by this development and sought legal redress. In late June, they sued Dr. Thomas for $50,000 for illegally acquiring the cave and Floyd's corpse. For the next two years wrangling between the Horse Cave dentist and the Collinses reverberated through the courts. Finally, in 1929, a decision was reached by Circuit Judge Porter Sims, who used Lee's own testimony to declare that both the cave and Floyd's body had been legally obtained without duress by Dr. Thomas. Much to the anguish of Floyd's brothers, Floyd's body remained in Crystal Cave.

But not always. Sometime on the night of March 18–19, 1929, his corpse was snatched from its glass enclosure and spirited away by a person or persons unknown. Discovering the theft at nine o'clock the next morning, Dr. Thomas sought help from the authorities of the three surrounding counties. The casket was dusted for fingerprints, and bloodhounds, after being given Floyd's scent, were sent scurrying through the countryside. Before the day was over, Floyd's body with its left leg missing was discovered no farther than eight hundred yards from the cave, wrapped in a gunny sack and half hidden in brush on the edge of the Green River. The following day, March 20, the peripatetic corpse was back in its coffin. The thieves were never apprehended and the missing leg was never found.

Dr. Thomas said he could not guess the motives of the body snatchers. But there were others who could. A few natives believed that Dr. Thomas himself had ordered the body stolen in order to stimulate the cave's tourist trade. Others maintained that jealous competitors, particularly the Great Onyx crowd, had taken the corpse hoping to hurt Crystal's business. Still others, and they seemed to be in the majority, speculated that Homer Collins had paid to have his body snatched but that the hirelings had dropped it along the way.

Whatever the truth of the matter, Dr. Thomas chose not to take any further chances with Floyd's roving corpse. Thereafter he locked the cave at night and closed a metal coffin lid over the glass cover. Although Floyd was no longer continuously displayed, tourists were still asked to pause respectfully at his casket as guides gave them a short spiel on his caving prowess. As late as 1952, interested visitors were still permitted a peek under the metal lid— for the proper tip, of course. Seeing a body inside, they were left to wonder whether it was really Floyd. "Sure it is," the guide would say, adding cryptically, "Floyd's wore out three coffins already." His coffin had, in fact, been replaced several times.

The publicity surrounding Floyd's various burials and the kidnapping of his body added new sensational and bizarre angles to the Collins tragedy. It also restimulated interest in the central Kentucky caves and helped touch off renewed cave wars. By the close of the 1920s no less than fifteen different caves were again competing for customers, with Dr. Thomas and Crystal leading in imaginative ways. Such competition raged with varying intensity for the next twenty-five years. When the prosperous days of the late twenties gave way to the depression years, the commercial caves worked even harder to capture their share of the tourist market. During World War II, some were forced for a time to abandon their activities while a few, such as Crystal, stayed alive by visits from Fort Knox soldiers. Then, immediately following the war, they viciously resumed their conflict as they sought to command a slice of the increased trade brought about by easier travel and a more mobile national population.

The decade of the 1950s saw the bitterest struggles yet between the competing caves in the central Kentucky region. As one oldster observed at the time, "It's a war, brother. Only difference between it and regular war is that they ain't killin' nobody." Sometimes it was close. Shots were exchanged and serious threats were made. Mainly, though, cave solicitors peaceably prowled the streets of Cave City, Horse Cave, and Park City watching for prospects and claiming their particular cavern was "the grandest of them all." In hawking for Floyd Collins Crystal Cave, Dr. Thomas's solicitors would ridicule its smaller rivals by stating, "My God, you could set that there thing in the main room in Crystal and still need a flashlight to hunt it."

As in the earlier period, tricks were played and property destroyed. Cave owners sent their agents out on the road in cars with out-of-state license plates to learn the pitch of rival solicitors. Signs pointing to enemy caves were torn down or the directional arrows turned around. "High winds" or "faulty flues" were claimed to be responsible for missing or burned-out ticket offices when the real causes lay elsewhere. As for ruses, cave country ingenuity knew no bounds. An agent might stand off a hundred yards or so from a legitimate repair crew working on a rival cave's access road, stop every arriving car, and send them back the way they came. Another might drive up the road leading to an enemy cave, pull off in a mudhole up to the car's axles, and inform everyone else passing by that this would also happen to them if they continued on. One favorite ploy was to tell a tourist who stopped to inquire about the entrance to Mammoth, "It's the first entrance just a mile up the road, friend." Of course, it was the solicitor's own cave.

Ironically, at the very time the Kentucky cave wars were reaching their zenith, Mammoth Cave, the historic *bête noire* of all the other commercial ventures, was leaving the private competitive scene. The groundwork for this development had been laid at the time of Floyd Collins's death. People were just then beginning to talk of a national park in central Kentucky. Two years before (1923), the national government had set aside Carlsbad Caverns in New Mexico as a national monument, and advocates of the Kentucky cave region believed that their claims were just as good. Strange as it may seem, Floyd's entrapment actually fed enthusiasm for a national park in the area. Many saw in Floyd's death an omen—a

sign that pointed toward placing all the central Kentucky caves
under government management. Indeed, a major highway, to be
called The Floyd Collins Highway, was proposed to provide easy
access for the rest of the nation to the cave region. Less than a week
after his death, the Louisville *Courier-Journal* wrote editorially:
"Floyd Collins has brought Kentucky before the world. He will not
have died in vain if you open the cave country, his country, to the
people of the United States."

In 1926, when the last of the original Croghan heirs died, plans
were laid for the eventual government takeover of at least
Mammoth Cave. In May of that year, President Calvin Coolidge
signed a bill authorizing the creation of a Mammoth Cave National
Park with the understanding that no less than 20,000 acres of
surrounding land would be donated to the government for that
purpose. Shortly thereafter, the Mammoth Cave National Park
Association, a private subscription organization, was formed to buy
up land and to clear titles. To aid it in doing so, the legislature of
Kentucky created a Kentucky National Park Commission which
was empowered to go to court to condemn property that the
association was unable to secure by voluntary means.

Gradually a park took shape. The old historic entrance to
Mammoth was acquired in 1930. In 1931, George Morrison sold his
New Entrance to the government. By 1941, over seven hundred
deeds, including the titles to Colossal and Salts caves, had been
liquidated and the park stood at 50,696 acres. This land roundup
was not accomplished without hard feelings and much animosity.
Most of the park land was bought at depression prices (thirty
dollars an acre instead of the normal sixty dollars) as hard-pressed
farmers were taken advantage of. Further, legal condemnation
action and forceable ejection of some families were necessary. In
the end, over two thousand persons were displaced, and the
abandonment of homes, churches, and schools was difficult for
many of them to accept. Even those who voluntarily surrendered
their property felt that they had been robbed of it.

Although Mammoth Cave was accorded full national park status
on July 1, 1941, its formal dedication waited until the end of World
War II when, on September 18, 1946, it became the nation's
twenty-sixth national park. In this transition, many of the cave's

guides and most of the cave's practices and routes were retained by the government. Actually, many of the surnames that are on the Mammoth Cave payroll today have been there for over a century. But some names are missing. As long as the cave remained under private management, black guides outnumbered white guides three to one. When the government took full control in 1941, all of the blacks were "furloughed." Black natives, many of whom had already been removed from their own community and lands by the government takeover, hated the national park all the more for this discriminatory action.

Aside from the various factors involved in the government's acquisition of Mammoth, one constant remained—the desire to make the cave a financial success. To this end, the National Park Service continued to charge a substantial entrance fee. Moreover, it kept all other government-owned caves within the boundaries of the park (such as Colossal and Salts) closed to the public and noncompetitive with Mammoth. But two caves—Great Onyx and Floyd Collins Crystal Cave—still remained open because the government did not own them yet. In the liquidation of the park's deeds and titles, the owners of these two caves had successfully escaped government control. As a result, they still fought for a share of the cave tourist business—for a portion of the half-million visitors who by 1952 were annually streaming into Mammoth Cave National Park.

The cave wars of the 1950s, therefore, involved Mammoth even though it was no longer privately owned or operated. Now a new facet was added to the cave war struggle: The private cave owners fought against a government takeover. In that fight they rarely overlooked any tactic to protect their interests. They encouraged their solicitors to dress in khaki and to wear guide caps or Smokey Bear hats to trick tourists bent on entering the park. Billboards advertising their caves sported the official National Park Service green. Driving along the main highway to Mammoth in the mid-fifties, one would see trim little huts flying American flags that could easily be mistaken for official ranger stations. But inside sat military-garbed private solicitors, blending blarney and hard-sell to detour Mammoth visitors to their own enterprises.

Naturally, the National Park Service detested these private

caves, and national park administrators constantly sought ways to eliminate them or negate their influence. Great Onyx and Floyd Collins Crystal Cave not only remained in direct competition with Mammoth but were a threat to bureaucratic survival. These two caves ate up maintenance appropriations by using the roads and general resources supplied by the government for the park. Also, the success of these caves had a direct bearing on the salaries of the employees at Mammoth. The park was subsidized and administrators paid according to the number of tourists it attracted each year. The fewer the tourists, the lower the park rating. Then, too, the more tourists at the private caves, the fewer the patrons at Mammoth to buy souvenirs and other concession items.

But the two remaining caves within the park boundaries continued to hang on despite all the National Park Service could do and, as late as 1959, within sight of the government-owned concession-operated Mammoth Cave Hotel a sign read: "Privately-Owned Floyd Collins Crystal Cave 4 miles."

On February 4, 1925, in the middle of the Collins tragedy, the *Chicago Tribune* quoted A.J. Musselman, a friend of Floyd's, as saying, "Floyd has the theory that all the caves of the district, Mammoth Cave, Colossal Cavern, Onyx Cave, Sand Cave, and the hundreds of others of lesser importance, are connected by passageways." Thirty years later, Matthew Bransford, a third generation guide at Mammoth, declared to an interviewer, "It's all one system. Just like a river, its branches are all connected."

The idea of cave connections had intrigued residents of the Kentucky cave country for almost a century, and neither the death of its primary exponent, Floyd Collins, nor the acquisition of much of the land by the National Park Service stopped such speculation. These two events, however, did drastically affect explorations leading to the finding of connections. The Collins tragedy understandably put a damper on enthusiasm for deep underground discovery, and for the next thirty years only isolated forays were mounted into the caves' inner recesses. Then, when the Park Service took over Mammoth and nearby caverns in 1941, it placed an official ban on such explorations, declaring everything in the government-owned caves off limits except for the regular Mammoth tourist trails. This government action was based on two related motives. First, no park superintendent relished the thought of a repetition of the seventeen-day circus surrounding the Collins affair. Second, the uncovering of a connection between Mammoth and any of the other caves in the area, especially the two remaining privately owned ones, would lessen the importance of Mammoth, inflate the value of the connecting caves, and make their ultimate acquisition by the government much more difficult.

In the same year that the government acquired Mammoth (1941), the National Speleological Society was founded. Refusal to permit underground exploration in Mammoth Cave National Park immediately conflicted with the society's aims, and it sought the means either to force government officials to change their minds or to circumvent their antiexploration edict. When the National Park Service remained adamant in its stand, the society turned to the owners of the two private caves—Great Onyx and Floyd Collins Crystal Cave (now known to cavers simply as FCCC)—for help in determining the extent of the region's cave system. Ultimately, the Great Onyx management decided to refuse exploration except to a handful of trusted friends. After more than a decade of vacillation, Crystal's owners proved more amenable, and in 1953 they opened their cave to scientific examination.

It was fitting that Floyd Collins's own cave became the base from which modern underground exploration of the Central Kentucky Karst radiated. The motive on the part of the cave's management was partly personal, partly scientific, and partly commercial. Exploration and scientific curiosity was in their blood, but they also foresaw publicity and monetary advantages in such a development. Should a connection with Mammoth be found, the value of FCCC would soar and the government would be placed in the position of having to buy it at a reasonable, if not inflated, price. Even if such a connection were not discovered, the publicity would help Crystal's tourist business.

Prior to 1953, when permission was given to the National Speleological Society to explore in Crystal, some mapping of the cave's passages had been undertaken by such local cavers as Luther Miller, William T. Austin, and James W. Dyer (Crystal's resident manager). But after the 1953 agreement, expert cavers from all over the country were drawn to Crystal like a magnet. Many admitted that their interest was heightened by the spirit of Floyd Collins, and most were fascinated by the prospect of proving his connections theory. The society, itself, sponsored an elaborate, highly publicized underground expedition in 1954 not only to map Crystal's passages but to uncover such connections. Known as the C-3 expedition (for Collins Crystal Cave), a group of thirty-two men and women worked underground from Valentine's Day, Sunday, February 14, until Saturday, February 20. Their entry date was almost twenty-nine years to the day after Floyd Collins's death.

How different this 1954 assault was from Floyd's lonely journeys! Nourishing food, cooking stoves, sleeping bags, spare parts, extra helmets and light, and even switchboards and telephones accompanied the expedition into the depths. Yet for the individual explorer out at the forward edge, the loneliness, isolation, and danger were still the same. There the basic tools were no different than those available to Floyd—hands, feet, rope, and carbide lamp. The explorers sometimes joked that Floyd's ghost was following them, calling out: "Wait for me!" Some of the cavers did not relish such talk, and all members of the expedition fell strangely silent when they were in the vicinity of Floyd's casket.

The C-3 expedition made a number of new discoveries and ended with an up-to-date map of Crystal's many passages. But connections with the surrounding caves were not uncovered. New probings for these were thereafter undertaken only by small groups of volunteers on a weekend or holiday basis. Such persistent efforts ultimately paid off when, in September 1955, a first connection was found. A small party, crawling in a remote passage, suddenly discovered a connecting route between Unknown Cave and Crystal Cave. This immeasurably added to the belief that other connections would surely be found. Now fully alive to the monetary possibilities, the management of Crystal enthusiastically cooperated in further efforts. Indeed, in 1957, Crystal's former manager, James Dyer, was one of the incorporators of an organization of elite cavers, called the Cave Research Foundation, which had as a specific goal the systematic discovery of such connections. The National Park Service, meanwhile, feeling both pressure and acute embarrassment from these developments, finally signed an agreement in 1959 with the Cave Research Foundation, permitting scientific research, including exploration, in all the region's government-owned caverns.

Progress was now rapid. In August 1960, under the auspices of the Cave Research Foundation, a second connection was discovered—this one between Colossal and Salts. Then, a year later, a third connection was found, tying these two caves into the Unknown/Crystal system. This same year (1961) also saw an end to the private cave problem. Great Onyx, which at no time had encouraged exploration on its property, was sold to the government. Lucy Cox, who had inherited the cave from her father, Reverend Edwards, reaped a $325,000 bonanza. After the sale, Cave Research Foundation teams immediately made their way into the cave's depths while the National Park Service closed it to the general public. Also, in 1961, Floyd Collins Crystal Cave was sold to the government—for $285,000—by its owners, Mrs. Carrie B. Thomas (Dr. Thomas's widow) and her two daughters, Mary Thomas Chaney and Ruth Thomas Pohl. Thereafter experienced cavers continued to go into FCCC, but it, too, like Great Onyx, was closed to the public.

Certainly the prospect of further connections boosted the price of these two private caves and encouraged the government to hurry to buy them. A final connection with Mammoth seemed just a matter of time, and government purchase was the only feasible solution. With these two purchases completed, Mammoth was finally left with no other competitors, having outlasted them all. Floyd Collins, meanwhile, must have stirred in his casket over the FCCC sale price of $285,000 cash. It was the kind of fortune that he had sought and was a far cry from the $1900 he had in the bank at the time of his death. Likewise, the ghost of Lee Collins must have shaken its head, wherever it was, as it remembered dreams of riches and the stark reality of gathering up pop bottles.

As for the final connection, it was not made until eleven years later. During the intervening time, myriad teams of cavers probed toward each other in both FCCC and Mammoth, reporting their findings to the Cave Research Foundation and adding to the miles of passages already marked on its maps. In the meantime, the old Collins homestead on Flint Ridge was converted into a bunkhouse for these underground explorers who sought to find in the caves' lower levels mud-encrusted passageways that branched out toward the Green River and served as interconnecting drainage tunnels for both Flint Ridge and Mammoth Cave Ridge. Finally, on September 9, 1972, one exhausted but jubilant team of six persons conquered "the Everest of world speleology" by leaving the Collins homestead bunkhouse on Flint Ridge and fifteen hours later emerging on Mammoth Cave Ridge from the elevator rising out of the Snowball Dining Room of Mammoth Cave. At that moment the Flint Mammoth Cave System, as it was thereafter called, became the longest cave in the world—144.4 miles.

Floyd Collins, were he alive, would have been pleased.

In assessing the significance of the Collins tragedy in mid-February, 1925, the *Louisville Herald* editorialized: "As the years progress and the story becomes embellished and embroidered, Floyd Collins may grow into a legend, a fable."

As the years have passed with their reburials and body snatchings, renewed cave wars, national park developments, and cave connections, the Collins story has indeed taken on the aspects of a modern legend. Floyd's own generation started the process by carrying to their deaths an exaggerated image of what had happened at Sand Cave and bequeathing to their progeny the framework for unlimited variations thereon. And, like Annie Oakley and Buffalo Bill, Floyd Collins did gradually metamorphose into a fabled figure. Floyd, however, remains unique. The central personalities in most legends are remembered for how they lived. Collins is remembered for how he died.

Legends are not easily begun. The contemporary circumstances must be right and the proper ingredients present. America during the 1920s was a silly, immature society. It gaped at flagpole sitters and worshipped less than competent actors on the silent screen. It fell for such strange movements as Couéism that had people murmuring to themselves "Every day in every way I am getting better and better." And it made superhuman heroes out of sports figures and aviators—Red Grange, Babe Ruth, Charles Lindbergh. Actually, the 1920s was a floodtime for heroes. Perhaps the rapid economic growth and the drastic social and cultural changes that characterized the period forced the nation to create them. Certainly the abounding materialism and the changing moral patterns made Americans feel a bit guilty as they looked back over their shoulders at their more sober puritanical past. Heroes, after all, could be endowed with the older historic virtues of thrift, strength of character, and godliness.

Floyd Collins was such a hero, and the sensational aspects of his situation fit the pattern of the other "events" of the Roaring Decade—the rush of antitoxin to Nome, the Loeb-Leopold murder of Bobby Franks, the disappearance of Aimee Semple McPherson, the Hall-Mills murder trial, and so on. Yet there were subtleties in the Collins case that made it unusual. The decade of the twenties was a time of intense social and cultural insecurity involving the erosion of status and the decline in political control by the older native Protestant stock. Floyd's entrapment in Sand Cave provided these Americans with a source of identification as well as a point of comparison. In contrast to Floyd, they were still relatively "safe." Yet his tragedy was a harbinger of things to come. Especially in the Klan-infested and Klan-dominated areas of the Midwest and South, Floyd Collins became a symbol. Not just by coincidence the widest and most penetrating coverage of the Sand Cave event was conducted by the press in these two regions. Floyd's precarious situation created in their inhabitants a strong bond of commonality with him—a feeling of being threatened and even trapped by forces over which they no longer had control.

There were other subtle factors operating in the Collins story. The nation was rapidly moving to an urban setting and was leaving its rural past behind. The Collins affair offered a psychological respite from this headlong rush. It appealed to nostalgia since it involved country folk. Also, as the nation was becoming more Roman Catholic in its composition and traditional Protestantism was succumbing to modernism, the Collins story contained God-fearing fundamentalists. Further, at a time when the average American was known only by his dogtag number on the battlefield, felt like a stranger on the streets of his own burgeoning city, and was losing his identity in the industrial mass-production system, Floyd Collins remained an *individual* to the very end. In a day when "rugged individualism" was being championed, Collins was the very personification of it—a self-reliant, independent loner. Also of tremendous significance was the geographic location where his entrapment occurred—the "old" frontier where the strength of the young United States had first been displayed. Out of this same milieu had come the legends of Daniel Boone and Davy Crockett.

As with most legends, this one was built on only a few hard facts. Legends are best created when detailed information is skimpy. This seems contradictory in view of the extensive press coverage given the Collins episode. Yet, the interrelationship of these conditions— elaborate press coverage and few facts—helped launch the Collins legend. Almost everything known about Floyd was hearsay. No one knew him intimately and he left no records. Salient bits of knowledge about his activities surfaced from time to time, but they were only disjointed fragments. This condition permitted fabrications, inventions, and additions to be joined into the Collins story. Gaps could be filled at will and human interest supplied whenever the need arose, not only while the tragedy was occurring but also at any time afterward.

There were, of course, inherent qualities in the Collins story that assured its continued appeal and also encouraged mythologizing. The utter hopelessness of the victim's situation as well as the Man versus Nature theme contained epic possibilities. Also, for legend purposes, it was essential that Collins lost rather than won his struggle to survive. The manner of his death and the circumstances surrounding it were all highly symbolic—the snow, cold, rain, and mud, and the loneliness, darkness, starvation, and isolation. The Greeks had soothsayers and oracles; Collins had his dreams. These dreams supplied a preternatural dimension to the tragedy. And, like most martyrs, Floyd became the prophet of his own death, which, in the end, was touched with controversy and consummate irony. He died while others went on to gain the riches he sought and make the cave explorations and connections he had aspired to.

Certainly the most critical factor in imparting a legendary flavor to the Collins story was the telling and retelling of it over and over and in a variety of art forms. Following the tragedy in 1925, songs, poems, movies, novels, articles, books, and television specials dealt with the affair. With each retelling not only were all the original errors and myths retained but new sensations and new errors were inserted. Wholly fictionalized recreations of the story encouraged further distortions and anomalies to creep in. The final result was not so much the perpetuation of a historical event as the creation of a folk saga.

In less than six months following Floyd's death, three books about the Sand Cave affair appeared. All three were privately published and are rare items today. The first, written by the court of inquiry reporter, Richard H. Lee, was given the title *The Official Story of Floyd Collins.* It contained only a meager and error-strewn narrative, concentrating instead on a verbatim report of the testimony given in the military probe. The second work, entitled *The Tragedy of Sand Cave,* was released just ten days after the shaft was closed by reporter Howard W. Hartley of the *Evening Post.* Consisting entirely of a rehash of his newspaper articles (including those about Alma Clark and Old Shep), this small volume was as unreliable as its raw material. The third book, produced jointly by Eldred B. Brannan and Cecil H. Alexander, was called *The Entombment of Floyd Collins in Sand Cave, Kentucky,* and supplied a ridiculously romantic version of the whole tragedy. Comparing Floyd to Christopher Columbus, the authors claimed that instead of embarking on an unknown sea, Collins set out alone and unafraid on the hundred thousand miles of passages that lay under "Old Kentucky."

Because of the paucity of information about Collins himself, and the difficulty in sorting out the facts relating to the rescue, the Sand Cave story did not again appear in book form. Instead, it was perpetuated and passed along by other means. First and foremost of these was phonograph records. According to one account, Polk C. Brockman, a talent scout and record distributor, while vacationing in Florida in the spring of 1925, came to the conclusion that a Collins ballad would sell. After broaching this idea to Andrew B. Jenkins, a blind Atlanta evangelist, Jenkins sat down at the piano and wrote the song in an hour while his stepdaughter, Irene Spain, arranged the music. Brockman paid them twenty-five dollars for it. He then sold the song to Columbia records, who gave it to Vernon Dalhart, a country singer, to perform.

The year before (1924), Dalhart had released "The Prisoner's Song," which became the first American phonograph record to sell

a million copies. In that same year, he also performed "The Wreck
of the Old 97," another smashing success. But neither of these
came close in popularity to Dalhart's "The Death of Floyd
Collins," which for the next two years sold over 3 million copies, far
outstripping all other contemporary country and western records.
By that time, six other artists had also recorded the song. The
Dalhart version alone, counting remakes and reissues, ultimately
turned up on nineteen different labels, including Victor, Cameo,
and Edison. The ballad simultaneously appeared on a song roll for
player pianos and sold for one dollar. Snapped up like hotcakes, it
filled many a parlor with its sad lyric as both young feet and old
pumped the pedals.

"The Death of Floyd Collins" remained in its original form for
only a very short time. Adopted by the rural and backwoods areas
of the border states and upper South, it was quickly modified to suit
local conditions. In some places it was called "The Ballad of Floyd
Collins," in others "The Doom of Floyd Collins." By the early
thirties it was being sung as far west as Utah and as far north as
Wisconsin. In the process, the structure of the lyric was constantly
changed. Sometimes a moral was emphasized by adding verses.
Sometimes new events were inserted. In the end, no fewer than
thirty-seven different versions existed. Still, all of them essentially
followed the pattern of the Jenkins original:

### The Death of Floyd Collins

#### 1.

Oh come all you young people
    And listen while I tell;
The fate of Floyd Collins
    A lad we all know well;
His face was fair and handsome
    His heart was true and brave;
His body now lies sleeping
    In a lonely sandstone cave.

### 2.

How sad, how sad, the story
   It fills our eyes with tears;
Its memories too will linger
   For many many years;
A broken-hearted father,
   Who tried his boy to save;
Will now weep tears of sorrow
   At the door of Floyd's cave.

### 3.

"Oh! mother don't you worry
   "Dear father don't be sad
"I'll tell you all my troubles
   "In an awful dream I've had;
"I dreamed that I was a pris'ner
   "My life I could not save;
"I cried, 'Oh! must I perish
   Within this silent cave?'"

### 4.

"Oh! Floyd," cried his mother
   "Don't go my son don't go
"'Twould leave us broken-hearted
   "If this should happen so"
Tho Floyd did not listen to
   Advice his mother gave
So his body now lies sleeping
   In a lonely sandstone cave.

### 5.

His father often warned him
   From follies to desist
He told him of the danger

And of the awful risk
But Floyd would not listen
To the oft advice he gave
So his body now lies sleeping
In a lonely sandstone cave.

6.

Oh! how the news did travel
Oh! how the news did go
It traveled thru the papers
And over the radio
A rescue party gathered
His life they tried to save
But his body now lies sleeping
In a lonely sandstone cave.

7

The rescue party labored
They worked both night and day
To move the mighty barrier
That stood within the way
To rescue Floyd Collins
This was their battle cry
We'll never, no we'll never
Let Floyd Collins die.

8.

But on that fatal morning
The sun rose in the sky,
The workers still were busy
We'll save him by and by.
But oh! how sad the ending
His life could not be saved
His body then was sleeping
In a lonely sandstone cave.

9.

> Young people oh! take warning
>   From Floyd Collins' fate
> And get right with your Maker
>   Before it is too late
> It may not be a sand cave
>   In which we find our tomb
> But at the bar of Judgment
>   We too must meet our doom.

Before the end of the 1920s, poetry was also being employed to retell the story of Floyd Collins and his death. Of the many early poems inspired by the tragedy few survive. Most were very poor quality doggerel and were passed along by word of mouth rather than being printed. Those that were published are now found mainly in private collections. Like the ballads, their emphasis and interpretations have varied. Yet, again, the basic outline remained the same. One example, which can serve for all, was written by John A. Logan, attorney for the Kentucky Rock Asphalt Company, soon after the shaft was sealed. Entitled "Echoes from Sand Cave," Logan first published this in a private anthology in 1930:

> All the world is in a nightmare,
> Because a man just tried to creep
> Through the bowels of the Earth's crust,
> And there he found his last long sleep.
>
> In the narrow slimy passage,
> Of this most awful sandstone cave,
> He by one foot was so fastened,
> His life the whole world could not save.
>
> All the wealth of this great nation
> Was placed then at his sole command,

But with it all, he could not move
A small like stone, just made of sand.

And the heroes of the country
Gathered there from far and wide;
But despite their noble efforts,
He remained, and there he died.

Through the countless awful hours
This great nation held its breath,
Pouring out its golden treasure
To prevent this poor man's death.

Now the sympathetic system
Of the world has been so wrung,
The amount of human suffering,
Cannot be told by human tongue.

This poor man of humble station,
With his courage and fortitude
Could by speaking one short sentence,
Fill the world with gratitude.

Yet the wise out of this Nation,
Say that we think of wealth alone,
But could they just feel our heart-throbs,
They would speak in different tone.

Could they hear from station broadcast,
The prayers now in the Nation's heart
For a lone man in a cavern,
They would no longer take a part

In unfriendly criticism
Of our frenzied strife for gain;
They would see it all as we do—
Just a great contested game.

With the coming of the Great Depression, the hero-making process of the 1920s slowed down. Hard times were unkind to the champions of the previous decade, and Floyd Collins was no exception. From 1930 to 1940, his name appeared only occasionally in print and was infrequently spoken of in the nation at large. However, in the Kentucky cave country and environs his memory remained very much alive. The very name "Floyd Collins Crystal Cave" assured it. Crystal's owner, Dr. Thomas, was not content merely to advertise Floyd's cave and grave during the decade; he even had a monument built to Floyd in 1939 in the center of the town of Horse Cave. A chimney-sized pile of stone, this memorial had a plaque fastened on it that told Floyd's tragic story. Placed in a location that made it a traffic hazard from the beginning, the memorial was struck by a truck in June 1965, knocking most of it down and the plaque off and killing Bosley Pettigow of Cave City, who happened to be standing nearby.

Floyd's name began to reappear in print with some regularity contemporaneously with the arrival of World War II. Thinly veiled adaptations of his plight were also broadcast over the radio. Certainly the most direct reminder of the tragedy emerged in July 1941, when the *Saturday Evening Post* ran an article entitled "Come, Let Us Go Spelunking" in which Floyd was a central figure and served as a "horrible example" of what not to do while caving. In this article a number of interesting new "facts" were added to the already error-ridden Sand Cave story. Among other things, it was claimed that "a ten-pound sledge hung about Floyd's neck" when he was trapped, that his rescuers had to dig a shaft "eight feet square in solid rock," and that Floyd's relatives and friends would have brought him out alive were it not for the intervention of the newspapers.

The postwar decade of the 1950s saw a marked increase in interest in the Collins affair. Hollywood found Floyd first. As if to commemorate the twenty-fifth anniversary of the event, a full-length movie appeared in 1950 called *Ace in the Hole* (later retitled *The Big Carnival*). Produced by Billy Wilder, it was set in the Southwest and had as its stars Kirk Douglas and Jan Sterling. In the screenplay, Sterling was the wife of the proprietor of a combination gas station and curio shop who was trapped by a cave-in in an old Indian cliff dwelling while hunting salable artifacts. Douglas, a has-been big-city reporter, prolonged the rescue and built up the suspense for his own purposes. Sterling, who hated her husband, encouraged this subterfuge, and in the end the victim died. The film not only emphasized the reporter's ambition and the wife's in-fidelity, but also pointed up the greed of political and business interests in the area. It particularly sensationalized the carnival atmosphere attending the abortive rescue attempt, even showing a ferris wheel in operation at the site. Roughly paralleling the Collins tragedy, this movie quite naturally recalled it to mind and added immeasurably to a growing distortion of the real Sand Cave situation.

Television discovered Floyd next. On May 27, 1951, the *Philco Television Playhouse* put on a drama entitled "Rescue." This was based on Skeets Miller's eyewitness accounts of the Collins affair. Fred Coe, producer of the program, happened to be in Miller's office one day (Miller was then night program supervisor of NBC), saw the framed Pulitzer Prize certificate and a map of the Kentucky cave country hanging on his wall, and asked him about them. Fascinated by Miller's reminiscences, Coe decided to bring the rescue attempt to the small screen. Homer Collins was flown in from Kentucky to advise the TV production people and was reunited with Skeets, whom he had not seen in twenty-six years. To add to the authenticity, Homer and Skeets were interviewed briefly at the end of the program. In general, the play was well done, but its unidimensional quality diminished its claim to accuracy. After it was over, Homer, who had never been to New York before, found he liked the bright lights so well that he resisted going home. Philco, which was paying his room and bar bills at the Dorset, experienced some anxious moments before he finally left town.

During the middle years of the fifties a number of things occurred to keep the Collins story alive. The National Speleological Society's C-3 expedition into Crystal in 1954, a pictorial article about this foray in *True Magazine* entitled "Seven Days in the Hole," and Joe Lawrence, Jr.'s and Roger W. Brucker's "official" history of the venture *(The Caves Beyond)* recalled Floyd's tragedy by means of the many references made about him and his caving adventures. At about the same time, "macho" magazines such as *Man's Magazine* and *Saga* recounted Floyd's ordeal. In 1955, Brucker also wrote a chapter on the Sand Cave affair for the book *Celebrated American Caves* (edited by Charles E. Mohr and Howard N. Sloane). The next year, 1956, the Collins rescue story was again retold by Franklin Folsom in his *Exploring American Caves*. Since the contemporary press served as the major source of information in all these various accounts, most of the original errors and interpretations were inevitably retained.

Then television struck again. In January 1957, *Robert Montgomery Presents* offered a dramatization called "Tragedy at Sand Cave." It was a mish-mash of fact and fancy. Long on excitement and short on accuracy, its main claim to authenticity was its use of the clothes and military uniforms worn at the time and a set that was a replica of the inside of the cave. Skeets Miller was listed in the credits as technical director, and again the presentation centered around his role. Far more sensational than the Philco TV program in 1951, this effort gave a totally slanted picture of the rescue. The conversations used in the script were unnatural and Floyd's words were filled with too much contemporary meaning. Moreover, the carnival atmosphere surrounding the cave's entrance was wholly exaggerated and depicted as being constant. Homer, who was piqued at not being reinvited to New York, saw the show on a TV set in Louisville and angrily stated afterward that there was nothing accurate about it at all. "Any eight-year-old kid could've beat it," he said. Some of Miller's former newspaper friends at the *Courier-Journal* felt that it overemphasized his actions. Neil Dalton, then public relations director of the Louisville Courier-Journal and Times Company, labeled as "ridiculous" the drama's claim that although he had sent Miller to the scene of the tragedy, he had ordered the young newsman to "stay out of the cave."

Nursing his anger concerning the *Robert Montgomery Presents* program for almost a year, Homer Collins finally released his own version of the rescue with the aid of a collaborator in an article in *Cavalier* magazine in January 1958. Advertised as "the FULL story" of the Sand Cave tragedy, it fell far short of that. Although clearing up a few matters, Homer confused others, with the result that his article was more detrimental than beneficial. He garbled the events of the first Monday and Tuesday (putting the harness attempt on Tuesday, for example). He claimed that he never offered $500 to have his brother's leg amputated (although dozens of bystanders heard him do so), and he asserted that he reentered the cave against Denhardt's orders on Thursday (it was Friday). Homer also gave the line of cars on Sunday, February 8, as being ten miles long (the longest estimate up to this time was four), and he set the number of guardsmen at the cave at three hundred (there were never more than fifty-nine present).

Whatever Homer might have accomplished in straightening out the record would probably have gone for naught anyway, since in the next year, 1959, the Pulitzer Prize–winning novelist Robert Penn Warren published a revamped version of the Collins tragedy in a work called *The Cave*. That Warren should have used this incident in one of his writings is not strange; he was born in Guthrie, Kentucky, in 1905, and was twenty years old when the Collins affair occurred. *The Cave* was an overdrawn novel that preached the idea that anyone who "lives with a guilty secret lives in a dark cave." The person in the book who had the darkest secret was Isaac Sumpter, son of a Baptist preacher, who pretended to talk to and feed Jasper Herrick, a Korean War veteran, who was trapped in a Tennessee cave. Besides Isaac, who was Jasper's partner, the plot revolved around Jasper's invalid father (Jack), a younger brother (Monty), and a girl (Jo-Lea) who was loved by both Jasper and Monty. Each of these harbored deep-seated reasons for not wanting Jasper rescued.

Containing lavish quantities of religious bigotry, personal fear, greed, and sex, the novel moved inexorably toward the inevitable climax. While exploring a cave worthy of commercial development, Jasper was caught on the edge of a deep pit by a rock falling on his foot. Rescuers thereafter hurried in and out, the main one being Isaac Sumpter. Ultimately, the press descended on the site and huge crowds milled about as Isaac reported fictitious news from below. Johntown, Tennessee, was the Cave City of the book where conniving businessmen were busily making an economic killing. There was also a professor of geology from the state university and a mine superintendent present. In the end, only one person ever actually reached the trapped man and that was Isaac's father, preacher MacCarland Sumpter, who at the conclusion of the novel realized that all of them, including his son, were liars. Jasper, of course, had long since died.

*The Cave* was not intended as history. Yet its similarity to the Collins affair easily caused its fictional aspects to rub off onto the real thing. The net impact was to reinforce in reader's minds a belief that Floyd Collins, too, had been done in by opportunists, money-grubbers, his friends, and especially his partners. The morbid nature of the crowd, the unending carnival atmosphere, the inexplicable slowness of the rescue, the commercial exploitation, the impure motives—these remained when all other details were forgotten.

Now and again, a few antidotes to a complete lapse in accuracy regarding the Collins tragedy surfaced. In 1959, Skeets Miller appeared as a guest on the Jack Paar show. Slightly heavier (140 pounds) than when he went into Sand Cave in February 1925, he was disarmingly frank about his adventure. Admitting that the incident was a highpoint in his life, he denied that his trips into Sand Cave were heroic. "That wasn't heroism, or courage either," he exclaimed. "That was pure ignorance." Recounting accurately the circumstances at the cave as he found them, he was just warming to his subject when, unfortunately, a commercial cut him off. When the show returned, George Jessel, another guest, took the conversation off in a totally different direction, and the moment of truth was lost.

A year later, 1960, Skeets Miller got another chance to set some of the record straight by writing his own account of the rescue for the *Reader's Digest*. Selected for the magazine's First Person Award, Miller's effort netted him $2500. An exception to the previous sensational popular stories that had appeared about Floyd, this one was unembellished even though it dealt with the emotion-filled Monday afternoon harness and Tuesday night jack attempts. Somewhat short on precise details, Miller's account nonetheless kept matters in perspective and captured the vacillating feelings of hope and despair that surrounded all the rescue activities.

But Miller's article in 1960 was an exception as slanted versions and damaging publicity continued to dog the Collins affair. One of the most distorted retellings of the story appeared in January 1964 in *American Legion Magazine,* which had a circulation of two and one-half million readers. Written by Clarence Woodbury, this article restated almost every cliché and myth now in existence about Collins, including reprinting a photo taken earlier of him in Crystal Cave but creating the impression that it was snapped while he was trapped in Sand Cave. Not only was the Woodbury account faulty in repeating all the former errors, but it initiated entirely new ones—the temperature in the cave was sixty-eight degrees, the rescue shaft was twelve feet square, and so on. Its most eye-catching false claim was that the Collinses, after unearthing Floyd's body, had placed it on display in an ornate casket "to bolster the tourist business." "During the dull seasons at the cave," the account continued, "the Collins family—father, stepmother, and children—took the casket on tour. They played small theaters and tent shows in the East Kentucky hills and the Ozark Mountains of Missouri and Arkansas, and the highpoint of their act came when they all stood around Floyd's casket and sang, 'The Death of Floyd Collins.'"

Surviving members of the Collins family immediately rose in anger. Imbued with the cave country habit of suing at the drop of a hat, Homer, Marshall, and Nellie (now Mrs. Nellie Collins Leach) each brought separate actions against the *American Legion Magazine* for a total of $1.5 million. Of the three, Nellie's suit was the most important. At the trial in May 1965, the sixty-five-year-old Nellie testified that she had never participated in a tour involving Floyd's body and had not authorized his interment in Crystal Cave. None of the Collins children had, she said. In his closing statement, Nellie's lawyer asserted that the Collinses had suffered much over the years as a result of irresponsible statements like those in the *American Legion* article and argued that an award of no less than $500,000 would be just. The court did not agree, although it did find for the plaintiff. On June 11, 1965, an all-male jury awarded Mrs. Leach $15,000—$10,000 in compensatory and $5,000 in punitive damages. Naturally, the reading public incorporated this juicy controversy into its already hazy and distorted recollection of the Floyd Collins tragedy.

That this process of uncritically retelling the Collins story has not ended was amply demonstrated only recently by a spate of articles and newspaper information appearing in 1975–76 at the time of the fiftieth anniversary of the Sand Cave affair. Once again, as in 1925, there were subtle economic, social, and psychological reasons why Floyd Collins's plight was particularly intriguing and meaningful. Concerned and confused by recent national racial and moral upheavals and especially by the growing manifestations of the implacability of nature—the limitations of a finite earth, diminishing energy resources, and the dangers of pollution—modern Americans, like Floyd in 1925, felt themselves trapped in a seemingly rescueless situation. It was Man versus Nature all over again, except this time it had serious national consequences.

Inexplicably, all the recent treatments of Floyd not only failed to perceive these subtle yet significant modern connections but were content to reiterate the Sand Cave rescue story with all its faulty interpretations, myths, and errors intact. For example, William Halliday, an expert on caves and caving, in a chapter in his *Depths of the Earth* (1976) again treated the Collins tragedy mainly as an exciting example of unsafe caving techniques and thereby added nothing to our broader understanding of the affair. Michael Lesy's impressionistic chapter on the Collins incident in his *Real Life— Louisville in the Twenties* (1976) could have helped clarify many matters since it dealt with the sensationalism and shortcomings of the press. Instead, Lesy merely repeated their exaggerated assertions, allowing their many distortions and misstatements to stand. Stating that these newspapers rarely told the truth, he left his readers to wonder what their mistakes were.

Again, there was an occasional effort to uncover the truth and to identify the most glaring errors in the growing Collins legend. Key questions were beginning to be asked and more careful and reasoned conclusions were attempted to be drawn. When Roger Brucker and Richard A. Watson wrote their account of the final connection made between Crystal and Mammoth *(The Longest Cave,* 1976), they agonized over the precise details relating to the Collins affair and suspected that much of what had previously been written about it needed scrutiny. As indicated earlier, Brucker's dissatisfaction led in part to the research and motive for this present book.

The two most recent attempts to reexamine the Sand Cave story illustrate once more the variety of means and the divergent approaches used to handle the Collins tragedy. In February 1978, Malcolm W. Bayley published an article entitled "The Man Who Tried to Save Floyd Collins" in *Yankee Magazine*. Although based on interviews with Skeets Miller, it is filled with too many errors. Excessively laudatory with respect to Miller's rescue role, it claims that Floyd was trapped "on his face," that "reporters from all over the country were on the job" by the time Miller arrived on the scene on Monday, that Miller himself had been ordered "to stay out of the cave," that the passage floor was covered with "ooze and slime," that the cave was composed of sandstone, and so on.

Fortunately, the year 1978 also saw the publication of Donald Finkel's *Going Under*, a long and intricate poem representing a lyric exploration of the experience of caving. Author of seven previous books of poems, Finkel was the 1974 winner of the Theodore Roethke Memorial Award and brought to the Sand Cave story an understanding and artistic creativity woefully lacking in all earlier poetic efforts. In his *Going Under*, Finkel first invokes Stephen Bishop for a guided tour through Mammoth, then follows Floyd into Crystal, and finally to Sand Cave. In doing so, Finkel captures the essence of Collins completely:

> across bottomless pits
> through corkscrews and chest-compressors
> scrambling through the clammy shadow
> a cave-rat, scuttling on all fours
> panting, lantern in his teeth
> came restless Floyd
> lone mole of Barren County
> sidling between thighs of limestone
> groping her wet flanks
> sleek with water, slick with clay

Far more perceptive and sensitive than most, in one section Finkel shows the contradictory emotions and motives tangled up in the rescue by having Skeets Miller say:

> I brought him a light so he
> could see himself die
> I warmed myself
> at the furnace of his hunger
> in the name of mercy and the fourth estate
> I stuck my thumb in his agony
> and pulled out a Pulitzer

In another section, Finkel depicts Carnival Sunday thus:

> His brother Homer plowed through the rabble
> Muttering in his weeklong beard
> —Where were you when he needed you?
> picking his way among
> pickpockets and preachers
> guardsmen and concessionaires
> peeping rubes and gaping samaritans
> pimps, hucksters, suckers, seekers
> moonshine and black balloons
> marked SAND CAVE, to where
> Lee their father straggled vaguely
> more lost than Floyd

Regardless of their various biases, approaches, or literary and research skills, by 1978 all writers and observers of the Collins rescue effort could still agree on one thing—it *was* one of the most sensational events in modern American history. Consensus ranked it as the third biggest single news story between World War I and World War II, topped only by Lindbergh's trans-Atlantic flight in 1927 and the Lindbergh kidnapping of 1932. On the fiftieth anniversary of Collins's death, a newspaper poll taken among Kentuckians placed Floyd's rescue story at the head of the list of those involving that state, outstripping even the Great Flood of 1937. The Louisville *Courier-Journal* still insisted that "No story ever captured and held the attention and stirred the imagination of so many millions of people as the experience of this Kentuckian." In 1975, after half a century of newspaper activity, Neil Dalton bluntly stated that the Collins story "has never been surpassed, in my experience, for dramatic setting."

Yet, paradoxically, as late as 1978, one could still read accounts of the Sand Cave affair that were no more sophisticated, analytical, evaluative, or accurate than the first ones a half century before. Even the original newspaper misspellings were retained. When new material was added, it was invented or borrowed from hearsay, poetry, TV scripts, sensational court cases, or the pages of a novel. In the end, one could believe or disbelieve anything about Floyd Collins. Incredible as it seems, even today a visitor to the Kentucky cave country can run into grizzled natives who will stoutly proclaim: "Don't pay no attention to any of 'em, mister. Floyd Collins warn't dead a-tall. It was jes' a dummy they took outa that sinkhole. Floyd lived out his life on a ranch in Arizona."

Such is the continuing nature of the Collins legend.

Old-timers in central Kentucky still like to sit around and swap tall tales about the Collins tragedy and also about the cave wars. Knowing winks about Floyd and laughter over rival solicitors' antics have replaced much of the former bitterness as oldsters rock and tell their stories. Although time has dimmed memories and passions have cooled, some of these natives still act as occasional "cappers" for the few remaining private neighborhood caves or man rickety stands that sell "cave souvenirs" to tourists.

Today, Cave City is located óne mile from I-65 on Ky 70, which still travels through it. The I-65 interchange is a garish, neon-lighted hodgepodge containing among other things three or four chain motels, several gas stations, half a dozen fast-food franchises, a wax museum, chair ride, and numerous rock shops—all living off the Mammoth Cave National Park tourist trade. Now largely bypassed, Cave City itself possesses a number of motels catering to cave visitors, but it is only a small place with one main street. Comfortable, modest-sized homes nestle into its surroundings. It is a peaceful town with few reminders of bygone days. The People's Bank is still there. The H.Y. Davis office of the Citizens Bank and Trust exists where the Dixie Hotel once was. Next to it is the Handy Building, where the military court of inquiry was held. The two-track L&N still runs through the town. Chiefly freight trains now rumble past, although an occasional Amtrak whisks by on its way between Chicago and Florida. The white wooden passenger-freight station with its green roof stands empty beside the main crossing, no one using it. Near the post office is a dilapidated shack. Floyd's body was twice embalmed there.

Memories and towns remain but people go. After marrying again and selling Crystal, Lee Collins had two more children—a little boy who died and a daughter named Leona. At the time of her birth, Leona was younger than the youngest offspring of Lee and Martha's youngest married child (Marshall). Lee died in 1936 and was buried in a grave on Flint Ridge, a hundred yards off the Crystal Cave Road. Unkempt and seedy, this little cemetery contains some forty stones, and Lee's two-foot-high sandstone marker is about the only one that remains legible. It reads:

LEE COLLINS
Born May 26, 1858
Died Mar 15, 1936
Gone But Not Forgotten

Homer Collins ultimately migrated to Louisville, got married in 1929, and had one child. During his later life he was a wallpaper and paint salesman. Remaining testy concerning the circumstances surrounding his brother's death, he frequently expressed bitterness about the rescue's failure. He persisted in believing that the only way to have gotten Floyd out was through the Sand Cave passageway. On the twenty-second anniversary of the event, he complained to the Louisville *Courier-Journal,* "If I had had only five good men who knew the surface conditions as I and Floyd knew them, I feel sure we could have rescued him within forty-eight hours after he was trapped." Homer lived until 1971, when he died of a liver ailment.

Andy Lee did not return to Illinois after the tragedy but remained in Kentucky. He farmed in Hart County for a while and then opened a small commercial cave that he called Floyd Collins Crystal Onyx Cave. He died in 1940 at age forty-five, leaving four children behind. Nellie, Floyd's younger sister, who was always in precarious mental health, got married and lived not too far from

Homer in Louisville until her death in 1971. Passing away just six months after Homer, she had no children. Annie, the older sister who left home in 1919 and settled in Moline, Illinois, had five children. Her life was tragic. One morning while she was fixing breakfast, her husband stabbed her three times with a butcher knife and, as she fled out the back door, chased her into the yard and emptied a gun into her. As she lay dying, her two young daughters clung to her skirts. Returning to the kitchen, her husband reloaded the gun and killed himself while their eight-year-old son cowered under the breakfast table.

Marshall, as of this writing (1978), is the only one of his generation of Collinses still alive, living in a neat, well-kept bungalow in Horse Cave, Kentucky. With him is Anna, his wife of sixty years. Two of their children live in the west and the other remains close by. A short, pixielike gentleman, Marshall would rather talk about his grandchildren than anything else, but he can also be voluble on the subject of Floyd. Like Homer before him, he still harbors considerable ill will about the tragedy, but unlike Homer, he blames Johnnie Gerald for much of the failure. Marshall continues to believe that the turning point in the rescue was Gerald's rejection of aid from the Woodson and Kratch men.

As for Johnnie Gerald, he returned to his car dealing and real estate pursuits after the rescue attempt was over. He was a habitual attender of auto auctions in the surrounding towns in central Kentucky where he bought new stock and unloaded his clunkers. In-between, he sold building lots to his neighbors. As time passed, Gerald gained a reputation for being a rough character. At least once he got into a scrape with the law for allegedly running illegal liquor. Johnnie remained bitter about the Collins affair to the end of his life and especially about his treatment at the hands of the military. He continued to claim that Floyd still could have been reached through the Sand Cave passageway and that the Carmichael shaft was worthless. He particularly resented lingering suspicions that his rescue motives had been impure—suspicions that to the day of his death helped make him a controversial figure. In 1965, while on a fishing trip to Lake Barkley, he was killed in an automobile accident, leaving a large family. His second wife, who was only fifteen when Floyd was trapped, still lives in Cave City as the manager of an apartment house.

Robert Burdon, Gerald's chief antagonist in 1925, lived out the rest of his life in Louisville. Frustrated at not having been able to free Floyd, he consistently maintained that Gerald and the Collins family had prevented him from effecting a successful rescue. He retained the belief that the only way to have saved Floyd was to have pulled him out even though it meant "busting up his leg." Burdon always felt that the key rescuer besides himself was Skeets Miller and often contended that the two of them would have accomplished the job if left alone. If it was any consolation to Burdon, he was made a captain of the Louisville Fire Department in 1941. Thereafter he became an authority on civil defense and was placed in charge of such matters in Louisville during World War II. Retiring in 1953, he divided his time between hunting and fishing and training volunteer firemen for small villages in Jefferson County. Prior to his death in December 1961, at age sixty-nine of a heart attack, Burdon suffered from stomach ulcers and lost an eye to glaucoma. His widow, Grovena, and a son and daughter still reside in Louisville.

Alma Clark, Floyd's mystery sweetheart of 1925, is today (1978) Alma Clark Short, a seventy-one-year-old woman who is five feet tall, plump, with light gray hair, quick bright eyes, and a face that still reflects the beauty of her youth. She lives with her husband, Floyd ("Barney") Short, only one-half mile from Sand Cave in a modest house with religious pictures, mostly heads of Jesus, adorning the walls. She and Barney worked for thirty-four years for the Mammoth Cave Hotel. Barney is retired but she still occasionally prepares fried chicken for the hotel, a dish for which she is justly famous. Recently asked whether she ever goes to Sand Cave, she replied, "No, I've never even been there—I had no reason to." She still smiles over all the press speculation about her and Floyd. "After the rescue was over," she said, "I got letters from all over the country. Letters of sympathy. Some even included stamped envelopes. I felt funny because I had no feeling for Floyd Collins. But the letters were so sincere—some of them." She also said that following the tragedy she received numerous songs that people had written. "They wanted my permission to use my name," she explained, "but I never gave it. There wasn't anything between Floyd and me."

Of the many others involved in the Collins drama, most went

their way unnoticed and the course of their later lives remains
unknown. But not all. Ed Estes was killed in a car-train accident in
1928, just three years after the Sand Cave incident. Ed's son,
Jewell, who first discovered Floyd, died in the early 1960s. Bee
Doyle lived until he was sixty, dying in 1947. By then he was a
rather extensive landowner. His son, Arthur, who was a mere boy
when Floyd set out on his last adventure, continues to live at the
edge of Cave City and possesses the rock that trapped Floyd's foot.

General Denhardt's later life was tempestuous. After returning
to Bowling Green following his state duties, he became active in
local politics. In November 1931, he was severely wounded in an
argument over a political matter and, although given less than a
fifty-fifty chance to live, managed to survive. In 1937, however, he
came to what the natives in the cave country called "a fittin' end."
After divorcing his wife, he took up with a forty-year-old widow
who was mysteriously shot while standing in the road beside his car.
Tried twice for her murder—the first trial ending in a hung jury—he
was on his way to court for the second trial when he was gunned
down by her three vengeful brothers. Denhardt left his name on the
Bowling Green State Armory.

Henry St. George T. Carmichael, one of the main heroes of Sand
Cave, went on to become very active in community and state civic
affairs—state disaster chairman of the American Red Cross, a
trustee of Washington and Lee University, and seven-time head of
Kentucky's annual March of Dimes. He also became vice-president
for operations of the Kentucky Rock Asphalt Company. Today,
that company is no longer operating, its mineral rights having been
sold to the Reynolds Metals Company. Carmichael died in 1949 at
age sixty-nine of uremic poisoning.

Professor William Funkhouser remained dean of the graduate
school of the University of Kentucky from 1925 until his death at
the age of sixty-seven in 1948. Funkhouser enjoyed the reputation
of being one of the best known scholars at his institution, dividing
his time between "deaning," serving as faculty advisor for athletics,
and traveling to the jungles of Central America to capture rare
entomological specimens. By the time of his death, he had been an
officer in or held membership on a score of scientific and educational organizations and had written more than a hundred papers.

He even had a bug named after him—the *Funkhouserini*. During his later life, Funkhouser rarely alluded to the Collins tragedy and in his official obituary the incident was not even mentioned. The local newspaper itself inserted the brief sentence: "Dr. Funkhouser helped direct recovery efforts when Floyd Collins was entombed in a cave near Cave City more than 20 years ago."

Such was not the case with William Miller. The Collins affair remained a key part of his existence. Skeets Miller always claimed that the Collins episode itself did not change his life, but winning the 1926 Pulitzer Prize did. Because of the prize, Arthur Krock of the *New York Morning World* invited him to join that paper in 1927. Miller quickly accepted because by doing so he could simultaneously pursue voice training in New York City. But music was again forgotten when he took over the news desk of WJAC and then went on to NBC when it was founded. In 1931 he was placed in charge of that network's special events programming. Success rapidly followed as he originated on-the-spot radio coverage of unusual happenings. Miller broadcast from submerged submarines, airplanes, dirigibles, and even lions' cages. He arranged for the first live transmission from a parachute jump and was one of the first passengers to fly the Pacific in Pan American Airways' famed clipper. Robert Ripley of "Believe It or Not" once designated Miller as "the bravest man in radio," and an NBC publicity handout asserted that "when the Angel Gabriel blows his trumpet to mark the end of the world, 'Skeets' will have him do it over an NBC coast-to-coast network."

On January 31, 1942, almost seventeen years to the day that he received orders from Neil Dalton of the Louisville *Courier-Journal* to go to Sand Cave, Miller was made eastern program manager for NBC. Three years later, on the occasion of the fortieth anniversary of the creation of the Pulitzer Prizes, his Sand Cave exploits were again singled out for special mention. In reviewing the history of the prizes, the Pulitzer committee said, "From the standpoint of individualistic enterprise and personal courage, the 1926 Pulitzer award to reporter William Burke Miller . . . stands forth as the most exciting."

Now retired from NBC, Skeets Miller presently (1978) lives in a handsome home in South Wallingford, Vermont, surrounded by mementos of his many adventures. Extremely articulate, he is quite willing to talk about Floyd Collins, but there is a sadness in his voice. Looking back over it, he does not yet see how Floyd could have been saved, but at the same time he berates himself for not having used something during the last jack attempt to hold the wooden blocks together. "I will regret it all my life that we didn't save Collins," he recently said when asked about it in the study of his home. "I worked so hard, and did not accomplish a thing." Turning and looking out the window, he added, "It still makes me shiver."

One final important member of the Collins rescue effort remains alive as of 1978. He offers a marked contrast to Miller, indicating that the Fates do play favorites. Ed Brenner, the cocky little miner who in 1925 risked his life in the bottom of the shaft to be the first to reach Floyd's body, is today only a toothless caricature of his former self. Living on Staten Island since 1926, he occupied from 1951 to 1976 a three-room dilapidated shack that some of the time was without heat, hot water, electricity, or adequate toilet facilities. Brenner is now past eighty and until the winter of 1976 was paying over one-half his Social Security check in rent. Until then his rent was only fifty dollars a month, but his landlord raised it to a hundred because he "wanted that old man out of there." This was the hero who in 1925 was reported by the *New York Times* as receiving the personal congratulations of President Coolidge.

Talking frankly about his situation recently, Brenner stated that his gas meter had been taken out in 1970 and his electric meter in 1973. During the three years from 1973 to 1976, he had walled off the back two rooms of his shack with tarpaulin and padded about in his bare feet in a ten-foot-by-twelve-foot anteroom that contained boxes, rags, empty food cans, a canvas sack on which he slept, and five cats. The cats, he said, were necessary to protect him from the rats, especially after one bit him on the hand in the winter of 1974 and his arm swelled to twice its size.

In 1976, following much renewed publicity on the occasion of the fiftieth anniversary of the Sand Cave rescue attempt, the *Staten Island Advance* learned of Brenner's plight and arranged for him to be moved to a boarding home. Welfare officials were amazed that he had survived the previous several winters. There Ed Brenner remains, somewhat uneasy in his new surroundings, but still loquacious about his past and particularly about his role in the Collins rescue. "Collins was a mighty plucky fella," he asserted recently, snapping his head back, "but they was all agin him." Lowering his voice, he added, "Ya know, that guy was really murdered." Quizzed specifically about what he meant, he refused to elaborate. "That family would get me, if I said anything," were his final words on the subject.

As for Sand Cave, the place where it all happened, few visitors go there anymore. Occasionally a park ranger from Mammoth brings over several tourists or caving enthusiasts who insist on seeing "where Floyd Collins was trapped." Actually, few people even know where Sand Cave is, although there is a historical marker along the highway about five hundred yards from the spot. Not far from this sign, a crumbling road turns off of old Ky 70 just beyond Turley's Corner. Four hundred feet in and off to the right is a ramshackle one-room shanty set among waist-high weeds, its tin roof sagging and its weatherboarding coming loose. This is what is left of Bee Doyle's Sand Cave ticket office. Miraculously, the tongue-and-groove ceiling is still intact as are the wall shelves on which artifacts such as Floyd's left shoe and the twenty-seven-pound rock once stood. Empty bottles and jars are strewn about and an old wrecked space heater lies on its side in the middle of the floor. Seventy yards farther on one can traverse the same route through scrub brush, around the edge of the stone ledge, and down to the cave that Floyd's rescuers used in 1925. There, at the cave's entrance, the National Park Service has posted a sign CLOSED. Across the small two-foot-square opening that drops into the depths at the overhang's rear wall is a steel grate, welded shut to discourage the adventuresome. Twenty feet away, in front of the overhang, is a prominent funnel-shaped depression, about fifteen feet deep, the sides sloping inward. This is what remains of Carmichael's shaft.

To the observant, other reminders of the earlier days abound. The dump site is still discernible under a growth of weeds, a furry tongue licking out from the cave and into the deep ravine beyond. A cable used to steady the hoist while rescuers and dirt were being lifted out of the shaft is buried in a large yellow poplar above the ledge on top of the hill. Heavily scarred wounds around the trunks of other trees suggest where similar cables were anchored. Projecting out of the bark of others are rusting nails that were driven in for the reporters' telephones. Occasionally, five short barbed-wire strands of the original fence can be seen protruding from the middle of seven-inch trunks, testimony to the fact that these trees were only half as large in 1925. Sticking out of some trees only two or three wires are visible, but they are enough to permit the tracing of the rescue camp's extent, if one is willing to crawl over rocks, push through brush and weeds, and keep an eye out for snakes.

The area all around the perimeter of the site is now heavily wooded with poplars, scrub pines, ferns, fallen tree trunks, dead branches, and dense foliage. Many of the larger rocks that dot the landscape are covered with lichen and moss. Vines hang down everywhere. Even when the sun shines it is a gloomy place. In the late afternoon it is gloomier still. And it is quiet. Only the flutter of a bird, the rustling of leaves by some small animal, or an occasional jet airplane streaming overhead disturbs the silence. But if one listens carefully, he can also hear the faint plop of ground water methodically dripping off the stone ledge above Sand Cave's mouth as it begins its slow dark journey into the depths where Floyd Collins once lay trapped.

# *Epilogue*

"Okay, Roger, you take the caving part, and I'll take the history."

With that statement to me by Bob Murray during our original phone conversation in November 1976, my first thought was: *Brucker, you've* got *to get into Sand Cave!* The saga of Floyd Collins would remain forever unfinished without knowing what that cave is really like. Only by going into the cave could some of the details surrounding the Collins entrapment and rescue effort be clarified. Contemporary newspaper articles, notes in diaries and on maps, and even eyewitness accounts were not enough to give a complete picture. There *had* to be some shred of fabric, some rusty tin can, some cold dollop of mud in Sand Cave that could reveal just a little more than we already knew. Murray agreed that as storytellers and explorers, we simply had to see for ourselves.

Cavers had been almost everywhere that Floyd Collins had explored. I felt that after my many years of caving in Flint Ridge I knew every rock that Floyd had touched. Stanley Sides, an old friend and past president of the Cave Research Foundation, had copied down nearly a dozen instances of Floyd's autograph scrawled with a pointed rock on the walls of Salts, Crystal, and Unknown caves. It was an awkward script, sometimes with a backward F. Often Floyd also scratched in the date. Good cavers do not deface cave walls anymore, but Floyd's marks provide the only record we have of his travels, so perhaps he can be forgiven. Yes, cavers have followed Floyd everywhere . . . except into Sand Cave.

Writing on the day after Ed Brenner found Floyd dead, one reporter said: "No man will ever enter the tunnel. Superstition and a solid barricade of timber will keep at bay curious youths, who might in the future decide to see for themselves where Collins died—and who might meet his end." In 1955, I myself wrote of Sand Cave: "To this day no one has been back to explore the cave. Its entrance is effectively blocked. Other approaches may be possible, and one day, perhaps, the headlamp of an explorer will fall upon a rotten rope hanging from the top of a pit where Floyd rigged it. A few feet farther on he may come to the gallery that Floyd found [but] with prudence and care, the explorer need not be victim of a watermelon-shaped rock and well-meaning but inept rescue attempts."

Actually, there have been several attempts to get into Sand Cave. In his *Depths of the Earth* (1966), William Halliday remarked that three decades after Floyd's death and before the National Park Service erected a steel barrier over the entrance, caver Larry B. Matthews crawled into the first room of the cave and found an opening still continuing. There is no indication, however, that Matthews ever pursued it. Also, after the final connection was made between the Flint Ridge and Mammoth cave systems in 1972, Cave Research Foundation teams continued to explore Mammoth systematically and pushed into the neighborhood of Sand Cave. The leader of the final connection party, John Wilcox, personally led a dozen or more groups into a wet, muddy area of Mammoth called Bransford Avenue, some of whose side passages fanned out below Sand Cave. Indeed, one of these passages lies directly beneath it. Another passes within a couple of hundred feet on the north. A third lies three hundred feet to the south. Wilcox investigated every foot of each of these for leads. If any had been found, hard-charging parties of cavers would have rushed in. But there were no leads up, down, or to the side. Not even a trickle of water for a drain, a telltale sign of a possible route into Sand Cave. The muddy walls of this deep set of passages extended unbroken a hundred and fifty feet below the lowest point Floyd claimed he had reached.

This was discouraging. Long before Bob Murray's phone call, I had very much wanted to enter Sand Cave and, on more than one occasion, I pored over the survey data and trip reports with Wilcox. "John," I pleaded, "are you sure there's no way up into the bottom of Sand Cave?"

"You could see for yourself," said John. That meant that Wilcox was as certain as a thorough caver could be. Sand Cave still remained untouched.

Bob's call and subsequent visit to my home in Yellow Springs in January 1977 spurred me to greater action. The time had come for a frontal assault. But there was a delicate problem. The Cave Research Foundation, of which I also am a past president, still explores, surveys, and supports scientific studies in Mammoth Cave National Park under terms of the agreement made with the Park Service in 1959. Desiring to comply with that agreement and not jeopardize the foundation's status, I wrote the park superintendent for permission to undertake a historical survey of Sand Cave, emphasizing that the information gained would be useful to the park's interpretive program. In February 1977, the superintendent gave his qualified permission, but he cautioned about the dangers involved. "Every week some fool wants permission to go into Sand Cave," complained Superintendent Albert Hawkins. "The bars are welded shut. Nobody goes in because the cave is so unstable. If you go in, make sure you weld it back up tight. And keep it quiet! We don't need any more requests to go in there."

Thus began our clandestine operations to unlock the secrets of Sand Cave.

On April 23, 1977, I and several other cavers I had recruited tramped through the woods to Sand Cave to look at it with a fresh eye. The previous fall I had made photographs of the shelter and of the stout grating that barred the entrance. This first scouting party carried a compass, steel measuring tape, and notepaper. We set up a survey point between the conical depression that marked the location of Carmichael's shaft and the barred entrance. From that point we sighted rays through the compass and measured distances to the walls and prominent rocks. Finally, we surveyed to a place on the wall directly over the rectangular entrance gate. There we noticed a rusty nail projecting from a crack in the rock. Could it be a relic of the 1925 survey? An original survey station?

In early May I constructed a full-scale cardboard model of the Sand Cave grating. My purpose was to devise a way to get through it without sacrificing any of its deterrent, or leaving a trail behind to invite inquiry. At the end of May, Murray and I examined the entire area around Sand Cave. Among other things, we paced off the broad, flat apron of rubble that fans outward from the shelter, consisting of rocks and muck from the shaft excavation in 1925.

Earlier I had asked engineer John Bridge to calculate the number of cubic yards of rubble in this dump. He estimated about a hundred and fifty cubic yards. This presented a puzzle: a shaft six feet square and fifty-five feet deep would contain about seventy-five cubic yards of material. When deepened another ten feet, as it was to remove Floyd's body in April 1925, the cubic yardage from the shaft would total ninety. Where had the additional material come from? After discussing the case of the extra sixty cubic yards with geologist Art Palmer, Bridge decided that thirty-five yards might be accounted for by air spaces between the loosely piled rubble, since mined material always takes up more space than its original solid form. The final twenty-five cubic yards probably represents material that slumped into the shaft from the side walls as it was sunk deeper.

Murray and I discussed these calculations as we took turns making the first of the nearly invisible modifications to the grating over the entrance. We plastered mud over our hacksaw cuts to keep the investigation a secret, stopping several times to look innocent whenever visitors arrived. Then, on June 3, I and a party of cavers set off by jeep in the dark of night for Sand Cave. Earlier, we had encountered a field party of archaeologists and told them we were off to survey a passageway in Mammoth Cave. Retribution for our lying came in the form of a tire that went flat before we had gone two hundred feet. We quickly changed it and drove on to the cave, arriving at 1:00 A.M. on June 4.

We carried heavy loads of tools, cameras, a tape recorder, surveying compass and measuring tape, a packet of maps made in 1925, a sketch of the end of Sand Cave drawn from memory by Skeets Miller, and an oxyacetylene cutting torch with ninety-pound bottles of gas. We expected to travel directly to the cave, following a cross-country route marked earlier with empty pop cans by Murray and myself. But I managed to lose the way, swearing and thrashing through the sawbriers and crashing through heavy brush for forty minutes. (Consult maps on pages 226–227.) The "quiet break-in" started with the antics of burglars in a Peter Sellers farce.

At the cave I made two final hacksaw cuts. Another caver fired up the torch to heat the metal. Two others started a survey at the old nail at the sandstone-limestone contact. Our survey's first shot was plumbed vertically, through a concrete collar buttressing a two-foot-by-two-foot opening. One side of the opening was near a bedrock limestone wall and all four walls were laid-up masonry. Within a few minutes the first explorers to slip inside the cave passed back word that the cave was formed by open spaces between large limestone breakdown blocks. They could find no passages dissolved out of limestone, as one expects to discover in most caves in the region. These immense breakdown blocks generally tilted downward away from the cliff face, as if they had once fallen into a void below—a void that could lead to a solid limestone ceiling.

Imagine, for the moment, that you are accompanying our expedition. From the top of the gate you can see a crevice about ten inches wide extending to the right. To enter you place your hands on the gate rim and lower your body down about four feet. Keeping your feet together, you slide your legs down a slope until your trunk is beneath the masonry wall. This steeply pitched floor is squishy mud. The left wall continues as limestone bedrock. The right wall and ceiling are the edges and undersides of fallen breakdown blocks. Above you, the ceiling block appears to be supported by steel bars jammed in place at the time the gate was constructed. At this point the chamber is snug but comfortable, eighteen to twenty-four inches wide. At the bottom, a slide or chute leads downward four feet through a small black hole.

The top of this hole is formed by the narrow edge of a wedge-

shaped limestone block five feet long by eighteen inches wide that
has slipped downward eighteen inches. Dozens of cave crickets
roost on the ceiling amid drops of water sparkling in the light. A
trail of dark brown stain, cricket or cave rat droppings, runs
vertically along the right wall. Feetfirst, you can twist your body to
the right to corkscrew through the ten-inch-by-eighteen-inch gap
that leads to a larger space below. The right-hand wall is formed by
several blocks that rest upon each other. They tilt away from the
bedrock wall. Your feet reach a soft earth floor. You slide your
body downward until your head clears the blocks overhead.

You are now at the southwest corner of a room that is
comfortable to sit in, but not high enough to do much else.
Irregular in shape, it slants downward gently along a northeast
bearing. Its dimensions are about six feet wide and fifteen feet long,
with three or four feet of headroom. Its ceiling is a very large,
smooth block of limestone divided by a two-inch crack. Two large
blocks make up the floor on the left side of the room. They are as
big as grand pianos.

Behind where the entrance route descends into this room is a
niche or alcove. You can crawl around the corner and see the
bedrock wall slanting downward. Rubble and earth slope to meet
this wall four feet below. Inside the alcove, the space to the left
pinches between breakdown blocks. The floor is covered with cave
rat feces, nut hulls, and twig fragments. The place smells of rat
urine. Under this organic material is a fine tan-colored sand with
pieces of limestone embedded in it the size of lunch boxes.

To the right a crawlspace leads three feet to a blind pocket that
terminates under the left wall of the room above you. You are
directly beneath the grand-piano-size slabs that floor that upper
room. A sandy chute eight inches high leads downward at a twenty-
degree angle for eight feet. You have to dig the sand out and
enlarge it if you wish to squeeze in. Then you can wriggle to the
bottom of the chute where the route ends at a bedrock wall. More
rat dung is piled here, and you can see small cracks between the
wall and the blocks that lean against it. There is no air movement.
By removing more sand you can follow the bedrock wall downward
ten feet in a three-foot-square pit. But there is no way out, and you
must climb back to the larger room above.

Here you feel a gentle breeze on your face; lamp flames flicker. The breeze blows out from a four-inch-high crack, a sand-floored opening that extends back horizontally about eight feet before it turns a corner. The breeze pulses, alternately strong then weak. It dies, then springs up again. It is the kind of breeze that cavers associate with large passages nearby. It whets the appetite for exploring and conjures up possibilities of discovery. You poke a finger into the sand and find it is loose enough to move easily. One caver scoops out a trench and earthworms his way back to the place where the opening turns the corner between giant boulders, only to find further progress blocked in this direction.

At the northwest corner of the room is a loose pile of limestone rocks on the floor. They range from brick size to the size of a typewriter case. They may have been left over from the 1925 pounding to enlarge the passageway, or perhaps Floyd piled them here during his weeks of labor to open the cave. Across from the pile it appears possible to squeeze over the top of a couple of dropped blocks. You try, but these squeezes dead-end.

Between the large rock slabs on the floor are a three-inch piece of aged rubber hose, the neck of a beer bottle and a rusty metal fragment the size of a fifty-cent piece. Alert to the possibilities of finding other artifacts in the shadows, your light suddenly strikes a modern flash cube, probably dropped down between the entrance bars by one of a handful of visitors each week. Undoubtedly it was carried here by a cave rat.

You creep to the north edge of the room and discover a five-foot drop over the lip of a block that leads to a chamber about the size of a Volkswagen Beetle interior. Here Sand Cave appears to stop. There is no way onward! We break out the old maps made in 1925 and they show the route leading on, directly through the pile of mud and rocks confronting you. Could this be a blockade put here by Carmichael to seal the cave?

We form a human chain and begin to remove this barrier with our hands. Soon an opening appears. In thirty minutes we uncover the beginning of a passageway extending sharply to the left. The rocks we have moved would half fill a bathtub.

You eye this lead out of the Volkswagen-shaped room, how it goes under a ceiling arch that is cracked. It looks unsafe; someone has pounded it with a sledgehammer. You peer beneath and see that the cracks do not go far. Just beyond the arch is a hole below two large sharp-pointed rocks in the ceiling. Clearance between the floor and the pendant points is about eleven inches. The rocks are ominous, so menacing they raise the hair on the back of your neck. If they let go they would sever your spine instantly.

This calls for care. You can see that they are wedged, anchored securely in place. You lie down and wiggle under them, willing yourself to be small. You move half a body length into a crawlway two feet wide and three feet high. Water drips off a block of rock on the right wall.

Now you are in a little chamber fifteen feet beyond the comfortable waiting room above. A mud slide slants in on the left wall. Sharp corners and edges of breakdown blocks jut down from the ceiling, but the roof is stable. Ahead is a triangular-shaped opening between a large slanting block on the right side and the vertical side of another block on the left. This looks like the thirty-degree pitch Skeets Miller described. Is it? "No, we just measured that. It's minus seven degrees," replies the notetaker. It certainly looks steeper than that.

It is a very tight squeeze with a soft, slippery floor. Your shoulder sinks into the mud like a plow and gouges a furrow as you move forward. The squeeze continues for twenty feet through successively deeper mud. Near the end the ooze is three inches deep. With relief you see that the passage becomes wider and higher, three feet by three feet. Chunks of rotted black wood lie on the floor near the right wall, remnants of 1925 shoring. Apparently these two- and three-inch blocks were wedged under some of the rocks jutting in on the right wall. They all seem to be quite solid. Was shoring at this location really necessary?

The passage turns to the right, still triangular in cross-section. Water plop-plops into the mud on your left. You try, but it is impossible to keep your left hand and forearm out of the water. What frustration! You want to move quickly out of the icy pinpricks of the drip on your skin, but the passage is too small to allow you to do more than squirm inch by inch. Then the ceiling yields upward to permit you to crouch amid boulders the size of television sets. You see a cheesy, green, shaley limestone along the left wall at the floor. White marks on wall rocks show where they have been pounded.

The passage now bears to the right again. It squeezes down to a roughly rectangular cross-section two feet wide by one foot high. One rock juts up to restrict the clearance to ten inches; it appears to have fallen recently. Beyond this squeeze is a turnaround room.

Here you are sixty-five feet from the entrance gate and forty feet beyond the end of the larger room we passed on the way in. Your depth is exactly thirty feet below the floor of the shelter. The turnaround room itself resembles the inside of a pup tent ten feet long and four feet high, erected at right angles to the passageway. The way in is under one slanting wall. The way out leads under the other slanting wall. You can see that the gray-colored roof of the room is formed by the surfaces of the two large breakdown blocks. The ends of the room are packed with loose rocks that appear to have been piled there for storage. Two persons can rest in the turnaround room, three in a pinch. But the place is cold from the strong breezes that flow through it. It is spacious only by contrast with the adjacent body-sized crawlways.

There are a number of artifacts in this turnaround room. It is exciting to inventory them. A fat green Coca-Cola bottle stands out. On its bottom are the molded letters *Bowling Green.* There is a clear glass light bulb with straight sides. Its filament zigzags vertically on glass supports. Voltage and wattage are not shown, but it looks like a thirty-two-volt bulb. Black fragments of shoring blocks, one inch thick and a few inches long, rest between the rocks. Other lengths of shoring obviously cut from small trees are rotting where they lay. There is a pipe-tobacco tin with a hinged lid, too rusty to make out any lettering. Strands of fine electric wire, vivid green, a few inches long, are easy to overlook because they blend with the mud. Here and there are also several other bottles, including a one-pint whiskey bottle, as well as fragments of rusty metal of various sizes, probably can fragments. Had anyone entered this part of Sand Cave since 1925, they certainly would have taken these artifacts as souvenirs.

A low crawl leads northeast out of the turnaround room. It makes a sharp bend to the east and after six feet appears to end in a rubble wall. But this is not the end. Your eye follows the right wall down to the boulder on the floor. Its shadow hides an opening eleven inches wide leading to a nine-inch crack between the boulder and the right wall. Headfirst? Or feetfirst? "Feetfirst makes it easier to feed you if you get stuck," says one of your fellow cavers dryly.

You lower your feet into the crack, back against the wall. It is the tightest squeeze thus far. You make a corkscrew twist to the left, assume a sitting position, and bend your knees to the limit of joints and wall. Your feet find a way and slip into a continuation of the passage below the crack. You remove your hard hat and hold your head sideways to pass through to the small chamber below. While catching your breath you observe that it is less breezy here than in the turnaround room. You conclude that the formidable nine-inch squeeze would have prevented all but the thinnest and shortest rescuers from reaching Collins.

You are now at the top of a chute. A wooden wedge has been jammed in the crack between the boulder forming the right wall and floor. Nearby is a four-inch diameter piece of shoring that appears to support a ceiling boulder. An empty whiskey bottle lies behind the shoring. Straight ahead an alcove opens in the slanting ceiling; a faint breeze issues from it. On either side of you are short pieces of timber shoring, wound about on one side by a pair of electric wires. One end of the wires is broken, as if flexed back and forth rather than severed by wire cutters. The other end of the wires trails off down the slope into blackness. The passage walls on both sides are vertical slabs of breakdown. The roof is jumbled boulders. The path itself angles downward fifty degrees, a steep pitch that is made slippery by mud. You descend feetfirst, back against the floor, eyes viewing projecting rocks that jut out from walls and ceiling a scant six inches away from your face. You bend to the right, then left. By now the electric wires have become buried in the mud floor. The walls appear to be a matrix of smaller rocks and mud. You continue to inch down the slope fifteen feet to the apparent end of the cave. There are depressions in the sloping floor of this chute that just fit your buttocks and permit you to rest between strenuous bouts of exertion. What drains your energy is a continuous struggle to brace your body against slipping, while keeping clear of ugly-looking walls and ceiling. In this tight place only one person at a time can stand, bent at an angle to occupy the end.

It is difficult to match what we are seeing with the old descriptions, and we are full of questions. Is this the final chute that Skeets Miller plunged down headfirst on his initial visit to Floyd Collins? Has the appearance of the passage changed in fifty-two years? We do not know for sure, but it resembles the sketch Skeets Miller drew for us before we came in. There is a jumble of rocks straight ahead that may be the result of a passage collapse or where the rescue shaft's lateral tunnel broke in.

You can see the floor from your semisitting position. It looks like gravel—water-deposited sediment, rocks, sand, mud. A small crack extends to the left. There is an exposed section of limestone running across the floor; it is a ledge, or perhaps the edge of a breakdown block. Next to it is a shallow depression that appears to curl back under the ledge. There are many football-sized rocks on the floor. You feel a light breeze spring up from tiny cracks.

This four-foot-by-five-foot-high chamber is a trove of artifacts. Many are hidden by rocks. The pair of twelve-gauge green copper wires that emerge from the slope leading down to this place run along for three feet on the right side of the passage, then plunge into the sediment at your feet. These wires were obviously part of the circuit for the bulb placed on Floyd's chest to give him light and keep him warm. Three old rusted L&N Railroad lanterns are on the floor. One has an intact globe and wick. A glint of white china proves to be half of a coffee cup. A three-eighths-inch-diameter steel rod, with a four-inch-diameter loop on the end, sticks out of the sediment. You tug on the rod and the sediment quivers like pudding. You discover that this rod is actually a four-foot-long steel bar with a seven-inch right angle on the end. When asked about the bar later, Skeets Miller couldn't recall whether the one he had used in the jack attempt had a loop handle on the end. He did not recognize it from a sketch we made.

There are also five bottles in this end room. Two are 400 cc (16 oz. liquid) medicine bottles with molded graduations at the corners. Three are whiskey bottles. There is a quart Ball jar, blue glass, with its metal top screwed on. You find a crushed, rusty can, No. 10 size. There is a pale blue Maxwell House tea can, rectangular, badly rusted. You brush the mud off a heavy chunk of steel to reveal a sledgehammer head. Bits of a woven textile are encased in the sediment, apparently the remains of an army blanket. You leave these artifacts where they are. As with those in the turnaround room, you do not collect anything.

After several hours in Sand Cave's cold air, your urge to urinate is suddenly unbearable. But the quarters are too tight to find some out-of-the-way spot, so a can is pressed into service. At once it becomes clear that those rescuers who reported smelling excreta and attributed it all to Floyd probably had themselves and fellow rescuers to blame as well. You pause to look around at the walls once more. Material appears to have collapsed in from the left, the direction of the shaft's lateral tunnel. Water enters this part of the cave from time to time, but drains away through cracks you do not find.

"Have you noticed these little walls?" one of the cavers yells down the chute. Rescuers in 1925 evidently built small retaining walls of rocks, and piled gravel and rocks behind them. These line the chute and have been constructed in every available niche. Some are only a few inches high and long. Others extend for several feet. Many are collapsed. All of them are the same muddy brown color as the rest of the chute. On your way in you could not see them because they blend with everything else. It is only when you are forced to wait in the cold that the eye and mind begin asking questions. Why do these walls look . . not quite right? Aha! They are not just natural walls. Some are man-made! Such is the discovery process in Sand Cave.

The wires plunging into the loose earth floor at your feet present a challenge. Could we possibly find the final light socket by digging? We take turns hour after hour, filling some coffee cans that we have brought along for the purpose. We dump the spoil where we assume the lateral tunnel came in. Slowly we excavate downward about three feet and back under the ledge five feet, still following the wires. When we decide to stop, the section we have dug resembles the 1925 descriptions of where Floyd's head and body filled a slanting tube beneath a rock ceiling. To dig farther, we would have had to turn upside down and work with our feet higher than our heads. It is extremely fatiguing to dig in such an inverted position and nobody wants to do it. Cold and tired, everyone now wants to get out as fast as possible. You look at the artifacts one last time and at the sediment itself. It is a filling of stratified yellow sand, mud, and surrounded limestone cobbles. Suddenly you spy one small piece of sandstone the size of a matchbox. It is the only sandstone you have seen in Sand Cave.

The last survey station we can place in Sand Cave before leaving we designate as A-15. But the 1925 survey of Roy Anderson required only ten stations to reach this assumed point. A quick comparison of our survey and a copy of the Anderson map that we have brought along reveals major discrepancies. Why? If our survey is correct, some of the 1925 Anderson bearings could not possibly have been sighted because jutting walls and bends of the ceiling would have interrupted the line of sight. We are puzzled, and as we emerge from the cave we are left to wonder: How close did we finally come to the precise spot where Floyd Collins had lain?

Even after rehashing our various exploring trips into Sand Cave (we actually made six in number), listening to our taped comments while we were there, rereading the historic accounts, and looking at our photos and the sketch made by Skeets Miller, we still remained uncertain about exactly where we had been in relation to the 1925 descriptions. Many questions gnawed on our minds. Why was the Anderson map wrong when we knew Anderson to be competent? Where was the collapse that had isolated Floyd from his rescuers? Why had we been able to reach the apparent end of Sand Cave, housing such rescue artifacts as a crowbar and L&N lanterns, when rescuers had been prevented from reaching it after the Wednesday morning cave-in?

The answer suddenly came. The cave-in was still there, seven feet beyond the turnaround room, just where it was supposed to be. *We had found a bypass!* The half-hidden nine-inch crack that we had barely squeezed through, leading to the top of the chute, had never been used by Floyd's rescuers. The tipoff was the jumble of rocks making up the ceiling over the chute. Those rocks were the *underside* of the Wednesday morning cave-in. The original route to Floyd lay slightly up and straight ahead from the turnaround room for a distance of about four feet to another hole that led downward.

That was the beginning of the final chute in 1925. Before the ceiling collapsed, this chute had contained one more bend, exactly resembling the sketch Skeets Miller had given us. The crack that we squeezed through was one of those through which rescuers in 1925 continued to talk with and hear Floyd but did not attempt to penetrate.

I was struck dumb by the implications. If the last parties of rescuers—led by Johnnie Gerald, the Kyroc crew, and Roy Hyde—had squeezed through this nine-inch crack, they would still have been able to feed Floyd, keep him warm, and work to release him. Instead, they had abandoned the scene because of fright and exhaustion.

Most of our questions were now answerable. The Anderson map was not wrong, and the extent of the collapse was now known. The first cave-in in 1925 blocked the top of the pit and chute, altering the chute by filling its topmost bend. The second collapse, only two or three feet away, was toward the turnaround chamber. Our map and profile diagrams show Sand Cave as it is today. Skeets Miller's sketch showed the chute as he remembered it before the collapse. We had definitely discovered a bypass route that Floyd's rescuers had not used or tried.

Or had they? Did Johnnie Gerald try to fit through this nine-inch crack late in the rescue? Was that one of the reasons why he brought a grease gun into Sand Cave, to make the crack slippery so that he could force his way through? Is this the reason he so persistently claimed that Floyd could still be reached in the Sand Cave passageway? We do not know and the dead Gerald cannot tell us. There is still one other nagging question. Although Anderson's survey was made after the collapse, his final map shows two additional bearings and distances. Was it possible that he carried his survey through the nine-inch crack? We think not. We believe that he saw the light from the bulb on Floyd's chest shining through the nine-inch crack and approximated his final two survey stations by sighting on it. This speculation seems to be confirmed by a look at the preliminary plot that Anderson made on a leaf of his survey notebook. On this plot he shows the last two bearings and distances only as dotted lines and has them clearly marked as estimated. This would explain why the shaft lateral found Floyd in a slightly different location than expected. It would also help explain why Carmichael, poking his head into the lateral tunnel at the end of the 1925 rescue attempt, could see the electric wires buried in the mud—just as we had. He erroneously concluded that he was looking at the far side of a terminal collapse that everyone said had sealed the passage.

In any case, we know that by squeezing through the nine-inch crack, we ultimately came within inches of the exact spot where Floyd Collins had rested. The ironic conclusion is inescapable: The Carmichael shaft was unnecessary, and the work to free Collins could have continued inside Sand Cave.

But human nature and frailty often guide decisions, and those early rescuers who used the regular passageway were shocked and frightened when it collapsed. They thought they faced as much as fifteen feet of almost impossible digging. They also assumed that there was no bypass because Floyd himself had said there was none. Later rescuers, like the Muhlenberg miners, were stopped after only a few feet into the breakdown by blocks that were too large to remove, and there was not enough room to pound them into smaller pieces. They also reasoned that Homer, Gerald, and the other cavers would have discovered any alternative way in, if there was one. To all of them, therefore, the situation *was* hopeless. In our investigation, however, our lead caver did not know that he was supposed to come to a terminal collapse. Hence, when he came to a rubble wall, he checked the shadows—where leads often are hidden—and found the nine-inch crack. He tried to squeeze through—and did.

There is one additional intriguing conclusion suggested by our Sand Cave experiences. We have no doubt that at the point where the cave ends, we were digging through layers of flood deposit as we followed the electric wires. In 1925, just before the Wednesday collapse, Skeets Miller and others had removed loose rocks and gravel down to Floyd's calves. Yet when Ed Brenner found Floyd dead twelve days later, his corpse was almost completely encased in gravel and a stream of water was running over his cheek. The Carmichael shaft on two occasions had been flooded to a depth of several feet. Is it possible that Floyd was drowned, or his corpse submerged, and that the light bulb on his chest was shorted out by water?

With Sand Cave at last carefully surveyed and most discrepancies clarified, it can now be said that it is not much worse than some caves people explore in Kentucky. It is formed in limestone, not sandstone. It is small and has tight squeezes. It is wet, but not as wet as cave passages that contain free-flowing streams or deep mud. The route in Sand Cave leads entirely through large and small breakdown blocks. Most Kentucky caves have passages developed by solution through solid limestone—tubes and canyons that are stable and safe. But most Kentucky caves also contain some breakdown blocks. Working in breakdown is always tricky, and sometimes downright scary, particularly where there is no well-defined route. In Sand Cave, the route is well defined by trampled mud, scuff marks, and artifacts, so it is not as frightening as some breakdowns.

Floyd Collins had explored in many such places. He had discovered Crystal through breakdown openings. He had joined his brothers and father to dig through a similar formation when they were hired in 1923 to reopen the back entrance to Salts Cave— where Pike Chapman had met his death through a collapse of rocks in 1897.

One aspect of Sand Cave, however, differentiates it from most other caves in Kentucky. To the untrained eye, as well as to the expert, it *looks* treacherous. Breakdown is objectively more dangerous than passages dissolved out of solid rock. In Sand Cave, menacing rocks dangle everywhere. Fist-sized rocks pop loose often enough to produce respect in cavers and terror in the inexperienced. To these, add gooey-mud squeezes and slopes where one can easily panic because movement seems impossible. Sand Cave *is* difficult at best.

Most cave explorers, no matter how experienced, would not return to such a cave after once venturing into it. Almost any other cave would seem more interesting and promising, as well as less dangerous—except for the breeze. A wind, such as the one in Sand Cave, means one thing in underground Kentucky: big cave. Floyd knew that. Its promise kept him digging and grubbing at the breakdowns in Sand Cave long after his sense of prudence must have told him the odds were against an easy breakthrough. But he had persisted in similar situations before and it had paid off in exciting discoveries.

What did Floyd find? Reports conflict. Those who retrieved his body reported a sizable pit behind the crawlway where he was trapped. That is all we know for sure from the Sand Cave end. Collins evidently had worked his way down from the top of a terminal breakdown into a segment of limestone passage or into a vertical shaft. He was trapped about fifty-five feet from the surface of the ground and claimed that his discovery lay some sixty feet below that. This would place it in a type of limestone (the Paoli Member of the Girkin Formation) that houses some large canyon passages in Mammoth. Such passages can contain beautiful gypsum crystals in the form of crusts and flowers. These passages in Mammoth are limited to areas where the sandstone caprock is intact and not eroded away. At the edge of the sandstone at hillsides such passages break down.

How long might the passages be that would lead out of such a pit as Floyd claimed he found? Since the base of the Big Clifty Sandstone is eight hundred feet above sea level, by tracing a pencil around the eight-hundred-foot contour line on the topographic map of the area near Sand Cave, one can be fairly certain that, if the passage ran south from Sand Cave, it probably would end at the hillside a thousand feet away. If it ran west, it might go a mile. If it headed north, it would go three thousand feet. If it headed east, it would extend only a few hundred feet where it would terminate in breakdown. On the other hand, if Floyd had found a cluster of vertical shafts, horizontal travel might be limited to less than a hundred feet.

One final question remains. Could Floyd Collins have been rescued from Sand Cave, and if so, how? Marshall Collins still maintains that the Woodson and Kratch monument carvers held the key to Floyd's release. Homer said that with five men as expert as himself and Floyd, rescue would have been accomplished in forty-eight hours. Burdon persisted in his contention that Floyd could have been pulled out. Skeets Miller believes that he might have freed him if he had been able to block up the jack properly.

Certainly there was no shortage of rescue alternatives or deter-mination in 1925. There was, however, a shortage of small cavers. Homer Collins has said that only three men besides himself reached Floyd and stayed with him long enough to feed him. Why, then, weren't small cavers aggressively recruited? The answer is simple. There were no organized groups of cavers to recruit from in 1925. Some local cavers who possessed the skills and small size were either kept out of the cave by Homer and Johnnie Gerald, or they concluded that the cave was too dangerous for them to handle. Volunteers were later encouraged to join the rescue work in the shaft, but neither caving skills nor small size were critical there.

Then, too, there was little coordinated organization and planning during the first crucial days of the 1925 rescue attempt. There was also a notable lack of accurate information with which to plan. Eyewitnesses to Floyd's situation gave conflicting stories. Nobody made an accurate survey until the passage to Floyd was blocked. By that time the last bearings and distances could only be estimated.

Given the ambiguities and numerous mistakes, together with Floyd's physical deterioration without adequate food and hot liquid, the authors are convinced that nothing and nobody then present could have saved Floyd Collins from death in 1925. The rescue effort at that time suffered from inadequate observations, insufficient experience in caves, and a poverty of resourcefulness. Even the monument carvers, promising as they seemed, would have failed. They would have required many hours of chipping to get at Floyd's trapped foot. Long before that, they, too, would have become chilled and exhausted like the rest. There were small pneumatic stone carving tools in 1925, but none of these were used at Sand Cave. The cave's close quarters would have caused both the user of such tools and the victim to choke on rock dust anyway.

Who, then, is to blame for Collins's death? Floyd himself bears the primary responsibility. Hence, it is hardly fair to shift the blame to the rescuers for their limitations and decisions. Yet, scapegoat-ing began the moment rescuers differed on an approach. Blame rose as half a dozen rescue leaders were damned for sins of commission and omission.

In attempting to identify the critical links in a chain of bad decisions, we are at once confronted by the intricate connection between the roles of men and fate. Henry Carmichael's Kyroc crew cleared out more debris on one trip on Wednesday, February 4, than other rescuers had removed during the previous three days. But Carmichael made a disastrous mistake when he trusted Reverend Roy Hyde's competence and accepted his observations about a "tunnel squeeze" and about the passage being completely closed. Homer Collins was correct in protesting Carmichael's decision, and so was Johnnie Gerald in maintaining that the passageway could still be used.

Upon the order of General Denhardt, however, and with the approval of nearly everyone, Carmichael turned to digging the shaft, a new and visible project whose progress could easily and directly be observed. The shaft offered a bold way to bypass the ambiguity, confusion, controversy, misery, and frustration of the earlier rescue attempts. Moreover, right or wrong, the shaft gave Carmichael his chance to control the work personally. We believe that this diversion of effort sealed Floyd's doom more certainly than any other link in the decision chain.

Following Floyd's death, and in view of the hopelessness of his situation, discussions have frequently arisen about what could be done if such an accident were repeated. Modern caving safety rules, of course, are designed to prevent such a repetition. A caver should never explore alone (Floyd was a solo caver). He should always wear a hard hat (Floyd wore a cloth cap). He should have at least three sources of light (Floyd had only one). And he should always leave word where he is going and how long he expects to be gone (Floyd usually did neither). But what if such an accident *did* happen again?

Given the present condition of cave rescue preparedness, two things would now happen if Collins were trapped today. If he were not part of an organized group, there probably would still be a long delay in getting expert help to him. No caver wants to organize a cave rescue if he can help it. Cave rescues take a long time. But if Floyd were part of an organized group he would fare better. Based on recent experience there would be an immediate call out of qualified cavers from lists compiled by the National Speleological Society and the Cave Research Foundation for this purpose.

Attention would first be given to life support, keeping the victim fed and warm to avoid hypothermia. Cavers today carry heat tabs—solid chemical fuel—to heat up cans of chicken, stew, or liquid on the spot. Wool clothing would be packed tightly around the trapped man. Several caving doctors would be summoned. If the ceiling threatened to collapse, rescuers would shore up the rocks and also install a length of garden hose to provide emergency means of feeding the victim. They would also set up a sound-powered telephone and install electric lines within the first few hours.

After the trapped victim was made warm and comfortable, information would be gathered systematically. A team would survey the cave and plot a map. They would question the victim extensively about the nature of the cave and the passages beyond, using such information to determine whether to alert the U.S. Bureau of Mines. It possesses a vertical rock-boring machine that is designed for mine rescue work and can bore a two-foot-diameter hole through solid rock at three feet per hour. One early task would be to set up a watch at the entrance to the cave, logging every individual time of entry and exit in order to keep track of the situation. Cavers on the scene would be assigned to shifts so operations could continue around the clock. If the accident occurred in Sand Cave, for example, National Park Service rangers and cooperating law-enforcement officials would establish crowd control and provide radio communication. Meanwhile, the logistics of the rescue effort would be organized by those who are qualified to handle myriad details such as travel, food, and lodging for experienced cavers.

Extricating the victim would obviously require rescuers familiar with working breakdowns in close quarters. Every means possible would be tried to bring the victim out of the existing cave entrance before excavating another one. In Sand Cave, chains of cavers would be appointed to relay materials out of the cave completely. They would use coffee cans, short crowbars, and garden trowels to dig out all loose material. Crews would change at least every three hours. On the surface, a diversion for the water seeping down the walls would be created immediately. Simultaneously, there would be a continuous search for alternative routes to the far side of the trapped man.

Would blasting be used? Probably not, although the art of controlled blasting with small shaped charges is a highly developed skill of some experts. Hydraulic wedges might also be used as a dynamite substitute. But modern Sand Cave rescuers instead would probably use small portable electric hammers and chisels to reduce the larger rocks that would not yield to manual pounding.

The plan outlined above would be put in motion today. Using it as the basis, we believe that a team of cavers, such as we had in Sand Cave to investigate it, could rescue a person trapped as Floyd was. This belief agrees with the opinions of the cavers themselves who spent more hours in Sand Cave than most of Floyd's rescuers did in 1925. The reasons for our confidence are twofold: First, every effort would be made to feed the trapped victim and to keep him warm and dry; second, small cavers are available today in sufficient numbers and with ample experience to work nonstop in a place like Sand Cave.

Still, we cannot be *absolutely* certain that we could get the victim out. Too many cavers die in caving accidents each year to be smug about the chances. As for the Collins rescue attempt, many of the procedures mentioned above *were* used at Sand Cave in 1925—and without success. Would those procedures that were not used have made the difference? No one can really say—and least of all Floyd Collins, who, in dark and seldom-visited Crystal Cave, lies in his casket, his face white, his gloved hands at his side, still waiting for the answer. . . .

# Epilogue 1999

Since *Trapped!* was published in 1979, the story of Floyd Collins continues to unfold in strange and fascinating ways. The basic facts remain as we described them. But tidbits of additional detail have been uncovered and, as time passes, the story simply refuses to end.

By 1999, none of Floyd's living relatives had personally known the man. His last surviving brother, Marshall Collins, died in Horse Cave, Kentucky, in September 1981, at age eighty-four. Skeets Miller died in Florida on December 29, 1983, at age eighty. William Douglas, one of the early rescue workers on the scene and prominent as the tallest of the rescue workers in some of the photos of the time, died in April 1994. Douglas was one of the few men who actually reached Floyd Collins with food and was the last person living to have seen Floyd Collins alive in Sand Cave.

Stimulated by the publication of *Trapped!,* some interesting material can now be added to the story. Genice Poynter, stepdaughter of Elkanah Cline, who used to guide tourists at Crystal Cave, claimed that the snatch-

292

ing of Floyd's body in March 1929 was a publicity stunt conceived by Dr. Thomas, who hired Oscar Logsdon, Alvey Logsdon, and Troy Burnett to steal it. That possibility had been rumored before, but the identity of the perpetrators was new.

Contrary to the earlier report that Wade Highbaugh's photo negatives of Floyd had been destroyed in a fire, most are actually preserved in Udolf C. Highbaugh's attic in Rockfield, Kentucky. Udolf is the son of Wade Highbaugh and was eight years old at the time of the event. He delivered his father's films for processing to their home darkroom a mile east of Sand Cave.

Udolf also remembered a fancy box of chocolates being delivered one day to his mother from Louisville. These chocolates were for Floyd; his mother had prepared and mailed the order since Floyd was illiterate. Allegedly, Floyd subsequently carried this candy to Alma Clark in his attempt to woo her.

Udolf also recalled his father being asked by a reporter to take a picture of a dog that was hanging around Sand Cave during the rescue effort. Wade told the reporter, "That isn't Floyd's dog." The reporter replied: "Doesn't matter. Just take the photo." Wade refused, but another photographer took it.

Udolf Highbaugh further claimed that he saw Bee Doyle repeatedly selling to tourists "the rock that trapped Floyd." Each time the new buyer left with his treasure, Doyle would reach under the counter at the Sand Cave ticket office and place another rock on the shelf. Udolf verified that the rock formerly in the possession of Arthur Doyle is the same rock now owned by Doyle's son-in-law, Billy Cassady, of Park City, Kentucky.

Shortly after *Trapped!* appeared, the daughter of Johnnie Gerald telephoned Roger Brucker to complain about her father being portrayed as a profane and outspoken man. "I never heard him say any of those swear words," she protested. She felt that we had slandered the memory of her father. However, numerous contemporary confirmations of his swearing left no doubt about his bombastic and colorful speech. Evidently, Johnnie loved his daughter enough to spare her his salty language. In any case, Gerald's ultimate contribution to the rescue effort was not his language but his courage, his convictions, and his loyalty to Floyd Collins.

Other interesting reactions came in the wake of the publication of *Trapped!* Fred Anderson, a Cincinnati filmmaker and video producer, interviewed Alma Clark Short before her death and reported that she said that Floyd Collins had asked her to marry him but that she had given him a firm "No."

In April 1983, George M. Crothers, a graduate archaeologist, conducted an archaeology investigation of Sand Cave and cataloged all of the 1925 artifacts that we had previously seen in 1979 but left in the cave. Crothers then removed them for preservation. Chief among the items were fragments of glass, a few bottles, pieces of a woolen blanket, a hammer head, cans, parts of kerosene lamps, a ceramic cup, a light bulb, some wood shoring, nails, and electric wires. These findings were totally consistent with the historic record described in *Trapped!*

A few years later Philip J. DiBlasi, a past president of the Cave Research Foundation and staff archaeologist at the University of Louisville, investigated the Collins home at Crystal Cave because of questions about its authenticity. While a water line was being replaced, an excavation unearthed refuse, artifacts, and the sandstone foundation of a house formerly sited next to the Collins house. An old photo, thought to be the original house but not the present structure, shows unidentified individuals on the front porch. A 1927 photo, however, shows the existing house. The present house contains a few machine-cut nails dating from 1880, but most of the structure appears to be more modern. DiBlasi concluded that the original Collins home had been located immediately to the southwest of the present structure. Apparently the present house was built between 1918 and 1927 using some salvaged materials from the original house.

On the entertainment front, the appearance of *Trapped!* provided a literary and historic gold mine for playwrights and magazine writers. *Time and the Rock*, a play by Warren Hammack and Beverly Byers Pevitts, opened and ran from July 24 through September 12, 1981, at the Horse Cave Theater in Horse Cave, Kentucky. The stage play dramatized the conflicts and interactions of the Collins family based on some of the scenes portrayed in *Trapped!* Hammack interviewed members of the Collins family and reviewed newspaper clippings. The play ran one season and was never restaged.

A highly fictionalized drama, *The Death of Floyd Collins*, by Tim Hatcher, opened in 1989 as an outdoor entertainment in the Green River Amphitheater in Brownsville, Kentucky. It has continued to run for ten years. Performed on Friday and Saturday nights during July and August, this two-act melodrama features community residents in all the parts. Names of characters other than Floyd were changed and, to spice up the action, Floyd is portrayed as having shot the sheriff. "You'll laugh, you'll cry," claims Ricky Skaggs, who plays the part of Ben (based on Lee Collins). Skaggs states he got the idea for producing the play after reading *Trapped!*

A far more serious undertaking was the creation of a musical, *Floyd Collins*, staged in Philadelphia in 1994. Tina Landau and Adam Guettel, inspired by a *Readers' Digest* story called "Deathwatch Carnival," made a short trip to Kentucky, interviewed a niece of Floyd's, a former cave guide, and a worker at the information desk at Mammoth Cave National Park. They bought copies of *Trapped!* The musical ran April 9-24, 1994, at the American Music Theater Festival. It received bad reviews. According to critics it tried to take in too much of the whole scope of the story told in *Trapped!*

The authors extensively revised the musical, combined Homer Collins and Johnnie Gerald into one character, and created a new character, Ed Bishop, who took on the mannerisms and perspective of a wise Stephen Bishop. This version ran off-Broadway in New York City at Playwrights Horizons Theater in February and March 1996. The production received mixed reviews. *New York Times* critic, Ben Brantley, contrasted the musical with the book *Trapped!,* faulting the musical's "billboard dialogue" and lyrics that "evoke not so much specific characters as abstract sentiments." But Brantley saw promise in the interesting music, which possessed "strands of the Americana of Copeland and the uneasy dissonance of Sondheim." Other reviewers liked the blend of acoustic bluegrass and hill music. The *USA Today* reviewer David P. Stearns gave it a four-star (out of four) rave review as "one of the most riveting events of the season."

Roger Brucker attended a performance. He was immediately struck by the theater lobby decorations, consisting of seventeen enlargements of all of the photos, maps, and drawings from *Trapped!* Prior to the show, cast members told Brucker they had read and re-read the book. Copies were on sale at the refreshment stand. Publicity interviews with Landau and Guettel quoted them as consulting *Trapped!* "over and over." *Trapped!* material served as the main underpinning for the musical's dialog, lyrics, and many scenes. In the "Special Thanks" section of the Playbill the authors listed Robert K. Murray and Roger W. Brucker but never specified the reason. As additional promotion for the musical, a six-minute segment of the National Geographic video "Mysteries Underground," for which Roger Brucker had served as a technical advisor, ran continuously in the lobby. Permission was not sought nor authorship acknowledged for either the book or the video.

As this epilogue is being written in March 1999, the Landau and Guettel musical *Floyd Collins* has re-opened at the Old Globe Theater in San Diego, California. Pre-show publicity included a four-page cover story in the *Los Angeles Times* entertainment section and a three-page cover story in the *San Diego Union-Tribune* arts section. Both stories make much of Landau and Guettel's research, but there is no mention of *Trapped!* Theater critic Michael Phillips of the *Los Angeles Times* gave it a mixed review: "When 'Floyd Collins' finds its voice, as it does, tantalizingly, about half the time, you hear a wonderful sound indeed." The musical is currently scheduled to run in Chicago, Cleveland, Philadelphia, and Brooklyn in 1999. Nonesuch Records released a CD, *Floyd Collins: Original Cast Recording*, a reprise of the Playwrights Horizons performance.

Other recent entertainment and educational versions of Floyd's story exist or are in the works. The video, "Mysteries Underground," was produced by Lionel Friedberg and released by The National Geographic Society in 1992. It includes a segment of carefully researched pictorial material about the cave wars and Floyd's entrapment. The Cave City Chamber of Commerce has obtained funding to produce a historic video of the Floyd Collins story in connection with a Floyd Collins symposium planned for year 2000. And in August 1998, photographer and writer Rob Rosenheck and filmmaker Sam Hoffman signed a formal option for making a major movie of *Trapped!*

The most recent research published on Floyd Collins was by Christine Quigley in a book entitled *Modern Mummies: The Preservation of the Human Body in the Twentieth Century.* She devotes four pages to summarizing the Floyd Collins entrapment story from *Trapped!* and adds new details of the embalming and restoration of Floyd's body. She also describes the 1989 removal of Floyd's coffin and monument from Grand Canyon Avenue in Crystal Cave and the subsequent earth burial in the Collins family plot on Flint Ridge.

Quigley carefully details the reasons three days were required to restore Floyd's body after its removal from Sand Cave in April 1925. The embalmer replaced his eyes, nose, and mouth, and rearranged other parts of his body. After this restoration, Floyd's stepmother told the undertaker she was pleased with her stepson's appearance. Quigley also reported that after the sale of Crystal Cave to Dr. Thomas, Floyd's body was again disinterred and once more considerable remedial embalming work was performed. Thereafter, it was placed in a glass-covered bronze casket in the Grand Canyon of Crystal Cave. The body continued to deteriorate and from time to time required "touching up." When Dr. E.R. Pohl took over the management of Crystal Cave, the casket was closed.

After Crystal Cave was sold to the government, Carol, wife of Donnie Collins, Marshall's grandson, repeatedly wrote the National Park Service requesting the reburial of Floyd's body. She finally sued the federal government to release Floyd's body. In 1988, National Park Service official Phil Veluzat informed the Collins family that the National Park Service was actively considering the matter. Veluzat found a federal ruling issued in 1961 stating that the Department of the Interior had no obligation to maintain anything so "totally repugnant" as an unburied body. National Park Service historian Bob Ward and superintendent David Mihalic made formal arrangements with Leona Ashe, Floyd's half sister, for a surface burial.

The National Park Service engaged Hatcher & Saddler Funeral Home in Glasgow, Kentucky, to remove and rebury the body. They rigged a block and tackle outside the cave entrance, welded together a steel sled, and placed a plywood skid track along the way. A fifteen-man crew pulled the heavy coffin, the massive tombstone, and its base—each weighing a thousand or more pounds—up and out of the cave. It took three days to move the coffin to the hearse. The undertaker performed some restorative work to the exterior of the casket but said that the lid remained unopened. Neither family members nor undertakers viewed the body. Leona Ashe said that she had "no desire to see it" because she had been told that "there were bones coming through."

Floyd Collins's fifth burial took place March 24, 1989, at the Mammoth Cave Baptist Church cemetery on Flint Ridge, less than seventy feet from the unmarked pauper's grave of Edmund Turner, Floyd's former caving companion. A pink granite monument marks his "final" resting place. Some forty family members heard Rev. Gary Talley read Psalm 40: "I waited patiently for the Lord; and He inclined unto me, and heard my cry. He brought me up also out of a horrible pit, out of the miry clay, and set my feet upon a rock." Mary Lou Carney, a relative from Chesterton, Indiana, remarked: "There is a real sense of relief now. It's been a nightmare for three generations the way he has been treated."

Jack Fincher, writing for the *Smithsonian,* also described this fifth burial in his article "Dreams of Riches Led Floyd Collins to a Nightmarish End." He supplied some clues that may explain why the National Park Service took extraordinary measures to keep the event secret and to block roads to the cemetery with law enforcement vehicles. Although directors of the Cave Research Foundation did not formally oppose the transfer of Floyd's remains, some individual members did. A director and former president of that organization, Sarah Bishop, wrote the superintendent: "To remove the American caving hero from his resting place of more than 50 years would appear to be callous, disrespectful—a travesty." She said the reburial plan threatened to diminish Collins' rightful place in caving history. Also, a former director of Cave Research Foundation complained that the action "flies in the face of Collins' wishes, as expressed to his father when he first found Crystal Cave. It's a slap in the face to every caver in the country." Red Watson, co-author of *The Longest Cave,* said that cavers in Europe were baffled that Floyd's body was taken out of the cave. Several famous European cave explorers are buried in the caves they loved and made famous.

Did the National Park Service fear some kind of caver demonstration, body snatching, or media circus? When asked about the secrecy surrounding the burial, Bob Ward, National Park historian, ducked the question. "Oh, it wasn't secret," he said. "It was private. We had reporters there."

Christine Quigley also may have provided some information in *Modern Mummies* that helps to clarify yet another part of the Collins saga. She reported: "For decades a sideshow was not complete without a mummy. The bodies were those of outlaws, outcasts, or merely victims of circumstance. They were seen by hundreds of thousands of persons and changed hands frequently." As reported in *Trapped!* the Collins family won a lawsuit against the *American Legion Magazine* for a fanciful story in which Clarence Woodbury claimed that the Collins family took the casket containing Floyd's body on promotional tours. Timothy Donley of Bowling Green, Kentucky, does possess a photo taken at Indianapolis, Indiana, in September 1925, showing a carnival sideshow tent. The main banner over the tent entrance reads: "FLOYD COLLINS TRAPPED." The photo shows a painting of Floyd in a stalagmite-encrusted cave, the rock pinning his foot and his face expressing pain and horror. To the left of the entrance is a huge question mark; on the right is a crude painting of a cave entrance.

Smaller signs read: "NO ADMISSION CHARGE" and "EVERYBODY WELCOME." This is the Indiana State Fair sideshow tent where Lee Collins appeared. Did Clarence Woodbury conflate his memory of this sideshow with the fact that in such cases mummies were often exhibited?

As with any sensational or newsworthy event, collectors love to gather memorabilia. Gordon Smith, co-owner of Marengo Cave in Indiana and past president of the National Caves Association, has several moth-eaten Sand Cave pennants, old books, and photos. Tim Donley, a periodontist from Bowling Green, Kentucky, owns the antique dentist's chair in which Floyd was fitted with his gold front tooth. Donley also has a fine collection of photo prints and glass plates. Russell Norton, a New England dealer in historic documents, has a white plaster bust of Floyd Collins, apparently sculpted by Floyd's nephew Russell Collins from a Highbaugh photo. The bust was displayed in a cave country restaurant for years. Fred Anderson tried to buy it but was unsuccessful. Later, Anderson talked to Russell Collins, who said he had a mold for the bust but not the original. Eugene Collins, a nephew of Floyd, has Floyd's 12 guage shotgun.

Some of the best photos of the Collins era recently appeared in Danny Fulks' condensed rewrite of *Trapped!* in an article for the Ohio Historical Society entitled "Buried Five Times, Floyd Collins Caver." William R. Halliday in 1998 published a thirty-two-page booklet, *Floyd Collins of Sand Cave: A Photographic Memorial.* It shows thirty-four Collins era photos with captions and a short summary of the story told in *Trapped!* Halliday identifies the figure in a widely published photo of Floyd in the Flower Garden of Crystal Cave as Floyd's brother, Homer Collins. The book contrasts the fake newspaper photo of Floyd dead in Sand Cave with a photo by an unknown photographer purporting to show the mud-caked corpse of Floyd in Sand Cave. The Wayfarer Inn's Floyd Collins Museum is located on Kentucky State Route 70 near Sand Cave at the entrance to Mammoth Cave National Park. It contains enlargements of newspaper clippings, artifacts of the times, and exhibits summarizing the story of Floyd's life and death.

Two new sources of information have recently come to light. The first is a book manuscript called "The Life and Times of Floyd Collins," by Homer Collins as told to John J. Lehrberger. Three versions of the manuscript are known to exist. Cave Books currently plans to publish the earliest of the three, which publisher Red Watson believes is closest to Homer's unedited narrative. Philip DiBlasi, who is assisting with the editing, says the bulk of the manuscript deals with Floyd's early life and only the last few chapters describe the accident.

An apparent treasure trove of documents has been delivered to the Cave Research Foundation. Equivalent to one file drawer, the material was assembled by the plaintiff's lawyer in the Nellie Collins Leach lawsuit against the *American Legion Magazine*. The papers have not been cataloged, but Philip DiBlasi, who has them in his Louisville office, claims they include a six-inch stack of photostats of newspaper front pages from 1925, numerous affidavits and depositions, and Homer Collins' book manuscript.

Those interested in popular culture can easily find Floyd Collins by searching the World Wide Web. Web sites change frequently, as do the search engines, but you can learn fascinating details. David Brison in France has collected more than twenty-five versions of "The Death of Floyd Collins." Cavers regularly create Floyd Collins paraphernalia. A bumper sticker that reads "Free Floyd Collins" was popular for many years. A number of T-shirts bearing Floyd Collins' likeness have been made, an inviting category for collectors. Finally, *Trapped!* is a classic reference for rescue squads and emergency medical technicians who can learn what *not* to do in a cave rescue emergency.

Fatal caving accidents still occur: William John Coughlin, age twenty-seven, died after a thirty-foot fall in Buzzard's Roost Cave, about three miles from Sand Cave, while on a guided "wild cave tour" on May 31, 1993. Ironically, a Cave Research Foundation expedition was being held nearby and a group of cave rescue specialists were meeting about twenty miles away. Neither group was called to help by the sheriff until too late.

And what of the caves in which Floyd Collins invested his life and hopes? In 1999 the combined length of Mammoth Cave, including Floyd Collins' Crystal Cave, is about three hundred sixty miles and is being increased yearly through Cave Research Foundation discoveries. Moreover, several additional nearby cave systems have been discovered and surveyed. When these are connected together, the total length may exceed five hundred miles. Ironically, the explorers are no closer to Sand Cave than we reported in 1979! The trail through the woods to Sand Cave has been widened and an interpretive sign placed at the edge of the sandstone overhang.

Finally, we sound a note of sadness over the passing of an era. The Cave Research Foundation moved its field headquarters out of the three buildings at Floyd Collins' Crystal Cave at the request of the National Park Service and is establishing a new headquarters outside the park. The old Austin house, remodeled several times as an expedition headquarters, was demolished, its site bulldozed, and rye grass planted. Only the rapidly deteriorating Collins home and Crystal Cave ticket office remain, sagging and weathered after twenty years of neglect. The surrounding once-open grounds are unkempt, taken over by a succession of brush and trees. The last environmental vestige of the old commercial cave culture within the Mammoth Cave National Park will soon fade into memory.

Unless official attitudes and funding priorities change, there is little Park Service interest in restoration and cultural interpretation of the Collins homestead and Crystal Cave ticket office. The example of Cades Cove in Great Smoky Mountains National Park shows the value of historic preservation to visitors and their enjoyment of the heritage of a vanished way of life. Without National Park Service protection after the Cave Research Foundation left the Crystal Cave property, the gypsum and cave onyx formations in Crystal Cave were heavily plundered by three energetic thieves, beginning in April 1955. Warnings to the National Park Service of the secret passageway under the cave gate went unheeded. In June 1995, the thieves were apprehended. They were convicted of stealing the formations and sentenced to prison on May 22, 1996. Their market was local souvenir rock shops, some of which cooperated with authorities to avoid prosecution under Kentucky law. Anthony Stinson and Leon Reynolds were sentenced to twenty-one months in prison and Anthony Hawkins to thirty-three months plus three years probation. National Park Service officials intended to make an example of these miscreants, but too little action came too late, as Floyd Collins's beautiful gypsum crystals and helictites lay in corrugated evidence boxes. Attempts were made to glue back together some of the broken formations in the cave but with limited success.

Today, one can park at the Flint Ridge road gate to Crystal Cave and hike the long mile in to see the depressing overgrowth of what is left of the Collins homestead and Crystal Cave ticket office. But nothing else remains to remind one of exciting cave wars and competitive cave explorations. Judge Thomas Russell commented in 1995, when sentencing the Crystal Cave thieves, that they had "stolen yesterday's time." Were Floyd Collins to survey the scene today, he would have to agree in more ways than one.

# Notes on Sources

These notes and their bibliographical information, together with the historiographical material already described in Chapter 10, contain all the sources currently available on Floyd Collins and the Sand Cave tragedy. Very little has been written about Floyd himself or about the Collins family, and, except for the contemporary press, not a great deal has been published on the Sand Cave rescue attempt. Although universally mentioned in history textbooks and in studies on the 1920s, this event has never been examined or reconstructed in detail before.

The authors, therefore, had to uncover new or previously unused evidence which ultimately included the papers of some of the participants, the complete testimony given before the military court of inquiry, and a large number of oral reminiscences. Some of the court of inquiry testimony was found in Richard H. Lee's rare *The Official Story of Floyd Collins;* the rest was pieced together from scattered information. Oral reminiscences were obtained from interviews conducted by the authors with residents currently living in the Kentucky cave country, and from interviews made earlier by the Cave Research Foundation with knowledgeable persons, some of whom are now deceased. Between the years 1958 and 1977, the foundation put more than a hundred and twenty hours of oral history on tape. The authors excerpted the most significant of this material relating to Floyd Collins and the Sand Cave rescue and placed it on twenty casettes of two hours each. These forty hours of foundation material, along with the taped interviews made by the authors themselves, constitute the most concentrated body of information extant on the Collins family, the Sand Cave tragedy, and the historical development of the central Kentucky caves.

Although the names of the oral contributors are mentioned in the note references in connection with the specific information they provided, we are listing them here as a group so that they can be collectively identified: Arthur Adwell (farmer-neighbor of the Collinses); Guy Blair (fireman on the old Mammoth Cave Railroad); William Travis Blair (next-door neighbor to the Collinses); Clifton Lewis Bransford (Mammoth Cave guide); Matthew W. Bransford (Mammoth Cave guide); Lawrence A. Burdon (son of rescuer Robert Burdon); Anna Collins (wife of Marshall Collins); Marshall Collins (younger brother of Floyd Collins); Perry Cox (husband of Lucy Cox); Lucy Cox (owner of Great Onyx Cave); Lyman Cutliff (neighbor and friend of Floyd Collins); Andrew Dennison (kitchen worker at Mammoth and later mail carrier in Cave City); Earl Dickey (Cave City banker); Lenny Dossey (Green River ferry operator); James W. Dyer (resident manager of Crystal Cave); Mrs. John B. Gerald (second wife of rescuer Johnnie Gerald); Carl Hanson (Mammoth Cave guide); Wade Highbaugh (Cave City photographer); Terry Jewell (solicitor for Mammoth Onyx Cave); Ellis Jones (Cave City garage manager); Elkanah Kline (Crystal Cave guide); Lute Lee (Colossal Cave guide); Paul McG. Miller (superintendent of Mammoth Cave National Park); William B. Miller (a chief rescuer and 1926 Pulitzer Prize winner); Mrs. Ben Monroe (owner of Park View Motel near Cave City); Dr. Elwood Rowsey, Sr. (owner of Diamond Caverns); Mrs. Nellie Sell (store owner on Flint Ridge); Mrs. Alma Clark Short (Floyd

Collins's alleged "sweetheart"); Irvin Stice (longtime resident of the cave country); Lawrence S. Thompson (professor at the University of Kentucky and "friend of the court" in the 1965 American Legion trial); John Vance (old-time resident of Park City); Mrs. John Vance (a close observer of the local scene); Lincoln Wells (solicitor and guide at Mammoth Cave); and Gordon Wilson (professor emeritus at Western Kentucky State University and an expert on Mammoth Cave region language and customs).

The references given below are designed to indicate the major sources for that particular section of the narrative. Since these references contain all relevant publication data, no separate bibliography is appended.

# 1

## *To Find a New Cavern*

Ellis M. Jones, "My Fifty Years of Cave Exploration in the Mammoth Cave Region of Kentucky" (unpublished memoirs), chapter 7, p. 5, says Floyd set the dynamite blast on Thursday, January 29. Richard H. Lee, *The Official Story of Floyd Collins* (Bowling Green: Times-Journal Press, 1925), p. 9, claims the date of the blast was Wednesday, January 28. Testimony before the court of inquiry puts the time at Monday, January 26. The latter is correct.

At the time of the Sand Cave tragedy, descriptions of the passageway varied enormously. Five different versions appear in the court of inquiry testimony alone. Bad as the passage is, hyperbole was the hallmark of all descriptions. One observer contended that after the first thirty-five feet, the "average" height of the passage was only eighteen inches!

Floyd's discovery of the sixty-foot pit and his subsequent entrapment is reconstructed from evidence given before the court of inquiry, oral interviews with some of the participants, Homer's recollections, and the statements of Floyd himself. Sources like Howard W. Hartley, *The Tragedy of Sand Cave* (Louisville: Standard Printing Company, 1925) and Ellis Jones, "My Fifty

Years of Cave Exploration in the Mammoth Cave Region of Kentucky" (which follows Hartley closely) have Floyd discovering "a wonderful cavern" whose walls "glistened with white gypsum and white stalactites." This is a fanciful elaboration on several of Floyd's statements made while he was semidelirious.

Floyd's personal reactions to his dilemma are gleaned from testimony given to the court of inquiry, from oral interviews, from Homer Collins's reminiscences, and from newspaper articles written by William B. Miller for the *Louisville Courier-Journal*.

For the geology of the Central Kentucky Karst, see George H. Deike, III, "The Development of Caverns of the Mammoth Cave Region" (Pennsylvania State University, Ph.D. dissertation, 1967); and William B. White, Richard A. Watson, E. Robert Pohl, and Roger W. Brucker, "The Central Kentucky Karst," *Geographical Review*, LX (1970), pp. 88–115.

Information on prehistoric man and the central Kentucky caves is found in Douglas W. Schwartz, *Prehistoric Man in Mammoth Cave* (n.p.: Eastern National Park and Monument Association, Interpretive Series, No. 2, 1965), and Patty Jo Watson, ed., *The Archaeology of the Mammoth Cave Area* (New York: Academic Press, 1974). Comprehensive information on the "mummies" is in Harold Meloy, *Mummies of Mammoth Cave* (Shelbyville, Indiana: Micron Publishing Company, 1977). The appendix in Roger W. Brucker and Richard A. Watson, *The Longest Cave* (New York: Alfred A. Knopf, 1976) is also excellent on ancient cavers. This source also contains much information on the history of Mammoth Cave. See also, Margaret M. Birdwell, *The Story of Mammoth Cave National Park* (n.p., 1959). For the most complete listing of sources relating to Mammoth Cave, consult Frank G. Wilkes, *Bibliography of the Mammoth Cave National Park, Mammoth Cave, Kentucky* (Louisville: Potamological Institute, University of Louisville, 1962). At one point, confinement in Mammoth Cave was thought to cure tuberculosis, and a rest center was established there. See Stanley D. Sides and Harold Meloy, "The Pursuit of Health in the Mammoth Cave," *Bulletin of the History of Medicine*, XLV (1971), pp. 367–379.

Stephen Bishop's tombstone is in the guide's cemetery in

Mammoth Cave National Park. The records of the Old Mammoth
Cave Hotel are currently in the possession of Ellis Jones of Cave
City.

The old-timer's quote is from Ben L. Burman, "Kentucky's Crazy
Cave War," *Colliers,* CXXI (June 6, 1953), p. 62. Exploration
history and cave war detail is based largely on oral interviews with
cave country residents by the Cave Research Foundation (CRF):
Lyman Cutliff, May 28, 1964, CRF Abstract, E side 2; Irvin Stice,
June 5, 1964, I side 1; Carl Hanson, July 2, 1964, I side 2; Lyman
Cutliff, August 28, 1964, L side 1; William Travis Blair, May 29,
1964, D side 1 and 2 and E side 1; John Vance, August 25, 1964, J
side 2; Guy Blair, July 5, 1965, M side 1; Ellis Jones, September 3,
1965, N side 2; and Lincoln Wells, July 2, 1964, J side 1. These
abstracts are currently in the possession of Robert K. Murray.

The appendix in Brucker and Watson, *The Longest Cave,* is the
best secondary account of the commercial development of the
Kentucky cave country. The Mammoth Cave appellate court
decision of 1926 involving Morrison's use of the words "Mammoth
Cave" is also found here on page 279. For another description of
the cave war see William R. Halliday, *Depths of the Earth: Caves
and Cavers of the United States,* rev. edn. (New York: Harper and
Row, 1976), pp. 29–30.

According to recent estimates, at least eighty percent of the white
residents in the Mammoth area were Scotch-Irish in background.
Area language patterns and mores are discussed in Gordon Wilson,
Sr., *Folklore of the Mammoth Cave Region* (Bowling Green:
Kentucky Folklore Society, 1968).

The exact date of Floyd's birth is ambiguous. His tombstone says
it was July 20, 1887. Floyd himself once indicated that he was born
sometime in 1890. Scattered family records show his birthdate as
April 20, 1887. This seems to be the most accurate.

Information on cave country family history and day-to-day
activities is from oral interviews with Clifton Bransford, July 7,
1965, CRF Abstract, M side 2; Lyman Cutliff, August 28, 1964, L
side 1; Mrs. Nellie Sell, June 3, 1964, H side 2; Earl Dickey, May
29, 1964, G side 2; and Anna Collins, August 26, 1964, K sides 1
and 2.

The material on Lee Collins and the Collins family is from oral interviews with Irvin Stice, June 5, 1964, CRF Abstract, I side 1; William Travis Blair, August 18, 1959, A side 2; Anna Collins, August 26, 1964, K sides 1 and 2; and the authors' interview with Marshall Collins, May 29, 1977.

Floyd's early caving activities are discussed by his brother in Homer Collins and John Lehrberger, Jr., "Floyd Collins in Sand Cave—America's Greatest Rescue Story," *Cavalier*, VI, No. 55 (January 1958), pp. 40–44, and by Mrs. Pace in the *Louisville Courier-Journal*, February 11, 1925. Other information concerning Floyd's caving adventures is from oral interviews with William Travis Blair, August 18, 1959, CRF Abstract, A side 2, and May 29, 1964, D sides 1 and 2; Irvin Stice, June 5, 1964, I side 1; John Vance, August 25, 1964, J side 2; Elkanah Kline, August 18, 1959, B side 1; Lyman Cutliff, May 28, 1964, E side 2; Anna Collins, August 26, 1964, K sides 1 and 2; Lenny Dossey, July 6, 1965, M side 2; and the authors' interview with Marshall Collins, May 29, 1977.

The compass story is from Halliday, *Depths of the Earth*, pp. 34–35. Floyd's discovery of Crystal Cave has been mythologized over the years. As one popular story goes, a raccoon carried the trap in, Floyd followed it, struck a match, and there was Crystal. For example, see John S. Douglas, *Caves of Mystery: The Story of Cave Exploration* (New York: Dodd, Mead and Company, 1956), pp. 33–34. Information about the family's first viewing of the cave is from oral interviews with Anna Collins, August 26, 1964, CRF Abstract, K sides 1 and 2, and William Travis Blair, August 18, 1959, A side 2.

Details about the development of Crystal and Floyd's explorations in it are from oral interviews with Terry Jewell, March 22, 1958, CRF Abstract, A side 1; Lyman Cutliff, May 28, 1964, E side 2; Lincoln Wells, July 2, 1964, J side 1; John Vance, August 25, 1964, J side 2; Anna Collins, August 26, 1964, K sides 1 and 2; Arthur Adwell, August 29, 1964, L side 2; Matthew W. Bransford, March 29, 1958, O side 2; and authors' interview with Marshall Collins, May 29, 1977.

Some of the legends about Floyd appear in various articles in the *Louisville Courier-Journal* in February 1925 as the tragedy was developing. See also Joe Lawrence, Jr., and Roger W. Brucker,

*The Caves Beyond: The Story of the Floyd Collins' Crystal Cave Exploration* (New York: Funk and Wagnalls, 1955; Teaneck, New Jersey: Zephyrus Press, 1975), p. 7.

C.L. Owens, assistant curator of anthropology at the Field Museum of Natural History in Chicago later asserted that Floyd told him there were undoubtedly connections between the other caves and Mammoth (see *New York Times,* February 16, 1925).

Floyd's contractual arrangement with the three farmers is discussed fully in the court of inquiry testimony of Edward Estes.

Hartley, in his *The Tragedy of Sand Cave,* p. 11, says Floyd called it "Sand Cave." He is wrong. The press named it.

Floyd's dream about angels was later widely reported in the press and in testimony given before the court of inquiry by his father, Lee. Miss Jane's quote is from *New York Times,* February 7, 1925.

The exact time of Floyd's departure for the cave on that last morning is in dispute. Homer, who knew only by hearsay, claimed it was 7:00 A.M. Others placed the time at 6:00 A.M. Lee, *The Official Story of Floyd Collins,* says he left Estes's house at 8:30 A.M. and that it was between 9:00 and 10:00 A.M. before he left Doyle's. J. Norman Parker stated before the court of inquiry that Floyd went into the cave about 10:00 A.M. The last is the best estimate.

# 2

## *Friends and Relatives*

The conversation between Doyle and Estes is from testimony given by Ed Estes before the court of inquiry. Jewell's trip into the cave is reported in Lee, *The Official Story of Floyd Collins.* Lee Collins's first meeting with Doyle and Estes is reconstructed from court of inquiry testimony given by Estes and others.

Marshall's rescue efforts on Saturday are from Collins and Lehrberger, "Floyd Collins in Sand Cave—America's Greatest Rescue Story," p. 67, and oral interview with Marshall Collins, August 26, 1964, CRF Abstract, K side 1. Other rescue information is from oral interviews with Lyman Cutliff, August 28, 1964, CRF Abstract, L side 1, and Clifton Bransford, July 7, 1965, M side 2.

Homer's actions on Saturday afternoon are described in Collins and Lehrberger, "Floyd Collins in Sand Cave—America's Greatest Rescue Story," pp. 42, 67–70. Some of the details, especially relating to the activities of other rescuers, are from the William D. Funkhouser Collection (Margaret I. King Library, University of Kentucky, Lexington, Kentucky), diary, entry for January 31, 1925 (hereafter referred to as Funkhouser diary); Lee, *The Official Story of Floyd Collins,* p. 10; and oral interview with Ellis Jones, August 28, 1964, CRF Abstract, L side 1.

Homer's first contact with Floyd is described in Collins and Lehrberger, "Floyd Collins in Sand Cave—America's Greatest Rescue Story," pp. 40–44, and in Homer's testimony before the court of inquiry. The *Louisville Courier-Journal,* along with the other Louisville newspapers, also carried a full account of Homer's Saturday rescue activities. Some of the details are from an oral interview by the authors with Marshall Collins, May 29, 1977.

The events of Sunday, February 1, are confused and the evidence is fragmentary. The narrative is an approximation of the truth based on a careful cross-checking of published and oral data. The basic information is from the Funkhouser diary; from testimony given before the court of inquiry, especially by Ish Lancaster and Bee Doyle; and from oral interviews with Lyman Cutliff, May 28, 1964, CRF Abstract, F side 2 and G side 1; Lincoln Wells, July 2, 1964, J side 1; Ellis Jones, August 28, 1964, L side 1; and Terry Jewell, July 6, 1965, M side 1.

The best source for Homer's Sunday evening rescue actions is Collins and Lehrberger, "Floyd Collins in Sand Cave—America's Greatest Rescue Story," pp. 70–71. The Hester episode is pieced together from portions of the court of inquiry testimony given by Hooper and Homer.

Homer's early Monday morning contact with Floyd is reconstructed from an interview with Homer and from William Miller's accounts in the *Louisville Courier-Journal.*

For a discussion of the effects of hypothermia see William R. Halliday, *American Caves and Caving* (New York: Harper and Row, 1974), pp. 126–130.

# 3

## *The Outside World Intrudes*

The Dalton decision to send Miller to Sand Cave is described in the *Louisville Courier-Journal*, January 12, 1975.

Miller's activities are from his own reminiscences. The number of persons at the cave when he first arrived is in doubt. The figures range from fifteen to seventy-five. The best guess is about fifty.

The activities of the early arriving newsmen are from their own accounts or from later court of inquiry testimony. Miller's first descent into the cave is based on his descriptions appearing in articles or interviews in 1925, 1942, 1957, and 1960. For the last one, see William Burke Miller, "Our Fight to Save Floyd Collins," *Reader's Digest*, LXXVI, No. 456 (April 1960), pp. 248–256. The authors personally interviewed Miller on July 30, 1977, in an attempt to clear up minor discrepancies.

Lieutenant Burdon's role is difficult to assess because his court of inquiry testimony and his various newspaper interviews are somewhat inconsistent. For his first trip in to Floyd, see *Louisville Courier-Journal*, February 9, 1925.

The arguments over proper rescue procedures are alluded to by all participants, but the details are sketchy. The Louisville press and Burdon's testimony before the court of inquiry are the best remaining sources.

The harness attempt is described in Miller's first newspaper accounts (as well as in a later one in the *Louisville Courier-Journal*, February 1, 1942), and in his *Reader's Digest* article of 1960. Other information is found in Collins and Lehrberger, "Floyd Collins in Sand Cave—America's Greatest Rescue Story," p. 71, and in testimony before the court of inquiry by Burdon, Homer, and Miller.

Homer's offer of $500 for the amputation of Floyd's leg was widely reported in the press. Howard Hartley in *The Tragedy of Sand Cave*, p. 43, pinpoints the exact time of the offer as 8:00 P.M. on Monday.

In an oral interview with the authors on May 29, 1977, Marshall contended that he returned to the cave the next day (Tuesday). However, all contemporary accounts indicate that he was not at the rescue site from Monday night until sometime on Wednesday. Even then, he took no part in any further rescue efforts.

Gerald's activities are from his own testimony before the court of inquiry and his newspaper interview published in the *Louisville Courier-Journal*, February 9, 1925. Additional information is contained in the Funkhouser diary.

Gerald's first trip in at 8:00 P.M. on Monday evening is described in the *Louisville Courier-Journal*, February 10, 1925. Besides Wells and Whittle, German Dennison (a neighbor) and Roy Cooksey (a black) were in his party.

Gerald's second and third trips are pieced together from information in the *Evening Post, Louisville Herald, Louisville Courier-Journal*, and from the court of inquiry testimony reported in Lee, *The Official Story of Floyd Collins*.

The February 2 issues of the *Louisville Courier-Journal, Times, Evening Post*, and *Herald* contain the first detailed accounts of Floyd's entrapment.

Miller's first eyewitness report appeared in the *Louisville Times* on February 2; his second one was published in the *Louisville Courier-Journal* on February 3.

A.W. Nichols, reporting for the *Evening Post*, and Howard Hartley, reporting for the *Louisville Herald*, were often in error concerning details of the entrapment, the events leading up to it, and the early rescue attempts. Their articles have to be used with extreme care.

In an interview with the authors in July 1977, Skeets Miller claimed that Hartley actually admired him and told him so. However, Hartley "had his orders," Miller said, and was forced to minimize or adversely color everything Miller did.

# 4

## *Human Chains and High Hopes*

Gerald's demand of Turner to keep traffic out of the cave is from *New York Times*, February 15, 1925, sec. VIII. The most complete account of the Woodson-Kratch episode is in Hartley's *The Tragedy of Sand Cave*, p. 51. The local Louisville press is best on the Gerald-Burdon altercation. See, especially, the Louisville papers for February 9, 1925.

For Carmichael's rescue efforts and the controversy over sinking a shaft, see the Funkhouser diary and the *New York Times*, February 4 and 18, 1925.

The rescue trips of Tuesday afternoon are pieced together from the Funkhouser diary, the Louisville press for February 4 and 5, 1925, and testimony given before the court of inquiry, especially by J.C. Anderson.

Jones in "My Fifty Years of Cave Exploration in the Mammoth Cave Region of Kentucky," chapter 11, p. 2, maintains that the terminal bulb had a protective cage around it. Miller insisted in the authors' interview with him in July 1977 that there was no such cage.

Miller's three trips into the cave on Tuesday evening were somewhat garbled by the general press. Even Miller's own descriptions leave some matters unexplained. For his first trip and the suppertime interview of Floyd, see *Louisville Courier-Journal*, February 4 and 5, 1925, and his testimony before the court of inquiry. A later description appears in the *Louisville Courier-Journal*, February 1, 1942.

The Pulitzer Prize–winning interviews of Collins by Miller on Monday and Tuesday, February 2 and 3, were published on February 3, 4, and 5 in proper newspaper English. Accounts by other newsmen and observers were oftentimes reported with spellings that attempted to capture the inflections of the central Kentucky citizenry. The court of inquiry testimony was printed both ways—sometimes imitating the local idiom and sometimes in generally accepted literary style. In the interest of accuracy and consistency, the present narrative has taken all conversations that appeared in standard form, including those reported by Skeets Miller, and altered them to reflect the cave country vernacular. In no case, however, has the sense or the sentence structure been tampered with.

In his court of inquiry testimony, Miller said his second trip in on Tuesday was 8:00 to 10:30 P.M., and his third 10:30 P.M. to 2:00 A.M. Other evidence, however, indicates that the time of his second trip was 9:00 to 10:00 P.M., the third from 10:30 P.M. to 1:00 A.M.

The Fishback episode is cloudy. Fishback's own testimony before the court of inquiry confuses not only the time but even the date. Burdon's testimony helps here, but the narrative still represents only an approximation of the Fishback incident.

For the final jack attempt, Miller's various accounts, some of them written long after the event, are the best sources we have.

Floyd's final statement to Miller was variously reported. The *New York Times,* February 5, 1925, contains an expanded and somewhat inaccurate version of this final encounter. For other reports, see *Louisville Courier-Journal,* February 5 and 8, sec. V, 1925. For Miller's later accounts, see *Louisville Courier-Journal,* February 1, 1942, and Miller, "Our Fight to Save Floyd Collins," p. 252.

Miller's comments to reporters on Wednesday morning appeared in all major papers on February 4 and 5, 1925.

The situation at the cave and the continuing controversies over proper rescue procedures are pieced together from testimony before the court of inquiry given by Burdon, Miller, and Matlack. Matlack's testimony must be handled carefully since it is self-serving. He uses dates and times inaccurately and his chronology of events is faulty.

In an oral interview with the authors in July 1977, Miller stated that he could not remember "a Matlack and his torch" at all.

The statement by the filling station attendant is from Burman, "Kentucky's Crazy Cave War," p. 65.

The church meetings are reported in *Chicago Tribune*, February 4, 1925, and *New York Times*, February 4, 1925.

Early reports of friction at the cave appear in the *Chicago Tribune*, February 4, 1925, and *Washington Post*, February 4, 1925.

For Dalton's role in getting Miller's stories into print, see *Louisville Courier-Journal*, February 28, 1954. For the various newsmen's comments about Miller, see *ibid.*, February 8, 1925.

# 5

## *Final Contact*

The Maddox-Fishback visit is reconstructed from news accounts and testimony before the court of inquiry.

The Gerard-Jones trip presents a real challenge in the authentication of data. We have only Casey Jones's and Gerard's word for some of this. Gerard was too frightened most of the time to be a reliable observer. Moreover, he later claimed that he fed Floyd, but this was clearly impossible. Jones, in turn, said that he was with Floyd for an hour and forty-five minutes. Funkhouser's diary, however, shows that he was with the trapped man no more than fifteen to twenty minutes. See Jones and Gerard testimony before the court of inquiry.

Miller's plans for Wednesday are described in the *Louisville Courier-Journal*, February 8, 1925, sec. V. For Miller's Wednesday morning activities, see *ibid.*, February 5, 1924.

There are several different versions of Miller's conversation with Floyd through the cave-in. The most reliable one is in Miller's own testimony before the court of inquiry. Much later, in 1960, and in an oral interview with the authors in July 1977, Miller elaborated on his original story somewhat, but the basic ingredients remained the same. See also Miller, "Our Fight to Save Floyd Collins," p. 254. Miller's Wednesday afternoon activities in Cave City are from the *Louisville Courier-Journal*, February 5, 1925, and February 8, sec. V, 1925.

\* \* \*

The Funkhouser diary sets the time of Gerald's first trip into the cave at 3:00 P.M. on Wednesday. This is wrong. Other evidence agrees that it was 5:00 P.M.

The substance of the Gerald-Collins exchange is reported in Gerald's testimony before the court of inquiry and in the *Louisville Courier-Journal,* February 10, 1925.

Carmichael's attitude toward Gerald is revealed in *ibid.,* February 18, 1925. Carmichael's warning to his men is from *Chicago Tribune,* February 5, 1925. The details surrounding the refusal to allow Miller and Matlack to enter the cave are described in *Evening Post,* February 10, 1925; in *Washington Post,* February 11, 1925; and in testimony given before the court of inquiry by Funkhouser, Miller, and Matlack. Morrison's activities are reported in the *Louisville Herald,* February 6, 1925.

The Williams-Lemay trip on Wednesday night is surrounded by confusion. Some papers erroneously reported that they reached Floyd and fed him at 9:30 P.M. (see *Louisville Herald,* February 5, 1925). Both men not only permitted this belief to circulate but later even insisted that they had done so. This was untrue. *No one* reached Floyd Collins after the first cave-in on Wednesday morning.

Gerald's last trip in at 10:30 P.M. on Wednesday night is reconstructed from these sources: *Louisville Courier-Journal,* February 9, 1925, sec. V; *ibid.,* February 10, 1925; *New York Times,* February 10, 1925; *ibid.,* February 5, 1925; and Gerald's testimony before the court of inquiry. There is disagreement about Floyd's final words to Gerald. Some reports claim that Floyd told Gerald to go home to bed rather than saying that *he* had gone home to bed. Gerald himself never cleared up the matter.

Accounts concerning the role of the Muhlenberg miners contain many contradictions. Some said that Lieutenant Burdon led them down. But it must have been Lieutenant Wells. Burdon did not go back into the cave until sometime on Friday afternoon. Further, one of the miners reported that he called to Floyd at 2:30 A.M. and Floyd responded, "Here I am, down here, come and get me." Floyd then allegedly added, "I'm all right. I'll be here waiting for

you when you get here." This is probably fiction. Floyd was in a
stupor when Gerald last talked to him at about 11:00 P.M. and
again when Hyde yelled in to him at 3:00 A.M. During this whole
time, Floyd was uttering only groans, grunts, or very short phrases.

Mining engineers and geologists throughout the nation immediately contested the "tunnel squeeze" theory of the Muhlenberg
miners. See *Louisville Herald,* February 11, 1925.

Floyd's last words are from testimony given by Roy Hyde before
the court of inquiry.

# 6

## *The State Takes Over*

The call-up and arrival of the guard is covered in all papers. The
Hanson telegram is from the *Louisville Herald,* February 4, 1925.
There are differences as to when General Denhardt arrived at the
cave, but it had to be before 2:30 A.M. on Thursday morning since
he held his first strategy conference at that time.

The Thursday morning surveying activities, like so much else
connected with the Sand Cave rescue, is a nightmare of confusion.
The best sources are the *Louisville Courier-Journal* and the
Funkhouser diary. Sample diagrams and a copy of the Mammoth
Cave Quadrangle are in the Funkhouser Collection, folder "Sand
Cave."

The Homer-Denhardt altercation is described in Collins and
Lehrberger, "Floyd Collins in Sand Cave—America's Greatest
Rescue Story," p. 73. At the time, the incident was also sensa-
tionally reported in all newspapers. Denhardt's statements to
Homer and to the volunteer crews are from *New York Times,*
February 6, 1925.

"This pitting of . . ." is from the *Evening Post,* February 6, 1925.
The distance of the shaft from the cave entrance is variously given.
The closest figure mentioned is eight feet and the farthest sixty.

Funkhouser says in his diary that it was "about twenty." Twenty is correct.

Early estimates of the time required to reach Floyd are given in all papers. So are the Lane radio experiments and the details surrounding Dr. Hazlett's arrival. The best description of the doctor's plane ride is in *Chicago Tribune,* February 5, 1925, and *Evening Post,* February 4, 1925. Dr. Hazlett's statement of late Wednesday night concerning the feasibility of amputation is from *New York Times,* February 5, 1925.

The newspaper statement about the Red Cross saving rescuers from moonshine is in *Atlanta Constitution,* February 7, 1925.

The most compléte description of the methods and procedures used in the digging process is in Lee, *The Official Story of Floyd Collins,* p. 28. The Carmichael comment about Floyd's meager chances is in *New York Times,* February 7, 1925. General Denhardt's telegram to Adjutant General Kehoe is quoted from the *Louisville Courier-Journal,* February 7, 1925.

Lee Collins's antics are alluded to by every major newspaper, but the most detailed coverage is supplied by the four Louisville papers. Lee's belief that the Lord would sustain Floyd until the shaft could reach him is from the *Park City Daily News,* February 5, 1925. His tearful comment about God wanting both him and Floyd is in *Louisville Herald,* February 7, 1925. His statement about Floyd being "saved" and joining his mother in heaven is from *ibid.,* February 5, 1925.

Miss Jane's and Andy Lee's reactions are taken from the *Washington Post,* February 7, 1925; *New York Times,* February 7, 1925; and *Louisville Herald,* February 7, 1925. Lieutenant Burdon's Friday activities are reported in the *Louisville Courier-Journal,* February 9, 1925, and *Louisville Herald,* February 7, 1925.

The actions of Homer and Gerald on Friday are recorded in all Louisville papers for February 6–7, 1925. The heated exchange of words in the Homer-Gerald-Denhardt incident are a composite. The exact sequence is difficult to ascertain because of differences in the various accounts. Gerald's final ejection is best described in the *Louisville Courier-Journal,* February 10, 1925.

General Denhardt's request for a conference with Kehoe is in

*New York Times* February 7, 1925. Although eight hundred rounds of ammunition were asked for, twenty-four hundred were actually sent according to one reporter who later examined the consignment from Frankfort.

The quotes of the crone and of the anonymous reporter are from the *Evening Post,* February 6, 1925, and *Washington Post,* February 7, 1925.

The sound test is described and evaluated in all major papers. Professor Funkhouser's search activities are recorded in his diary. Homer's attempt to find a new way into Sand Cave is reported in *New York Times,* February 8, 1925. General Denhardt's security preparations are revealed in *ibid.,* and *Louisville Courier-Journal,* February 8, 1925, sec. I. Carmichael's gloomy prediction to reporters on Saturday is in *Evening Post,* February 7, 1925.

The history of Cave City, as well as the information on the impact of the Collins tragedy on the town, are from oral interviews with: Earl Dickey, May 29, 1964, CRF Abstract, G side 2; Terry Jewell, March 22, 1958, A side 1, and July 6, 1965, M side 1.

The town's two hotels were the Dixie and the Gardner. The latter was the inferior of the two, and most action took place at the Dixie.

Neil Dalton's bathtub experience is told in the *Louisville Courier-Journal,* August 27, 1963. The Cave City crime picture is revealed in *Louisville Herald,* February 7, 1925.

The exact number of reporters present during the rescue was never determined. The highest number mentioned is a hundred and fifty; the lowest sixty. One story in 1965 claimed that there were "several hundred newsmen there." An example of such exaggeration can be found in Laurence Greene, *The Era of Wonderful Nonsense: A Casebook of the Twenties* (Indianapolis: Bobbs-Merrill Company, 1939), p. 125. There may have been as many as a hundred and fifty *media* people there, but certainly not a hundred and fifty *reporters.* The best estimate is seventy-five to eighty.

The *Baltimore Sun* quotation is from "The Floyd Collins Tragedy," *Literary Digest,* LXXXIV, no. 9 (February 28, 1925), p. 8.

The editorial comparing fictional creations to Floyd's situation is in the *Evening Post,* February 5, 1925, sec. II.

Information about radio and movie coverage is taken from the daily press and from Kay F. Reinartz, "Floyd Collins: Hero of Sand Cave" (unpublished paper), pp. 9–10, 19. The long quotation by Miss Jane is also from *ibid.,* p. 17. Reinartz's paper was ultimately published in a tightly edited form as "Floyd Collins, Hero of Sand Cave," in Bruce Sloane, ed., *Cavers, Caves, and Caving* (New Brunswick, New Jersey: Rutgers University Press, 1977), pp. 229–51.

The *Evening Post*'s comment about Floyd and Alma Clark is from the issue of February 6, 1925. The *New York Times* reference to Miss Clark is in the issue of February 6, 1925. The *Atlanta Constitution* quote is in the issue of February 7, 1925. William Travis Blair's observation about Floyd and women is from oral interview, August 18, 1959, CRF Abstract, A side 2. Lee's quip to reporters about Floyd and marriage is from *New York Times* February 15, 1925, sec. VIII. The concluding material about Alma is from oral interview with Alma Clark by the authors, March 17, 1978.

Speculative psychiatric insights concerning Floyd, caves, and sex are a result of interviews by the authors with Dr. Albert L. Ingram, April 13, 1978.

The *Evening Post*'s statement about the relationship between Old Shep and Floyd is in the issue of February 7, 1925. Information about Obie is from Collins and Lehrberger, "Floyd Collins in Sand Cave—America's Greatest Rescue Story," p. 72. Anna Collins stated in an oral interview (August 26, 1964, CRF Abstract, K side 1) that Obie was with Floyd at the cave the morning he was trapped.

Local attitudes toward the press are from oral interviews with Mrs. Ben Monroe, May 29, 1964, CRF Abstract, G side 2, and Earl Dickey, May 29, 1964, G side 2.

The *New York Times*'s comparison of Sand Cave with Times Square is in the issue of February 17, 1925. The banner headline and the subhead concerning the "tunnel squeeze" theory are from the *Evening Post,* February 5, 1925. The *Washington Post*'s elaboration of this theory is in the issue of February 6, 1925. The *Atlanta Constitution*'s description of "Joe Wheeler's" rescue attempt is from issue of February 7, 1925. The *Los Angeles Times*'s comment on Floyd's lunacy is the issue of February 6, 1925.

Samples of shaft measurement discrepancies are to be found in *Louisville Herald,* February 7–8, 1925, and *Washington Post,* February 8, 1925.

For examples of the telegrams received in Cave City, see *Louisville Herald,* February 4, 1925, and *Atlanta Constitution,* February 5, 1925. The two headlines concerning Floyd's slim chances are from the *Louisville Herald,* February 6, 1925, and *Louisville Courier-Journal,* February 6, 1925. The quote about Collins retaining the spark of life is from *ibid.*

The epic meaning of the Sand Cave episode was first alluded to by the *Washington Post,* February 6, 1925.

# 7

## *Carnival Sunday*

The blasting and radio circuit tests are described in the *Louisville Courier-Journal,* February 9, 1925. The banana oil experiment is covered in *ibid.,* and in the Funkhouser diary.

The crowd estimates are from the Turner testimony in Lee, *The Official Story of Floyd Collins; Chicago Tribune,* February 9, 1925; *Louisville Courier-Journal,* February 9, 1925; Hartley, *The Tragedy of Sand Cave,* p. 97; and oral interview with Lincoln Wells, July 2, 1964, CRF Abstract, J side 1.

The Sand Cave scene on Sunday, February 8, is reported in all major newspapers on February 9, 1925. The comment about the rooster is from *Louisville Courier-Journal,* February 14, 1954. Lee's quixotic actions are described in *ibid.,* February 9, 1925; *ibid.,* January 12, 1975; *ibid.,* August 23, 1976; and *Chicago Tribune,* February 6, 1925.

Religious activity at the cave is reported in *Louisville Courier-*

*Journal,* February 8 and 12, 1925; *Chicago Tribune,* February 9, 1925; and *Washington Post,* February 9, 1925. Hartley's statement about the skylark is from the *Louisville Herald,* February 9, 1925.

For the Woodson and Kratch interview, see *Evening Post,* February 4, 1925, and *Louisville Herald,* February 4, 1925.
   The Hartley article about Floyd being a victim of "greed for fame" is in *Evening Post,* February 5, 1925, sec 2.
   Lieutenant Burdon's comments are reported in *Louisville Herald-Post,* February 8, 1925. For examples of Burdon's charges appearing in other papers, see *Atlanta Constitution,* February 8, 1925, and *Philadelphia Inquirer,* February 8, 1925.
   The Killian AP dispatch is printed in the *Louisville Courier-Journal,* February 10, 1925.

# 8

## *Investigation and Frustration*

The opening headlines are from the *Evening Post* and *Atlanta Constitution,* February 9, 1925. The subheading is from the *Philadelphia Inquirer,* February 9, 1925. The best airing of Floyd's "shiftless qualities" and Gerald's "skulduggery" is in *Atlanta Constitution,* February 9, 1925. For the *Evening Post*'s and *Herald*'s justification for "muckraking," see their issues of Monday, February 9, 1925.
   The various Burdon charges are reviewed in *Atlanta Constitution,* February 10, 1925, and *Louisville Courier-Journal,* February 9, 1925. Gerald's defense appears in *ibid.,* February 10, 1925.
   For Killian's statement about the advantages of the tragedy for Cave City, see *Chicago Tribune,* February 9, 1925. The Killian death threat is published verbatim in *ibid.* The death threat headline is also from *ibid.*

Pertinent portions of all testimony given before the court of inquiry can be found in the pages of the *Louisville Courier-Journal, Times, Herald,* and *Evening Post* for the days in question. The actual court of inquiry transcript came to about seven hundred typescript pages. Some of this is republished in Lee, *The Official Story of Floyd Collins*.

Funkhouser's collapse at the end of the first day's testimony was caused by fatigue rather than excitement over Matlack's charges. The professor had been working at the cave with very little rest throughout the preceding week.

The impostor from Kansas was reported in all papers. The Miller and Denhardt telegrams are printed verbatim in *Louisville Courier-Journal*, February 12, 1925.

The Denhardt statement concerning Killian and the AP dispatch is from *ibid.*, February 15, 1925.

Carmichael's promise to keep going no matter what the odds is from *Chicago Tribune*, February 10, 1925. Carmichael's statement that Floyd was still alive is in *Evening Post*, February 9, 1925. Dr. Hazlett's comment about keeping up worker morale is in *Atlanta Constitution*, February 14, 1925.

For scientific evaluation of the validity of Lane's radio tests, see *Philadelphia Inquirer*, February 12, 1925. The Posey statement of February 10 is from the *Chicago Tribune*, February 11, 1925. The sample headline for Wednesday, February 11, is from *Atlanta Constitution*. Carmichael's Thursday statement is in *ibid.*, February 13, 1925.

The Louisville press is the best source for the injuries, personalities, and activities of the rescue crews at Sand Cave. Carmichael's key role in maintaining worker morale is from an interview by the authors with Skeets Miller in July 1977. The information on Eddie Bray is from Reinartz, "Floyd Collins: Hero of Sand Cave," pp. 21–22. The words of the Cincinnati miner are in *Louisville Herald*, February 14, 1925.

The Washington rumors are from the *Washington Post*, February 14, 1925. For details on the military-press compromise and accommodation, see *Louisville Herald*, February 14, 1925. The Friday night and Saturday morning official bulletins are in Funkhouser Collection, folder "Sand Cave." The Saturday morning Brenner statement is from Hartley, *The Tragedy of Sand Cave*, p. 125. The reference to chocolate ice cream appears in the *Evening Post*, February 16, 1925.

The two headlines concerning Floyd's imminent rescue are from *Los Angeles Times*, February 13, 1925, and *Boston Globe*, February 14, 1925. Miller's and Carmichael's observations concerning the lateral tunnel are in *Louisville Herald*, February 17, 1925.

The hillside scenes at Sand Cave on Sunday, February 15, are described in all newspapers on Monday, February 16, 1925. Miss Jane's brief comment on Floyd's rescue chances is from *New York Times*, February 16, 1925. For some of Lee's antics and statements on Sunday, see *ibid.*, and *Louisville Herald*, February 16, 1925.

# 9

## *The Struggle Ends*

The events surrounding the discovery of Floyd's body are reported both in the press and in court of inquiry testimony given by Brenner, Carmichael, and others. The official Funkhouser "death" announcement is in Funkhouser Collection, folder "Sand Cave."

The reaction of Nellie and Miss Jane to the news is in *Chicago Tribune*, February 17, 1925. Marshall's and Homer's reaction is in *Louisville Herald*, February 17, 1925. Lee's, too, is in *ibid.*

The medical examination of Monday, February 16, is variously described, and many of the details are in controversy. The sequence of events in the narrative is reconstructed from the best available evidence in the *Chicago Tribune*, February 17, 1925; *Louisville Herald*, February 17, 1925; and *New York Times*, February 17, 1925. Dr. Hazlett's statement on the precise time of Collins's death is from the *Chicago Tribune*, February 17, 1925.

The Carmichael bulletin promising the removal of Floyd's body by 5:00 A.M. Tuesday is in Funkhouser Collection, folder "Sand Cave." Dr. Hazlett's final medical assessment is in *New York Times*, February 18, 1925.

Lindbergh was flying a 150-horsepower Hispano-Suiza-equipped Jenny. This was a souped-up high-performance model used by the Army Air Service as a trainer. Lindbergh was actually an air cadet at this time. His various activities throughout the rescue are well known to Ellis Jones of Cave City, who shared them with the authors in an oral interview, May 27, 1978.

Carmichael's statement about the angle worm is in Lee, *The Official Story of Floyd Collins,* p. 107.

The hearings and decision of the coroner's jury are found in all papers on February 18, 1925. General Denhardt's final statement to reporters is in *Louisville Herald,* February 17, 1925.

Governor Fields's intention to attend the funeral is reported in *New York Times,* February 17, 1925. A.W. Nichols exaggeratedly claims in the *Louisville Herald,* February 18, 1925, that a thousand persons were present at the funeral. Details concerning the funeral are from the Louisville papers. The governor's note of sympathy is in *Louisville Courier-Journal,* February 18, 1925.

The rapid evacuation of Sand Cave is reported in *ibid.,* and in the *Louisville Herald* for February 18 and 19, 1925. See also, Funkhouser diary, entry February 19, 1925. Carmichael's statement on sealing the shaft appears in *Louisville Courier-Journal,* February 17, 1925.

The sample headlines are from *Philadelphia Inquirer, Chicago Tribune, Los Angeles Times,* and *Atlanta Constitution.* The flowery quote on death appears in *Louisville Herald,* February 18, 1925. The quotation about surrendering to Mother Nature is from Greene, *The Era of Wonderful Nonsense,* p. 131. The *Washington Post* statement is in the issue of February 19, 1925.

Carmichael's comment about the human race is from the *Washington Post,* February 17, 1925. The *Cleveland Plain Dealer* quote is in its issue of February 19, 1925. The *Chicago Tribune* headline is for February 17, 1925, and the *Atlanta Constitution* quotation is in the issue of February 15, 1925.

Killian's comment on heroism appears in *Chicago Tribune,* February 17, 1925.

The WHAS religious analysis is taken from a clipping book originally owned by Mary Frank Jones, but now in the possession of June M. Dyer.

Vance's comments are from an oral interview with Mr. and Mrs.

Vance, August 25, 1964, CRF Abstract, J side 2. Lyman Cutliff's observation is from oral interview with him, May 28, 1964, CRF Abstract, G side 1. Mrs. Ben Monroe's comment is from an interview with her, May 29, 1964, CRF Abstract, G side 2. Marshall's attitudes are from an interview with him by the authors on May 29, 1977.

The remarks about Floyd's stupidity are from oral interview with Carl Hanson, July 2, 1964, CRF Abstract, I side 2; *Louisville Herald,* February 18, 1925; and Burman, "Kentucky's Crazy Cave War," p. 64.

The concluding editorial appears in *Louisville Courier-Journal,* February 18, 1925.

# 10

## *Making of a Legend*

For Doyle's post-rescue activities, see *Louisville Courier-Journal,* March 1 and April 15, 1925. The $7000 figure is from an interview with John Vance, August 25, 1964, CRF Abstract, J side 2.

For Funkhouser's and Carmichael's subsequent actions, see various letters, Funkhouser Collection; *Louisville Herald,* February 13, 1925; *Chicago Tribune,* February 17, 1925; and *Louisville Courier-Journal,* February 18, 1925.

Like Carmichael, Skeets Miller made numerous speeches on the Sand Cave rescue. In May 1925, he wrote to Professor Funkhouser that from February 21 to April 15 he did not get one full night's sleep because of his speaking commitments.

Homer's first mention to reporters that he would get Floyd's body out is in *Evening Post,* February 17, 1925. For Lee's post-rescue activities, see *ibid.,* March 4, 1925, and *New York Times,* February 19, 1925. The eyewitness comment about Lee's vaudeville performance is from *Louisville Courier-Journal,* February 23, 1975, magazine section.

The legal maneuverings over the management of Floyd's estate are in *ibid.,* February 26, 1925, and February 27, 1925. For the Hunt contract and details concerning the recovery of the body, see

*Park City Daily News,* April 23, 1925; *Louisville Courier-Journal,* March 13, 1925; *New York Times,* April 23 and 24, 1925; and *Louisville Courier-Journal,* April 24, 1925. Supplying the interesting sidelights of the recovery are oral interviews with Lyman Cutliff, May 28, 1964, CRF Abstract, G side 1; Earl Dickey, May 29, 1964, G side 2; Wade Highbaugh, May 25, 1964, B side 2 and F side 1; and authors' interview with Marshall Collins, May 29, 1977.

While on the embalmer's table, Floyd's corpse was photographed in the nude by Wade Highbaugh, who claimed that Floyd had bruises on his left leg and a dislocated right shoulder. Unfortunately, Highbaugh's negatives were later lost in a fire.

The second funeral is covered in *Louisville Courier-Journal,* April 27, 1925, and *Louisville Herald,* April 27, 1925. The twenty-seven pound rock is described in Halliday, *Depths of the Earth,* rev. edn., p. 28.

For concern about the safety of the Kentucky caves, see *Louisville Courier-Journal and Times,* February 8, 1925, sec. I, and February 22, 1925, sec. V; and *New York Times,* February 17, 1925.

Lee's third marriage is described in *Park City Daily News,* May 25, 1926, and *Louisville Courier-Journal,* May 25 and 26, 1926. The widow Ebinger's first name was Bena.

The Thomas purchase of Crystal Cave is reported in *ibid.,* June 17, 1927. Other details are taken from oral interview with William Travis Blair, May 29, 1964, CRF Abstract, E side 1. The body-snatching incident is reported in *Louisville Times,* March 19 and 20, 1929. The missing left leg is sometimes disputed because Floyd's corpse still appears to have two legs. It is actually impossible merely by looking in the coffin to determine whether the left leg is fake or not. Local comment is from a number of oral interviews, especially from the above-mentioned interview with Blair. See also Brucker and Watson, *The Longest Cave,* p. 284.

The best published source on the cave war of the 1950s is Burman, "Kentucky's Crazy Cave War." Other cave war information is from oral interviews with Terry Jewell, March 22, 1958, CRF Abstract, A side 1, and July 6, 1965, M side 1; Guy Blair, July 5, 1965, M side 1; and Lute Lee, August 18, 1959, A side 1.

The *Louisville Courier-Journal*'s editorial on the Collins tragedy and national park is in its issue of February 22, 1925, sec. V.

Details regarding the government's takeover of Mammoth Cave and the surrounding area are from oral interviews with Terry Jewell, March 22, 1958, CRF Abstract, A side 1; Dr. Gordon Wilson, May 21, 1964, C side 1; and Lenny Dossey, July 6, 1965, M side 2.

The *Chicago Tribune* quotation is from its issue of February 4, 1925. The Bransford comment is from an oral interview with him, March 29, 1958, CRF Abstract, O side 2.

The history of "connections" is condensed from Brucker and Watson, *The Longest Cave,* especially pp. 286–93. For the history of the C-3 expedition and the first connection, see Lawrence and Brucker, *The Caves Beyond.*

The biggest "loser" in the sale to the government of the two remaining private caves was Edmonson County, which suddenly lost its two largest taxpayers.

For the history and description of the final connection, see Brucker and Watson, *The Longest Cave.*

The editorial quote from the *Louisville Herald* is from its issue of February 18, 1925.

The Brannan-Alexander book has no copyright date (although it appeared in 1925) and was published by Bradford-Robinson Printing Company of Denver.

The information concerning the Dalhart record is from Kay Reinartz and her paper, "Floyd Collins: Hero of Sand Cave," pp. 33–34.

Various versions of the Collins ballad can be found in Jean B. Thomas, *Blue Ridge Country* (New York: Duell, Sloan, and Pearce, 1942), and Thomas G. Burton and Ambrose N. Manning, eds., *Collection of Folklore: Folksongs* (Johnson City, Tenn.: Institute of Regional Studies, Monograph No. 4, East Tennessee State University, 1967). The original "Death of Floyd Collins" is reprinted here with the permission of Shapiro, Bernstein and Company, New York, which secured the copyright from Brockman.

The Logan poem is reprinted from John A. Logan, *Echoes From the Hills of the Mammoth Cave Country* (Bowling Green: Porter-Coombs Printing, 1930).

During the decade of the 1930s, the only piece published about Collins was by Oland D. Russell, entitled "Floyd Collins in Sand Cave," in *American Mercury,* XLII, no. 167 (November 1937), pp. 289–97. It contained nothing new. The Clay Perry article of 1941 is in the *Saturday Evening Post,* CCXIV, no. 2 (July 12, 1941), pp. 14–15, 36–37.

For a discussion of Billy Wilder and *Ace in the Hole,* see Tom Wood, *The Bright Side of Billy Wilder, Primarily* (Garden City, New York: Doubleday and Company, 1970), pp. 103–6. The movie was judged by critics to be neither a commercial nor artistic success.

The Mohr and Sloane book was published by Rutgers University Press, New Brunswick, New Jersey.

"The Ordeal of Floyd Collins" is in *Mans' Magazine* (June 1954), pp. 28, 30; "The Death of Floyd Collins," by Booton Herndon, is in *Saga* (Sept. 1956), pp. 18–21, 82–84.

The full title of Folsom's book is *Exploring American Caves: Their History, Geology, Lore and Location,* and was published by Crown Publishers (New York).

For the comments by Homer Collins and Neil Dalton on the 1957 *Robert Montgomery Presents* show, see *Louisville Times,* January 22, 1957.

The Homer Collins first-person article has been alluded to before in these notes: Collins and Lehrberger, "Floyd Collins in Sand Cave—America's Greatest Rescue Story," *Cavalier,* VI, no. 55 (January 1958), pp. 40–44, 67–74. Warren's *The Cave* was published by Random House (New York).

The 1960 Miller article has also been referred to in these notes before—"Our Fight to Save Floyd Collins," *Reader's Digest,* LXXVI, no. 456 (April 1960), pp. 248–56.

For the Woodbury article, see Clarence Woodbury, "The Death of Floyd Collins," *American Legion Magazine* (January 1964), pp. 10–11, 47–50. Material concerning the trial is in *Louisville Courier-Journal,* May 27–28, and June 12, 1965.

Lesy's book, *Real Life—Louisville in the Twenties,* was published by Pantheon Books (New York). The chapter on Floyd and Sand Cave was republished as an article entitled "Dark Carnival: The Death and Transfiguration of Floyd Collins," *American Heritage,* XXVII, no. 6 (October 1976), pp. 34–35.

The Bayley article appears in *Yankee Magazine* (February 1978), pp. 180–88. Finkel's poem, *Going Under,* was published by Atheneum (New York).

The poll, the *Courier-Journal* comment, and the Dalton statement are from the *Louisville Courier-Journal,* January 12, 1975.

Homer's statement to the *Louisville Courier-Journal* on the twenty-second anniversary of the event appears in the issue of February 5, 1947.

Information on the subsequent activities of the Collins family is from an oral interview by the authors with Marshall and Anna Collins on May 29, 1977. The material on Robert Burdon is from the morgue of the *Louisville Courier-Journal* and from an interview by the authors with his son, Lawrence A. Burdon, May 2, 1978. The information on Alma Clark and Johnnie Gerald is from interviews by the authors with Alma Clark Short and Mrs. John B. Gerald, March 17, 1978.

Material on Professor Funkhouser is from the Funkhouser Collection, and also from the *Louisville Courier-Journal,* June 10, 1948. The Denhardt information is from Henry H. Denhardt Collection (Margie Helm Library, Western Kentucky State University, Bowling Green). Carmichael's obituary is in the *Louisville Courier-Journal,* September 30, 1949.

Information about Miller is from the morgue of the *Louisville Courier-Journal,* press releases from NBC, and several oral interviews with him. The statement by the 1957 Pulitzer Prize Committee is taken from a press release.

For information on Ed Brenner, see *Staten Island Sunday Advance,* October 24, 1976.

---

*Epilogue*

The opening quote is from Greene, *The Era of Wonderful Nonsense*, p. 131. Brucker's quote is from his chapter in Mohr and Sloane called "The Death of Floyd Collins," p. 171. Halliday's mention of Larry B. Matthews' trip into Sand Cave is from *Depths of the Earth* (rev. edn., 1976), p. 49.

Information on the various rock strata and formations in the Mammoth area is condensed from Arthur N. Palmer's paper, "A Guide to the Limestone Formations in Mammoth Cave National Park," (Yellow Springs, Ohio: Cave Research Foundation, 1975). Conclusions relating to the nature and extent of Sand Cave passages are based on principles described in Roger W. Brucker, "Truncated Cave Passages and Terminal Breakdown in the Central Kentucky Karst," *National Speleological Society Bulletin*, XXVIII (1966), pp. 171–78, and in Roger W. Brucker, John W. Hess, and William B. White, "Role of Vertical Shafts in the Movement of Ground Water in Carbonate Aquifers," *Ground Water*, X, no. 6 (1972), pp. 5–13.

Observations concerning the Sand Cave passageway as it appears today are consolidated from six trips into the cave totaling more than two hundred man-hours. Roger Brucker, leader of these trips, was not able to squeeze through the nine-inch crack, but all other party members who tried were able to do so. Richard Zopf, who spent more time at the end of Sand Cave than any of the contemporary investigators, spent about twenty-five of his thirty-three hours at the spot where we believe Floyd Collins lay trapped. Zopf's stay there equaled or exceeded that of any rescuer in 1925.

A detailed account of current cave safety procedures and rescue exercises is contained in John P. Freeman (ed.), *Cave Research Foundation Personnel Manual*, 2nd edn. (Columbus, Ohio: Cave Research Foundation, 1975).

For a comprehensive review of fatal caving accidents, see Richard L. Breisch, "Fatal Caving Accidents in North America

Since 1940," *NSS News,* XXXV, no. 11 (November 1977), pp. 227–29. Statistics have been compiled on sixty-eight fatal caving accidents between 1940 and 1976. An estimated one hundred fatal cave scuba-diving accidents are not included. Of forty-eight general accident fatalities, twenty-three drowned, eight were asphyxiated by fumes, five disappeared mysteriously, five died of hypothermia, three died of injuries from falling objects, and four died from miscellaneous causes. Of the twenty vertical caving accidents, nine of the victims were unroped. A "typical" victim is a male, fifteen to twenty-five years old, usually not affiliated with an organized caving group and possessing little caving experience.

Several interesting parallels to the Collins case occurred in the most recent "buried alive" incident to capture public attention. On March 1, 1977, Ronald Adley, a miner for the Kocher Coal Company at Tower City, Pennsylvania, was trapped alive in a fifty-foot seam of coal in a flood mine disaster. The next day, a six-inch-bore hole was made through which chewing gum, tobacco, coffee, and a blanket were passed to him. One of his first requests was for a shot of whiskey, but he was given juice instead. In constant contact with his rescuers by voice, he was in a pocket where the temperature was about fifty degrees. He finally emerged through a waist-sized hole on March 6 after officials changed their predictions three times as to how soon he would be reached. Explosives were avoided for fear of a cave-in as twenty-three miners toiled with jackhammers and picks to reach him. There was no carnival on the surface, but again at the shaft entrance stood a brother, a mother, and other relatives hoping and praying. And again commercialism was present. In the midst of the rescue, Adley's wife, Anna Mae, received a dozen red roses and a promise of $10,000 for an exclusive story of her husband's ordeal. Not normally a religious man, Adley, while trapped, expressed hope that he might be out by Sunday so he could attend church. Freed on Sunday, his first words as he emerged were, "I want to get the hell out of here." "It's a miracle," said tearful Kate Adley, Ronald's sister-in-law, when she saw him alive. Anna Mae hugged him all the way to the hospital while he, black and grimy, worried about getting the ambulance dirty. Adley, like Collins, was thirty-seven years old.

## *Epilogue 1999*

Information concerning Douglas is found in Norman Warnell, *Mammoth Cave: Forgotten Stories of Its People,* privately published, 1997. Genice Poynter's claims concerning the snatching of Floyd Collins' body are from her November 1996 interview with Fred Douglas, related in a letter to Roger W. Brucker dated December 23, 1996. Fred Douglas also talked with Irvin Thompson in his Bonnieville, Kentucky, home. Thompson was one of the shaft diggers. He said he quit when the shaft reached forty feet because it slumped out of plumb and was too scary. The Highbaugh material was told to Roger W. Brucker by Udolf Highbaugh on March 12, 1999, in a telephone interview. Additional details were supplied by Timothy Donley in February and March 1999. Donley interviewed Udolf Highbaugh several times and cataloged his photographs. The complaint of Gerald's daughter came in a phone call to Roger W. Brucker in May 1980.

Anderson's interview with Alma Clark Short was described by him to Roger W. Brucker in February 1999. His interview took place in 1988. George M. Crothers's archaeological findings are in "The Archaeology of Sand Cave, Kentucky," *NSS Bulletin* 45, no. 2 (April 1983), pp. 19-33. Philip J. DiBlasi's findings are from "The Real Floyd Collins Home," *CRF Newsletter* 16, no. 2, p. 15, Cave Research Foundation. Roger W. Brucker obtained information about the play *Time and the Rock* in a telephone interview with Warren Hammack and Shawn Alexander in February 1999. Information about *The Death of Floyd Collins* as well as the quote was given to Roger W. Brucker in a telephone interview with Ricky Skaggs in March 1999. A promotional brochure published by the Barren County Visitors Bureau also describes the play.

The various reviews for the musical *Floyd Collins* are found in *American Theater Review,* April 1994; *Philadelphia Enquirer,* April 10, 1994; *New York Times,* March 4, 1996; *USA Today,* March 7, 1996; *Los Angeles Times,* March 17, 1999. Information about the research performed by Landau and Guettel is from "An Interview with Adam Guettel and Tina Landau" by program director Dana Williams, handed out at Playrights Horizons Theater during the musical's run. Pre-show publicity for the

San Diego opening appeared in the *Los Angeles Times,* February 14, 1999, and *San Diego Union-Tribune,* February 14, 1999.

The formal option for a movie of *Trapped!* was signed with Robert K. Murray and Roger W. Brucker on August 26, 1998.

Quigley's discussion of Floyd's entrapment can be found on pp. 189-94 in her book. The Psalm read at Floyd's funeral is from the King James version. Jack Fincher's article is in the *Smithsonian* 21, no. 2 (May 1990), pp. 137-50. Bob Ward's statement to Roger W. Brucker is from a conversation on May 11, 1998. Information about the intent to rebury Floyd Collins appeared in a story by Byron Crawford in the *Louisville Courier-Journal,* January 30, 1989. Roger W. Brucker has a copy of Sarah Bishop's letter to Superintendent Mihalic, dated February 16, 1989. The information about mummies being used in sideshows is found in Quigley, p. 59. Information about Floyd Collins memorabilia is from Roger W. Brucker's telephone conversations with Gordon Smith, Timothy Donley, Russell Norton, and Red Watson in February and March 1999. Roger Brucker has four T-shirts with portraits of Floyd: He made one in 1978; he obtained two from Jeff Middleton, director of the C.A.V.E.S. state educational caving program for gifted teens in Arkansas; and the newest is from Timothy Donley.

For the Fulk article and photographs, see Ohio Historical Society, *Timeline* 15, no. 3 (May-June 1998), pp. 2-17.

*Index*

# Index

337

CPSIA information can be obtained
at www.ICGtesting.com
Printed in the USA
LVHW050320090422
715532LV00005B/17

9 780813 101538